THE HIDDEN LIVES OF
TUDOR WOMEN

THE HIDDEN LIVES OF
TUDOR WOMEN

A SOCIAL HISTORY

ELIZABETH NORTON

PEGASUS BOOKS
NEW YORK LONDON

THE HIDDEN LIVES OF TUDOR WOMEN

Pegasus Books, Ltd.
148 West 37th Street, 13th Floor
New York, NY 10018

First Pegasus Books paperback edition August 2018
First Pegasus Books hardcover edition July 2017

ISBN: 978-1-68177-804-4

10 9 8 7 6 5

Printed in the United States of America
Distributed by Simon & Schuster
www.pegasusbooks.com

For David, Dominic and Barnaby

CONTENTS

Preface I

The First Age

1 Of babies and bellies
   Elizabeth of York and the first Elizabeth Tudor 7

2 Of nurses and nurseries
   Cecily Burbage, Elizabeth of York and the infant
   Elizabeth Tudor. 20

3 Of toys and terminations
   Elizabeth Tudor's brief life 33

The Second Age

4 Of young ladies and learning
   The Countess of Surrey's girls, Jane Dormer,
   Lady Bryan and Margaret Beaufort. 53

5 Of servants and masters
   Elizabeth Barton, maidservant. 73

The Third Age

6 Of love and marriage
   Cecily Burbage and Elizabeth Boleyn 85

7 Of apprentices and aspirations
   Katherine Fenkyll, wife and business partner 102

The Fourth Age

8 Of City trade and London life
   Katherine Fenkyll, independent businesswoman. 115

9   Of visions and revelations
    Elizabeth Barton, the Holy Maid of Kent 131

10 Of mistresses and mystics
    Catherine of Aragon, the Boleyns and Elizabeth Barton 142

11 Of politics and prophecies
    Elizabeth Barton and Anne Boleyn 156

12 Of inquisitions and treasons
    Elizabeth Barton and Anne Boleyn 170

The Fifth Age

13 Of pilgrimages and punishments
    Margaret Cheyne, Lady Bulmer 191

14 Of bibles and burnings
    Joan Bocher, Anne Askew and Catherine Parr 207

15 Of conscience and Catholics
    Joan Bocher, Princess Mary and Jane Grey 232

16 Of Protestants and pyres
    Queen Mary, Rose Hickman, the Marian martyrs,
    Margaret Clitherow and the new Queen Elizabeth 253

The Sixth Age

17   Of settlements and proposals
     Queen Elizabeth and Rose Hickman 271

The Seventh Age

18 Of wigs and witchcraft
    Queen Elizabeth in her sixties, and the witches
    of England. 291

19 Of frailties and finalities
    Jane Dormer, 'Gloriana' and the poor women
    of England. 305

Epilogue – Stuart women 328

Notes on the Text 330
Bibliography......................................376
Acknowledgements 394
Picture Credits...................................395
Index 397

PREFACE

This is a biography. It looks at the life of a woman, who was born in 1485 and died in 1603. She was a princess, a queen, a noblewoman, a merchant's wife, a servant, a rebel, a Protestant and a Catholic. She was wealthy, she was poor. She married once, twice, thrice and not at all. She died in childbirth, she died on a burning pyre, she died at home in her bed. She spent most of her life in the house, and she left home when young and did remarkable things. She changed England and was celebrated forever, and she was forgotten, a mere footnote. She was all these things and more. She was Tudor woman, and this is her story.

∞

The ruling Tudor dynasty was bookended by two princesses named Elizabeth Tudor – the one born in 1492, whose brief years passed into obscurity, and the other who dominated her era and brought the dynasty to its close with her death in old age, in 1603. Their lives are the full-stops between which countless lives of other Tudor women were lived.

This book is a collective biography, sampling, to different extents, the diverse lives enjoyed – or endured – by women living in Tudor England, and together constituting a multi-faceted impression of female humanity of the period: a Tudor Everywoman. It is a concept contemporaries would have been familiar with – after all, it was the early Tudor period that produced the allegorical play *The Summoning of Everyman*.

To the people of fifteenth- and sixteenth-century England, life could be divided into phases – the Seven Ages of Man, articulated most famously by Shakespeare, in *As You Like It*, as infant, schoolboy, lover, soldier, the justice of the peace, the ageing retiree and, finally, the infirm elder. From the female perspective, those Ages could never apply in quite the same way, in an era when women were largely denied any official, public role; but even where the Ages differ, there are yet analogies.

If, at birth, our Tudor Everywoman was a princess named Elizabeth, and at death a queen named Elizabeth, in between she was – among many other people – a daughter named Anne Boleyn, a servant girl-turned-prophetess named Elizabeth Barton, a businesswoman named Katherine Fenkyll, a widow named Cecily Burbage, a rebel named Margaret Cheyne, a heretic named Anne Askew, and an expatriate of advanced years named Jane Dormer. These particular names have lived on in the history books, and they provide major nodes in a network whose 'minor', but no less illustrative, points comprise much of what follows: the poor wool-spinners of East Anglia, the 'witches' of Surrey and the female apprentices of Bristol; the women who taught and those who fostered learning; the women who vowed to remain chaste and the women who made a living from sex; the women who kept their communities morally upstanding and the women who were driven to slander, thievery and murder; the women whose horizons seemed sunlit, and those whose lives ended in despair, in a noose tied by their own hands.

For some, the experience of Tudor womanhood ended very early – as it did for the first Elizabeth Tudor and for the unfortunate, illegitimate Mary Cheese: she, like a number of other newborn girls, found no welcome in an unsentimental world. For those that survived infancy, there was the stuff of girlhood and play, a variable education (according to social class and geography), and perhaps some temporary employment or domestic service before marriage and (for many) motherhood. With marriage, 'employment', in any modern sense of carrying out a paid or public role outside the home, was usually over. But other women remained unmarried, and ran independent businesses as a *femme sole* or continued in a career. Some ended up on the wrong side of the law, others were entirely law abiding – and a few spent a good while *inside* the law, embroiled in suits and counter-suits.

Women were not isolated from the turbulence around them, as a contested Reformation gathered pace in England, its catalyst being Henry VIII's desire for a divorce. Some women saw the light – or saw their own particular light – and in an age where public toleration of diverse opinions over religion or kingship was anathema, there were consequences for women who spoke out. Women could not be soldiers – one of Shakespeare's middle 'ages' – and neither could they, with the unusual exception of two ruling queens, dispense justice by holding any public office. But a surprising number of women were highly political, deliberately or implicitly – whether they were motivated by desire for power, devotion to their faith, support for their family, or the myriad of other reasons that could draw them away from the home.

The final two of the Seven Ages saw the descent into old age for women who had escaped the hazards of childbirth and the risks of disease, accident or execution. For those who did get that far, the final years presented new challenges and great contrasts. Alice Taylor, an 'aged and impotent wench' of Ipswich, spent her last years very differently to Elizabeth I in the 1590s, who by this time had reached her summit as 'Gloriana'. But as both of them looked around, they would have seen more women of their own age than men. With their greater longevity, many more women than men saw out all of the Seven Ages.

It is perhaps fitting, therefore, that the Tudor era itself reached the end of its Seventh Age in the last breaths of one of its most adept, extraordinary women.

Elizabeth Norton

The First Age

1

OF BABIES AND BELLIES

Elizabeth of York and the first Elizabeth Tudor

Towards the end of January or early February 1492, Queen Elizabeth of York, felt a familiar fluttering in her womb – a fluttering that provided proof she had conceived for the fourth time.

Henry VII's queen was, by then, close to the midway point of her pregnancy. But in the first months of pregnancy, the condition was notoriously difficult to diagnose. Could her symptoms merely be 'her natural sickness or store of water'?[1] Alternatively, could her increase in girth be due to 'some windy matter' rather than an expected baby? There were signs, of course, which *could* indicate pregnancy; but few physicians were prepared to confirm their diagnosis until the child actually began to stir in the womb. A mistake could be highly embarrassing for all concerned, and so for months women were left on tenterhooks.[2]

The first gentle movements, when they came, were testament to the fact that a new life had begun. For as far as most Tudors were concerned, life did not begin at conception.[3] The man's seed entered 'the woman's privitie' as one physician coyly called the neck of the womb,[4] there to be met by a matching seed, released by the woman.[5] To contemporaries, these were the raw materials for a child.

Most Tudor parents had a preference for boys, and once pregnancy was confirmed they were anxious for some hint that their wish had been gratified. It was theoretically possible, asserted some physicians, to tell the sex, since boys occupied a right chamber to a sub-divided womb and girls the left.[6] This segregation was, of course, a myth ('but dreams and fond fantasies'), as others rightly realized.[7] Life itself was deemed to begin when the soul entered the fully formed foetus, which occurred at 46 days for a boy and 90 days for a girl.[8] A Tudor girl was thus nearly three months in the womb before her contemporaries considered her to be a living person.

The question of gender would gnaw at the minds of many Tudor parents as the mother's sickness subsided and her stomach began to swell. The wealthier sort of parents could interrogate their physicians on the sex, their questioning filling the doctors with despair. 'It is very hard to know at the first whether the woman be with child or no,' complained the French royal physician, Dr Guillimeau, towards the end of the sixteenth century, and 'so by great reason must it needs be far more difficult to discern and distinguish the difference of the sex, and to determine whether it will be a boy or a wench'.[9] They were not miracle workers. But even Dr Guillimeau believed there were certain signs a mother could look for. Everyone knew that men were hotter than women, which gave them strength, intelligence and vigour. It stood to reason then that younger women, who became hotter than their seniors, would bear boys.[10]

There were, it was thought, some helpful things prospective parents could do to better their chances of conceiving the right gender. Those most anxious for a boy should refrain from sexual intercourse when the wind blew southwards, since this was almost sure to result in a girl.[11] The pregnant woman could also scrutinize her reflection – was her complexion clear? If so, it could be a boy. Carrying a girl was harder work, and so the mother would have 'a pale, heavy, and swarth countenance, a melancholic eye'. Boys reputedly lay higher in the womb than girls – again due to their heat – while a girl would lie 'at the bottom of the belly, because of her coldness and weight'.[12] Carrying a girl was even believed to affect a mother's health more adversely than carrying a boy.[13] In early 1492, at least Queen Elizabeth of York could content herself that she had already fulfilled her dynastic duty with the births of two fine sons – even though death could strike down seemingly healthy children at any moment.

Once pregnancy was established, it behoved a mother to ensure the health of both herself and her child. Spending her time in 'good tempered air' was particularly important, as was a good diet.[14] Pregnant women also had to think about clothing, since few women owned an extensive wardrobe. Even queens adapted their existing clothes, with extra panels added to their dresses.[15] They could supplement them with more-specific maternity wear, such as 'self grow' waistcoats, kirtles and gowns, which could be let out as the wearer's pregnancy advanced.[16] To begin with, gowns could first be unlaced to make them roomier, before more drastic changes were required. Women would also think about clothes for the birth itself. It was common for Tudor women to wear a hood with a shoulder cape in which to give birth.[17]

Elizabeth of York may initially have had concerns over her fourth pregnancy, because she had conceived only three months after the birth of her third child, Henry, on 28 June 1491. Her husband, heir to the House of Lancaster, had won his crown on the field at Bosworth in August 1485 – inaugurating the Tudor dynasty – and his marriage to Elizabeth, who was the eldest daughter of the Yorkist King Edward IV, had helped cement his position by unifying the houses that had fought for decades. To the royal couple, who were frequently surrounded by proud demonstrations of the new dynasty, each of their 'issue lawfully born' helped to symbolize their union and their hold on the throne.[18] Nonetheless, such a rapid new pregnancy in 1492 – almost certainly an accident – was a cause for concern, given the very real dangers that threatened women in pregnancy and childbirth.

'Pleading the belly'

Pregnancy was always a possibility for sexually active Tudor women of childbearing age, and heirs to crowns or great estates were always deemed a blessing to their parents. In quite different circumstances – the abject misery of the Tudor prison system – women also ardently prayed for pregnancy, not for continuation of the line but so they might defer execution by 'pleading the belly'.[19] In such cases, while pregnancy did not mean release from prison, it did usually serve to keep a convicted woman alive for several months, giving her supporters time to appeal for a royal pardon.[20]

Unsurprisingly therefore, many women deliberately sought to conceive in the crowded, mixed prisons of the period. They usually had plenty of time to do so. When Edith Sawnders, a London spinster, was caught rifling through the silver cabinet of a local gentleman, she pleaded her belly at her arraignment on 7 August 1565.[21] It was only on 3 December – nearly four months later – that this claim was tested by a jury of matrons, who confirmed that she was, indeed, with child. A little short of two months later, the expectant mother was granted a royal pardon. Her pregnancy had saved her life.

Catherine Longley, who was brought before the Kingston Assizes in March 1579, accused of stealing a woman's cassock and hat, also pleaded pregnancy.[22] It took four months for her and three other women convicted around the same time to be examined, with all but one – by that stage – pregnant.[23] She must have given birth in prison, since she remained incarcerated until at least March 1581, when she was finally pardoned.[24]

Not all women were so lucky. Katherine Harrison was also convicted of stealing women's clothing, at a hearing at Westminster on 28 November 1561, and declared herself to be pregnant.[25] Three months later, when her claims were investigated, the jury of matrons carried out their investigation. After an intimate examination, they pronounced pregnancy. But when she failed to display any symptoms, she was examined again on 26 June 1562 and found not to be pregnant. She was sentenced to be hanged.

Yet, most convicted women – even those beyond childbearing age – attempted a plea of pregnancy, since the punishment for almost every offence was hanging.[26] Old Alice Samuel, who was convicted of bewitching her neighbour's children in 1593, promptly declared herself with child on hearing the sentence, setting 'all the company to laughing greatly', including herself.[27] Her daughter, Agnes, who was still of childbearing age and also convicted of witchcraft, was actively urged by those around her to plead her belly too. 'No,' she said, 'this I will not do. It will never be said that I was both a witch and a whore.' Both women were hanged.

When pleading the belly resulted in a genuine birth, misfortune was very likely to pass down the generations, for where a baby was born in penal conditions, its prospects were not good, particularly if the mother failed to secure an eventual pardon and was subsequently executed.

It was well known that a pregnancy lasted approximately nine months, although it was possible for premature babies to survive being born up to two months early.[28] The queen's eldest child, Prince Arthur, had been born only eight months into her pregnancy, on 20 September 1486.[29] In 1492, given Elizabeth's rapid fourth pregnancy, she had probably only just begun menstruating again when she conceived. It may have been with the pregnancy in mind that the king and queen took up residence early at Sheen Palace arriving there in April 1492.[30]

There was much to prepare. The baby must have a cradle, filled with a wool mattress and down pillows, as well as furniture ready for the bedchambers of the child's nurse and rockers.[31] Other high-status babies were similarly provided for, although lower down the social scale preparations could be rather more *ad hoc*.

There were also preparations to be made for the mother. Giving birth was the single greatest danger that any Tudor woman could expect to face, and many mothers endured it upwards of five or six times in their lifetimes. The dangers were starkly illustrated by the fact that of the five English Tudor queens to give birth, three of them died in child-bed.[32] Any divine help was greatly appreciated. Elizabeth of York favoured the girdle of Our Lady, which belonged to Westminster Abbey, sending for it in good time for her deliveries.[33] She could lay this precious relic over her stomach while she was in labour, the Virgin's grace alleviating the queen's pains, as it had done for royal women over centuries.[34] Other Tudor women relied on similar charms. As late as 1584 – when superstition was supposed to have been expunged by the Reformation – the pregnant women of one town would 'run to church, and tie their girdles or shoe latchets about a bell, and strike upon the same thrice, thinking that the sound thereof hastened their good delivery'.[35] There was little other prospect of pain relief.

For Elizabeth of York, more than for other women, there was a ceremony to be followed as she prepared for the birth. Luckily for the queen, she had a set of ordinances to follow, giving her step-by-step instructions on exactly how to proceed for every confinement.[36] First, it was up to Elizabeth to select a room in which to give birth.[37] With 'her pleasure being under-stood', her attendants got to work, covering the ceiling, walls and even the windows with rich hangings to create a dark, stuffy space in the early summer heat. Elizabeth could, at least, afford candles, which were out of the reach of her poorer sub-jects; but the atmosphere must still have seemed oppressive. Only one window was curtained with fabric that could actu-ally be removed, allowing her to 'have light when it pleaseth her'. Sounds were muted in a room so swathed in fabric that even the floor and furniture were covered. Yet, it was a gorgeous, luxurious space, with hangings specifically chosen for the queen, depicting golden *fleur-de-lis* on a rich blue background.[38] Elizabeth was careful to keep the images neutral and uncomplicated, since figurative representations were 'not convenient about women in such case'.[39] It would not do for either the mother's mind or the child's to become unsettled, reasoned contemporaries.

This cushioned space was dominated by a rich bed, heavily embroidered and gloriously fine.[40] But while this hefty statement of her royal rank took up much of the room, Elizabeth would have baulked at using it for her labour. Women of all classes were advised to set up a little pallet bed on which to give birth.[41] This was a sensible precaution, since beds and their coverings were often the most expensive items that a family owned – and birth was messy.[42] Poorer women brought out their bearing sheets for each confinement, and in spite of their utility these sheets could have sentimental value and be passed down the generations as family heirlooms. It was common for women to leave them to their daughters in their wills.[43]

Elizabeth's pallet was rather more grand than the usual and hung with rich curtains suspended from the ceiling.[44] While it was not mentioned in the ordinances, the queen insisted that an altar be erected in her room for her private devotions, ensuring that it be 'well furnished with relics'.[45] It would have been on this that Our Lady's Girdle rested until such time as it was required. With everything ready for the birth, there was nothing to do but wait. The queen was best placed to know when the moment had come to enter her confinement[46] – it was usually around a month before the birth.

∽

In spring 1492, while a heavily pregnant Elizabeth looked for quiet, her husband was restless at Sheen. He needed something to occupy himself, and in May he ordered his clerk of works to build lists at the palace for a great tournament. He also paid, out of his own purse, for spears and other jousting weapons.[47] The tournament lasted more than a month, sometimes taking place within the palace and sometimes moving to the green outside. Elizabeth's last few weeks of pregnancy proved far from restful for her, as competitors and spectators packed the palace.[48] For others it was a jolly, companionable time. King Henry himself took part in archery contests on 4 June (taking his losses in good part too).

For Elizabeth of York, the festivities were marred by news that her mother had fallen gravely ill. Elizabeth Woodville had been a regular presence at her daughter's earlier confinements, but by 1492 she had been living in retirement at Bermondsey Abbey for some years. Twice widowed and fiercely devoted to her children, the fifty-five year old widow of Edward IV made her last will in April 1492, sensing that her death was imminent.[49] The eight-months pregnant Elizabeth of York could not make the journey to Bermondsey to be present at her mother's death on 8 June, nor attend the funeral service at Windsor, four days later.[50] The queen thus cast a melancholy figure, swathed in blue – the colour of royal mourning – as she ceremonially entered her confinement a few days later.[51] Tudor women relied on their female relatives to assist them at the births of their children, and to provide good cheer and support; but for her fourth birth, Elizabeth of York had to make do without her own mother.

After taking to her chamber, Elizabeth entered a female-dominated world, where the door was guarded by women determined to admit no man save the king. To facilitate this, the ladies of Elizabeth's household took on the official male roles, such as butlers and servers.[52] It was a tradition that the usually active queen was, however, prepared to break. During one earlier confinement, while sitting in her rich bed hung with curtains embroidered with crowns of gold and royal arms,[53] she received visits from two French ambassadors.[54] It was a substantial breach of protocol, but a harmless one, since she was chaperoned by her mother, her mother-in-law, and her other ladies. Henry could also slip in quietly during the queen's long and tedious days if he so wished. But for most of the time, Elizabeth tried to rest, in her comfortable smocks, which, even in the privacy of her apartments, could be lavish in their gold collars and silk cuffs.[55]

Outside Elizabeth's chamber, life at court continued much the same as before, enlivened by the tournament. Its jollity was marred somewhat by the death at the lists of Sir James Parker, who swallowed his tongue when hit by a strike from Hugh Vaughan. Many others were also hurt; but such matters were, after all, expected at jousts.[56] The king certainly did not appear openly concerned, spending the night of 1 July playing cards in his apartments. Perhaps his mind was on other matters, for apart from losing the high sum of £4 to his fellows, he had already been informed that Elizabeth had felt her labour pains begin.[57]

Contemporaries believed that a woman could recognize the coming of labour when 'certain dolours and pains begin to grow about the gutters, the navel, and in the rains of the back, and likewise about the thighs and the other places being near the privy parts'.[58] Some women, such as Joan, the unmarried mother of the unfortunate Mary Cheese, were taken by surprise. Indeed, Joan might not even have known she was pregnant.[59] She was out in 'a public place' on 1 March 1573 when she gave birth with such suddenness that the baby dropped to the ground head-first beneath her mother's skirts. The little girl lingered long enough to be baptized, but the head injury was such that 'she died through mischance and from no other cause' seven days later. By contrast, Elizabeth of York was already an experienced mother and knew well what to expect. She moved to her pallet and, perhaps, put on the mantle of crimson velvet and ermine that had been provided for her to wear, though it was a far from practical item in the heat of early July.[60]

The queen's trusted midwife, Alice Massey, was summoned as soon as labour began, as she had been for most – if not all – of her mistress's confinements.[61] Good midwives, who learned their trade by shadowing older practitioners, were highly sought after by all classes of women. The profession – which was one of the most important occupations that a Tudor woman could undertake – was a potentially lucrative one if the midwife could attract the wealthiest clients. Since no formal qualifications were required to be a midwife, mothers of sufficient social status were advised to be choosy. Manuals proclaimed the need to ensure that the woman engaged should be 'pleasant and merry, of good discourse, strong', as well as experienced.[62] This was prudent advice, since labour could easily last two or three days, requiring considerable stamina in both the mother and her midwife. Alice Massey was a master of her trade, who could pride herself on the fact that she had lost none of Elizabeth's babies at birth.[63]

While birth was dangerous for the mother, it was infinitely more so for the child, and the death rate was very high. The stakes were high, too, for unbaptized children were automatically barred from Heaven – arguably, to contemporary eyes, a greater tragedy than their all-too-brief existences. In recognition of this hazard, midwives were permitted to baptize children who seemed unlikely to live, which was a remarkable concession from a male-dominated Church. So necessary was baptism while the child was still breathing that midwives would sometimes carry out the ceremony even before the child had fully emerged from the mother's womb or before the sex was known – in which circumstance, a unisex name would be given to the baby. Unsurprisingly, the Church staunchly regulated the ceremonies. One midwife who failed to invoke the Holy Trinity in a baptism was publicly censured by her local priest: 'in evil time were you born, for in thy default, a soul is lost'. As a punishment, the woman was banned from attending future births; the faultless child's coffin was turned away from the churchyard.[64]

Elizabeth of York need not have worried. On 2 July 1492, she gave birth to her fourth child safely. Even in summertime, it was considered advisable for there to be a warm fire in the birthing room, towards which Alice Massey carefully carried the naked baby as the child uttered its first cries. The midwife had already expertly tied the umbilical cord with a double thread, before taking sharp scissors from her bag to sever the tie to the mother.[65] As the baby was wiped clean or washed and wrapped in a blanket,its sex was announced.[66] It was a girl.

'Ripped out of his mother's womb'

Julius Caesar was commonly – but erroneously – believed to have been 'ripped out of his mother's womb' at the very instant she died.[67] Nonetheless, Caesarean sections, which were named after him, were a long-standing if rare practice. Examples in England are documented from the medieval period.[68] One fifteenth-century image in a medical manuscript held by London's Wellcome Institute Library depicts a woman lying on a table, her womb gaping open, as a nurse holds her swaddled newborn child.[69]

The practice was recognized by medical practitioners in the Tudor period; one medical manual included a chapter on 'the means how to take forth a child by Caesarean section'.[70] But such an operation was intended as an absolute last resort, and the surgeon had first to ascertain whether the mother had already died during labour and, secondly, whether her child was judged to be still alive.[71] Many surgeons, though, were prepared to perform the operation even if the foetus was almost certainly dead. One commentator considered that 'lawyers judge them worthy of death, who shall bury a great-bellied woman that is dead, before the child be taken forth because together with the mother, they seem to destroy the hope of a living creature'.[72] No one realistically expected a baby born in such a manner to survive long. But, if born breathing, he or she could at least be baptized.

The operation was ideally carried out as soon as the mother had died, the surgeon making an incision in her stomach, about four fingers long, before cutting through the muscles to reach the womb. While holding the skin apart with one hand, he then sliced into the womb and carefully extracted the child for immediate baptism.[73] There were sixteenth-century rumours that Queen Jane Seymour had been forced to undergo a Caesarean section in order to save the life of Henry VIII's son in 1537. According to the ballad of the 'Death of Queen Jane', the exhausted consort asked her physicians to 'rip open my two sides, and save my baby!'[74]

However, the fact that she survived the birth by nearly two weeks makes this scenario impossible. It was not until the very end of the sixteenth century that some physicians began to advocate carrying out the operation on a living woman.[75] Indeed, Francis Rousset provided the example of Anne Godart, who had apparently given birth six times by Caesarean, although she died on her seventh attempt under the care of a new surgeon.[76] No evidence of this woman's existence was provided, however, and her story is unlikely. Dr Guillimeau, who wrote a medical tract on birth, counselled against operating on living women, having tried it twice himself with no happy outcome. Instead, he considered that 'I know that it may be alleged, that there be some have been saved thereby: But though it should happen so, yet ought we rather to admire it then either practice or imitate it.'[77] In an age without anaesthetic, effective painkillers or antibiotics, most surgeons would be condemning their unfortunate patient to an agonizing death, even if it already looked as though she would die anyway from the inherent dangers of childbirth. Until the modern period, it was almost impossible for a woman to survive a Caesarean section and very unlikely that her child would. In the Tudor era, Caesarean sections were all about salvation in a religious, rather than a physical, sense.

2

OF NURSES AND NURSERIES

Cecily Burbage, Elizabeth of York and the infant Elizabeth Tudor

Carefully wrapped and only a few minutes old, Elizabeth of York's second daughter was handed to her nurse while the midwife turned her attentions back to the mother. The woman who first swaddled the tiny princess was not her mother, who did not expect to carry out the day-to-day care of her children. Instead, it was probably the child's wetnurse, Cecily Burbage, the woman who was to provide the bulk of the child's care. The queen, like most higher-status Tudor mothers, did not intend to nurse her own child.[1]

Wetnurses were always carefully chosen. A nurse, believed contemporaries, should be of no 'servile condition', and instead possess a good birth and background.[2] Cecily Burbage, who was found conveniently close to Sheen at Hayes, to the west of London, fulfilled the job description admirably. She was highly respectable, the daughter of Sir Robert Greene, a gentleman, who had died more than a decade before.[3] The family was reasonably wealthy. They held the small but pleasantly situated manor of Hayes Park Hall, as well as the manor of Cowley Peche, which lay close to London, and smaller parcels of land in nearby Northall and Northwood.[4] The family also owned Theobalds in Cheshunt, Hertfordshire, as well as the manor of Cressbroke in the same parish.[5] With these scattered holdings, the Greenes were firmly members of the gentry even though they were of modest financial worth.[6]

By the summer of 1492, Cecily was a married woman of twenty-five or twenty-six years old, which was, it was thought, the perfect age for wetnursing.[7] The robustness of her eldest son Thomas (who went on to live to an old age) was noted favourably by the royal agents who first came to Cecily's house.[8] They also examined her youngest child – then aged only seven or eight months at the most – for signs of good health; Cecily's milk would be considered stale if the youngest were older than this.[9] Their report was favourable, as was the assessment of Cecily's person, behaviour, mind and milk (which may have been tasted by her royally appointed visitors).[10] She was a sensible, respectable woman, well-loved by those who knew her. These qualities, as well as her 'pleasing countenance, a bright and clear eye, a well formed nose, neither crooked, nor of a bad smell, a ruddy mouth, and very white teeth',were enough for her to be hired.[11]

The personality of the nurse was believed to be transmitted through her milk, so Cecily Burbage presented a reassuring figure. Nevertheless, her conduct was carefully monitored from the moment that she kissed her husband and children goodbye and made her way to Sheen.[12] As she took the new baby princess into her arms for the first time, she was closely observed. The instilment of virtue was essential to a young girl's prospects, and no-one had more influence than the wetnurse over the character of an upper-class Tudor girl, since, as one contemporary noted, 'the first person she will hear and the first person she will see is the nurse'.[13] It was well understood that 'what she will learn as an immature child she will try to reproduce when she is more practised and experienced'.[14] Cecily Burbage was simply the most important figure in the life of the young princess.

Almost as soon as a child was born, thoughts turned to baptism. Although this ceremony was usually carried out on the day of birth, healthy royal infants – who were entitled to greater ceremony

– waited longer. Still at Sheen with Cecily, the princess lay swaddled in her cradle, spending much of her time asleep.[15] It was well known, contemporary texts asserted, to be harmful for a baby to be left to cry, and so Cecily was ready with her breast or a lullaby when the princess stirred.[16] Rocking also helped; two gentlewomen, Jane East and Alice Day, were engaged to serve as the child's rockers.[17] The two women could gossip quietly as they fulfilled their monotonous, but gentle, task of soothing their charge to sleep 'not harshly or too fast, for fear of making the milk float in [her] stomach'.[18] To prevent an accident, the pair tied the baby into her cradle with strings to ensure that she could not fall.[19]

Swaddling

Swaddling, which fell out of favour in the eighteenth century, was considered essential by Tudor parents of all classes.[20] It was an old practice. On tombs and monuments from at least the fourteenth century, babies were depicted tightly swaddled like little Egyptian mummies. Swaddling not only kept the children warm, but, contemporaries considered, ensured that their limbs grew straight.[21]

At birth, a baby was wrapped in a piece of flannel or linen, ready to be washed.[22] Once clean, and while the midwife attended to the mother, the nurse or other attendant gently placed a linen shirt over the baby's body.[23] She would also prepare the baby's 'breechcloth' or nappy, which would be a piece of linen often doubled over or lined with some absorbent material, before being fastened into place with pins. The nurse next took out the swaddling bands, which were long, narrow pieces of linen, often tapering to a point at one end.

The bands could be around three yards long.[24] It took considerable skill to wrap a baby, with girls usually perfecting the art in their youth on younger siblings. The bindings had to be tied tight and the limbs bound straight to ensure that they grew correctly, since children were 'tender twigs'.[25] The bands would be removed only when babies soiled themselves or two or three times a day when they were bathed.[26] For obvious reasons, the bands were washable. Given the ineffectiveness of the nappies used, most families would have possessed several sets of bands.

Swaddling bands, such as the late sixteenth-century example on display at the Victoria and Albert Museum in London, could be highly decorative.[27] This rare Italian survival, made of white linen and decorated with white-work embroidery and lace, would have been worn by a royal or noble child. Even then, such finery was only worn on special occasions and would have made up the final layer of swaddling, covering plain, white linen bands. Woollen bands, for colder weather, were also in use; Henry VIII's first wife, Catherine of Aragon, ordered a set for one of her confinements early in the sixteenth century.[28]

The famous *Cholmondeley Ladies* painting, which dates to the very end of the Elizabethan period and now hangs in the Tate (Britain) Gallery in London, portrays two infants, held by their mothers and dressed in their best swaddling bands.[29] The children wear crimson mantles, which were associated with baptisms.[30] Both babies are swaddled in bands decorated with gold embroidery, while their heads and necks are covered in lace. The patterns on the embroidery match their mother's bodices, showing that they had coordinated their outfits for the occasion. Poorer children would not be swaddled in anything so fine, but even they might have a 'best' set of bands, for special occasions.

For most children, swaddling ended around eight or nine months of age, although the timing varied according to the development of the child. Princess Elizabeth's younger brother, Prince Edmund, was out of his swaddling by the time he was five months old, when hose and a coat were purchased for him.[31] Once released from their bands, Tudor girls would wear gowns, while boys wore coats

– although both garments were, in practice, almost identical.[32] Lower down the social scale, infants of both sexes might wear smocks. All young children wore biggins, which were tight linen caps tied under their chins. Bibs were also commonly tied around their necks.

Baptism was not only essential if a child were to reach Heaven. The ceremony also brought newborn children into the life of the parish and made them part of the local community. And from 1537 onwards, baptism gave them a kind of immortality, since – for the first time – it became a legal requirement for churches to record baptisms (as well as marriages and burials) taking place within their walls. In this way, the names of even the tiniest and most insignificant members of the community were recorded. The ceremony itself was usually a brief one, because most parishes saw a regular stream of births in a period of considerable population growth.[33] Ordinarily, it was the godparents who attended, rather than the parents, with the mother – who had still not been ritually purified by 'churching' following the birth – almost certainly absent.

Royal baptisms were much more lavish affairs, overseen by the queen's officers. For the christening of Prince Henry in 1491, 'necessary stuff' worth more than £6 was ordered from the royal wardrobe, including eight ells of cloth 'that went about the timber work that the font stood on', as well as fabrics costing 11s 10d to line and cover the font, the chapel ceiling and to provide a canopy above the baby.[34] The font had been even more richly dressed in fabric for the baptism of Henry's older sister, Princess Margaret, necessitating an expenditure of 15s 8d.

In the same manner as her birth, everything for the young Princess Elizabeth's baptism was regimented in detailed ordinances, which set out how the chapel should be furnished – hung with rich hangings of cloth of gold and carpeted in the chancel and aisle from the altar to the door – as well as who should attend.[35] Princess Elizabeth was carried into the chapel at Sheen in the arms of a duchess, while a countess assisted by holding the baby's long train of cloth of gold furred with ermine.[36] Two hundred unlit torches were carried before the child in the procession. The attending bishops were waiting at the door of the church, beside a canopy to be borne over the princess's head as a mark of her royalty.[37] There was a squeeze among 'the gossips' of the court as they jostled for position under the small canopy over the font, while one of the child's godmothers (whose names are not recorded) took care to ensure that she was ready for her baptism. Baby Elizabeth would have had three godparents – one male and two female – who would have been drawn from the higher ranks of the English Church and nobility.[38] She was then brought to the font, where she was anointed with water and finally given her name – Elizabeth. The first Elizabeth Tudor.

Once baptized, a 'little taper' was pushed into her pudgy hands, while all around her the torches were lit in celebration. At the altar, money was offered on her behalf, before she was confirmed in the Church. It was now time for those assembled to present their christening gifts to the child, which were ranked according to their value before being brought directly to the queen.[39] Once the ceremonies were over, Princess Elizabeth was taken home.

∽∽

'Home' for the princess, who was then just days old, remained her nursery at Sheen Palace, presided over by the already famil-iar figures of her nurse and her two rockers. Her mother, who was still in her darkened room, quietly recovering, was already a somewhat distant figure.[40] Traditionally, the sex of their infant was supposed to affect the mother's recovery time, with 'churching' – when the mother was ritually purified in church – permitted at an earlier time after the birth of a male child than after the birth of a girl.[41] But such niceties were rarely adhered to. Most contemporaries considered that a woman needed at least a month to recover from a birth. During this time, she would receive female visitors, and it was, according to contemporary writers, a companionable, gossipy time.

Elizabeth of York could, of course, receive visits from her new daughter as she whiled away the hours. It was still far from quiet at Sheen, as the tournament reached a bloody conclusion with an accidental shooting on 7 July.[42] Perhaps to royal relief, the festivities finally died down on 19 July, when the king briefly visited Windsor, before moving to Greenwich three days later.[43] After a short trip to Canterbury and the shrine of St Thomas Becket, Henry was back in London on 17 August, probably in time for the queen's churching, since he made the gift of a rich communion cloth to her nine days later.[44] With that, Elizabeth of York's fourth confinement was over and she could return to everyday life.

Princess Elizabeth could not stay indefinitely in the overcrowded court, and she soon moved to join the main royal nursery at Eltham Palace. This palace, which was very close to the larger royal residence at Greenwich, was the place that she would come to know best. Used by royalty since 1311, and standing high above the surrounding area, it had breathtaking views over London.[45] Elizabeth's grandfather, Edward IV, had ensured that it was one of the most magnificent buildings in England; he had completely replaced the old medieval hall with a new, imposing structure, which still stands today.[46] Indeed, such was Edward's desire to obliterate the earlier medieval past, that the remains of the old hall were comprehensively burned on the spot, and the fire-cracked floor tiles and charred timbers buried in pits.[47] The great hall at Eltham was vast in size, its imposing beamed ceiling rising high above the room's occupants. In late 1479 there had been fifty-one masons and forty-eight carpenters all busily working on a roof so elaborate that it was a wonder to see even fifteen years later when the royal nursery was in occupation.[48]

By the 1490s, Eltham was the height of luxury. The palace sat snugly within its moat, which was traversed by a fine hundred-year-old stone bridge. The building could even boast a flushing toilet in its north-east corner, containing a cistern inundated with water by a simple trap.[49] As in everything, Henry VII was canny in choosing Eltham as the royal nursery, since little was required to ready the royal apartments for his children.[50] Although ruined today, these rooms were, at the time, extensive. Later royal children enjoyed their own private chapel and separate gallery too, as well as rooms with glazed windows, decorated in soothing yellow ochre.[51]

At Eltham, the young Elizabeth entered a nursery already occupied by her two-year-old sister Margaret and her brother Henry, who had only just turned one. The star of the family – Prince Arthur – was also its most distant member. The king's eldest son, who was then aged nearly six, had been whisked away after his birth to Farnham, in Hampshire, there to be nursed.[52] There was, however, some contact between the two nursery establishments. Prince Arthur was attended by his own 'lady mistress, nurses, and other gentlewomen' from the time of his birth.[53] His dry nurse, who was in charge of the everyday running of the nursery, was probably Alice Bywimble, who was listed as serving in his household in 1488.[54] By June 1491, she had secured her appointment as dry nurse to the younger children's nursery. She had good reason to be pleased with this move, since it was something of a promotion. Eltham was the larger establishment, and it contained the younger children who would remain in the nursery for longer.[55]

The nursery was a remarkably stable establishment, in which promotions tended to happen from within. Princess

Margaret had lost one of her rockers, Margaret Traughton, at her younger brother's birth, when the experienced gentle-woman transferred to the new baby's cradle.[56] Her wetnurse though, Alice Davy, was still present in the nursery in the summer of 1492 when Princess Elizabeth arrived. So too was Anne Mayland, Margaret's second rocker, and Margaret (or Margery) Gower, who served as replacement rocker – a role that the toddler no longer really needed. Princess Margaret's attachment to the women who had rocked her cradle was such that they remained with her as servants throughout her early childhood, still drawing the same salary they had when they soothed her to sleep.[57] This was far from uncommon, given the very strong emotional bonds built up between the children and their nurses. Prince Henry's rockers would also remain with him long after he had left his cradle.[58]

Cecily Burbage was introduced to Anne Oxenbridge, who was still nursing Prince Henry. Present also in the nursery was Frideswide Puttenham, who rocked his cradle alongside Margaret Traughton, as well as Jane Collins, who served (as Henry VII put it) as 'gentlewoman to our said son'.[59] In 1492, Elizabeth's servants completed the establishment.[60] The entire nursery staff – although largely assigned to the care of individual children – also worked together collectively as 'servants unto our right entirely well-beloved son the Lord Henry and the Ladies Margaret and Elizabeth'.[61]

For the tiny princess, by far the closest bond was with her wetnurse, who had given up the care of her own young family to nurse her. Raising babies – then, as now – was relentlessly hard work, embracing all 'the filth, the sitting up late, the bawling, the illnesses, the never sufficiently attentive watching' identified by contemporaries.[62] Each of the royal wetnurses received the very generous salary of £10 per year from the king – far in excess of that paid to the dry nurse and to other nursery staff. Since considerable affection could develop between nurse and child, there was also the possibility of honours in later life. Right up until she died, Elizabeth of York was sending gifts to the woman who had nursed one of her brothers.[63]

Anne Oxenbridge, too, would later be provided with generous honours by the notoriously parsimonious Henry VII, expressly for 'her services to the king's son Henry, Duke of York'.[64] This trend continued long after she left her charge, was widowed, and had remarried. In 1509, the former wetnurse was remembered by Henry VIII at his coronation, when she was provided with a personal invitation from the king and a fine gown to wear. One of the new king's first grants, made shortly after his eighteenth birthday, was to Anne and her husband, to top up her pension by £20 a year (followed by an increase in May 1512, as well as other, later, payments).[65] Clearly, she retained a special place in her foster-son's heart. He also always remembered Alice Davy, who had suckled Princess Margaret, employing her in the household of his first wife, Catherine of Aragon.[66]

The bond between a wetnurse and child could be very strong, as an unusual early manuscript edition of a *danse macabre* in Paris's Bibliothèque Nationale shows.[67] Dating from the late 1400s, it depicts women and girls of various classes, ages and roles in life meeting with a sudden death. Here, a wetnurse is shown holding a plague-ridden, swaddled baby, as both are lured away by Death who commands: 'Wetnurse, follow your fair child', before declaring: 'you both will die together'.[68] Nurse and child are portrayed as so inseparable that they must die together.

The evidence of closeness and affection between children and their wetnurses would not have surprised contemporaries, who noted the rivalry between mothers and the nurses they employed.[69] Juan Luis Vives, who wrote an early sixteenth-century tract on the education of girls, believed that character was transmitted to the child in the milk. It was therefore essential that a virtuous woman was selected as a wetnurse, since 'we are often astounded when the children of virtuous women do not resemble their parents. Either physically or morally.'[70] Erasmus was rather more brutal; in a colloquy addressed to a new mother, he declared that a woman who 'banished' her child 'just as if you had put him under a sheep or a goat' would be horrified to hear herself called 'half-mother' by the child as soon as he could talk; in fact, as far as the Dutch scholar was concerned, 'The woman who refuses to nurse what she bore is scarcely a half-mother.' It was no surprise, believed Erasmus that the child would turn to their nurse for affection, since their love was divided 'between two mothers'.[71] Thomas More agreed. Where a baby boy was nursed, he would 'taketh his nurse for his own natural mother'.[72]

Such writings would have been hurtful to Elizabeth of York, who was, by all accounts, a relatively attentive mother for a woman of her class. Her privy purse accounts survive only for the last year of her life, but they show her to have been a fond and concerned parent, with regular contact with members of her children's household, as well as frequent purchases of clothing and other necessaries for her daughters.[73]

'My duty in this motherly office'

In modern times, views have ranged back and forth about the benefits of breastfeeding as opposed to those of formula milk. Today, though, twenty-first century mothers are assured by medical practitioners that 'breast is best'. Hundreds of years before the development of formula milk, it was not so much a debate about whether breast was best for Tudor babies, as *whose* breast was best.

Most writers on the subject considered breastfeeding to be the mother's duty. 'It were fit, that every mother should nurse her own child', asserted the author of *The Nursing of Children*.[74] There was nothing so good to nourish a child, agreed the influential physician Dr John Jones, than its mother's own milk.[75] For other scholars, breastfeeding created an unbreakable bond between mother and child, with Erasmus going so far as to liken wetnursing to 'a kind of exposure'.[76] It was a mothers' duty, said Thomas More, and only 'death, or sickness' should prevent it.[77] Elizabeth Clinton, Countess of Lincoln, put it more forcefully in the early seventeenth century when she wrote a tract – ostensibly addressed to her daughter-in-law – on the godly duty of 'every mother' (as she declared) 'to nurse her own children'.[78]

The countess acknowledged, among other common objections, 'that it is troublesome; that it is noisome to one's clothes: that it makes one look old'. But she pooh-poohed these, since 'all such reasons are uncomely, and unchristian to be objected', as 'they argue unmotherly affection, idleness, desire to have liberty to gad from home, pride, foolish finesse, lust, wantonness, and

the like evils'. In any event, she assured her reader, 'behold most nursing mothers, and they be as clean and sweet in their clothes, and carry their age, and hold their beauty, as well as those that suckle not'.

It was the greatest regret of the countess, who had been a Tudor mother herself, that she had been discouraged from breastfeeding. 'I should have done it', she candidly told her reader, but had been overruled by another's authority. She had also not considered properly 'my duty in this motherly office'. Now she knew the correct path, but lamented that 'it was too late for me to put it in execution'. It was unnatural to send a child to be nursed, she declared, both for the mother's own child and also that of the nurse, and she warned: 'be not accessory to that disorder of causing a poorer woman to banish her own infant, for the entertaining of a richer woman's child, as it were, bidding her unlove her own to love yours'.

Yet, while poorer Tudor women had little choice but to feed their children for themselves, most upper-class women did not nurse their own babies.

All but a few mothers of Lady Clinton's class employed wet-nurses. Elizabeth of York would certainly have been aware of the debate surrounding maternal breastfeeding, but social pressures – to cede the daily care of the infant and to quickly return to fertility – were the more powerful drivers. There was no question of her, or a great many other Tudor mothers, nursing their own child.

3

OF TOYS AND TERMINATIONS

Elizabeth Tudor's brief life

For most Tudors, the first of life's seven ages, infancy, lasted up to around the age of seven, its early years characterized by Shakespeare as the time of 'mewling and puking in the nurse's arms'.[1] But Tudor adults found infants adorable too, with contemporaries speaking of their 'sweet baby-talk' and the delightful first word: 'mamma'.[2] Many Tudor parents struggled not to laugh when their tiny children were cheeky or emulated their own speech just a little too closely.[3]

Infancy was also the stage of experimentation and play, universal for children of all social classes, which could begin in earnest when the swaddling was finally removed. It was Cecily Burbage who was responsible for taking Princess Elizabeth out of her cradle to play,[4] and it was she who, when Elizabeth was around a month old, released her hands from the swaddling bands, after which her arms were covered by loose little sleeves.[5] This was the first freedom of movement Tudor babies enjoyed, allowing them to 'use and stir' their hands.

At the same time, the nurse could begin to take the child out into the fresh air. For the young Elizabeth, this time coincided with the height of summer, and care would have been taken to shield her from the sun in the garden, while rain and 'rough wind' would also have been considered dangerous to the infant. The gardens at Eltham had once proved troublesome to the king. His first appointee as keeper of the gardens, Robert Palmer, neglected his duties, leaving them overgrown and tangled.[6] In late 1487 a new gardener, Robert Hart, had been appointed, and he took better care than his predecessor, ensuring the gardens were lovely.[7] And thus the three royal children, out with their nurses in the summer sun of 1492, could enjoy the pursuits of infancy and early childhood in the freedom of the moated surroundings. Contemporaries believed that children needed suitable playmates and companions,[8] and as Princess Elizabeth grew, she turned to her siblings for her own, with Prince Henry, only one year her senior, likely to have been her most particular friend – despite the cautions by some writers who considered that young girls should only play with other girls and be closely supervised by their mother or nurse.[9]

The little girl also had to accustom herself to a change in dress, wearing gowns which, for ceremonial occasions, could be very fine, such as the rich crimson velvets or cloth of gold regularly worn by the nobility.[10] Perhaps Elizabeth appeared decked out in a green velvet gown, edged with purple tinsel and lined with black buckram, as her younger sister, Mary, did when she was aged four.[11] Alternatively, Henry VII and Elizabeth of York would have thought nothing of clothing their toddler daughter in dresses of black velvet, edged with crimson, or a kirtle of tawny damask and black satin, edged in black velvet.[12] For extra layers against the long cold winters, she could wear woollen hose.[13] She was certainly surrounded by every luxury, with carpets, wall hangings and the other trappings of royalty adorning her chambers.[14]

With Princess Elizabeth on the move and learning to speak, it was time for Cecily to introduce solid food to the girl's diet. This was a delicate stage in an infant's life and highly worrying for anxious parents and attendants. Milk alone was supposed to be given until the front teeth appeared, cautioned one manual, before some simpler foods – such as chicken legs, on which the baby could chew – might be introduced.[15] Since infants have few teeth, it was necessary for a nurse to chew the food herself before spitting it out and placing it in the child's mouth.[16] Anxious parents would wait to see how their child did, and a nurse might come under suspicion should the baby fail to thrive. Erasmus, for one, considered that 'nurses put very little of the food they chew into the baby's mouth, most of it they swallow themselves'.[17]

There was also some argument that boys and girls should be weaned at different times, with three years suggested for boys and up to a year earlier for girls.[18] Boys were, after all, expected to live longer and have more active lives: they needed their mother's (or wetnurse's) nurturing milk for longer. If such a rule was followed in the royal nursery at Eltham, then Prince Henry and his younger sister, Princess Elizabeth, would have been weaned together. Henry's weaning was completed by at least March 1495.[19] Since Elizabeth was then nearly three, it seems likely that she was largely fed with solids by that date.

'A pleasant pastime for the child'

In their royal play at Eltham, Elizabeth, Henry and Margaret had a wealth of toys and games from which to choose. Toy manufacture began to reach an industrial scale in early sixteenth-century Germany, when toys could be made cheaply and quickly for export and sale. There were toys to suit almost any parental purse, ranging from the inexpensive cup and ball to intricate tin toy animals.[20] Babies were given gender-neutral playthings, including rattles, which are known from the sixteenth century, windmills and, for older infants, hobby horses. There were baby walkers, too, with their wooden frames to help the toddler learn to walk.[21]

Certain toys were aimed at girls. Dolls had been in

existence for centuries before Elizabeth's birth, having originally been made of clay.[22] Dolls' houses and miniature furniture are known from at least the mid-sixteenth century, again in Germany.[23] These could include dolls' kitchens with dishes, meat plates, cutlery and furniture, all carefully wrought.[24] Wealthy girls, such as Princess Elizabeth, could also receive fashion dolls, modelling the latest in clothing, while poorer children's dolls were made of rags and stuffed with straw.[25]

A few sixteenth-century dolls survive in museum collections, but to get a true idea of the lavishness of some examples, it is necessary to turn to portraiture. In 1577, the two-year-old Arbella Stuart, who was a great-great-granddaughter of Henry VII, sat for a portrait that now hangs in Hardwick Hall, her childhood home.[26] Clutched in her left hand is a doll, depicting an adult woman in Elizabethan dress, with a ruff at her neck, puffed sleeves and a full skirt.[27] It was probably a fashion doll, given to this wealthy and aristocratic little girl as a toy. Perhaps it was a favourite of hers, which she

refused to part with even as she sat for her first portrait.

Children from every walk of life were capable of finding a toy in almost anything, including animal knucklebones, wooden wheels or household implements.[28] A famous painting (1560) by Peter Brueghel, which now hangs in the Kunsthistorisches Museum in Vienna, shows more than 200 children playing around 80 different games, providing an unprecedented insight into childish pursuits of the period.[29] Many of the games are familiar: girls play knucklebones and dolls, while a group of boys and girls act out a mock bridal procession and another group plays blind man's bluff. One girl is also depicted pretending to keep a shop; other children play 'paper, scissors, stone', roll hoops and rock barrels.[30]

There were some adults who looked for educational value in these games. Juan Luis Vives considered that the well-bred girl 'in the form of play' should be permitted to 'exercise herself in things that will be of benefit to her later'. He favoured 'chaste tales' told to the girl, rather than dolls, 'which are a kind of image of idolatry and teach girls the desire for adornments and finery'. Nonetheless, as he said, 'those toys made of tin or lead that represent household objects' were still permissible, since they provided 'a pleasant pastime for the child, and in the meantime she learns the names and uses of various things without even being aware of it'.[31]

Through play and the accoutrements of play, as she sought to imitate her mother or nurse, a Tudor girl began to learn about the world and her place within it.

The infant Elizabeth's parents remained a distant but very real presence in her life. Henry VII, of course, had no intention of being a hands-on father to any of his children. Indeed, in the days and weeks after Elizabeth's birth he was busy with a proposed invasion of France, for which he set sail in October 1492.[32] It was to be a brief, but successful campaign. He returned to his kingdom just over a month later, richer by a pension of nearly 60,000 crowns per year – and without a single skirmish being fought.

Although affairs of state kept King Henry constantly occupied, he managed to keep an interested eye on his children, particularly his sons, as evidenced in regular purchases of clothes and other items for them in his accounts.[33] The king and queen had spent the Christmas before Elizabeth's birth at Eltham, arriving there on 23 December,[34] where they received visits from Margaret and little Henry. The king had been minded, on 31 December, to order the immediate payment of the nursery staff's wages, which were by then overdue by more than a month.[35]

At New Year 1494, the king surprised the nursery at Eltham with the delivery of two horses for Prince Henry.[36] He also loaded his two sons with offices – although this allowed him, effectively, to keep them in his own hands.[37] Little Prince Henry was fetched from Eltham later in 1494 for the greatest of these appointments, with the three-year-old riding ceremonially through the City of London on a fine courser.[38] Two days later, on 1 November, he was created Duke of York.[39]

To celebrate young Henry's elevation, great jousts were held at Westminster, in which challengers ran in the lists, and there was sword-fighting and other sports. The event lasted several busy days,[40] during which the king, queen and at least their eldest daughter, Margaret, then aged five, attended: indeed, the tournament was held in the little girl's honour, allowing her to pick the winners each day.[41] Because her brother and sister were present at Westminster too, it is possible that the two-year-old Princess Elizabeth was also permitted to attend. Royal children were often expected to appear in public at a young age.[42]

If so, Cecily Burbage cannot have failed to notice the gallant William Craythorn, who would later become a significant figure in her life. This Yeoman of the Horse[43] had been in the king's service since at least November 1491, and he was considered by the king to be a 'well-beloved servant' who gave 'true and faithful service'.[44] He provided the comic relief one day when the challengers were late arriving, riding comically into battle with a horse 'apparelled in paper in manner of a bard', while his mount's apron showed an image of two men playing at dice. Craythorn, who was not known for his martial prowess, wheeled his horse around to face another courtier, Henry Wynslow, with his lance, before dismounting for hand to hand combat.[45] Everything they did, Wynslow later confided to one chronicler, was 'to cause the king to laugh'; but unfortunately it went a little too far. When Wynslow knocked Craythorn's sword from his hand, his opponent picked it up and launched himself at him – forgetting, for the moment, the merry purpose of their sparring. It was up to the king to separate them, commanding them to leave the field so that the true knights (who had, by then, arrived) could enter.

Cecily Burbage's wider life continued even as she undertook her duties in the royal nursery. On 14 January 1493, when she had been at Eltham for less than a year, her younger brother died.[46] In one swoop, she became heiress to her father's moderate estates. In the Tudor period, the daughters of a man without sons shared his estates as co-heiresses – but Cecily did not even have any sisters with whom to share this boon. Nonetheless, although her husband would have moved to claim the inheritance at once, Cecily was still preoccupied with her young charge at Eltham. She rarely, if ever, found the time to visit home.

As a younger daughter, Princess Elizabeth did not rate highly in the hierarchy of royal children. Indeed, she appears to have been so insignificant that her grandmother, the formidable Margaret Beaufort, neglected to record the date of her birth in her Book of Hours, unlike those of her other grandchildren.[47] It is not even clear what Elizabeth looked like, although babies were expected to resemble both their parents ('two persons in one'), with perhaps the father's nose and eyes and the mother's brow and chin.[48] There is only one recorded 'likeness' of her, in *The Family of Henry VII*, which now hangs at Hampton Court and shows her as an adult, crowned and kneeling in a line of daughters behind her mother. She displays a serene, calm expression in a thin and pointed face; but the image is a fantasy.

In March 1493 the princess was included – implicitly – in a grant made by her father to St Michael's monastery in Dover, the price of which was that 'the prior and convent may pray for the good estate of the king, Elizabeth his consort, Arthur Prince of Wales his first born son and the rest of his children and of the king and his progenitors after this life'.[49] But these prayers did Princess Elizabeth no good at all. She would not reach her fourth birthday, let alone adulthood.

∽

Death stalked the nurseries of Tudor England, with disease a major peril of the young.[50] Indeed, in York, at the end of the Tudor period, infant mortality represented more than 15 per cent of burials.[51] These were not isolated cases. A third of deaths in the late Tudor and early Stuart period are thought to have related to children under ten, while approximately 15 per cent of burials in the 1580s were of children aged less than one year.[52]

Most children who died were killed by infectious diseases. The dreaded sweating sickness, bubonic plague, typhus and syphilis were all present in England, among other horrors in an age where medicine was rudimentary.[53] Childrearing manuals abounded with purported cures for childhood ailments, yet most of them had only a limited effect. Pious Elizabeth of York once told her husband that children were only 'lent' to their parents, something which did little to alleviate the bitterness of each crushing blow.[54] She, like others, could take some comfort in religion, but losses were still harshly felt by most parents.

'Most inhumane murders'

Although most deaths of Tudor children were the result of illness or accident – and the subjects of regret and sorrow, but ultimately acceptance, in the face of fate and God's will – violence could play a part too.

On 1 June 1593, an unmarried woman named Jane Little, who lived in Hoxton, Middlesex, felt her labour pains begin.[55]

She had been concealing her pregnancy for the past nine months, but there was gossip enough about her increasing size. Gathering her clothes about her, she hurried away from her lodgings and out into the fields, a little way from town. There, she laboured alone, before giving birth to a baby girl. Whether in shock or in panic when the baby cried, or carrying out a premeditated plan, Jane dug a hole and buried her daughter alive, before returning home again. But she did a poor job of concealing her crime, and the infant's body was soon found. At a subsequent trial, Jane pleaded guilty and was sentenced to hang.

Such tales were far from unusual in Tudor England, where there was considerable stigma attached to illegitimacy, as well as little in the way of poor relief.[56] Four years after Jane Little gave birth, Jane Gamble, an unmarried servant from Edmonton, north of London, gave birth to a boy in her room in her employer's house.[57] She immediately crushed his skull, a deed for which she was condemned to hang. Another unmarried mother, Elizabeth Colpitt of Cobham, Surrey, gave birth at an inn in 1568, before throwing her infant daughter into a sawpit, where she was smothered.[58] Colpitt was immediately apprehended, but not tried for three months – in which time, she was able to conceive another child and plead her belly.[59]

Most recorded infanticides were committed by the mother, using whatever means she had to hand. Tudor court records note babies being suffocated by their mother's hands,[60] rolled in a piece of cloth, stabbed with a meat knife, buried alive, or having their skulls crushed or necks broken – among other methods of dispatch.[61] A mother who bore a daughter in Maldon, Essex, panicked and hid the child in a chest in her room, only to find it dead the next day. After consulting with the probable father, she then buried it in a heap of horse dung in the garden, where it was quickly discovered.[62]

Occasionally, the baby's father would commit the crime, as was the case with Francis Shoesmith. He visited the house of Elizabeth Edlyn in Little Wembley, Middlesex, on 19 July 1580, around eight hours after she had given birth.[63] Shoesmith took the baby out into the fields before attempting to kill it with his bare hands. When he found himself too squeamish to continue, he simply buried the child. In Epping, a father was found guilty of throwing a newborn into the 'mud or slud' of a ditch, allowing it to drown.[64] In another, unusual case, a clergyman named James Ellis, who was the rector of Chiddingfold, was found not guilty at the Southwark Assizes in March 1560 of murdering his mistress's day-old baby within the rectory.[65]

Infanticide was actually quite hard to prove, given the fact that most of the children were born without witnesses and could, therefore, have been dead at birth. One Agnes Hughes was arraigned in Middlesex, accused of suffocating her baby son in 1584, but found not guilty 'on account of the uncertainty of the evidence'.[66] Other women, who had more successfully concealed both their pregnancies and the babies' bodies, would not have been discovered at all.

Older children, too, could become victims. On 8 March 1588, one Margaret Young was sentenced to hang in Middlesex for the murder of James Young, 'an infant of seven years', whom she had held over the fire to burn.[67] Nearby, and only three years later, Mary Hill was hanged for suffocating the six-month-old son of a neighbour with a linen cloth.[68]

Despite this ostensible prevalence of infanticide, it was seen as a particularly unnatural and barbaric crime, and it attracted considerable public attention. One pamphlet (1610), entitled 'The Bloody Mother', recounts 'the most inhumane murders, committed by Jane Hattersley upon diverse infants, the issue of her own body and the private burying of them in an orchard'.[69] Jane Hattersley was a servant in the house of Adam Adamson of East Grinstead, Sussex, who became her lover. The affair went on for ten or twelve years, 'in which time,' as the pamphlet related, 'the full number of the babes they have had, cannot be known, but three she confessed, besides one that is yet living'. 'This common and most imprudent bastard-bearer' gave birth to her first in a neighbour's house, where she was discovered by the wife, Mrs King, who, for five or six days kept a close watch on her to ensure that she did not harm the child. One morning, when her hostess was out, Jane suffocated the child with a hand over its mouth, before cleaning the baby to ensure that – when the constable arrived – it looked as though it had died naturally.

While this baby received Christian burial, her second was born more secretly and smothered at once. She then carried it to a nearby orchard and buried it beside a tree. Adamson then killed the third child in the same way and buried it close by its elder sibling. When the fourth pregnancy became apparent, suspicious neighbours drove Jane out of town. Staying with her sister, who evidently kept her under supervision, Jane sent her fourth infant to live with a nurse. Although there were rumours in East Grinstead, it was only with the discovery of a body under the tree in the orchard that Jane was imprisoned, before being hanged in 1609. Adamson went unpunished since – thanks to Jane's 'simplicity' – she took all the blame on herself.

The account of Jane Hattersley's crimes made lurid reading in the early seventeenth century; but, in an age with limited contraception, it was no surprise that similar stories were played out throughout the Tudor period. More fortunate illegitimate children were boarded out by their parents. Jane Pusie was 'great with child' in 1583 when the curate of Bampton – and presumably the father of her baby – paid for her to lodge in the house of one William Cooke in a neighbouring parish.[70] After giving birth, Jane returned home alone, and the curate made a payment of 12d a week to Cooke 'for keeping the said child'.

In the manuscript of the *Danse Macabre of Women*, musing on female mortality, a poignant illustration shows Death snatching away a young girl, who cries out for her mother: 'look, the dead woman is taking me away'.[71] The girl's thoughts turn to her few precious things: 'please take care of my doll, / My five stones, my beautiful coat'. The fifteenth-century poet John Lydgate portrayed the death of a 'little infant that were but late born' in his own version of the *Danse Macabre*.[72] For him, Death was the child's music tutor, teaching how to dance the dance of death. In September 1495 it was Princess Elizabeth's turn to take a new dancing master.

Christmas 1494 – Princess Elizabeth's last – was spent apart from her parents, with the king and queen still busy with their festivities at Westminster, where they were entertained with masques.[73] Her royal parents were similarly preoccupied in the summer of 1495, as they set out on a great progress, heading first north-westwards, towards Bewdley, Ludlow and Shrewsbury.[74] As summer began to wane, and the evenings shortened, they went north, up past Derby and then to Northampton. There, King Henry took care of nursery business, ordering the payment of the half-yearly salaries of the staff serving 'our right dearly well-beloved children the Lord Henry the Ladies Margaret and Elizabeth'. The first was due to 'our well-beloved Cecily Burbage, Nurse to our right dearly well-beloved daughter the Lady Elizabeth'.[75] The familiar nursery staff were still all in place, and there was no hint that anything was amiss at Eltham.

The weather that September was unusually stormy, with hot, humid days and 'exceeding thunder'.[76] On 8 September, chroniclers recorded a notable and sudden death, of Sir William Hussey, Chief Justice of England.[77] It was during this unsettled weather, too, that a small royal tragedy was played out in the nursery at Eltham: the death of Princess Elizabeth on 14 September.[78]

Claims that she died of atrophy, a slow, painful wasting disease, are based only on a reference to the goddess Atropos in her tomb inscription; but the association of this deity with death was well established by the Tudor period, particularly in relation to female death.[79] More likely, she died of some simple childhood disease or from an accident, her death sudden and unexpected.

Elizabeth's parents were on the road between Northampton and Banbury when messengers set out to intercept them with news from Eltham.[80] No hint of the emotion can be discerned in Henry VII's privy purse accounts from the period. Life on the progress continued the same as before, with small purchases of gloves and cheese made as they continued with their itinerary. On 1 October 1495, the royal couple arrived at Windsor, and two days later were at Sheen. The king attended the opening of Parliament on 13 October 1495, which sat, as usual, at Westminster; the business that winter was dominated by the attainder of the king's step-uncle and former supporter, Sir William Stanley.[81]

Henry VII had accepted the news of his daughter's death with equanimity. On 27 October, for his remaining offspring at Eltham, he placed an order 'for diverse yards of silk bought for My Lord of York [Prince Henry] and My Lady Margaret'.[82] His nursery had shrunk in size. But it was expected soon to grow, for Elizabeth of York was, by then, reaching the halfway point of her fifth pregnancy: life went on.

For the first funeral of a member of the Tudor royal family, the notoriously penny-pinching king was, however, prepared to open his hands, laying out the enormous sums of 1,000 marks and then £318 9s 7d on the funeral and tomb.[83] On the appointed day, a procession of gentlemen set out from Eltham. Riding two-and-two, they crossed the narrow stone bridge at Eltham Palace and along the winding road that led away from Elizabeth's final residence.[84]

Behind them were the officers of arms in all their heraldry, riding beside a chariot covered in black cloth and pulled by six large horses similarly draped with the colour of mourning. Amid the snaking procession, along the autumn roads still muddy from the recent storms, lay the three-year-old, carried in her coffin on the chariot. It was a mournful company, but also stately. Merchant knights, all in the robes of their livery companies, followed behind, four on each side of the corpse. The seven official mourners then followed, the first of which was the fifty-year-old Elizabeth, Duchess of Suffolk – sister of Edward IV and thus a royal princess herself. This Princess Elizabeth followed the coffin of her tiny great-niece, her hood pulled up in the expected show of grief. Six other ladies followed her, again with hoods over their faces and no mantles, riding in the solemn line.

It was a journey of nearly ten miles, through fields and settlements, to London, which at that time was still very far from extending its sprawling suburbs to Eltham. The route was quiet, but still took the best part of the day. Their arrival was noted when it was time to cross the Thames. As the party approached Westminster Abbey, a canopy was raised over the deceased Elizabeth by four of the knights, while at each corner of her hearse a banner was unfurled, showing the Holy Trinity, the Virgin Mary, St George and, finally, the king's own royal arms.

With her final journey over, the little girl was brought into an abbey bedecked in sombre magnificence. Black sarcenet covered much of the interior of the great church, embroidered all over with red and white roses to depict the young princess's importance as a symbol of the united royal houses of Lancaster and York.[85] These flowers had previously decorated the chamber in which she was born, less than four years before. In spite of the great size of the abbey, it was a packed assembly, with the Archbishop of York, the royal chaplains, many lords, the Lord Mayor of London and representatives of the guilds and livery companies all in attendance.

Once everyone was inside, the services began. The Earl of Northumberland led the mourners. It must already have been dark outside, with only the flickering flames inside the church to illuminate the mournful scene.[86] Towards the end of the final mass, the Duchess of Suffolk, who had, in her time, buried six of her own children, was led to the altar. She made an offering of money before returning to her place. Following her went the other ladies in pairs, giving their own alms for the good of the princess's soul, before the rest of the company joined them.

It was time now for the coffin to be brought forward. Once again, it was the women who took the lead, with Lady Daubeney, Viscountess Lisle, the Countess of Wiltshire and, of course, the Duchess of Suffolk (among others) offering palls of cloth. If Cecily Burbage or any of Elizabeth's nursery attendants were permitted to attend, their names were not recorded – they were certainly not high-ranking enough to serve as official mourners, although their grief was considerably more genuine.[87] By custom, Elizabeth's parents stayed away.

Finally, as one contemporary put it, 'when the mass and all other ceremonies pertaining to the funeral of this noble young lady were solemnized, then was the corpse taken up out of the hearse, and borne with all reverence in like sort and manner as it was brought to the church and so entombed'.[88] With the body now interred, the company returned home again.

For this first Tudor royal burial, Henry VII had decided upon Westminster Abbey, where he and his wife and his formidable mother would later be buried. Close to the altar of St Edward the Confessor – the holiest location in the great abbey church – a tiny tomb was erected, of black and grey marble.[89] It once included Elizabeth's effigy, carved in copper and gilt, but this has long since been lost.[90] The child's epitaph was written in Latin and sums up the loss felt by her family at her death:

Here, after death lies in this tomb a descendant of royalty, the young and noble Princess Elizabeth, daughter of the illustrious king, Henry VII, who swap the flourishing sceptres of two realms. Atrophy, most merciless messenger of death, snatched her away. May she inherit eternal life in Heaven![91]

A life that had begun with such promise had proved disappointingly brief. It was, in essence, a common story; so many Tudor girls failed to grow into Tudor women. Even a princess, such as Elizabeth, could all but disappear from the records, and her place in the royal nursery was soon filled by another daughter – Mary – who would live to adulthood. Elizabeth's death also meant the end of her nurse's service: Cecily Burbage's place was taken by Anne Crown, who came to nurse the new baby.[92]

There are a few hints that, among her family, Elizabeth was still remembered. A beautiful medieval breviary in royal ownership was later augmented by at least three and, possibly, four Tudor hands to provide a calendar of royal dates in order of the year.[93] All the important dates are there, including the birth of Henry VII and the death of Henry VIII. Princess Elizabeth's birth or death dates were not recorded, but in the record for 18 March, which marked the birthday of her sister, Princess Mary, it stated that Mary was the *third* daughter of Henry VII. Implicitly, at least, the short life of the first Elizabeth Tudor was acknowledged.[94] Perhaps she was loved and missed after all.

Memorials for minors

Parents did the best for their dead children, usually giving them the most honourable burial to which their means could stretch, with wealthier children receiving the more expensive coffins, rather than a simple shroud.[95] Princess Elizabeth was not the only Tudor child to be remembered with a tomb memorial, but when it came to memorials of this kind, it was more common for infants to be commemorated with their parents rather than have their own monuments. Indeed, inscriptions of this type are often the only evidence for the brief life of an infant. In one such example, the names of only nine of the children of Sir John Blount and his wife Katherine (the parents of the famous Bessie Blount, mistress to Henry VIII) are known, yet their tomb is adorned with the representations of eleven children – two of whom are now forgotten.[96] In this case, all the children are depicted as adults; but it was also common to show young children as they had been in life: as swaddled infants.

One of the most poignant examples is the brass in Blickling Church, Norfolk, dedicated to Anne Astley, who died in 1512. Anne had been visiting her sister at Blickling when she went into labour. She had twins (a boy and a girl), who died at birth, along with their mother. Anne's effigy shows her in the clothing of a pregnant woman, with the laces spread wide on her bodice to accommodate her increasing girth.[97] She holds a baby tucked within each of her arms, with no distinction made for the sex of the infant. Both are tightly swaddled.

Swaddled children have been depicted on tombs since the medieval period, and such images highlight the personal tragedy of each infant death.[98] An individual monument to little John Eyre at Knipton, Leicestershire, dating to 1523, shows the baby lying tightly swaddled with decorative bands, very much as though he was still in his cradle. A similar monument for Elyn Bray at Stoke d'Abernon, Surrey, which dates to 1516, also shows the child swaddled. As with Anne Astley's effigy, in children this young it was rare for the sexes to be distinguished.

The Second Age

4

OF YOUNG LADIES AND LEARNING

The Countess of Surrey's girls, Jane Dormer,
Lady Bryan and Margaret Beaufort

On Thursday 8 May 1495, only a few months before Princess Elizabeth would die, and well over 200 miles away from the quiet of Eltham Palace and the bustle of London trade, the poet John Skelton arrived at Sheriff Hutton Castle in Yorkshire. In spite of its wooded location in the primordial Forest of Galtres, the fortress was no backwater. It loomed mighty to those who approached, standing quadrangular and solid, its five floors of accommodation and high galleries strung out along its walls.[1] Skelton could reflect that the road there was one more travelled by soldiers than poets, as he passed through the castle gates and under a narrow archway into the inner courtyard. Nonetheless, it was also a family home; and Skelton's errand lay with the castle's mistress, Elizabeth Tylney, Countess of Surrey, and with the women and girls that attended her.

At seven, a Tudor girl was generally regarded as entering her second age, that of adolescence.[2] For Shakespeare, this was the time of the 'whining schoolboy with his satchel', 'creeping like snail unwillingly to school'. It is an engaging image, but it held less true for girls.

Records of the education of Tudor women are extremely sparse.[3] Girls were, for the most part, taught informally in their homes. Religious education was, of course, essential, but whether girls received much else in their early training is less clear. By the 1530s, it was becoming fashionable for the gentry and nobility to educate their daughters, and many girls were able to read and write.[4] In this trend, many families strove to follow the example set by Sir Thomas More in the education of his three highly accomplished daughters.[5] His friend Erasmus, too, recommended the education of women. It was their considered opinion that it would provide girls with the tools to assist their husbands in creating a Christian home after marriage and to raise their children virtuously.

Richard Hyrde, who wrote the Introduction to Margaret More's translation of Erasmus's *Treatise on the Paternoster*, echoed contemporary sentiments to the contrary. 'I have heard,' he wrote, 'many men put great doubt whether it should be expedient and requisite or not, a woman to have learning in books of Latin and Greek. And some utterly affirm that it is not only neither necessary nor profitable, but also very noisome and jeopardous.' He had heard it said that such studies would 'inflame their stomachs' towards vice.[6] Hyrde considered such a view erroneous, but it was a widely held one.

Thirty years later, Thomas Becon considered the subject of women's learning, regarding it as a biblical duty for them to be taught 'to be sober minded, to love their husbands, to love their children, to be discreet, chaste, housewifely, good, obedient to their husbands; that the word of God be not evil spoken of'.[7] To raise a godly woman, he believed, schools for girls should be erected in every town, presided over by 'honest, sage, wise, discreet, sober, grave and learned matrons' as teachers. Becon asked an obvious question:

*If it be thought convenient, as it is most convenient, that
schools should be erected and set up for the right education
and bringing up of the youth of the male kind, why should
it not also be thought convenient that schools be built for
the godly instruction and virtuous bringing up of the youth
of the female kind?*

He did not go so far as arguing for the same curriculum,
however. Latin, Greek and even 'good letters' were to be left
to the boys. And although the provision of education for girls
grew in the Tudor period, no one was seriously asking that
they be taught to the same level as boys. In the 1580s, Richard
Mulcaster, addressing the issue, was quick to assure his readers
that he would speak of boys' education first, since 'naturally the
male is more worthy'.[8] Girls should not, he considered, be permitted to attend grammar schools or universities; but they had
some capacity for learning. 'We see young maidens be taught to
read and write and can do both with praise; we hear them sing
and play and both passing well; we know that they learn the
best and finest of our learned languages to the admiration of all
men.' He had noticed that girls actually seemed to learn faster
than boys, although he was quick to assure his readers that 'for
all that seeming yet it is not so', since 'their natural weakness,
which cannot hold long, delivers very soon'. Nonetheless, they
should certainly be taught to read, since they needed this skill
to fully embrace religious teaching. There was also no harm in
teaching them to write if that was possible, while music was also
useful. Principally, girls should strive to be good housewives,
but (he considered), a little learning could not hurt.

In aristocratic households, it was mothers who were primarily responsible for the early education of their daughters,
providing instruction in reading, religion, sewing, embroidery,
music, dancing and cooking.[9] It was through the instruction
of her own mother that the London merchant's daughter,

Rose Hickman, learned of Protestantism during the 1530s and 1540s. Her mother, as she recalled, had sent for reformist texts from overseas and 'used to call me with my 2 sisters into her chamber to read to us out of the same good books very privately for fear of trouble because these good books were then accounted heretical'.[10] A generation later, Grace, Lady Mildmay received her early instruction also from her mother, who had strong ideas about reading, considering 'it ever dangerous to suffer young people to read or study books wherein was good and evil mingled together'.[11] Instead, her curriculum contained only the Bible, John Foxe's compendium of Protestant martyrology, *Acts and Monuments* (*Book of Martyrs*), and two other approved religious works. This was enough, considered Grace's mother. As her daughter later recalled, her mother would often say 'that she would teach me not to subject myself unto mine own will and frame me to bear patiently whatsoever adversity should assault me in this world'.

Samplers and stitchery

Sometime in 1598, Jane Bostocke, a young Shropshire gentlewoman, finished a long worked-over project, carefully stitching her designs and lettering into a piece of linen with various coloured silks, and decorating the result with small beads and seed pearls. As well as intricate geometric designs, she carefully stitched a dog with a collar and a lead, as well as a rather more exotic chained bear. She included trees and flowers and a small heraldic lion. It is clear that Jane changed her mind on more than one occasion, carefully unpicking a castle on an elephant, a squirrel cracking a nut and a raven.

Jane intricately stitched the letters of the alphabet, too, before recording her name, the date and the birth of her cousin, Alice Lee, on 'the 23 of November being Tuesday in the afternoon 1596'. She may already have begun the work before her cousin's birth, later deciding to present it to her as a gift.[12] Undoubtedly, the piece of stitchery must have taken her many hours of careful work – sometimes by the light of the window, sometimes with a candle burning close at hand. The result is the earliest surviving English sampler that is dated, and it now resides in London's Victoria and Albert Museum.[13]

Upper-class Tudor girls, such as those at Sheriff Hutton, and women such as Jane Bostocke spent much of their time at their needlework. A sampler of the kind on which Jane worked was intended for the beginner, allowing girls and young women to perfect different types of stitching. Another surviving Elizabethan example, by a girl who stitched her name as 'Susan Neeadri',[14] contains the queen's arms and initials accompanied by heraldic beasts.[15] This sampler, which is long and narrow, is extremely intricate, its top panel embroidered in red and gold silk and the second panel in black and silver. The remaining bands were worked with cheaper, linen thread.

Lower down the social scale, too, girls were taught embroidery. Thomasine Wolters, an orphan living in Sandwich, Kent, in the 1580s–90s, was boarded out in the home of a Mistress Smythe. There, she was taught to sew; she later purchased her sampler from her old mistress when she left to marry. The Sandwich Board of Orphans, which oversaw Thomasine's modest inheritance and paid for her maintenance, also periodically purchased silk thread for her work.[16] As well as producing beautiful embroidery, Thomasine had been taught to stitch her own gowns and coifs to cover her hair, and to make lace.

Sewing was, after all, a practical skill. Tudor women commonly made and repaired their own clothing, and even high-born women stitched clothes. Henry VIII's first wife, Catherine of Aragon, was skilled at shirt-making.[17] The future Elizabeth I sent her half-brother, Edward VI, a shirt 'of her own working' as a New Year's gift when she was just six years old. Women frequently made vestments and other items for churches, too. Elizabeth's lady-in-waiting, Blanche Parry, gave an altar cloth that she had made to the church of St Faith's in Bacton in Herefordshire in 1589.[18]

There was nothing unusual in seeing Tudor girls and women of all classes sitting with their heads bent, stitching.

Another young gentlewoman who was educated at home was Jane Dormer, who was born in 1538. She was entrusted to the care of her grandmother after the early death of her mother and, as Jane later recalled to her biographer, 'the first thing she learned was her duty to serve God, and her obedience to her father, grandfather, and grandmother, by conforming herself with affectionate humility to their commands'.[19] Before she was seven, she could read, practising on her primer. She was a highly accomplished needlewoman, producing both samplers and church ornaments, and she acquired her own governess.

While still a young child, Jane Dormer was chosen to attend Prince Edward (the future Edward VI), who was only three months older than her. She quickly settled into the role, 'passing her time with the prince, either in reading, playing, or dancing, and such like pastimes, answerable to their spirits and innocency of years, and in playing at cards'. Jane's grandmother later used her influence with Henry VIII's eldest daughter, Princess Mary (the future Queen Mary), who had already taken on two of Jane's aunts, to accept Jane into her household. As Jane recalled proudly, this was really prestigious, since 'in those days the house of this princess was the only harbour for honourable young gentlewomen, given any way to piety and devotion. It was the true school of virtuous demeanour, befitting the education that ought to be in noble damsels.' As such, 'the greatest lords in the kingdom were suitors to her to receive their daughters in their service'. Young Jane would read to the princess, as well as carry out more menial duties.

Jane Dormer was far from alone among her peers in finishing her education and upbringing away from home. One Venetian visitor to the country, who arrived at the start of the sixteenth century, regarded the standards of English parenting as woefully lacking and exhibiting an alarming want of affection.[20] As he noted, 'after having kept them at home till they arrive at the age of 7 or 9 years at the utmost', parents would put their children out of the house and set them 'to hard service in the houses of other people, binding them generally for another 7 or 9 years'. When he pressed his hosts for an explanation, the ambassador was assured that this practice was intended to teach the children 'better manners'; but he considered that there was a darker motive. It was, he was sure, 'because they like to enjoy all their comforts themselves, and... they are better served by strangers than they would be by their own children'. Parents did not even bring their children home again at the end of their service in another's household, 'for the girls are settled by their patrons', while the boys went into business with the assistance of their benefactors.

This was a rather bleak assessment of a practice so commonplace that it was almost universal. The Venetian missed the fundamental point of it, at least in relation to Tudor girls: gentry parents sent them away to a higher-status household in the hope that they would marry up. The habit of 'placing out' girls for their advancement and education was already well established by the beginning of the Tudor period.[21] It outlasted the dynasty itself. Young Anne Clifford, who was the daughter of the Earl of Cumberland, actively sought a place serving Queen Elizabeth I. The girl's hopes that an influential aunt would (as she put it) 'prefer me to be of the Privy Chamber' were scuppered only by the queen's death in March 1603.[22]

∞

More than a century earlier, Elizabeth Tylney, Countess of Surrey, was also staffing her household with young gentle-women. They hoped that she would help them find their way in life. At Sheriff Hutton Castle, the beautiful countess saw herself as a literary patron. Born an heiress, she was used to the splendour of her manor house at Ashwellthorpe in Suffolk. She had thought herself settled into comfortable middle age when Fortune's Wheel turned against her in August 1485. Then, her second husband, Thomas Howard, Earl of Surrey, had found himself on the losing side at the Battle of Bosworth Field, along with his father, the 1st Duke of Norfolk. The battle's victor, the new King Henry VII, had been in no mood to be lenient towards the vanquished Richard III's greatest supporter, and the wounded (and now fatherless) earl was taken straight from the battlefield to the Tower of London. Terrified and unpro-tected, the countess had swept up her children and fled to the windy and sparse Isle of Sheppey to await the outcome of events. It was four long years before she saw her husband again, and even then they were not to return to the comfort of Ashwellthorpe.[23]

The suspicious and untrusting first Tudor king needed good soldiers, a factor that finally secured Surrey's release in 1489, when he was sent north with an army to quell a rebellion. The countess, with her children, packed up her fine woven tapestries, cushions and plate, before making the slow journey northwards to unruly Yorkshire.[24] It was Surrey's appointment as Lieutenant of the North that brought him and the countess to Sheriff Hutton Castle. There was 'no house so like a princely lodging' in all the North,[25] but nevertheless the wind whipped around the turrets and battlements. The stone walls, though thick, let in a chill so biting that the green and red velvet cushions and carpets, 'sore worn' with the hurried feet, could do little to make the place homely.[26] It was a cheerless administrative seat, from which the exiled countess craved culture.

The household at Sheriff Hutton woke early. Servants dressed hurriedly and began their tasks for the day. It was the marshal – a senior household officer – who roused the more lowly residents, who slept on their rolled mats in the great hall.[27] This hub of castle life served many functions. In the morning, the previous day's filth was swept away and the dogs chased out, before table boards were set out on trestles to fill the room.[28] Others bustled around, preparing breakfast as the fires roared in the stuffy kitchens, or fetching water from the well. The line between servant and family was often blurred in Tudor England, with kin frequently placed to serve their greater family members.[29]

Space was at a premium. Only the Countess of Surrey's married daughter, Anne Bourchier, Lady Dacre of the South, had rank enough to have her own chamber when she visited.[30] The unmarried girls shared a single chamber for young ladies, which lay close to the earl's and countess's own rooms, for propriety's sake.[31]

It was a noisy and chaotic environment, but also companionable, allowing the two Howard daughters – fifteen-year-old Elizabeth and ten-year-old Muriel – to learn from the chatter of the older girls. Apart from bed curtains, there was little privacy.[32] In such households, it was usual for the young ladies' chamber to be locked at night, and the key brought safely to the mistress. But such security measures were easily circumvented. A quick hand could steal the key or a copy could be made, allowing for illicit picnics with men and even love affairs.[33] Elizabeth Howard was, in 1495, on the brink of womanhood – 'freshly embeautied with many a goodly sort of womanly features'[34] – and it was essential that her mother guard her reputation and honour if she was to make a good match.

Elizabeth Howard rose early, at around the same time as her parents, climbing out of the featherbed that she shared with a female companion. Too much sleep dulled girls' wits and could cause illness, according to contemporaries.[35] It was better not to stay too long in bed. Instead, the girls said their morning prayers,[36] before cleaning their teeth and washing behind their ears in a basin. Then they combed their hair, before dressing for the day. For noble girls, such as Elizabeth and Muriel, there were fine cloth gowns and dresses lined with fur.[37] Underneath, they each pulled on a thick pair of hose and a smock, which, unlike the more elaborate outer garments, were at least washable. Once dressed, the girls attended mass in the castle chapel, before being released for breakfast. The household tasks could then begin.[38]

There was nothing remarkable about 8 May 1495 at Sheriff Hutton Castle, save for the fact that John Skelton later recalled it poetically. The scholar had every reason to be pleased with himself as he prepared for his meeting with his hostess. With long, flowing hair he looked younger than his thirty-two years, and in his fashionable short gowns and furred hanging sleeves, he seemed gallant. In recent months his court career had taken off. He had been appointed to serve the king's own mother, Lady Margaret Beaufort, as her official poet – an honourable but largely honorary post. He would later use this influence to secure an appointment as tutor to her grandson, Prince Henry. But that was years in the future; for now, the boy was still playing in his nursery with his sisters, Margaret and – for not much longer – Elizabeth.

The summer of 1495 proved to be one of enjoyment and jollity for Skelton, his hostess and the young girls of her household. On that morning of 8 May, he took time to visit the gardens, crunching lightly over the sand-covered pathways to admire the rose bushes and 'birds on the briar', which 'sang on every side'.[39] Ambling along, he came upon one of the countess's grooms, who led him from the gardens up a winding stair to the countess's chamber of estate.

The Countess of Surrey sat surrounded by a 'bevy' of 'fair ladies'. She was still a strikingly attractive woman. Years earlier, she had been beautiful enough to attract the attentions of the eligible Thomas Howard, a comrade-in-arms to her battle-slain first husband.[40] Although almost continually pregnant during the early years of her second marriage, she had maintained her slender figure, allowing her to wear the latest fashions.[41]

The countess's daughters were striking too, as Skelton noted. He would later become a priest, but in his youth John Skelton was something of a womanizer,[42] and the countess's married daughter, the glamorous Anne Bourchier, reminded him of the beautiful, mythical Helen of Troy. He cast an appreciative eye over her half-sister, Elizabeth Howard, as well, again by way of literary allusion.[43] She was Criseyde, the treacherous, but deeply alluring, lover of Troilus. He gazed on her with a poet's eye, but perhaps also with an appreciation of a different kind, finding her ripe for love – 'lusty to look on, pleasant, demure and sage'.

The countess's daughters were not the only women that Skelton noted at Sheriff Hutton. He came across Margery Wentworth, either on this visit or during an earlier one. The girl was somewhat mousy, being 'benign, courteous and meek'. Her mother – the countess's half-sister – had used the family connection to good effect in placing her at the castle.[44] The Wentworths hoped that the teenaged Margery would secure a good husband through her aunt's lofty connections.[45] A younger girl present, Isabel Pennel, was another relative. She was still only a child, but she had a good chance of marrying well. Skelton was impressed by her, too, declaring to her: 'by Saint Mary, my lady, your mammy and your daddy brought forth a goodly baby!'[46] Teenaged Agnes Tylney, who was a distant cousin of the countess, had left her parents and the quiet society of Lincolnshire to attend the countess when she moved north to Sheriff Hutton.[47] She went on to make the best match of all the Countess of Surrey's women – none other than her mistress's widower, just four months after the countess's death in 1497.

The career of a lady mistress – Lady Bryan

The Countess of Surrey oversaw the education of her daughters and the girls in her care herself, as was usually the case for aristocratic women. But even higher up the social scale, princesses were governed by a 'lady mistress'. This woman, charged with the princess's early education, would be drawn from the ranks of the aristocracy and was often appointed at birth.

In 1516, following the birth of his daughter Mary, Henry VIII turned to a familiar pair of hands. He selected the experienced Elizabeth Denton, who had once served as mistress in the nursery that he had shared with his sisters.[48] She was already elderly and cannot have been expected to serve for long. But her replacement had already been identified.[49]

The Countess of Surrey's eldest daughter, Margaret Bourchier, had already left home by the time that John Skelton visited Sheriff Hutton in 1495. By 1516, she had been married to the courtier, Sir Thomas Bryan, for many years.

She was a solid matron, with a reputation for learning that was originally fostered under the care of her mother. To ensure that she was of sufficient status to teach his only child (at the time), the king made Margaret a peeress in her own right. He also offered the new Baroness Bryan the very substantial salary of £50 a year.[50] At first, Margaret's role was largely that of a senior nanny and mother figure. She was still in the princess's household early in 1518 when her husband died. Shortly afterwards, Lady Bryan married the lowly David Zouche.

In the summer of 1519, Margaret was replaced as lady mistress to Mary by the royal Countess of Salisbury, and Margaret immediately transferred to the service of a new royal baby – Henry VIII's illegitimate son, Henry Fitzroy.[51] Nothing is known of her time with him, but she was certainly still employed in 1520.[52]

Since Princess Mary held the position of heir apparent, the governance of her education was a matter of state importance. When she was nine, her household moved to Ludlow. The first instruction issued to her council by the king required that every month, 'or further as the case shall require', they should assemble to consider the girl's health and 'her virtuous education in learning'.[53] They were instructed to send both for the girl and her governess to enquire of progress if necessary, while her lady mistress and her schoolmaster, Dr Featherston, were permitted to sit on the council along with the rest of the dignitaries.

Lady Bryan was not forgotten. When, in 1533, Anne Boleyn gave birth to the future Queen Elizabeth, Lady Bryan joined the princess's household as lady mistress. She found herself in an establishment that was unwieldy and expensive, with the household unfortunately beginning to expand just as winter came, with the additional expenses of 'wax white lights fuel as coal and other things'.[54] At the same time, the household officers took advantage of the lack of direct royal supervision, many of them bringing 'more servants then

they were allowed by the standing book signed with the king's hand' to be fed in the household. As a consequence, economies had to be made: the 'mess of meat' for dinner, the shared portion formerly divided between two household members, was now to feed four.

Margaret Bryan was, herself, involved in these economies when she came up against her former charge, the teenaged Princess Mary. The girl, who had by now been declared illegitimate and forced to join her infant half-sister Elizabeth's household, was regularly ill. Perhaps, her doctors reasoned, she would feel better if she could have dinner (which was then usually served mid-morning) as soon as she was dressed in the morning, at between nine and ten o'clock.[55] The Countess of Salisbury agreed, but Lady Bryan vetoed the idea, considering that 'the service of Her Grace conveniently could not be served before xi of the clock at the least any day'. The kitchens were simply too busy: she must take a larger breakfast, before skipping dinner entirely and eating again at supper time. As the lady mistress of the 'legitimate' Princess Elizabeth, Lady Bryan now outranked her replacement who served the 'illegitimate' Princess Mary.

Lady Bryan was determined that Princess Mary should accept her authority. She made this very clear, reading the elder princess's mail and only passing it on if she deemed the content suitable.[56] Once, when she passed a letter from her own daughter, Lady Carew, to Mary at Hunsdon, she declared that 'for the passion of Christ' the princess should be prepared 'in all things to follow the king's pleasure and in so doing she trusted that the King's Grace would be good and gracious Lord to her and other wise she was utterly undone'.

Through her service to each of Henry VIII's children in turn, Margaret Bryan had to walk a tightrope as the political sands constantly shifted. In 1536, following Anne Boleyn's execution, she was forced to petition the king's chief minister for clothes for the growing Princess Elizabeth. The following year, she transferred to the service of Prince Edward, whom she served with devotion.

By the time she made her will, in 1551, Margaret Bryan was in receipt of an annual pension of £70 – an enormous sum.[57] As she acknowledged, this was 'granted unto me by the virtue of his gracious letters patents, for my poor service done as well unto His Majesty [Prince Edward] in his tender age, as also unto his dearly beloved sisters the Lady Mary's Grace and the Lady Elizabeth's Grace'. She had helped to raise and educate three future sovereigns of England.

It was a cheerful meeting at Sheriff Hutton on 8 May 1495, filled with merriment. The countess had, she told Skelton, 'contrived for you a goodly work' by ordering her girls to weave a garland of laurel for the poet to wear. On the countess's command, servants hurried in, carrying rugs and carpets on which 'these ladies softly might rest', while another menial provided the embroidery frame. Noble girls were always proficient at embroidery. 'With fingers small, and hands white as milk', they expertly weaved Skelton's garland. Some used a needle over fine silk, while others worked gold thread into the gift. They used the scraps of 'broken work' that they had to hand, as they decorated the garland with roses and buttons, as well as hurriedly embroidering birds into the cloth. It was a gorgeous work and eminently suitable to ladies of their class.

As well-born young girls, the countess's young charges sat erect and still, being sure not to twist their heads from side to side – as the conduct manuals enjoined – since stillness and poise would give them 'the reputation of being straightforward and to be depended on'.[58] The Countess of Surrey could pride herself in the way that the girls in her care performed. They would surely all marry well.

∽

The Countess of Surrey's charges could expect to learn, in her household, the skills deemed fitting for girls of their class. But the majority of Tudor women had little access to formal education of the sort provided for boys.[59] They could, very occasionally, attend boys' grammar schools. In 1615, one Alice Shaw is known to have attended the prestigious Rivington Grammar School, founded in the 1560s,[60] which sent pupils on to the universities – though Alice, as with all other young women, would have been barred from university entry. But at Rivington there was Latin and Greek on the curriculum, so that Alice, along with the handful of other female students there in the early seventeenth century, could have received a school education comparable to the best on offer to boys. But such an opportunity was a rarity, and most schools resisted admitting girls, with many grammar schools, such as Harrow, expressly forbidding the education of girls in their statutes.[61]

More usually, where girls did go to school they attended their local village school. One such, in London, was run by an aged priest named William Barbour between 1504 and 1515. He took in thirty students, teaching them both religious doctrine and 'further learning'.[62] At Wigston, in Leicestershire, a small free school was assembling daily by the 1580s, in the nave of the old parish church.[63] That girls as well as boys attended is clear from the record of an incident when, one day, a drunkard entered the schoolroom, breaking the teacher's hour-glass.[64] After ushering out this unwelcome visitor, the schoolmaster made a point of giving one end of the hourglass to a boy and one to a girl, demonstrating his class was co-educational.

At Norwich, even the very poorest girls were sent off to the schoolroom, although typically girls' formal education often ended earlier than their brothers', when financial need made it necessary for girls as young as six to begin working for a living. Of the three daughters of Anne and Geoffrey Roberts, who lived in the city in 1570, the eldest – aged nine – had been pulled out of school to work, although her sisters still attended.[65] The six-year-old daughter of a very poor neighbour – Elizabeth Skyver – also attended school, as did the seven-year-old daughter of a widow named Katherine Gabone. These girls usually returned home to take up spinning work after their lessons each day.[66] Martin Luther, for one, considered that there was easily time for girls to spend an hour a day at their lessons while also keeping up with their household tasks.[67] They could, he supposed, reclaim the time needed for lessons from the otherwise idle moments used in play, dancing and sleep.

Such small local schools tended to teach reading, writing and accounting. Occasionally, rudimentary Latin would also be on the curriculum. Most of the institutions were run by men, although a few schoolmistresses are known from the period.[68] The wife of Richard Dawes was running a school in Barking, Essex, in 1590, where she taught both boys and girls to read.[69]

She fell foul of the Church courts for failing to obtain a licence to teach, although she was still permitted to teach any girls that wanted to be scholars and boys under the age of ten.

Girls were sometimes boarded out with a schoolmistress. Young Thomasine Wolters, the orphan living in Sandwich, Kent, had an inheritance amounting to property rents of around £10 per year. The Wardens of the Orphans of the town administered her money and had a duty to ensure that she was well brought up.[70] By 24 June 1589, she had been boarding for two years in the house of a brewer, William Evans, whose wife took on the task of raising their young charge, for which money was supplied for 'necessaries laid out about her and teaching her'.[71]

In late 1591, Thomasine moved to the house of Mistress Smythe, to continue her education. Precisely what this lady was teaching her under the general heading of 'board and learning' is not clear, although Thomasine was certainly taught to sew and to read. In 1592, the Wardens purchased a book for Thomasine, 'containing all the Service and the singing Psalms'.[72] Whether Mistress Smythe had other pupils is not known, but Thomasine remained with her until April 1594, shortly before she married.[73] Thirty years later, in another example, the wife of William Maye of Ash was paid by the Sandwich Wardens 'for schooling and mending of shoes and apparel for the child she keepeth'.[74] Such women may have effectively run small boarding schools.

Higher up the social scale, nunneries also tended to take in young girls and boys for their education, although the extent to which they did so has probably been overstated.[75] St Mary's, Winchester, contained twenty-six children in 1535, with an equal number of nuns, while Polesworth in 1537 housed up to forty-two children. More usually, the numbers were smaller, with only one or two girls at any time – hardly enough to be considered a girls' school. The girls educated at nunneries tended to be high–born, as was Bridget Plantagenet, daughter of Viscount Lisle, a notable occupant of St Mary's in 1536. She was there with Henry VIII's kinswoman Mary Pole and several other daughters of the gentry and nobility.

The education that the nuns provided was, highly variable, since nuns were often little more than literate themselves.[76] Elizabeth Barton, on becoming a nun, received the two daughters of the gentleman Thomas Gold to 'be brought up by her in virtue and learning' – despite the fact that she had had scant education herself.[77] She was certainly no scholar. But Elizabeth Barton would nevertheless go on to have an impact on her age far in excess of her humble beginnings.

Margaret Beaufort, patroness of learning

Although Tudor women were never permitted to study at university, their patronage was more than welcome. Margaret Beaufort, who was a wealthy heiress, had long been interested in education. She became a patron of the printer William Caxton following her son's accession to the throne, and she published her own translations of popular religious works, as well as inviting Caxton to print editions of works that she wanted to see brought to a wider audience.[78]

Margaret, through whose line Henry VII claimed the throne, had first begun to show an interest in Oxford University when her servant, Sir Reginald Bray, became steward of the university in 1493. Three years later, she founded a lectureship in theology there. But she also established one at Oxford's rival, Cambridge, at the same time,[79] and it was this ancient university upon which she focused her attentions. This may, in part, have been due to the influence of the cleric John Fisher, who was a Cambridge man and Margaret's greatest friend.[80] In 1501 he was appointed as vice-chancellor of Cambridge, becoming its Chancellor in 1504.

Margaret's patronage was not merely honorary: she expected to be consulted. When, in 1500, her theology lectureship fell vacant at Oxford, she wrote to the university to confirm the choice of one Mr Roper 'to read our lecture there', confirming that 'we be right glad, and trust with God's mercy it shall be to the great honour and wealth of your said university'.[81] She also used her influence to secure university appointments for her friends and dependents.[82] The university was grateful for her not insubstantial funding, offering its 'never-ceasing thanks' in a flattering letter as it sought to solicit more money.[83]

Margaret Beaufort's patronage was not unprecedented. Her ancestor Queen Philippa of Hainault had founded Queen's College, Oxford, in the fourteenth century, while Margaret of Anjou, wife of Henry VI, had founded Queen's College, Cambridge, in the mid-fifteenth century.[84] But Margaret resolved to outdo them both.

The tiny college of God's House, at Cambridge, had been founded in 1439, originally with ambitious intentions to house sixty scholars.[85] These grand plans never came to fruition, and the foundation was so poor that there were never more than four students in residence at any one time.[86] It was ripe for refoundation. On 1 May 1505, Margaret's son granted her a licence to expand the college to achieve its sixty members.[87] In the same document, he gave her permission to change its name to Christ's College.

She gave generously to her new foundation, as well as reserving rooms in the college, at which she could stay whenever she was in Cambridge. She even oversaw the building works there, in order to ensure the magnificence of what was intended to be her lasting memorial. Margaret Beaufort was so regularly at Christ's during the last years of her life that the poor from the surrounding area would come to see her.[88] She also took a personal interest in the students. Once, when looking out of a window, she saw a scholar being punished by the dean for some misdemeanour; she cried out 'Gently, gently!' in Latin, urging the master not to treat his charge too harshly.[89]

Margaret's educational ambitions did not stop at just the one college. In 1508 it came to her attention that the Hospital of St John the Evangelist at Cambridge was in a poor state of repair. She resolved to take charge of this religious house, organizing the licences needed to turn it into a college. She was, by now, in her late sixties and in poor health. Aware that she would not live to see the foundation of her second college, Margaret left detailed instructions in a codicil to her will.[90]

Thus, Margaret Beaufort is remembered, too, as the founder of St John's College, Cambridge. Modern visitors to the city will sometimes come face to face with the indefatigable benefactress if they notice the nineteenth-century statue of a severe-looking woman, veiled and wearing a wimple, glaring down at them from above the main door to St John's.

5

OF SERVANTS AND MASTERS

Elizabeth Barton, maidservant

I n late 1524, or early 1525, Elizabeth Barton, a young girl from Aldington[1] in Kent, walked over to the house of Thomas Cobb, a gentleman of the parish.[2] Verbally, they agreed their terms, and within a few days she had moved into the servants' quarters of his house, high in the attic. She was nineteen years old, but she probably had several terms of service behind her already – stretching back to the beginning of her adolescence. It was the way for most of her peers.

She had received little in the way of education; indeed, one contemporary considered her to be 'a poor wench without learning'.[3] She knew no Latin, although she could probably read and write, and had probably attended a village school until she entered service.[4]

Service was far from unusual for both boys and girls of her class: the vast majority of them spent a period of time as agricultural or household servants. In Tudor Salisbury, for example, in the parish list of 1533 one-third of women and half of men were in service.[5] The parents of adolescents usually assisted in finding a suitable first placement from among families in the local area or from connections further afield. A verbal agreement was then made, tying the teenager into work for one year's service, in return for a wage.[6]

With that agreement, the adolescent was ready to leave home, packing up their belongings and walking over to the house of their new master or mistress. This period of service was looked on as a transitional stage, in the same way that most girls' social betters were sent to serve in the households of the nobility.[7] Agricultural servants were young and unmarried – it was not a career, and cases of married women staying in service were rare.[8] While they learned skills and saved for their future, they were also looking to marry and start their own households. And with so many young people entering service, it was also possible for them to gain useful social connections that would benefit them later in life. Young Elizabeth Cooper from Norwich, for example, became lifelong friends with Thomas Sutton, who served in the same household.[9] He would serve as a Sheriff of Norwich in the 1550s and show Elizabeth some favour when she found herself in trouble with the law.

Since service was more of a life-stage than a career or an indicator of social class, it is unsurprising that the dividing line between the servant and the served in houses such as Thomas Cobb's was not always strictly drawn.[10] Indeed, it was expected that Cobb – and other masters – would stand in *loco parentis*. They were obliged to maintain their servant for the term of his or her service, regardless of whether there was enough work or whether the servant was fit to do it.[11] Conversely, servants were not free to leave their employment early, and the courts regularly ordered those who absconded back unless they could prove that they had been mistreated.

Runaway servants might have hoped that they could quietly melt away by securing a better offer elsewhere; and it is true that new employers were often less than rigorous in their checks when employing new servants. Mawdlin Gawen, a young servant from Oxfordshire, found this to be the case in 1575, after running away, with her lover, from service in Teddington.[12] In London, they claimed to a prospective employer, Mr Fluett, that they hailed from Collyweston. Evidently suspicious, Fluett questioned them on the distance of Collyweston from Stamford;

but he took them into his employment even when they failed to answer. The pair would have been constantly aware that their former master might seek them out.

In 1520, John Smith, a servant of a London draper named Thomas Howell, ran away, after which Howell and his wife expended great efforts and sums in chasing him. Mistress Howell ordered men to ride after him, following his trail for over four weeks all the way to Plymouth.[13] When Smith was finally located, he refused to return until forced to do so by the court. It cost his master more than £6 to secure his return to unwilling service – a sum Howell intended that Smith should reimburse. Howell was not considered a bad master, as suggested by the fact that one of his maidservants stayed in his household for at least five years and another for six. They were paid 13s and £1 4s a year respectively, which was considered a good wage, and they each received a new gown every year.[14]

More common than absconding, for dissatisfied servants, was simply moving on at the end of their term, and many maidservants often passed through the service of a number of employers. There would usually be plenty of choice, for even quite lowly households could employ servants. For example, one William Blunte, of Richmond in Surrey, worked as a labourer yet was known to have kept an eleven-year-old girl as his servant in 1559.[15]

Sin and servitude

At the opposite end of the spectrum from servants anxious to escape their masters were the relationships that evolved into something much closer than a master–servant agreement.

Illicit relationships were far from unknown between maidservants and the men of the house in the Tudor period.

Contemporaries warned girls to be wary of the 'flattering

tongues' of young men.[16] They could beguile them with 'crocodile tears', but were a danger. Indeed, girls should 'trust not a man at the first sight / But try him well before'. It was not at all uncommon for servant girls, away from the watchful eyes of their parents for the first time, to become pregnant. In just one example, Anne Prescold, who was a servant to John Nott in Abberley, Worcestershire, found herself with child and out of job in 1598, leading her to petition the local courts for her paramour – John Hey – to 'contribute towards her support'.[17]

Matters were not helped by the fact that sometimes the quarters in which the men and women of the household lived were very close indeed. Edward Glascocke of Easthampfield was brought before the Church courts in 1587 charged with sharing a bed with both his wife and his maid, a state of affairs that was held responsible for the three arriving very late for church in the mornings.[18] In another case, the parson of Alphamstone in Essex and his wife were furious when their maid, Joan Reyner, confessed

to being pregnant in 1572.[19] Nonetheless, their attempts to end her employment early received short shrift when she took them to court over the matter. The parsonage contained only three beds, which, when the parson quarrelled with his wife and needed to sleep elsewhere, meant that his stepson was moved in to share with Joan. Unsurprisingly, the pair were soon getting up to rather more than sleep in their narrow bed, leading to the maid's predicament. The parson and his wife were ordered to maintain her for the remainder of her year of service.

Things were less clear-cut for Milson Parker, a servant in the house of Thomas Garner in Adderbury, Oxfordshire, in 1583.[20] On promise of marriage, she began to sleep with another servant, Michael Garner, who was probably a relative of her master, continuing until after Christmas when she discovered she was pregnant. On being hauled before the archdeacon's court at Oxford, she was forced to admit that on one occasion 'she lay by the space of two hours in bed alone in the night season with a shepherd called Robert Widows', who also served in the household.

Serving-women who fell pregnant would usually lose their positions and their livelihoods. It is not surprising that many cases of infanticide were committed by unmarried servants who had attempted to conceal their pregnancies.

By far the majority of servants – including Elizabeth Barton – worked on farms. Her master, Thomas Cobb, was a prominent man, charged as bailiff and steward with running the Archbishop of Canterbury's substantial estates in the parish. As the archbishop's most senior manorial officer, Cobb held considerable sway in the local community, his daily life centred on both church and the farm.

Life in rural Aldington was dominated by the grand archiepiscopal palace, sitting close beside the parish church. It loomed large over the little town that nestled close to the winding road taking travellers to and from the ancient port of Hythe.[21] The palace – with its five kitchens, nine barns, six stables and many other agricultural buildings, all set within more than a thousand acres of farmland – dwarfed the other buildings in the settlement.[22] The townspeople proudly displayed their ambitions in the great new church steeple, which was slowly rising, stone by stone, as donations and bequests trickled in.[23] It was a project that would never be completed, though it was already the tallest local structure in 1525.

Elizabeth Barton was too young to remember the great Erasmus's brief tenure as Rector of Aldington, which had begun in 1511; but she was certainly familiar with the new priest, Richard Masters, who had arrived in 1514 and would remain for well over fifty years. He was a scholarly, conservative man, who spent most of his time with his head bent over his enormous library of 113 books, stowed carefully in his chamber in the parsonage.[24]

Farming life was a busy, hard life, but, as contemporaries asserted (based on the Book of Job), 'a man is ordained and born to do labour, as a bird is ordained to fly'.[25] The year was an annual cycle, with ploughing and sowing to be done, alongside animal husbandry. The main crops were always peas and beans, corn, barley and oats, while horses, cattle, sheep and pigs were usually kept on mixed farms.

Women, whether of the family or servants, were expected to play an active part in farm life, and this would have been no less true for Elizabeth Barton. They had their own specific and vital jobs to do; not for nothing did the old saying maintain that 'seldom doth the husband thrive, without the leave of his wife'.[26] On waking, the women of the house were enjoined to first say their prayers, before sweeping and tidying. It was then time to milk the cows, feed the calves, and wake up the children of the family before preparing breakfast.

Women carried corn and malt to the mill, as well as attending to brewing and baking, and making butter and cheese. They fed the pigs and dealt with the poultry. It was also the wife's job, assisted by the female servants, to prepare a kitchen garden in March, sowing the seeds and herbs that would 'be good for the pot and to eat'. They would need to plant flax and hemp, too, which they would later spin into cloth for towels, sheets, shirts and smocks, while they also prepared the sheep's wool for clothes and blankets. For servants such as Elizabeth, there was at least variety within the yearly cycle of hard toil. In towns, servants' work could be even more varied, where a good position could see some girls involved in their employer's trade, either through work in the shop or in manufacture.[27]

Thomas Cobb was by all accounts a diligent master, aware of his contractual obligations and prepared to fulfil them. At Easter

1525, which can only have been weeks, at most, after Elizabeth Barton was hired, she fell dangerously ill – 'touched with a great infirmity in her body'.[28] Sometimes her throat would swell so much that she writhed in agony, struggling for breath as 'though she had suffered the pangs of death itself'. There was considerable fear that the swelling 'was like to stop her breath'.[29] At other times she was quieter, but still very sick, her illness coming in fits and starts. As her sickness progressed, she was carried out of the servants' attic and down to a room that she shared with one of Cobb's young children. The baby, which slept in a cradle close to her was also dangerously ill, so it was thought the pair could be nursed together.[30]

Elizabeth was still very ill in November 1525. During all this time her master had been paying for her food and care, in spite of the fact that she could carry out none of her duties. He must surely have been intending to end her employment when her year's term was set to conclude, at the start of 1526.

Many young girls were less fortunate in their master than Elizabeth Barton. The entire relationship between servant and master was based upon trust. Poor Elizabeth Bannister made the mistake in the late 1490s of taking up a position as a servant in the London home of Henry Mappe.[31] Almost as soon as she arrived, the girl realized her error, as her master threatened her with weapons before he 'ravished her'. The servant was then locked away in the house for eleven weeks, while her employer used her, by her own account, to 'his pleasure in sinful living'. When Mappe's wife, Alice, discovered what had been going on, she turned on the maid, demanding that she 'set no foot in the house' again: Mappe then sent the unfortunate girl on her way with threats to her life should she speak of what had happened. Homeless, Elizabeth Bannister went before the Court of Aldermen to plead her case, only for her past to be raked up against her. She had, she said, 'never used sinful living' before; but she did admit that 'she was no maid when she came to

[Mappe's] service for a Ralph Talbot kept her' in the town where she had been born.

The rape of girls

On 26 November 1563, a twelve-year-old named Agnes Wevell was walking through fields near Ashford, in Kent. According to her testimony, she was suddenly set upon by a labourer named James Purser, who 'ravished' her before she was able to hurry away and raise the alarm. Purser was brought before the assize court to answer these accusations, but was found not guilty.[32]

At the Rochester Assizes on 25 February 1586, a tailor named John Henshaw, from nearby Deptford, was dragged in from his cell, protesting his innocence.[33] The judges heard accusations that, on 3 February 1583, while at Deptford, he had raped Elizabeth Rowson, the eight-year-old daughter of a townsman there. Eighteen months later, on 18 August 1584, he had, it was claimed, struck once more, while visiting the house of Richard Halpeny in the town. There,

he was alleged to have raped a six-year-old girl named Alice Keeling, before repeating the offence again on a second visit ten days later. After hearing the evidence, the jury deliberated before finding Henshaw not guilty of all charges. He was free to return home.

Rape was an all too common charge brought before the Elizabethan assize courts, and some of the victims were very young girls. It was a crime that was difficult to prove, particularly when it occurred within the privacy of a man's household. Servant-girls were particularly vulnerable, and many accusations were levelled by them against their employers. Joan Lee of Debden, in Essex, accused her master, Nicholas Ratcliff of raping her in his house on 2 July 1559; he too was found not guilty at trial.[34] Another Essex woman, Joan Hasserd, who was a servant in the house of George

Male at Ilford, accused a local yeoman of raping her in 1559, while she was in her master's house.[35] He was found not guilty, as was John Ryston of Chigwell, who allegedly raped his servant, Agnes Dowson, on 27 June 1559.[36] Eight years later, in the same court, one John Stonerde of Feering was accused of raping his servant, Priscilla Knight, but he too was found innocent.[37]

From the records, the conviction rate appears woefully low. In the case of a clerk named Robert Scrymger of Rochester, who was accused of raping four-year-old Jane Vycars on 6 September 1573, he was probably only convicted because the jury knew that his life could be spared with a plea of clergy.[38]

The threat of sexual violence remained a very real one for many Tudor women. And despite these known cases, the damage that reporting such offences would do to their own reputations provided women with a powerful incentive to say nothing.

Although there were dangers and disagreements in the master–servant relationship, service could be very beneficial to all parties involved. Many masters and mistresses remembered their own youths working in the households of others, and were accordingly kind. Servants could expect a small bequest in the event of their master or mistress dying during their employment. In 1499, Katherine Lorkyn, who was serving the London draper Sir John Fenkyll and his wife, Katherine, received four marks under her master's will, although his male servant, Richard Thomson, did somewhat better, accepting five marks.[39]

At the end of 1525, Elizabeth Barton was still lying desperately sick at Aldington, in her master's house. She had proved a poor employee, and she must have been fearful of her future position. Her mind was also troubled, and being 'brought into such weakness and idleness of her brain' she 'often times trifled and spake such words as she remembered not herself when she came to good advisement'.[40] In her delirium she spoke out, raving about the Seven Deadly Sins, the Ten Commandments and other scriptural passages that she had learned in church. Even more surprisingly, the people around her began to listen. As soon as Elizabeth Barton was well enough to sit up, her master commanded that, from henceforth, she should dine at the table with him and his wife – a considerable honour for a lowborn female servant.[41]

The Third Age

6

OF LOVE AND MARRIAGE

Cecily Burbage and Elizabeth Boleyn

For Tudors, the third age, following infancy and adolescence, began around fourteen and was, in Shakespeare's words, the time of the 'the lover, sighing like furnace, with woeful ballad'. This phase of later adolescence and early adulthood, when the possibilities of love stretched out promisingly, could last for fourteen years, taking a man or woman up to the age of around twenty-eight. It was also thought to be a dangerous time, when young people were most prone to sin.[1] They needed the guiding hand of someone in authority as they negotiated the end of their childhoods.

This was particularly the case for girls, cautioned writers such as the educationalist Vives. Young women should appear in public as rarely as possible, he considered, since their good name and reputation 'seem to hang by a cobweb'. The danger was that 'if some slur has attached to a girl's reputation from men's opinion of her, it usually remains forever and is not erased except by clear proofs of her chastity and wisdom'.[2]

A plethora of rules and expectations surrounded young women. Tudor girls should not sit silently in company, since they would seem uneducated; yet, they might be called light-headed if they spoke too much. To laugh openly was to be flighty, while to speak with a man was to appear flirtatious and an 'easy conquest'.[3] All this, and more, the Tudor girl was expected to understand and negotiate on the road towards adulthood. On the successful management of these challenges, her marriage prospects hung.

At all social levels, it was expected that there would be some love or, at least, liking between a couple about to marry.[4] Where a girl or boy was 'beaten and compulsed' by their parents into marriage, it was an ungodly match, in which the young couple were marrying 'in a forgetfulness and obliviousness of God's commandments'.[5] It was considered not right to join two young people 'not for any love, or godliness in the parties, but to get friendship, and make them strong in the realm, to increase their possessions, and to join land to land'. After all, as some contemporaries reasoned, wasn't there every possibility that a penniless young man, even the 'son of a harlot', could rise to great wealth?[6]

Love in marriage was deemed essential to some extent, since 'the greatest joy and sweetest comfort that a man may have in this world is a loving, kind, and honest wife'. As such, a man should closely observe the behaviour and reputation of his prospective mother-in-law, in the expectation that her daughter would follow her conduct. Men were advised to seek out meek and demure wives, skilled in sewing, spinning, knitting and keeping bashfully out of the way when strangers came to call.[7]

The importance of some semblance of love notwithstanding, few men or women expected to choose entirely for themselves. Those that eloped, without their father's consent, were embarking on a 'marrying' that was 'ungodly'. Where money or estates were at issue, the stakes were higher. In the mid-sixteenth century, the firebrand Bishop Hugh Latimer would lament that 'there was never such marrying in England as is now'. He could only marvel at the reports he heard: 'I hear tell of stealing of wards to marry the children to. This is a strange kind of stealing: but it is not the wards, it is the lands that they steal'. It was theft indeed, where an heiress or a young male heir could be carried off and forcibly married. Indeed, the danger for young heiresses was so acute that an Act of Parliament was passed against those 'as shall take away maidens that be inheritors, being with the age of xvi years, or that marry them without consent of their parents'.[8] At the very least, advice should be taken by family and friends.[9]

In spite of the arguments over just who should be responsible for arranging a marriage, almost all writers were in agreement that some matches were simply beyond the pale. No girl should be forced to marry a man considerably older than her; it was distasteful. In the words of one Elizabethan writer, 'I must needs confess that to match a young maid with an old man, it is miserable'. It was 'unseemly' for a young woman to marry an old man 'that carrieth a countenance rather to be her father than her husband'.[10] Most young girls would go more willingly to their graves, he considered.

There is no doubt that forced marriages did happen in Tudor England, affecting even the mightiest in the land: Henry VIII complained in January 1540 when he was compelled to put his neck 'in the yoke' to marry Anne of Cleves. The unfortunate Anne had only arrived in England a few days before, but was required to marry the horrifying king with whom she did not even share a common language. Henry's sister, Princess Mary, was similarly afflicted when required to marry the aged Louis XII of France in 1514. Only a promise that she could choose her next husband persuaded her to accept the role of Louis's bed-mate – a role that would probably have gone to her deceased elder sibling, Princess Elizabeth, had she lived to marriageable age.

Girls often came to regret marriages into which they found themselves pushed. In January 1559, both Thomas Merkingfeld and Isabella Ingleby brought a suit for the annulment of their marriage in the Chester Church courts.[11] They had been married between nine and ten years earlier, when Thomas was less than fourteen years old and Isabella still under twelve. Almost immediately, it was clear that the young couple loathed each other, with Thomas declaring when he reached his majority that 'he could not fantasise the said Isabella as his wife nor so would not take her and use her as his wife'. Young Thomas had been 'compelled by his friends to marry the said Isabella'; but the pair refused to consummate their union. This was a sensible move, since it represented the only basis on which they would be likely to get the marriage legally dissolved.

In most cases, a courtship began with a young couple demonstrating some interest in one another, perhaps by way of the prospective groom shyly begging his beloved to 'give me a kiss withal I pray thee'.[12] To that entreaty, the only chaste answer was: 'I would keep my virginity whole, and undefiled for you.' Nice girls saved themselves for marriage; but there still lurked dangers.

Jane Singleton from Halsall, Lancashire, thought that she had done everything right when a young gentleman named Gilbert Halsall came courting.[13] She arranged for a local man named James Spencer to go with her to the church one afternoon in 1558, to witness her marriage. The couple stood together at the altar, as Gilbert took Jane by the hand, telling her that 'I Gilbert take thee Jane to be my wedded wife and thereto I plight thee my troth'. The pair released their hands, before Jane took Gilbert's fingers into her own, swearing that 'I Jane take thee Gilbert to my husband and thereto I plight thee my troth'. The couple then kissed before spending the night together. But to Jane's dismay, Halsall promptly abandoned her. The bride was forced to petition the Church courts at Chester for them to uphold the marriage. Technically, the pair did not even need to plight their troths in church, since all that was required for a valid marriage was a mutual promise to wed, followed by consummation.

'Those things that prohibit conception'

Sexual intercourse in Tudor England is usually portrayed as a risky business for women, with pregnancy the seemingly inescapable outcome. Inevitably, accidental pregnancies occurred, but the role of women was not always passive. Henry VIII's fifth wife, Catherine Howard, when discovered to have indulged in pre-marital sex, was reported to have said that 'a woman might meddle with a man and yet conceive no child unless she would for herself'.[14] Knowledge of contraception was not as rudimentary as is often supposed.

The official position of the Church in the period was always that sexual intercourse was for procreation.[15] Contraception – and abortion, after the time when the foetus was deemed to have gained its soul – was therefore illegal in England, and had been since the thirteenth century.[16] To seek to prevent pregnancy was a sin against God. However, many people were prepared to risk this sin.

Queen Elizabeth of York and Henry VII may well have employed some method of contraception after the birth of their sixth child, Prince Edmund, in February 1499. When the couple's eldest son, Prince Arthur, died suddenly on 2 April 1502, the queen promised her husband that they could have more children. On 2 February 1503, only ten months after Arthur's death, the queen duly gave birth to another child. She had evidently conceived with ease, suggesting that she had been actively trying not to in the previous few years.

For sexually active women in the sixteenth century, there were really three ways to avoid bearing a child. The first – and most straightforward – was abstinence. This could be difficult, contemporaries agreed. Before he became pontiff, the medieval Pope John XXI had written a medical manual, which was first translated into English in 1560. In it, the churchman devoted an entire chapter to remedies 'against great desire to fleshly lust'.[17] For the really committed, he considered that a paste of hemlock, applied to the man's genitals, was guaranteed to 'take utterly away all desire of copulation', while anointing with deadly nightshade could have a similar effect. Similarly, eating the flowers of a willow or poplar tree would be sure to 'make cold all the heat of carnal lust in him'. The prospect of a lover who had swathed himself in deadly hemlock would have been enough to put off most women, even if their partner's 'desire of copulation' had been entirely unassuaged.

Failing abstinence, if a woman was to be sexually active she could take steps to prevent conception, as Catherine Howard appears to have done. Some methods were as simple as a jumping up and down after intercourse, or hurrying down a flight of stairs – although their effectiveness is debatable.[18] The withdrawal method, or the timing of intercourse for a day when the woman was less fertile, were popular methods, although neither was infallible, then as now.

Less passive methods also existed. In the 1980s, archaeological excavations were carried out on a privy in the keep of Dudley Castle.[19] The archaeologists discovered what looked like small scraps of leather in layers of material, originating from the Civil War-era occupation of the castle in 1642–7. When taken to be analysed, they were discovered to be ten condoms, five of which were stored carefully inside a single one.[20] The condoms, made not of leather but of sheep or pig intestines, were designed to cover the tip of the penis. They were of a standard size and thickness, suggesting that they were mass-produced. Such items would have required considerable preparation by the manufacturer, in soaking, cleaning and stretching the intestines, and so would have been very expensive to buy; but at least the owner would have been able to economize later by rinsing them out and re-using them.

The Dudley Castle examples are the earliest known condoms in Europe. While they post-date the Tudor period, similar condoms were available in the sixteenth century and first noted in sources from the 1560s.[21] The scholar Hercules Saxonia, in his *Luis venerae perfectissimus tractatus* of 1597, described condoms as a way of preventing both venereal disease and pregnancy. They were, nevertheless, sufficiently rare that few women will have come across them in the Tudor period.

Instead, women found herbal and plant-based contraceptives of more use – many of them known since Antiquity. Medieval writers had written of them in their own publications. The thirteenth-century Italian physician William of Saliceto, for example, included a chapter in his *Summa conservationis et curationiis* on 'those things that prohibit conception and cause abortion'. Rue, savin or juniper were particularly effective, he considered, providing that the woman took them within ten days of intercourse. Indeed, pretty, innocuous-looking rue was commonly considered to act as a contraceptive, the knowledge of it passed down through generations of women. This, and other leaves believed to inhibit fertility, would commonly be eaten in meals, allowing women to take some control over their own fertility by way of the food they chose to cook.

The discovery of the New World also opened up new possibilities for birth control. By the mid-sixteenth century, it was understood in Europe that *Montanoa tormentosa*, known as zoapatle, could help to prevent conception[22] – though in practice it would have been near-impossible for most European women to obtain a sample.

If abstinence and contraception both failed, the only remaining method of birth control was abortion. This was usually considered permissible until the foetus had become animated and obtained its soul. Abortion could be procured through herbal means, which were usually inhaled.[23] More drastic measures could also be taken. The Elizabethan noblewoman, Grace Mildmay, noted in her diary that a medicine taken from the Guaiacum plant, which grew in the Caribbean but had become well-known in England, could be applied directly to the womb, if tied to a stick, and held in place 'even until it bleeds'.[24] She was quick to assure her readers that 'I take this medicine to be very dangerous and evil to be applied unto women in this manner.' But sometimes, needs must. For unmarried women, such as Catherine Howard, a pregnancy could be ruinous. Even a married woman, whose house was already full of hungry mouths, could view another pregnancy as disastrous. It is not surprising that some Tudor women did what they could to take control of their own fertility.

Tudor marriage was a family affair, connecting not just husband and wife, but involving their parents and other kin firmly expecting to be included in deliberations.[25] This was not surprising, since, given the subordinate status of wives, property was always transferred at marriage, even among the lowliest members of society. Materially too, therefore, women had a good deal to lose if they made a mistake in their choice of husband.

Poor Alice Carre of Greenwich, a widow, learned this to her cost when a comely baker began to pay his addresses to her in 1577.[26] Thomas White arrived in town with his friend, an innkeeper named Thomas Dove, boasting of his great wealth and success in baking bread. This piqued the widowed Alice's interest. Soon, she found herself being entertained in White's house in nearby Stratford-at-Bowe. Alice was seduced by the alluring baker and agreed to all he asked, 'making and concluding a marriage'. She then happily signed documents presented to her by Dove, although, as her suitor and his friend knew, she was illiterate. She began emptying her house, passing a featherbed and bedding, as well as her household utensils, to Dove. With this, Alice's fiancé disappeared. The widow soon discovered that, in spite of her visit to White's 'house', 'in truth he had no house nor possession in Stratford-at-Bowe'. To add insult to injury, she soon learned that the documents she had signed acknowledged a debt to Dove of 26s 8d, which was promptly demanded.

Alice Carre was at least fortunate that she found out the truth before marrying her fortune hunter. For another Alice, Alice Carter, realization came later. She brought a case in the Church court at Chester in February 1559, during which her new husband's motives became all too clear.[27] She wanted the marriage annulled, since, as she claimed, 'Thomas Barrow did never favour her this respondent as his wife nor she him as her husband'. Instead, she had come to 'credibly believe' that the marriage had been arranged by her husband's father 'only to get money of her father'. Alice Carter was very lucky that her marriage had not been consummated, since it was a relatively simple matter for such unions to be dissolved: sexual intercourse between husband and wife was an essential ingredient of any valid marriage.

∽

Widowhood potentially put women back on the marriage market, as Alice Carre knew; it could also revive the frisson of courtship in later years, as Princess Elizabeth's wetnurse was to discover. Following the royal toddler's death in 1495, Cecily Burbage, finding herself unemployed, returned home to Hayes. As a wife and mother, she was expected to settle back into domesticity, running her household and supervising her children's education. This was what she – and all other Tudor women of her class – expected of marriage. But by August 1497, her husband's health was failing. From his sickbed he made his will.[28] He was still 'of good memory', as he assured those who were present to witness his testament, but the time had come to look to the health of his immortal soul. He lingered for some months, but did not last the year. The Christmas of 1497 must have been a muted one for Cecily, since it was on that day that William Burbage's will was proved. As her household plunged into mourning, she found herself a widow and a single woman once more.

Cecily Burbage was still only around thirty years old; she was also an heiress of moderate wealth; and she may already have had a new husband in mind. Her second marriage took place only a couple of months – at most – after her first husband's death.[29] She had almost certainly become acquainted with William Craythorn, a well-liked member of the king's household, during her time with Princess Elizabeth.

He was certainly interested in Cecily's lands, launching himself, after their marriage, into legal disputes to secure them by Easter 1498.[30] In April 1501, he and Cecily sold some of her inheritance in Northcliffe and York for £100.[31] Wives were expected to be submissive, with one conduct book advising them 'not only to avoid that which may anger her husband, but also to frame herself to do that which may please him'.[32] A man could always mould his bride's personality and 'frame her to his fancy', but such things took time.[33] As a wife, Cecily was legally and by convention considered entirely subject to her husband, who could deal with her goods as he saw fit.

While Cecily arranged her second marriage herself, at around the same time the Earl of Surrey began to consider a husband for his eldest daughter. Elizabeth Howard had probably once been intended for Henry Bourchier, Earl of Essex, whose wardship (and, thus, the rights to his marriage) had been acquired by her grandfather when she was an infant. Such arrangements were common. Elizabeth's younger sister, Muriel, later married another family ward.[34] However, the Howard men's battlefield 'treason' in backing Richard III in 1485 had put an end to the Essex match. Surrey was forced to look elsewhere for his elder daughter, after he was finally released from the Tower.

Tudor marriage was often described as a bargain.[35] In the case of gentry and aristocratic marriages, this was apt. Sir William Locke, a prominent London alderman and merchant, insisted on seeing the account books of one prospective son-in-law, Anthony Hickman, only being content to allow him to wed his daughter Rose when he proved to be worth £1,000.[36] For a girl such as Elizabeth Howard, who was born into one of the highest families in the land, it was essential that she maintained or even furthered her social position, as well as obtain financial security. In the last years of the fifteenth century, when she was approaching twenty, her parents arranged a marriage for her with young Thomas Boleyn.[37] This was a solid, respectable match; and Thomas, with his dark good looks, was an interesting proposition. He was highly intelligent and well educated, as well as being physically a fine specimen – well schooled in jousting and dancing.[38] At only three years older than Elizabeth, he was very eligible. Thomas was the grandson of the fabulously wealthy Earl of Ormond and, although on his father's side he hailed from London trade, his wealth made up for his deficiencies in breeding. His social connections in Norfolk, too, were potentially useful, since Surrey's lands were mostly held in the county.[39]

Who suggested the match is not recorded, but it began with the two fathers sitting down together to discuss the terms. These meetings were congenial, since both Surrey and the groom's father, Sir William Boleyn, knew each other and later became friends. Surrey, like all aristocratic fathers, would supply a dowry of course.[40] This payment, usually made in instalments, was the groom's to keep and was also intended as Elizabeth's inheritance. She could expect nothing more from her father's estate.

The dowry helped set the size of her jointure – the income on which she was expected to live during her widowhood. The Boleyns were *nouveau riche*, but to secure Surrey's daughter, Sir William was prepared to be generous. Elizabeth could have a life interest in his lands in Sussex which would, he was sure, go a long way to supporting her in widowhood. She could also have the income from two Norfolk manors, as well as the 'advowson' – the often lucrative right to appoint the vicar – of Holkham church. This was a start, but not enough for the daughter of the Earl of Surrey, who was, after all, marrying down socially. To these gifts, Sir William Boleyn also added the income from three Kent manors, to take effect after his own death.[41] Surrey's lawyers would have hurriedly calculated the income that these lands could produce, before multiplying the sum by ten to set a value for Elizabeth's dowry.[42] It was a generous settlement.

The young couple married in around 1499 and took up residence at Blickling Hall in Norfolk. As she settled down into domesticity, bearing her husband 'every year a child', the new Elizabeth Boleyn could reflect that her parents had settled her reasonably well.[43] There were, however, economies to be made, since the couple were living on an income of £50 a year – tiny for a young husband and wife with court ambitions. Yet, as she focussed on childbirth and child rearing, Elizabeth could look forward to a brighter future when, in due course, her husband inherited the Boleyn estates. With a young, handsome and ambitious husband, she could reason that she had done rather well for herself.

Cecily Burbage, on the other hand, learned a hard lesson in the financial disadvantages of being a wife. Her second husband suddenly died on 12 August 1505. Shortly afterwards, she was at home at her own manor of Theobolds in Cheshunt, Hertfordshire, when the calm of the local area was broken raucously.[44] As she later recalled in court, John Copwood, secondary of the king's remembrancer's office, arrived at the gates. He was accompanied by a force of men, armed to the teeth with 'swords, staves, bows and arrows'. When she refused to let them in, they broke down the door, entered and carried off her household goods worth £30, before turning to the barns and fields and leading away her livestock. Surveying the consequences later, Cecily and her servants estimated it as amounting to at least a hundred marks and lamented the damage done 'against the peace' of the king.

Copwood's account was rather different. He had acted entirely properly, he later assured the court; the widow had exaggerated. The goods he had taken were nowhere near so valuable. As to breaking the king's peace, he countered, he had been doing anything but. He had come armed with a writ dated 12 July from the king, in which he instructed the Sheriff of Hertford to seize the goods. Henry VII had concerns over the accounts of William Craythorn, who had been serving as Escheator of Yorkshire. He had 'not accounted', as far as the financially scrupulous king could see, for debts that he owed by virtue of the office, or for the profits of the office itself. Indeed, he owed at least £40. On this basis, the sheriff assembled a jury at Waltham Cross to consider just what Craythorn owned, right down to the six featherbeds held in the house at Theobolds. While this was going on, Craythorn suddenly died, leaving his widow liable to pay his debts. It was only then that they 'entered' Theobolds and took custody of the goods, Copwood assured the court, passing them directly into the king's own hands. In court, Cecily's lawyer argued that the goods had been invalidly seized by a man that was 'not an officer of the king and is not privy to the king's patent'. Her argument failed. The former Cecily Burbage must have lamented the position that meant her own property was entirely subsumed by a spendthrift husband.

The London draper's wife, Katherine Fenkyll, had her own views on the subordinate position of wives, which she made very plain. A few years after she was widowed, in 1499, her 'familiar and old acquaintance' Joanne Johnson, a wealthy widow, came to visit her on confidential business.[45] It was, she admitted, a delicate matter, since she had agreed to marry a gentleman, Robert Long of Windridge, but there was the small matter of both her personal effects and her debts. She had, she believed, around £500 in goods, including furniture, plate, money and jewels, which Long was anxious to acquire as his own property on their wedding day. Nonetheless, the widow wanted to protect herself.

She agreed with Katherine, as well as two other friends, that they would hide away £300 of the goods, intending to 'cloak and colour the same' from her husband so that she 'might give and have or otherwise bestow the same at her liberty and pleasure'. Instead of acquiring his new wife's fabulous jewels, Long therefore found himself liable for her existing debts of more than £200. This was a bad bargain and he was furious, rushing to the courts with a bill of complaint asking that a '*subpoena* be directed to the said Katherine, William Broke and Joanne his wife commanding them and any of them by the same severally to appear before the king in his honourable courts of Chancery' to be examined. Joanna Johnson, however, as a wife, could not be sued in court independently of her husband. She got off scot free. With no clear evidence against her, Katherine, as she would have realized, was in no danger. But she understood the potential troubles wives could face in being financially dependent on their husbands.

Cecily Burbage was a wife for the vast majority of her adult life. She took her third husband around a year after Craythorn's death, marrying the upstanding William Bedell.[46] He, a largely self-made man, had begun his career as receiver of the lands of the young Duke of Buckingham, before transferring into the employment of Henry VII's mother, Margaret Beaufort.[47] He was devoted to her, later crediting his good fortune in life solely to his patroness, from whom, as he said, 'I had all that I have.'[48] She was fond of him, too, appointing him to act as her treasurer for the final eleven years of her life. After her death, Bedell transferred to the household of Cardinal Wolsey, again serving as treasurer.[49]

With such important contacts, Bedell was a good match for Cecily, and he allowed her to continue her comfortable life, on the fringe of the royal court.[50] Her third husband was a charitable, faithful man, while to Bedell, Cecily was the one whom 'I trust above all creatures'.[51]

Cecily was widowed for a third, and final, time in 1518, when she was past fifty. The devoted Bedell had paid her the complement of making her his sole executor, charged with disposing of the residue of his estate 'to the most profit of my sinful soul as trusty and lovingly as she would I should do for her'. Although she had family connections to London trade, she lived out her remaining years as a country gentlewoman.[52] Her days at Eltham Palace and the brief life of Princess Elizabeth must, by now, have seemed a distant dream. These final years of widowhood were her longest, but short compared to a long career of marriage. She died in 1521 and was buried beside her third husband, in the south transept of Westminster Abbey.[53]

'To make the best pancake'

A Tudor wife who could not cook was, reasoned one contemporary, a woman who had broken her marriage vows. 'She may love and obey, but she cannot serve and keep him with that true duty which is ever expected'.[54] Those expectations being high, a Tudor housewife equipped her kitchen with a variety of mostly pottery vessels for the purpose, such as the small sixteenth-century cauldron held by the Museum of London.[55] This plain, handmade pot has two small handles for lifting it when hot. Other typical items included mugs, bowls and other, different types of cooking pot, all essential to the smooth running of the kitchen.

At the lowest level of society, cookery was fairly basic. Most people ate a simple diet of bread and pottage (a vegetable and, sometimes, meat stew).[56] Pottage was easy to make; it could sit, stewing over the fire, while the house's occupants got on with other tasks. As for bread, very few poorer houses had an oven in which to bake it, so when bread was required, a housewife would either have to purchase the loaves or make use of a communal bakehouse. This last was a common feature of many villages, providing several ovens under one roof, and available for use for a small fee.[57] Bread was a staple of most diets, so women would make regular use of these communal facilities.

Cookery could be rather more elaborate in the homes of the well-off. At the end of the Tudor years, in 1604, the aristocratic Eleanor, Lady Fettiplace, compiled a book of more than 200 recipes, complete with her marginal notes and amendments indicating that she had tried and tasted them herself.[58] Inexperienced housewives of sufficient means could also make use of published texts, with Gervase Markham's *The English Housewife* being particularly influential in the early seventeenth century. He considered that the first step to gaining a profound understanding of cookery was to 'have knowledge of all sorts of herbs belonging to the kitchen, whether they be for the pot, for salads, for sauces, for servings, or for any other seasoning, or adorning' This, the young wife should learn through her own labour and experience. She must know what to sow in her garden, and when to sow it.

The middle and upper classes had the time and resources to make more elaborate meals, in which context sugar became more commonplace in the Elizabethan period. And writers such as Markham fed the need for new and interesting recipes incorporating sugar. 'To make,' as Markham asserted, 'the best pancake,' a housewife should:

> ... *take two or three eggs, and break them into a dish, and beat them well: then add unto them a pretty quantity of fair running water, and beat all well together: then put in cloves, mace, cinnamon, and a nutmeg, and season it with salt: which done, make it as thick as you think good with fine wheat flour: then fry the cakes as thin as may be with sweet butter, or sweet seam, and make them brown.*

They should then be served, strewn with sugar. He had further, helpful tips, warning that 'there be some which mix pancakes with new milk or cream, but that makes them tough, cloying, and not so crisp, pleasant and savoury as running water'. The housewife who wanted to try something else sweet could attempt white pudding, which was made with 'the best, thickest and sweetest cream', and to which the cook could add oatmeal, egg yolks, currants, dates and other dainties.

Boiled meats and broths were popular. An 'ordinary stewed broth' was a simple dish, made from the neck of veal, or a leg of beef or mutton, or a chicken. When the meat was washed, it would be put in a pot with water and then boiled. After straining the resulting broth, half a pound of prunes, half a pound of raisins and a quarter of a pound of currants could be added, with some mace and two or three cloves, and left to boil for some time. A white broth was a similar dish, but made with veal, capons, chickens or other fowl (or fish) and including a pint of white wine, as well as slices of ginger.[59]

Cooking was labour-intensive, and even a joint of boiled meat was not entirely straightforward. For a leg of mutton, the housewife needed to wash the meat, boil it a little, and then place it on the spit over the fire for half a dozen laborious turns. It then had to be slashed with a knife and pressed between two dishes to obtain the gravy, before being turned half a dozen more times and pressed again, and the whole process repeated as many times as moisture could be got out of the meat. The mutton could then be boiled until tender in white wine and mutton broth. While it was cooking, the gravy would be heated, to which salt, sugar, cinnamon, ginger and lemon slices might be added, as well as orange and some crumbs of white bread.

7

OF APPRENTICES AND ASPIRATIONS

Katherine Fenkyll, wife and business partner

I n 1511, two years into the reign of King Henry VIII, the widow Dame Katherine Fenkyll arrived at the Guildhall in London, accompanied by a young man named Henry Lenton, who had recently left home for the first time in his life. He followed her into the building, where she confirmed before witnesses that she had taken him on as an apprentice. At the same time, she also sponsored his admittance to the Freedom of the City.[1] The formalities over, the pair returned home to Thames Street, not far from London Bridge. There was work to be done and much that Katherine needed to teach her apprentice over the long years of his service.

Two years later, Katherine Fenkyll returned again to the Guildhall, this time with Raynold Love in tow, who had also come to learn a trade from her. Business was booming for the intrepid female entrepreneur. She was reaping the rewards of everything she had learned and practised in more than a decade of commercial enterprise, which began with her marriage to one of the City's leading traders.

For many women in Tudor England, early adulthood was never going to embrace any sort of trade, because so often the conventions of law, society, class and marriage eschewed those possibilities, instead directing women's time and energy inwards, into the domestic sphere. Yet, the picture was more complicated than that. At many levels, 'women's work' was vital – in the East Anglian cloth industry, for example, and, as Elizabeth Barton would have known, in the smooth operating of any farm. Apprenticeship was not a totally male domain, either in the learning or in the training, and while for girls it was often in contexts predominantly identified with women, such as dressmaking, it was not always exclusively so. As for married women, wives came to share in the work of their husbands' businesses, and some, such as Elizabeth Fenkyll, were even able to use their experience as a basis on which to become influential players in the City of London.

This is not to say that it was easy for unmarried girls or married women to ply a trade. The City merchants and tradesmen, organized into their livery companies, reigned supreme in Tudor London.[2] It was through these organizations that a member could obtain sponsorship of his admission to the Freedom of the City, allowing him to pursue his trade.[3] There was normally nothing in the way of legality to stop women taking the Freedom too – but very few did.[4] One draper who, in 1570, arrived in the company's hall with a female apprentice, seeking her Freedom, was turned away by the master and wardens. The case caused much murmuring, since many in the company suspected that the woman did indeed have the right to be enrolled – but it was not a trend they wanted to encourage. Indeed, only seventy-three women are known to have been enrolled as apprentices in sixteenth-century London, among the many thousands of men who did so.[5] Girls could sometimes have their apprenticeships secured by charitable institutions: the destitute Margaret Gyllam, for example, who had been a patient at London's St Thomas's Hospital, was sent after her discharge to learn needlework and button-making with one John Delow and his wife in 1564.[6] But in some cases, women were even banned. The 1550 Ordinances of the Weavers' Company confirmed that no weaver could reveal anything of his trade to 'any maiden, damsel, or other woman'.

Although only a tiny number of London women were formally apprenticed in the period, women frequently did appear as sponsors for men seeking the Freedom of the City. Elizabeth Lewin, who was the widow of a baker, brought her apprentice John Jankyns to the Guildhall to secure his Freedom in September 1546. Two years later, Richard Tothill arrived at the Guildhall with Elizabeth Middleton, the widow of stationer William Middleton, both of whom Tothill had served. Joan Alynson, the widow of a horner (a craftsman working with horn products), had remarried by the time she brought her apprentice to the Guildhall in 1544; but her second husband appeared only as a witness rather than as a master.[7] As these examples, and that of Katherine Fenkyll in 1511, suggest, such women were frequently widows who had taken over their husbands' businesses; but they were also sometimes wives.

Although female apprentices in London were rare, they existed in small numbers in other cities. Sixteenth-century Bristol saw a number of young girls bound by indenture both to masters and their wives, although in rare cases a girl could be apprenticed to a single man.[8] Often, these indentures make it clear that it was the mistress who would train the girl. Helen ap Richard arrived in Bristol from Tintern, Gloucestershire, in October 1542, when she agreed to become apprenticed for seven years to a grocer named Roger Jones and his wife, Elizabeth, who plied her own trade as a seamstress.[9] She was to work with Elizabeth in learning how to cut, fashion and fit clothes, so that she too could earn her living.

Dressmaking was considered an entirely respectable business for a woman, whether married or single – and many examples are known. In 1542, Eleanor Harnage, the daughter of a yeoman farmer from Shrewsbury, finished her apprentice-ship under Matilda Sexby, wife of a draper and an independent seamstress.[10] Agnes Newman, whose father was a Gloucester labourer, served a mistress rather than her master, for it was the seamstress Joanna Tewe who promised to teach her, when she arrived in 1532, rather than Joanna's merchant husband.[11]

Girls were also commonly apprenticed to learn the 'art of housewifeship', a uniquely female occupation;[12] but, since wives assisted their husbands in their businesses, the girls probably learned something of these trades, too. In a small number of cases, girls were apprenticed in the male-dominated trades. On 2 November 1534, Alice May entered into an indenture in her home town of Bristol. She was to serve a pin-maker named Thomas White and his wife, Margaret, with it expressly set out in the indenture – for the avoidance of doubt – that Alice was to be trained as a pinner.[13] Five months later, Alice Lower was apprenticed to a mercer to learn his trade.[14]

Some successful female mercers already plied their trade in Bristol. The unmarried Sibyl Garvey was one of them, taking on Jane ap David as her apprentice in June 1552.[15] Agnes Bishop, also unmarried, was another; she negotiated and made the arrangements for young Alice Saxby to travel from Wiltshire to learn the seamstress trade from her in 1534.[16] Girls could also take decisive action themselves, in arranging their own apprenticeships. Margaret Come, the daughter of a deceased cardmaker in Bristol, arranged her own apprenticeship with the draper Roger Walker and his wife in 1553.[17]

Apprenticeships for women were taken seriously by the parties concerned. Constant Wale, who was apprenticed to a mercer and his wife for eight years in 1553, undertook to serve them for a further two years after the end of her term, for a wage of 40 shillings and her food and drink.[18]

There were young women, therefore, who bucked the trend. Yet, Bristol's female apprentices were still a minority, and the numbers of young men and women taken on to learn a trade tell their own story: for the period 1552–65, there were 38 female apprentices as opposed to 1,571 male apprentices. More than 97 per cent of apprentices were male.

∽∾

On the other side of England, in London, it proved far easier for wives to involve themselves in their husband's trade or run their own independent business than for an unmarried woman to take up a trade.

Katherine Fenkyll had been a widow for twelve years by the time she arrived at the Guildhall with Henry Lenton. Nothing is known of her early life, but she first left home in the latter years of the fifteenth century, when the Tudor dynasty was still new. She may, like so many of her contemporaries, have begun her working life as a servant. There was certainly no shame in that. Indeed, it was seen as desirable, since the wives of even wealthy merchants were required to do their husbands 'service' and play a part in the family business.[19] Men were advised to look for a capacity to work rather than riches when choosing a bride, even if it meant selecting a wife who was a 'servant in degree'. Thus, it was far from unusual for the wives of London tradesmen to have been in service, and Katherine's contemporary Thomasine Percyvale, for example, worked her way up from service to become a leading London trader.[20]

Katherine became the second wife of the draper Sir John Fenkyll at some point between 1497 and 1499.[21] It was a highly prestigious match for her and one that threw her into the centre of London trade. Her new husband was regularly called to official service during his lifetime of trade in the capital.[22] He was part of an elite social group, diligently walking over to the Guildhall every St Matthew's Day to cast his vote in the City elections.[23] The same names appeared again and again in

London's important positions; John himself served as an alderman from 1485 until his death, as well as Sheriff of London on occasion.[24] He also represented the City in Parliament and had the personal satisfaction of being known to King Henry VII.[25] When he was knighted on 6 January 1487, after which he obtained a coat of arms, it must have seemed as though he could rise no higher.[26] Nonetheless, he threw himself into civic administration, something which – although important – could be deadly dull.

Sir John Fenkyll had a wide range of contacts in the City, through which he could buy and sell his wares. On one day he might trade with a stockfishmonger, the next an ironmonger or a linen-draper. Sometimes he did business with mercers, grocers or even the tiremongers, who sold an exotic sweet wine imported from the Continent.[27] As a side-line, he bought and sold iron goods and imported wine.[28] He was opportunistic, with a good nose for what would sell, once bringing a barrel of marmalade home with him from Portugal along with his more usual wares.[29] His business connections stretched right up to the king. For the most part, he sold cloth, exporting fine fabrics to the Continent regularly, sometimes in his own laden ships[30] and sometimes in vessels that he had hired.[31]

During Katherine Fenkyll's short marriage to Sir John, her business activities were subsumed by those of her husband. Because, as a general rule, English wives had no independent legal status, they could own nothing – not even the clothes they wore or the property that they brought to the marriage – and neither could they sue or be sued. Any debts incurred by them were their husbands', as were any wages they earned. Katherine assisted her husband in his business and was trained by him; but she had no *official* role.

Medicine makers

Whatever trades or occupations women's aspirations or needs led them to, there remained also the many domestic roles that women were expected to perform. And in an age when doctors were expensive, this included proficiency in preparing medicines for their families. Indeed, this was the first virtue of 'a complete woman', considered the writer Gervaise Markham in his 1615 tract on the *The English Housewife*. He provided recipes for treating a wide range of disorders, from excessive sweating to headaches and the alarmingly named 'frenzy'.

The English housewife was, contemporaries considered, almost a doctor in her own home. Were one of her household struck down with a fever, she should take spoonfuls of rosewater, aquavite (an alcoholic spirit), running water,

vinegar and the fascinatingly named dragon water, as well as half a spoonful of mithridate – a semi-mythical remedy that would be rather hard for the average Tudor woman to obtain – and beat them all together before offering it to the afflicted person.[32] If a family member were to be troubled by a sore, she could make a poultice from elder leaves soaked in milk, and then strained, before boiling the concoction until it was thick.

For the dreaded 'frenzy' or inflammation of the brain, beetroot juice should be squirted up the nose in order to 'purge and clean [the] head exceedingly'. Ale could then be drunk, to which boiled violet leaves and lettuce were added to 'suddenly bring [the patient] to a very temperate mildness, and make the passion of the frenzy forsake him'.[33]

This was not, however, always the position for female traders in the capital. London wives had the potential for considerable autonomy. According to the custom of the City of London, a married woman who 'follows any craft within the said City by herself apart, with which the husband in no way intermeddles' would then 'be bound as a single woman as to all that concerns her said craft'.[34] Even if she was brought before the court, she would be treated as a single woman – a *femme sole*. Married women in London could rent houses or shops without their husband's involvement, as well as enter into contracts.[35]

The gap between married women's lack of legal status and the realities of commercial life could make for difficulties – as Sir John Fenkyll found to his cost a few years before his marriage to Katherine. Joanne Horne, the wife of the influential William Horne, ran her own business and approached John to sell her some valuable silk remnants.[36] He knew her well and had, indeed, been one of the aldermen who had elected her husband as Mayor of London in October 1487.[37] She was, she assured him, a 'sole merchant' and could buy and sell and enter into contracts and agreements in her own name. Accordingly, Joanna sent – by her servant – confirmation of the debt attested by her own seal.

Happy with this, John waited for his money. After some time, he began to ask for it, before finally he 'demanded' it. It was then that she told him that she was not, after all, trading as a *femme sole* and that (as he recalled) she 'would not consent nor pay anything of the said sum in the life of her said husband'. John would have to wait, she declared, if he wanted his money. He did want his money, and after William Horne's death he requested that Joanna – now a widow and in charge of the administration of Horne's estate – pay him what was owed; yet she still refused, to John's 'great loss and damage'. It was a confused situation and one that the customary law of London was not able to deal with. Was the contract valid? It only was if she had truly been a *femme sole*, but that was not clear. He was 'without remedy', complained John, when he took the matter before the Chancery courts. How on earth could someone hoping to do business with a married woman truly tell that they were on firm ground in doing so?

∽

In other parts of the country, married women were also working for a living or running businesses. In the mid-sixteenth century, the enterprising Mistress Conye, a woman 'authorised to keep a victualling house' in Norwich, came into conflict with the authorities when she was caught selling the beer at her inn at a premium.[38] She followed in a proud Norwich tradition of female entrepreneurship, going back centuries and often skirting close to what was legally permitted.[39]

The truth was that women's incomes were often essential to support a family, as, sometimes, was the child labour that was rife. The destitute are often invisible in the records, but a 1570 census of the 810 poorest citizens of Norwich highlights just how bleak conditions could be.[40] In a house belonging to John Hennings, who rented rooms in the building to three other families, lived Alice Reede, a forty-year-old woman whose husband, a thatcher, had 'run away', leaving her with four children, including a breastfed infant. She took to spinning wool to make ends meet. At the same time, she also set her eldest two children, a girl of fourteen and a boy of nine, to work in spinning to keep the rent paid and food on the table. They were, the census bluntly put it, 'very poor'.

In another room lived Margaret Palmer, a widow of forty-eight. She both spun and took in washing to survive. Her room neighboured that of another widow, Anne King, who spun cloth and carried out other small jobs, while her seventeen-year-old daughter went out to work. The final room was occupied by a couple equally as desperate: the elderly Robert Hemmyngs, unable to work since he 'lieth miserably of a disease of his body', and his wife Muriel, who also spun fabric to keep the family's heads above water. Their six-year-old daughter was too young to take on such work, but within a few years she would have been assisting her mother. So many girls could expect a future dominated by the clacking and whirling of the spinning wheel; it is no surprise that, for example, Christopher Smith and his wife sent their two daughters, aged just eight and six, to learn the trade (with 'Mother Mallerde'). The girls would soon have been helping to fill the family coffers.

The type of work available to women depended, in large degree, on where they lived. In Cornwall, many of the poor women and children were employed in digging for lugworms in the ooze of the riverbeds, in order to sell them to fishermen for bait;[41] other women would spend their evenings washing, pickling and packing fish for export to foreign markets.[42]

Despite everything they actually did to earn themselves, and their dependents, an income, for Tudor women it remained their marital status that defined them rather than the type of work, business or trade that they might pursue.[43] Katherine Fenkyll, immersed in London trade, understood this too. On her marriage to Sir John Fenkyll, she had immediately become one of the *doyennes* of London society, her life suddenly filled with glamour.[44] But in 1499 – on her husband's death – she was able to come out of his shadow as a businesswoman in her own right.

The Fourth Age

8

OF CITY TRADE AND LONDON LIFE

Katherine Fenkyll, independent businesswoman

In the Tudor conception, the fourth age of life, beginning around the age of twenty-eight, was traditionally a time of action. For William Shakespeare, it was represented by the very masculine image of 'a soldier, / full of strange oaths, and bearded like the pard, / Jealous in honour, sudden, and quick in quarrel, / Seeking the bubble reputation / Even in the cannon's mouth'.

Women, of course, were almost never soldiers. Yet, this phase of adulthood – when they were settled as wives and mothers, or staring in the face of spinsterhood, or experiencing the independence of widowhood – could become a time of great dynamism and self-realization. As the era unfolded, Tudor women made their presences felt in a diverse range of roles, and some launched themselves onto a public stage in a manner they can scarce have expected, often transgressing the expectations of their sex in the process. For the widowed Katherine Fenkyll, it was in trade and business that she would excel.

In 1527, 'My Lady Fenkyll' was sitting at the top table of the Drapers' Company Election Day feast. To her left was the guest of honour, the Prior of Christ Church. Ranged around her were the heavyweights of this London livery company, for this was the high point in the Drapers' Company social calendar. On this day, the worthies of the trade and, indeed, of the City were invited to sit and feast in the company's hall.[1] Around her was a table festooned with silver-gilt plate borrowed from her house earlier that day.[2] She could sit and make merry, feasting on dates and capons, and on the exotic meat and fish. And she was secure in the knowledge that she had become the grand dame of one of the greatest livery companies in London.[3]

Katherine Fenkyll had still been a relatively new bride when her husband, Sir John, had died in 1499; but he had judged her more than capable of taking over his business affairs. By the custom of the City of London – which was cast in iron – a childless widow was entitled to one half of all her husband's chattels and goods.[4] Sir John had gone further than this, leaving Katherine a life interest in the marital home on Thames Street, as well as lands outside London, while the remainder of his estate passed to her absolutely. Of even greater significance, he had named her an executor of his estate, along with his brother-in-law and fellow draper Thomas Cremor and a friend, Thomas Spence.[5] The two senior executors were quickly able to see off Spence, leaving Katherine and Cremor thrown together in the administration of the large and complex estate.[6]

In London, widows were the most visible Tudor women.[7] Joan Bradbury, for example, who died in 1530, ran her husband's tailoring business after his death in 1491, taking her own apprentices and ensuring that her children were well settled in trade.[8] Katherine Fenkyll took a similar approach, although it took her time to establish herself as an independent business-woman. Under the terms of his will, John had requested that two of his associates, John Squire and William Sakfeld, 'or any other' who would 'take the labour to occupy' one of his ships should be permitted to use the vessel for three years after his death.[9] In return, they would be liable for all the charges, but would also receive a third of the profit, with the remaining profit passing back to Katherine. It was only at the end of the three years that the ship was to pass to 'the free will and discretion of mine executors': it was then that Katherine found herself fully in control.

Katherine was left extremely wealthy, and she had little need to involve herself in the draper's business. She could have contented herself with fulfilling her late husband's wishes. She supervised his burial in the parish church of St Michael's, Crooked Lane, as he requested, alongside the body of his first wife.[10] She could have busied herself with the charitable bequests that John left to the church for the good of his soul. She could, indeed, have retreated into her house on Thames Street, which was only a stone's throw away from St Michael's. The church, which stood at the heart of the parish, engaged five chaplains to sing mass each day, their salaries paid by ancient and generous endowments from members of the Fishmongers' Company. The voices rang out into streets crammed with dwellings and people, where often several families crowded into the narrow buildings fronting the roads.[11]

Much of what is now thought of as Central London consisted of fields in Tudor times. Animals grazed close to Covent Garden and in the green spaces around the buildings clustered in the Inns of Courts.[12] The lawyers could hear the cows lowing even as they hurried into court. But just a few streets away, within the boundaries of the old City, things were quite different. The City ditch and wall, once so important for defence, were already in sad decline. John Stow, in the late sixteenth century, lamented that the ditch was 'now of late neglected and forced either to a very narrow, and the same a filthy channel, or altogether stopped up for gardens planted, and houses built thereon, even to the very wall, and in many places upon both ditch and wall houses be built'.[13] These ancient structures delineated a city that, in Katherine's time, was rapidly growing. Fifty thousand inhabitants at the start of the sixteenth century had increased to more than a hundred and fifty thousand by the end of the century – making it one of the largest cities in Europe.[14] Narrow streets were packed tight with slender timber-framed buildings, often rising five storeys above the street below. The only gaps in the facades were the dark, tunnel-like alleyways, winding their way towards further residences behind.[15] For extra space, the upper storeys could stretch across the street as jetties, so when the property opposite did the same, the street below was almost roofed by the resulting canopy.

In this crowded metropolis, the houses of rich and poor bumped up against each other. Many of the more modest buildings occupied a small area of just one small room, before rising precariously high above the street. At ground level, there was usually a shop of some kind; on the floor above a hall, and then sleeping quarters higher still. Those people who were lucky enough to have a small yard squeezed into their property's tiny footprint could keep the privy a reasonable distance from the main living quarters. For others, with no outside space, there was only the attic, leaving residents with a long trek upstairs to answer a call of nature. The inhabitants of these poorer dwellings did, though, have one advantage over the residences of their social superiors: the single chimney-stack running up through the house, like a spine, allowed fireplaces in every room. The house could be cramped, smelly and noisy, but at least the occupants would not be cold. Fire was, of course, a constant danger, and Tudor householders were always vigilant. A careless neighbour could relatively easily burn down the entire street.[16]

Larger houses, such as those occupied by Katherine Fenkyll, were still narrow edifices, dominated by the shop below. But they could stretch back far into their plot. Such dwellings would include an upper hall for entertaining and a parlour to give a more comfortable environment. Kitchens, too, were often part of the main house, while there would be a bedroom for the master and mistress, and perhaps two or three further chambers for the children and servants. John Fenkyll may well have had his warehouse directly behind his shop in Thames Street. As well as this, he would have had a study in the living quarters, providing him with a private space in which to work, perhaps overlooking the street below.[17] A well in the yard behind the house meant that the well-to-do had a private water supply, rather than relying on the nearest street pump or conduit.

One of Katherine's neighbours, on nearby New Fish Street, lived in a house rising to six storeys, which included the attic, one or two small rooms on each floor and a hanging jetty.[18] Many larger houses were shared, with tenants renting various individual rooms and spaces, to create a rabbit warren behind the solid wooden front doors.[19] Another house, on Pudding Lane, close to Katherine's, was so large that it was divided into four units – two at the front, abutting the street, and two behind.[20]

The Fenkyll house, lying just off the major thoroughfare of Candlewick Street, with its maze of tiny lanes running down from it to the Thames, was well situated to allow Katherine to take up her husband's trade. She was but a short walk from the river and London Bridge. This structure over the Thames, connecting the City of London with Southwark, was enormously high, and lined with houses on both sides so that, as one contemporary marvelled, 'it seemeth rather a continual street than a bridge'.[21] On account of its importance, it was guarded on both sides by gates and towers, manned by wardens and officers at all times. It was on the towers of London Bridge that the severed heads of traitors – grisly mementos of Tudor justice – were displayed for all to see, first on the side closest the city and, after 1577, at the Southwark end.[22]

To add to this hub of activity, foreign traders also flocked to London, travelling from the Low Countries, France, the

German and Italian states, and beyond to conduct their business. In 1593, when a survey of foreign householders living in London was carried out, more than 7,000 of them crammed the streets, mostly within the City walls. They often stayed for many years, becoming all but English; and they were women and children, as well as men. One Mrs Agostyn, from Seville in Spain, arrived in England in 1570, accompanied by her husband and one-year-old daughter; she stayed on in the city after she was widowed, though she remained a gentlewoman and plied no trade. But other foreign-born women set to work. We know of a French silk-lace worker named Louise Ahere, who in 1593 was living in Aldgate Ward with her adult daughter, who helped her mother in the trade. A Dutch immigrant, Gillian Mescart, was supporting her young son and daughter by working as a silk weaver in England after the death of her husband, having spent thirty years already in the country. She remained in contact with her roots by attending a Dutch church in the city.[23] Many of these foreign-born women and their families in London would have been Protestants escaping the violent strife that afflicted France and the Spanish-controlled Netherlands in the last decades of the seventeenth century.

Unsurprisingly for such an international hub, England's capital was exotic and glamorous. Katherine had only to take a short stroll from her front door to purchase gold from Arabia, spices, frankincense and Babylonian oil, Indian purple cloth, gems from Egypt and ambergris from the cold Arctic.[24] Like her late husband, Katherine dealt primarily in fine cloths, and her own trading business, with its wares sailing for distant ports and ships in foreign harbours, now contributed to the glamour of the City.

'Women of evil life'

Katherine Fenkyll's career as a savvy businesswoman selling cloth brought her success and respect in a man's world. For the far more numerous women who earned a living by selling their bodies, there was little chance of rising to such heights.

Prostitution in the Tudor period existed mainly in towns, encouraged by the anonymity of large transient communities.[25] In most towns, this ancient trade was actually outlawed; but a few were rather more progressive. A man in the port towns of Southampton and Sandwich, or in Southwark just outside the City of London, could visit a licensed brothel if he so chose.[26] Such brothels were tightly regulated. The prostitute paid rent to the brothel-keeper, but was then able to keep her earnings for the night. There was money to be made in selling sex.

Elsewhere, brothels were not always so accepted by their communities. One winter's evening in 1567, Mistress Cooe of Chelmsford, Essex, was leaving church when she received word that her husband, Henry, had been seen entering the house of Mother Bowden nearby.[27] Furious, the wife marched over to the house and knocked at the front door, at which point her husband quickly slipped out of the back entrance, leaving Mother Bowden 'and the harlot her daughter' to face the wrath of Mrs Cooe. She beat the old woman, who was prostituting her own daughter, before grabbing the daughter by the hair and dragging her about the house. Breaking free, the girl rushed into the street screaming that her assailant would kill her mother.

Henry Cooe, not to be dissuaded, returned to the brothel a few days later – only to be interrupted once again, this time when a crowd came to arrest him, perhaps sent by his angry wife. He fled out of the back door, before leaping over a gate into a neighbour's yard, but was captured and dragged to the constable's to be charged with immorality, along with Mother Bowden.

The magistrates were keen to clean up the town; they rounded up two other brothel-keepers at the same time, one of whom, George Blacklocke, was known for luring in the young people of the town with the promise of gambling and alcohol, as well as the pleasures of the young women under his roof.

The worthies of Chelmsford were not unusual in trying to root out prostitution in their town. From at least the start of the fifteenth century, brothel-keepers had been banned from living within the walls of the City of London, since 'thieves and other persons of light and bad repute are often, and more commonly, received and har-boured in the houses of women of evil life within the City'.[28] Punishments for brothel-keepers and 'women of evil life' were severe, intended as deterrents. In August 1495, a man named John Merell was hauled before the Court of Common Council in London.[29] After being dragged from his prison cell, he soon confessed when confronted with proofs that he was a 'bawd'. This brothel-owner had conveyed the thirteen-year-old Alice Wilson to his house in order to permit her to be 'rav-ished' by a client named Alan Redman. Whether Alice con-sented to this or not is not recorded, but it was Merell who was punished, being first humiliated in the pillory before being banished from the City on pain of imprisonment. It was his third offence.[30]

The punishments were largely the same for both women and men caught in the sex trade. Seven and a half years later, one Agnes Dryver appeared before the London authorities, having been 'indicted for a common woman of her body'.[31] She was found guilty of whoring and sen-tenced to be led in shame through the streets of London, while wearing a striped hood over her head and carrying a white rod in her hand – a pun-ishment enacted according to the letter of the medieval laws of the City.[32] At the same time, minstrels played to alert the population to Agnes's shame.

It was, perhaps, better than the prison she had been kept in, although time in the pillory in Cornhill was also a hard punishment; an hour a day was considered enough of a deterrent. She was also then evicted from London, being barred on pain of imprisonment of a year and a day and more time in the pillory. It was her third offence.

In spite of the severity of the laws, desperation or the desire to make money provided sufficient incentive to turn people again and again towards London's sex trade.

Following her husband's death, Katherine worked closely with her fellow executor, Thomas Cremor, to resolve the estate's affairs. It was a lengthy process; the pair were still chasing up outstanding debts ten years after Sir John's death.[33] They also had to deal with a case brought by Sir John's nephew, who believed that he should have been allocated more of the estate and business.[34] When Katherine noticed that he even claimed her house on Thames Street, to which she had a prior life interest, she angrily pronounced, in court documents, his claims to be 'untrue', their matter 'imagined'.[35]

Such issues were vexing when Katherine had a business to run. But, as a businesswoman, she always had to be on her guard. In 1515 she brought a claim before the Drapers' Company regarding silk that she had bought from the wife of Matthew Boughton, which was, in her, judgement, 'non-lawful and not after the sample'.[36]

The two apprentices that Katherine had engaged, in 1511 and 1513, worked directly under her, learning the trade from their mistress. Sponsoring them for their Freedom of the City was not cheap,[37] and the two young men may have been interested in more than Katherine could teach them. After finishing a term of service, an ambitious apprentice would look to start a business, something which required capital of at least £40 to £50 in the greater companies, in order to build a stock;[38] and marriage to a wealthy widow was an attractive way of gaining the necessary funds. The attraction could work both ways, and at least one contemporary reported gossip about wealthy City dowagers marrying the apprentice living in the house 'who is most pleasing to her, and who was probably not displeasing to her in the lifetime of her husband' and in whose 'power she places all her own fortune'.[39]

Katherine Fenkyll did indeed have her eye on a second husband, but it was her co-executor and brother-in-law – not one of her apprentices. She may have had to wait, for Thomas Cremor was still married to his previous wife in February 1511.[40] A Norfolk man, who had come to London to make his fortune,[41] Cremor had begun a habit of snaffling wealthy widows when he married Jane Hariot, a middle-aged mother of five.[42] He was neither as influential nor as wealthy as Sir John Fenkyll, but he was nonetheless well connected in the Drapers' Company.[43] He had also been a Member of Parliament. Katherine had grown to like him over the years in which they worked together on Sir John's estate – and the couple married as soon as he was widowed, some time after 1511.[44] Taking a new husband, after years of freedom, was a major gamble for Katherine. She enjoyed her status as the widow of a knight, insisting until the end of her life in being referred to as 'Dame' or 'Lady' Katherine Fenkyll.[45]

In this marriage, Katherine probably made a love match. She moved immediately into her new husband's 'mansion' in the large parish of St Dunstan's, in the east of the City, not far from Crooked Lane. It was a large, fine residence, which, unusually for London at the time, included a garden – a luxury indeed when most citizens made do with a yard, at most.[46] It had also been Cremor's former matrimonial home, which had passed to him from Jane following their marriage.[47] He was attached to the place, and there was no question that the couple would remain at Katherine's house on Thames Street.

Only a few years later, Cremor would resist strongly pressure that he and Katherine move into the living quarters over the cloth market at Blackwellhall. He held the wardenship there, thanks to a timely 100-mark donation to the Drapers' Company in 1516.[48] It was a hugely lucrative post, but by 1520 complaints were being made about Thomas's 'ordering' of the hall, as well as about the conduct of his servants. Two years later, the Drapers ordered Thomas and Katherine to move their household to the hall, so that they could keep a better eye on it.[49] When King Henry VIII then attempted to grant the keepership instead to his own candidate, the Drapers' Company, alarmed at this potential loss, had to lean on Katherine's husband to stump up for a bribe to the lord chancellor, Cardinal Wolsey, 'to be good for us for Blackwellhall'.[50] This calmed matters somewhat. Not long afterwards, Cremor was able to reach a *quid pro quo* deal with the Drapers' Company: if he allowed them to pass off his expenses relating to Blackwellhall as their own, then they would 'grant that if he decease before my lady his wife that she shall continue there without any let expulsion or impediment of this house for the space of time of vi months after his death'.[51] For Katherine, this was an important concession.

Thomas Cremor did indeed die before his wife, on 25 September 1526. Shortly beforehand, he had made his will.[52] He left Katherine well provided for, asking that his goods and chattels be divided in half so that she could receive one part 'to do therewith her own will and pleasure as her part and portion of my goods to her belonging and appertaining after and according to the custom of the City of London'. The other part was to be used for his bequests, including those to the Church for the good of his soul. After gifts to his sister, nephews and nieces, and servants, he left the residue of his estate to Katherine, who was the only executor. She also received a life interest in the house in St Dunstan's. Twice widowed, once again Katherine was in sole charge of her business.

Within hours, she was called upon to defend her right to the lucrative Blackwellhall.[53] Meeting the day after Cremor's death, the Company – in violation of their agreement – voted to elect one of their number as the new warden, having seen off the king's own candidate with a substantial bribe. They waited only three weeks after Cremor's death before going, *en masse*, to Blackwellhall with the Company officers and aldermen of the city.[54] There, Katherine was presented with the new warden – Peter Starkey.

After much discussion, the dignitaries returned to Drapers' Hall. Two days later, the Company declared that they had concluded an agreement 'that the Lady Dame Katherine shall have that one half on all the revenues present and received that shall or may come or grow of and by the office of Wardenship of Blackwellhall aforesaid for a period of six months'. It was not what had been agreed in Thomas Cremor's lifetime, but it was probably as much as Katherine could expect. She had certainly taken steps to protect herself, spiriting away 'all the goods belonging and pertaining' to the wardenship to hold them hostage until an agreement could be reached.[55] She also bought herself some time, declaring that she would retain the warden's lodgings until Christmas.

Katherine's second widowhood was as busy as her first; but she had to defend her interests, as there were many determined to take advantage of a wealthy widow. She was no one's fool. When she received word of a suit against her second husband's estate, she took decisive action. It might be, she considered, exactly as the claimants – James and Nicholas Lewson – said, that her late husband had guaranteed the debts of one Thomas Barnaby, a London citizen and haberdasher; but, she continued in her plea, of the two possible witnesses to the agreement, Barnaby was 'beyond the sea about his business' and Cremor was dead.[56] She was certainly not about to pay out more than £270 to the two Lewsons just on their word.

As Katherine herself lamented, she was 'likely to be condemned because she knoweth not whether it be paid or no nor where there be any bond or other writings of the same among her said husband's writings or in the hands of the said Barnaby'. She had not been privy to any deal, and now, once again finding herself in charge of a business, she needed time. She would have to make a search of Cremor's study and offices, requiring 'reasonable time to search her books and bills', since she 'also supposeth to find it sufficient discharge for the same'. They were *her* books and bills now, and it was her business. She would pay nothing without making further enquiries, particularly since she strongly suspected that this was an attempt to defraud her. Frustratingly, the records of the Tudor Chancery are often incomplete, and we do not know the outcome of this claim, Katherine's counter-suit or other matters that she contested; but she is unlikely to have given in without a fight.

This was not the only suit that Katherine had to deal with following Thomas Cremor's death. She soon received a visit from one George Hubbard of Bishop's Lynne, Norfolk, who arrived brandishing a bill. Thomas had owed him £100, he claimed, asking Katherine to pay it at once.[57] She was highly suspicious; it was surprising that Hubbard had not attempted to claim such a high sum during her husband's lifetime. Indeed, Katherine soon got the measure of her visitor, believing that 'the said Hubbard knows privately' that no debt was due. At first, he was bullish, demanding the full sum at once; but then he lowered his expectations, offering to leave if she would only pay him 'a little sum of money'. Katherine scrutinized Hubbard's document carefully. She noted that 'it was not sealed with his [Thomas's] seal nor subscribed with his hand', whereupon she refused absolutely to countenance it, refusing to pay 'one penny for the same'. Let him take her to court, if he dared.

Having failed to extract money on this occasion, the troublesome Hubbard had not yet finished with Katherine. He immediately resorted to bad-mouthing her about the City in an attempt to damage her business and extort the money from her.

Once again, she instructed her lawyers to bring a case against him. It was vitally important that her reputation in business remained strong.

Cutpurses and arsonists

The type of fraudsters Katherine Fenkyll had to ward off were generally men who saw potential rich pickings in a wealthy widow. In the Tudor period, as in most periods of history, fewer women than men were accused or convicted of crimes,[58] and their participation in violent crime was particularly rare. When it came to female crime, the predominant offence was petty theft. Women, in particular, tended to steal clothing and household items.[59] These were often of no insignificant value, since clothing was expensive in Tudor times.

Pickpockets operated in the towns and villages of Tudor England. They would either cut the purse from the victim's clothing or rifle through it as they walked by, and women were perpetrators as well as victims of such crimes. In one incident from 1602, a purse containing 4 shillings was stolen from Alice Broane in Braintree in Essex, but the pickpocket was captured – and sentenced to hang.[60] In another example, one Mrs Ansell of Billericay was assaulted by a sailor, who cut the purse – containing a penny, three pieces of ginger and two thimbles – from her girdle.[61] A female pickpocket from Brentwood was the culprit in another incident, targeting a gentleman and getting away with a valuable gold angel and 30 shillings, until she was caught.[62]

Elizabeth Godesdon of Newington, Surrey, was hauled before the Croydon Assizes on 3 March 1578, accused of grand larceny. She had, the judges were told, carried out something of a mini crime spree. On 5 September 1577, she had entered the house of Richard Alee in Little

Bookham and stolen ten pieces of linen worth 5 shillings, six lower-value pieces of linen worth 5 shillings, and 13s 4d in coin.[63] Just under a month later, she had returned to Newington, where she had stolen a smock worth 20d and eight other pieces of linen. Then, two months later, in December, she had gone to Chertsey, where she purloined a valuable cassock and a petticoat worth £1. Selling off these items would have provided Elizabeth with a good living; but she was soon apprehended. At her trial, she was convicted of the last two offences, and she took recourse to pleading her belly.[64] She was lucky enough to secure her release in 1581 under a general pardon – but was soon back to her former profession. On 22 March 1582, Elizabeth Godesdon was again before the Croydon Assizes, accused of breaking into the house of one William Perkyn of Cobham and stealing a gown and two shirts.[65] Such career criminals were not uncommon in sixteenth-century England.

Theft remained a dangerous business under the Tudors. If the goods stolen were worth more than one shilling, then a convicted thief would likely be sentenced to hang. For smaller offences, the thief would usually be whipped. But women were also sometimes involved in more serious crimes, too. Mary Mascall of Great Leighs, who was a clergyman's wife, was accused in 1596 of leaving her house at 2am,[66] going to the barn of a neighbouring rector, which was filled with corn and barley from the recent harvest, and placing a pan of gunpowder within it before igniting the powder with a pistol. The resulting explosion and fire must have woken the neighbourhood: she was soon apprehended and imprisoned, but later escaped from Colchester Castle to go on the run for two years. And there were female murderers, too, throughout the period.

Katherine was an old woman when she was widowed for a second time. She had been active in London trade for thirty years. As a woman, she could never be a member of the Drapers' Company, but she nevertheless remained an important figure in the life of the trade.[67] She was always invited to attend the Drapers' renowned feasts during her second widowhood, where the menu for the ladies (at the 1516 election feast) included brawn and mustard, boiled capons, roasted swan, pike, baked and roasted venison, and quails and other delicacies, while the liverymen ate beef.[68] And she usually supplied her own silver to augment the Company's tableware.[69] As she dined at the top table, surrounded by those familiar to her over a lifetime of trade, Katherine Fenkyll could reflect on her success. Although sometimes a wife, she was primarily a draper, her identity tied up in the management of her business and affairs.

∽

By 1526, Katherine Fenkyll had reached the pinnacle of her career – and was close to the end of her life. At around the same time, Elizabeth Boleyn was just beginning to notice her comfortable married life change. More dramatically still, the career of Elizabeth Barton, serving woman to Thomas Cobb of Aldington in Kent, was about to explode on an international stage. For these Tudor women – and many others – life would never be the same again.

9

OF VISIONS AND REVELATIONS

Elizabeth Barton, the Holy Maid of Kent

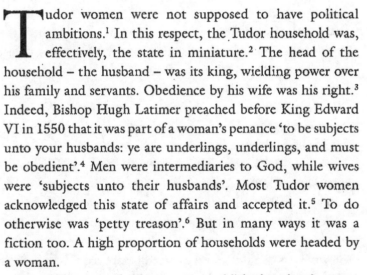

Tudor women were not supposed to have political ambitions.[1] In this respect, the Tudor household was, effectively, the state in miniature.[2] The head of the household – the husband – was its king, wielding power over his family and servants. Obedience by his wife was his right.[3] Indeed, Bishop Hugh Latimer preached before King Edward VI in 1550 that it was part of a woman's penance 'to be subjects unto your husbands: ye are underlings, underlings, and must be obedient'.[4] Men were intermediaries to God, while wives were 'subjects unto their husbands'. Most Tudor women acknowledged this state of affairs and accepted it.[5] To do otherwise was 'petty treason'.[6] But in many ways it was a fiction too. A high proportion of households were headed by a woman.

In 1589, a remarkable tract was published under the name 'Jane Anger'. In it, the author, whose real identity is unknown, sought to defend women from the slights of men.[7] Was not, she asked, the biblical Adam made of clay, which was then purified when he became flesh? 'Then, lacking a help for him, God making woman of man's flesh – that she might be purer than he – doth evidently show how far we women are more excellent than men.'[8] Indeed, as she continued, 'from women sprang man's salvation. A woman was the first that believed,

and a woman likewise the first that repented of sin.' Men relied
on women for their very survival, she asserted, since:

> ... *they are comforted by our means; they [are] nourished
> by the meats we dress; their bodies freed from diseases by
> our cleanliness, which otherwise would surfeit unreasonably
> through their own noisomeness. Without our care they lie
> in their beds as dogs in litter and go like lousy mackerel
> swimming in the heat of summer.*

Men, she said, 'confess we are necessary, but they would have
us likewise evil'.

Jane Anger was, however, a lone voice in a world where the
Homily on Matrimony, as read regularly to parish congregations,
stated that:

> ... *the woman is a weak creature, not endued with like
> strength and constancy of mind: therefore they be the sooner
> disquieted, and they be the more prone to all weak affections
> and dispositions of mind, more than men be; and lighter
> they be and more vain in their fantasies and opinions.*[9]

Women were, the homily asserted, 'the weaker vessel'.[10] Men
had the whip hand, sometimes literally so. For example, in 1598
William Hylls of Sandon was dragged before the Church courts
of London and charged with being 'a very lewd and uncharitable
man with his wife' for he 'hath used her most ungodly; not only
by refusing her company, but also by beating her most cruelly,
without any pity or compassion'.[11] In his defence, he claimed
that his wife had beaten and misused his sister, as well as some
orphans then living in his house, so he 'gave her viii strokes with
a wand'. He was sorry, he told the court, and promised not to
do so again. On the one hand, the very fact that the matter came
to court demonstrated that there was some recourse for a beaten

wife; on the other, the only sentence handed out to Hylls was that he should publicly acknowledge his fault in church. The law left women largely at the mercy of their husbands or, if unmarried, their male relatives.

At first glance, the status of women in the Tudor era seems to have denied them any sort of political agency. But there were exceptions. Most clearly, these lay at the upper end of the social scale. Aristocratic women could have real political input from within their households, in particular helping to build connections which could be utilized to promote both the family into which they were born and the family into which they married.[12] It was widows who arranged their children's marriages. Women paid regular visits to each other, which facilitated political bonds between families. Although public office was largely closed to women, those of sufficient status could intervene effectively in Parliamentary elections, pressing for and supporting their own candidates.[13]

∽

Lower down the social scale, there were some quite surprising avenues of political activity, as Elizabeth Barton, in service with farmer Thomas Cobb, was to discover in 1525. As she lay on her sickbed that year, her words, spoken in her delirium, appeared marvellous to her master. He called on the well-read parson Richard Masters to visit her, along with a curious local gentleman, Edward Thwaites. Elizabeth's symptoms appeared to be those of epilepsy, considered Thwaites, but he then dismissed this diagnosis.[14] Perhaps Masters did indeed inform Elizabeth that her visions 'preceded of the inspiration of the Holy Ghost' as it was later alleged.[15]

What happened next is unclear.[16] Did these men concoct a plot to exploit her? Later, there were claims that Masters used the girl to increase his 'advantage and lucre', but that appears to have been unlikely.[17] The credible Edward Thwaites, taking notes at the bedside as he witnessed the trances, had a stronger financial motive.[18] But his later bestselling pamphlet on Barton, entitled 'A Marvellous Work of Late Done at Court of Street in Kent', suggests that he too took everything at its face value.[19] They probably were, genuinely, beginning to regard her as a prophetess.

Listening to Elizabeth speak of 'many high and godly things', the perplexed Richard Masters sat down to write a report to the Archbishop of Canterbury, into whose episcopal authority the matter fell.[20] He hurried to his horse, riding at once to Canterbury.[21]

Archbishop William Warham was, by 1525, already well into his seventies, a veteran of Church politics and controversies, and something of a relic of a bygone age. He had been Archbishop of Canterbury for more than twenty years. When Masters arrived, he was granted a personal interview, setting out all he had seen and heard in Aldington. It was a fascinating case, considered Warham, and one that required further analysis. 'If she had any more such speeches', the archbishop informed his guest as he sent him home again, Masters 'should be at them as nigh as he could and mark them well'.[22] It should be done as rigorously as possible. Warham enjoined his subordinate to report everything to him, 'to the intent to maintain uphold and verify such report as he had made'.[23] It was all very strange and required more investigation.

After sending Masters away, Warham sent his comptroller to the monastery of Christ Church, Canterbury, with orders to the prior to send two of his monks to Aldington.[24] The task fell to the cellarer there, Dr Edward Bocking, a highly educated man with a doctorate in divinity, as well as another university graduate, William Hadley. Both men went 'against their minds', as they told their prior. He agreed that it looked very much like a fool's errand, since such prophetesses were often proved to be false. Yet, he had to obey the archbishop's express command. Another monk there – one Barnes – and a Father Lewis from the Observant Friars went too, to 'examine the matter, and to inform him [Warham] of the truth'.[25]

At home in Aldington, Elizabeth Barton waited for Masters' return, still lying on her sickbed. According to a state-sponsored sermon later preached against her, during the parson's absence, she suddenly began to vomit, before finding herself 'restored to perfect health'.[26] If this had been the case, she told no-one, appearing still deeply unwell. Years later, she was described as 'fat and ruddy'.[27] Yet, when she was sick, Elizabeth could neither eat nor drink.[28] Examples of anorexia in holy women were known since the medieval period, when women had been venerated as saintly for their extreme abstinence; it is possible that this had originally caused Barton's mind to wander.[29]

Following Masters' return, the trances continued. Barton's early utterings focused on religion and piety. She spoke often of visits to Heaven, accompanied by 'our Lady of Court of Street' – referring to the image of the Virgin set up in a tiny chapel at the hamlet of Court-at-Street, only a few miles away on a hill overlooking Romney Marsh.[30] It was a place fast disappearing, notable otherwise only for its ruined castle close beside the almost forgotten chapel.[31] But already in the sixteenth century, the isolated hamlet had a mystical feel. The chapel's only occupant was a ragged hermit, who eked out his days in service to the Virgin. Never a parish church, the chapel was already falling apart when Elizabeth first spoke of it. As everyone assembled around her bed, she pronounced that she must go there, 'boldly', to offer the Virgin a taper. This was the price of her healing, she asserted, and – when it occurred – the Virgin would require that the bell 'should be rung for a miracle'.

This was the standard way that miracles were proclaimed and made known, but it immediately aroused suspicion. 'There were no bells at the chapel', Thomas Cobb pointed out curtly.

To this objection, as the more credulous Thwaites recalled, Barton herself made no answer; yet 'the voice that spake in her proceeded': 'Our blessed Lady will show more miracles there shortly, for if any depart this life suddenly, or by mischance, in deadly sin, if he be vowed to our Lady heartily, he shall be restored to life again, to receive shrift, and housel [i.e. confession and communion], and after to depart this world with God's blessing.' She then told those gathered around her bed what the hermit, who lived in the chapel, had had for his supper, as well as many other things which concerned him, to the marvel of those there.

Elizabeth had saved the situation by deflecting the questioning and by speaking of other matters. Nonetheless, her reference to bells at the bell-less Court-at-Street was a telling error. The miracles of which she spoke were vague and unsubstantiated, and it was probably not too difficult to guess what a poor hermit would have to eat. Had Cobb been at the point of catching her out? If so, why, when the group duly accompanied her to Court-at-Street, did she declare suddenly in the chapel that her cure would be delayed 'for a certain season'.[32] If Barton was indeed a fraudster, why did she not leap up from the floor declaring herself well again? It is just one of the many contradictions in her story. She, herself, would later confess that she had been 'perfectly whole' before she had even arrived at the chapel.[33]

Warham's commissioners arrived at Aldington after this first, unsuccessful visit to Court-at-Street. They immediately set to work examining her on her faith, and found her sound, before confirming that they believed her. Almost immediately, Barton formed a close bond with Dr Bocking, who took the lead in the investigations. Like Masters, he was a highly educated man and one that would later be accused of pulling the holy woman's strings.[34] However, the girl's relationship with this Doctor of Divinity was not necessarily as submissive as the authorities would later suggest. At one time, she cruelly prophesied the time and date of his death, before claiming that 'she heard the disputation between the angels and the devils for his soul'.[35] This was Barton's favourite means of ensuring that those with authority over her heeded and acted on her requests and demands – she held the key to their salvation. Bocking did, however, open up a wider educational world to Elizabeth. While she waited for the appointed day for her miracle, she began to attack the new religious reform movement as a heresy. In this, she was probably influenced by Masters and Bocking.

On the day appointed for the miracle, between 2,000 and 3,000 people gathered from miles around, waiting outside Cobb's hitherto quiet farmhouse for the prophetess to emerge.[36] All social classes were there, clamouring to see the eighteen-year-old serving maid.[37] She emerged, carried on a bed[38] and accompanied by Bocking and Masters, as well as Cobb and Thwaites, before leading a snaking procession down country lanes, singing the litany and psalms as they walked.[39] Aldington had witnessed nothing like it before, while the hermit living quietly at Court-at-Street must have looked up in shock at the sight.

As the crowd surged towards the pocket-sized chapel, most were forced to wait outside, peering through windows where they could. As a sung mass began, Barton fell into a trance, appearing at once disfigured as she 'lay upright upon the ground, her eyes staring, her tongue appearing abroad (somewhat without her teeth), her nether jaw some time let down and some time moved towards the one side and the other, wresting her body and her arms as she had been in a pang of sickness'.[40] Her face was truly terrifying, with 'tongue hanging out, and her eyes being in a manner plucked out and laid upon her cheeks, and so greatly disordered'.[41] All the while, she lay prostrate at the feet of the Virgin's statue.[42] With her lips 'not greatly moving', a voice was heard coming from her stomach.[43] She appeared even to those that disbelieved her, as though 'she had been in another world'.[44]

To Edward Thwaites, who would later note it all down, it seemed miraculous. He listened rapt as Barton began to speak in rhyme, with the voice that emerged from her sounding 'so sweetly and heavenly' as it touched on the joys of Heaven, and 'horribly and terribly' as her words turned to Hell. She, at times, 'ravished' those who listened to her words and, at others, 'put the hearers in great fear'.[45]

For three hours, she kept her audience rapt, touching on the chapel at Court-at-Street, which she wished were better maintained and occupied by a priest to sing mass daily. She spoke of the importance of pilgrimages, of trentals, of hearing mass and confession, as well as other tenets of orthodox belief.[46] She should, she said, become a nun, 'for such was Our Lady's pleasure'. It was the Virgin's pleasure, too, that Dr Bocking be appointed as her 'ghostly father', or confessor: the pair should not be parted.[47]

After the mass, Barton appeared to come to her senses. She kneeled before the image of the Virgin, declaring that she was now healed. Those present believed that they had witnessed a miracle, and although Court-at-Street had no bells to be rung, those of nearby churches pealed out to tell the world.[48]

Within days, the whole county was talking about the 'Holy Maid of Kent'. The archbishop, too, was concerned enough to put together a roll of paper, containing a list of the girl's revelations, before sending it to the king.[49] It seemed that God was speaking to England through humble Elizabeth Barton, and even Henry VIII turned to gaze her way. After reading the report himself, the king, who was then in his mid-thirties and in his glorious prime, passed it to his friend Sir Thomas More, 'commanding' him, as the humanist later recalled, 'to look thereon and afterward show him what I thought therein'.[50] The king was interested enough to ask his friend's opinion a short while later. More replied: 'in good faith I found nothing in these words that I could anything regard or esteem'. There was nothing there, he continued, that 'a right simple woman might in my mind, speak it of her own wit well enough'. But even he was not *convinced* that she was a fraud, for 'because it was constantly reported for a truth, that God wrought in her, and that a miracle was showed upon her, I durst now nor would not, be bold in judging the matter'.

This was the crux of the matter. Since God had the power to act upon the world, he might – just might – be speaking through a simple serving maid. To Thomas More, it appeared that Henry little esteemed Elizabeth Barton or her prophecies; but the king would soon come to know both rather better.

'The manifold number of scolding women'

When Elizabeth Barton spoke out, people flocked to her, full of expectations, welcoming her words. But Tudor society generally looked askance at women who spoke out of turn, and when it was deemed any were to have gone beyond what was acceptable, action was taken.

Visitors to the parish church in Leominster in Herefordshire are often struck by a wooden see-saw like device, with wheels at one end and a seat perched at the other. This is a cucking, or ducking, stool and was one of the last used in England. It was finally retired in 1809, following the punishment of one Jenny Pipes for using abusive language. In the Tudor period, cucking stools were features of most towns and villages – and they were contraptions used almost entirely on women.

Vocal women were often seen as a threat in the local community. And women's gossip, and its ability to make or break reputations, was regarded as a challenge to the social order, which could undermine the power of the authorities.[51] 'Scolds' were accordingly seen as turbulent, subversive individuals and their verbal abuse of their families and neighbours as a disturbance to the peace.[52] 'Scolding' was regarded, almost exclusively, as a female crime.

The punishment for scolding became noticeably more severe after 1550.[53] Previously, penance or a fine had been the usual method of dealing with such women. By the mid-sixteenth century, however, cucking had become the favoured punishment. A number of popular legal handbooks, including John Kitchin's *Court Leet, et Court Baron* of 1580, considered that every manor had a duty to keep a cucking stool.

One popular early seventeenth-century text, *The Cucking of the Scold*, outlined just what the punishment entailed. In this fiction, it was to be meted out on a woman who 'lacked no tongue' and would 'scold with anyone'.[54] This 'little devil, with her unquiet tongue' scolded all her neighbours and made a 'brawl' against the constable, before she was apprehended. After being sentenced by a justice of the peace, she was taken, under the guard of a hundred armed men, and carried in a wheel barrow. She was stripped down to her smock, 'Then fast within the

chair / she was most finely bound, / which made her scold excessively, / and said she should be drowned'. She was ducked repeatedly into the cold and muddy water, appearing like 'a drowned rat' to observers. It was not a punishment to be taken lightly.

The local cucking stool could get considerable use. By 1579, the one in the town ditch in Southampton had broken, which was deemed 'a great lack' because of its usefulness for 'the punishment and terror of harlots, scolds and other malefactors'.[55] It urgently required fixing, but then it broke once more in 1601, thanks to it being left 'standing abroad' in the salty sea air.[56] Repairs were again somewhat makeshift, and the wooden device broke again two years later.[57] This time, it could not be mended. A replacement was quickly required, considered the town authorities, 'to punish the manifold number of scolding women that be in this town and other evil living women'. They took the opportunity to order an improved model, equipped with wheels so that the scold could be collected from the door of her house.[58]

She could then be paraded through the streets during the journey to the town ditch, all the while receiving the jeers of her neighbours. It should be made quickly, it was decided, since the mayor was 'daily troubled with such brawls'.

Cucking was not the only punishment meted out to a scolding woman. The well-known scold's bridle, or brank, consisted of a metal frame attached to a scold's head, with a clamp to hold down her tongue. It was first recorded in Scotland,[59] and it also made its appearance in the sixteenth century. After the Tudor period, it became a popular method of punishment in England and Scotland.

10

OF MISTRESSES AND MYSTICS

Catherine of Aragon, the Boleyns and Elizabeth Barton

Fifty miles away from Aldington, at Hever Castle, on the other side of Kent, the former Elizabeth Howard – now Elizabeth Boleyn – was settled into a life of quiet domesticity punctuated by visits to court. She cannot have failed to hear of the county's new Holy Maid or the stir that she was causing. But in 1525, the stage was also set for Elizabeth Boleyn's youngest daughter to be transformed into the woman who would 'set our country in a roar'.[1]

In the early sixteenth century, Hever Castle, then as now, sat deep in the wooded countryside. It was a small place, but the extensive works carried out by Sir Thomas Boleyn had made it a comfortable family home. Thomas and Elizabeth moved their young family there in 1505, on the death of Sir William Boleyn. Her children, and the frantic, dazzling court of which she became a part, formed the stages for the political dramas of Elizabeth Boleyn's life.

At first, both Thomas and Elizabeth were much at court. Thomas was a proficient jouster, something which caught the interest of the young Prince Henry during the latter years of Henry VII's reign.[2] He was prominent enough in 1509, when the seventeen-year-old prince succeeded to the throne, to be made a Knight of the Bath at the coronation.[3] By this time, England had been without a queen or other major royal female household for six years, following the death of Elizabeth of York. Soon after becoming king, Henry surprised everyone by marrying his widowed sister-in-law, Catherine of Aragon. Elizabeth Boleyn was one of the ladies deputed to serve her at her coronation; she received the gift of a gown from the royal wardrobe for her pains.[4] Thanks to her father's eminence, she punched above the weight of a mere knight's wife, being accorded the rank of a baroness at the coronation.

Elizabeth Boleyn immediately took up a role in the queen's household.[5] She was held in high esteem. At New Year 1513, a messenger from the king arrived bearing one of the most expensive gifts that he would give that year.[6] Four fine gilt cups with covers, weighing an impressive 28 or 29 ounces, would soon follow.[7] By 1519, Elizabeth was also entitled, as a member of the queen's chamber, to be fed at the expense of the court.[8] She was already riding high on a wave of family prestige, since her father had finally been restored to his father's dukedom of Norfolk in February 1514, after winning a stunning victory against the Scots at Flodden Field the previous year.[9] And in 1520, she accompanied her husband and much of the English court to Calais for Henry's impressive and showy Field of the Cloth of Gold meeting with the French king.

Ladies in waiting

Tudor queens were never alone. As well as more menial servants, who tended to their needs, they also employed a household of women to serve as companions and attendants.[10] Following her marriage to Henry, Catherine of Aragon was provided with a household to reflect her rank. Her great ladies, who included the royal Margaret Pole, Countess of Salisbury, the Countess of Oxford and the Countess of

Surrey, were drawn from the highest levels of the nobility. These ladies were not expected to give daily service, instead serving the queen on great state occasions.

The queen received more regular attendance from the ladies of the Privy Chamber, who were her daily companions. These were married women, lower in rank than the great ladies, but still of prestigious families. Below them were the maids of honour, who were unmarried and were there both to finish their education and to secure a good marriage. Most of these girls were also the daughters of the nobility, although lower-ranking maids, such as Elizabeth Blount, who was the daughter of a country gentleman, sometimes also secured a place. Elizabeth arrived at court in 1512 when she was aged between twelve and fourteen years old.[11] Twelve was usually regarded as the minimum age to serve the queen.

The women and girls who served the queen were expected to provide her with company and entertainment. There was often dancing and music in the queen's apartments, while they would also sit sewing with their mistress or read to her. The queen's ladies were usually prominent in court masques too, which were lavish affairs. Only a few months after her marriage in 1509, Catherine of Aragon had written to her father that she passed her time in continual feasting and festivities.[12] The queen herself took part in these court festivities, dancing in masques with her ladies up until January 1513.[13] On New Year's Eve 1514 Henry VIII himself took part, in disguise, alongside the gentlemen of his household and some of the queen's ladies,[14] who appeared masked in rich yellow sarcenet, dressed in white satin dresses and mantles of blue velvet to match their bonnets, with their hair covered by coifs of damask gold. The king sometimes supplied the costumes: in an inventory taken after Henry's death, it was noted that he possessed eight Italian gowns for women with ruffs and sleeves made of cloth of gold striped with silver, as well as '12 dozen visors and masks for men and women'.[15]

A queen's maids and ladies were also expected to carry out certain personal duties. The countesses of Oxford and Worcester were privileged to hold a cloth before Anne Boleyn's face at her coronation banquet, allowing their mistress 'to spit or do otherwise at her pleasure'.[16] The queen's ladies would also perform the role of carver while their mistress dined, or hold the bowl for her to wash her hands during the meal. Though ostensibly menial, such service was much sought after because of the personal contact with the queen that it allowed.

There was also scope for personal contact between the king and the women who served his wife. Most of Henry VIII's mistresses and English wives were drawn from the households of his queens. The teenaged Elizabeth Blount, for example, caught the king's eye within two years of arriving at court; she would provide Henry with his only acknowledged illegitimate child. Mary Boleyn, too, served the queen before joining the king in bed, as would her sister in due course. It was perhaps unsurprising that Anne's successor as queen, Jane Seymour, who had herself been one of Anne's maids, strictly observed standards of dress in her household. She insisted that one comely French-educated maid replace her daring French hoods with the more modest English gable-hood, even though it 'became her nothing so well'.[17] For Jane, that was almost certainly the point.

Although her duties took her to court, Elizabeth was often at home at Hever, where her children were growing up. Three of her five children survived to adulthood.[18] Thanks to Thomas's ambassadorial connections, the couple's younger daughter, Anne, was sent to serve Margaret of Austria, regent of the Netherlands, in 1513, when she was aged around twelve. She later joined her elder sister, Mary, in Paris, to serve France's new English-born queen – Henry VIII's younger sister, also Mary. Elizabeth almost certainly played a role in the early education both of her daughters and her son, George, but no record survives.

In the countryside, she enjoyed a largely quiet, domestic life. The family lived comfortably – the women dressing in furs and other finery, purchased from fashionable London suppliers, and at dinner they sipped imported Gascon wine, poured by their servants in the intimacy of Hever's snug dining hall.[19] Elizabeth's husband, too, liked to appear well dressed, in black satin doublets, embroidered extravagantly.[20] When not at Hever, the couple still ate off familiar plates and had their usual furniture, which they had carried between lodgings on hired carts. Elizabeth received spending money from her husband, which allowed her to purchase necessaries for herself, while her larger bills – and those of her unmarried daughters – were sent directly to Thomas to be paid. Elizabeth Boleyn enjoyed the gilded life of a noblewoman, at home and at court.

Elizabeth was well-travelled, finding the time to build and maintain social networks through visits to friends and relations. She was particularly close to Anne Shelton, Thomas's niece, helping to arrange a marriage for the girl with her sister Muriel's son. It was this double niece who introduced Elizabeth to the Norfolk gentlewoman Anne Lestrange, whom aunt, niece and nephew visited in 1526.[21] Lestrange's residence, at Hunstanton, lay high in the north of the county, close to the coast and more than thirty miles from the Boleyn manor of Blickling. The three visitors stayed just one day. It was a long way to go merely for a dinner of heron and fresh rabbit, and was probably part of a longer trip to visit the homes of friends and acquaintances in the county. Elizabeth was also friendly with Lady Lisle, who kept in touch with her from her residence in Calais. Such visits helped oil the patronage networks and so were highly political in nature – albeit also pleasurable.[22]

Both of Elizabeth Boleyn's daughters followed her to court as adults. Her younger daughter, Anne, was dark, graceful and witty. She soon caused a stir after her return from France in 1522, secretly entering into a relationship with Henry Percy, heir to the Earl of Northumberland.[23] This would have been an excellent match for Thomas and Elizabeth's daughter – but her lower social status caused it to be broken. 'I considered that I was of good years,' Percy complained, when confronted by Cardinal Wolsey, 'and thought myself sufficient to provide myself with a convenient wife whereas my fancy served me best'. But this was not how such matters worked. Even Percy's defence of Anne's lineage fell on deaf ears. She might, as he said, be 'descended of right noble parentage' on her mother's side, but it was her father's side that counted more. As Percy admitted during the fraught interview with the all-powerful cardinal, 'she be a simple maid, and has but a knight to her father'. For all the wealth of the Boleyns, the former Lady Elizabeth Howard had married down. Percy was hurriedly married off by his father, while Anne was sent home to her mother in Kent.

Anne Boleyn spent some years at home at Hever after the Percy affair, although she was back at court in 1525. For the aristocracy and gentry in England, the court was the centre of all power and preferment. It was dominated, of course, by the gilded, bejewelled figure of Henry VIII. His people wanted to love him. He was, wrote one contemporary, a prince of 'extraordinary and almost divine character'.[24] The man that Elizabeth and her daughters knew so well was truly gorgeous to look upon, with a 'complexion very fair and bright', framed by wispy 'auburn hair'. He had a 'round face so very beautiful that it would become a pretty woman', all set within a body that was muscular and overwhelmingly masculine. One visitor to his court in 1515 spoke for many when he called him 'the handsomest potentate I ever set eyes on'.[25] Henry VIII was a godlike figure at a court filled with splendour and gaiety. The clever, witty Anne Boleyn found herself very much in her element.

The king had loved pretty, blond Catherine of Aragon when he had swept her off her feet in 1509. In turn, the widow of Prince Arthur was devoted to him, and the marriage was, at first, filled with love and fun. The young king delighted in surprising his queen by appearing in her chamber – disguised as Robin Hood or some other mythical figure – to dance and make merry. But there were dark times, too. The couple's first son, Prince Henry, died in February 1511, having lived for less than two months, while his two younger brothers failed to survive their births in October 1513 and December 1514/ January 1515. Following the birth of a healthy child (Mary) in February 1516, Henry was heard to declare that 'we are both young: if it was a daughter this time, by the grace of God the sons will follow'. But his confidence was misplaced. At the end of 1518, Catherine's final pregnancy ended in stillbirth.

While Catherine channelled her hopes for the future into her surviving daughter, Henry's perspective on achieving a male heir was changed in 1519 by the birth of a healthy – but illegitimate – son to his mistress, Elizabeth Blount. It appeared that he was capable of begetting a son. The fault surely lay with Catherine. By 1525, Catherine of Aragon was approaching forty and had no prospect of bearing another child. Instead, she took solace in her religious devotions. The contrast between her and the young and lively Anne Boleyn was striking.

By late 1525 or early 1526, Henry VIII had begun to show an interest in Anne. He hoped, at first, that she would become his mistress. Indeed, why not, because Anne's elder sister Mary had already been the king's bedmate. But the prospect of becoming yet another discarded royal mistress was an alarming one for the ambitious Anne, who had once hoped to become Countess of Northumberland. She retreated to Hever, but this only whetted the appetite of her sovereign, who pursued her with ardent letters.[26] 'My heart and I surrender ourselves into your hands, beseeching you to hold us commended to your favour, and that by absence your affection to us may not be lessened', he wrote, before informing her that 'it would be a great pity to increase our pain'. After all, was it not well known in astronomy that 'the longer the days are, the more distant is the sun, and nevertheless the hotter; so is it with our love, for by absence we are kept a distance from one another, and yet it retains its fervour, at least on my side; I hope the like on yours'. Henry's letters to the unobtainable Anne were full of frustrated lust and longing, speaking of that which he was 'forced to suffer', her absence 'almost intolerable, but for the firm hope I have of your unchanging affection for me'. To keep him firmly in her thoughts, he sent her a miniature of himself, set into a bracelet.

During this courtship in letters, Anne was with her mother. The younger woman was in a quandary, at times appearing willing to come to court, before changing her mind, prompting the king to complain 'that you would not come to court either with your mother, if you could, or in any other manner'. Elizabeth was acting as chaperone for her daughter, but she must also have counselled her. They had to be careful, since there was danger in displeasing the king. Indeed, on hearing that Anne would not return to him, he replied darkly that 'if true, I cannot sufficiently marvel at, because I am sure that I have since never done anything to offend you'. 'It seems,' he said, 'a very poor return for the great love which I bear you to keep me at a distance both from speech and the person of the woman that I esteem most in the world.' He was besotted with her even after continuing rebuttals. Months later, he wrote that he had 'been for the whole year stricken with the dart of love, and not yet sure whether I shall fail or find a place in your heart and affection'; he had to know whether she loved him too.

The king's ardent suit, although flattering, was hardly what Elizabeth would have desired for her daughter, particularly having witnessed the way in which her elder daughter had been picked up and discarded by Henry. Nonetheless, she threw her support behind Anne in the spring of 1527, when the king finally made an offer that Anne could accept. In spite of her own misgivings, expressed in the present of a jewel shaped like a maiden in a stormed-tossed ship, Anne had returned to court by May 1527, when she was led out in public as the king's dance partner for the first time. Only days later, a secret ecclesiastical court opened to examine the validity of Henry's marriage to Catherine, in order to clear the way for his new fiancé, Anne Boleyn. Elizabeth Boleyn could not have thought to marry her daughter any higher.

∞

While Henry VIII was pursuing Anne with letters, the eighteen-year-old[27] Elizabeth Barton was continuing to build her own reputation and career on the other side of Kent. At Court-at-Street, she informed everyone present that the Virgin had told her to become a nun. Accordingly, Dr Bocking rode at once to Archbishop Warham to request that both his appointment as Elizabeth's confessor and her entry to a convent be arranged.[28] Warham, who was convinced by all he had heard at Aldington and Court-at-Street, complied, arranging for the girl to enter the Benedictine House of St Sepulchre's, just outside the gates of Canterbury. Once this was done, Bocking sent letters to Richard Masters, requesting that he send Elizabeth secretly to him at Canterbury in the company of his own servants. She accordingly arrived that evening, spending the night at Bocking's monastery, before riding out with him the next day.[29]

Barton's new home was a venerable one, having stood on the site for around 400 years.[30] For a girl who had hardly left her home parish, Canterbury itself must have seemed impossibly large. The nunnery, nestling close to the main road to Sandwich, Deal and Dover, was a haven amid the bustle.[31] High walls shielded the nuns from the outside world, and only the small parish church that lay inside offered an inlet to visitors. She was entering a house that was dominated by its charismatic prioress, Philippa John, who would eventually have to surrender it during the dissolution of the monasteries in return for a pension.

The girl entered through a high arched gateway, large enough for a cart to pass through. Although grand, the nunnery was of only modest value – £40 a year was the best estimate of the royal commissioners charged with assessing the house's annual worth only a few years later. For most of its history, it was home to just five black-veiled nuns at any one time, in addition to the prioress. They must have been eager to meet a new sister, whose reputation preceded her and who was, by all accounts, 'not a little esteemed' by the people of Kent.[32]

∽

By the late 1520s, Elizabeth Barton was probably one of the most famous women in England. But it was undoubtedly Elizabeth Boleyn's younger daughter who was the most well known. Henry VIII's attempts for a quick annulment of his marriage, on the grounds of the biblical sinfulness of marrying his brother's wife, were quickly dashed. Word of the secret court headed by Cardinal Wolsey was soon leaked, and Catherine alerted her powerful nephew, the Holy Roman Emperor Charles V. For Charles, it was a point of family honour. He would, as he bluntly told the English ambassadors to his court, 'defend the queen's just cause'.[33] He acquired the power to do so on 16 June 1527 when, after sacking Rome, he took the pope prisoner. Henry and Anne were also both uncomfortably aware that Catherine was hugely popular in England, particularly among women.

Indeed, such was Catherine's popularity that Anne Boleyn found herself the victim of a mob of angry women in October 1531. In cases of known or suspected adultery, and given a husband's king-like powers over his family, if there was going to be a confrontation it was more usual for wronged wives to confront their husbands' mistresses. For this purpose, they would often enlist the help of female friends and neighbours, in order to publicly shame the rival.[34] To many in England, Catherine of Aragon, who was greeted by cheers whenever she appeared in public, was just such a wronged wife. On hearing, one day, that Anne was having supper at a house by the Thames, without the king, a mob of London women began to organize itself, soon numbering 7,000 or 8,000 strong. Surging out of the city, they intended to kill Anne. The king's fiancée hurriedly abandoned her dinner so that she could escape. All was not quite how it appeared, however, for among the crowd were men disguised as women, which was a canny ruse. As the Venetian ambassador noted, little was done about the disturbance, since 'it was a thing done by women'.[35]

Riot girls of Tudor England

Although women had little official political role in Tudor England and were considered, in law, entirely subject to their husbands, there was scope for them to take direct action – and examples of their doing so. Organized groups could be particularly difficult for the authorities to deal with, allowing women to exert some limited social pressure and, locally, effect change.

One such rising occurred on 5 August 1577, when thirty women stormed the chapel at Brentwood in Essex, after hearing about its planned closure. They were heavily armed with items that they had found around their homes, including pitchforks, spits, hammers and kettles filled with hot water, as well as a 'great sharp stone' that someone had picked up on the road to the chapel. The women presented a fearsome spectacle. They dragged out and beat an unfortunate schoolmaster that they found within the building, before locking the doors. During the commotion, the sheriff arrived with his men to storm the place; seventeen of the women were able to escape, although the others were taken to gaol. The ringleader, Thomasine Tyler, made an escape attempt later that day, but the women need not have worried about suffering harsh retribution. Thanks to their ambiguous legal status, they were soon released.[36]

The riot at Brentwood was far from an isolated incident. Groups of women often vigorously enforced standards of morality in their communities. The lecherous parson of Abchurch, in London, found this to his cost one day in June 1563.[37] After asking a local woman whether he might 'have his pleasure on her' in exchange for money, the married parson duly arrived at the appointed time. Upon removing his gown and jacket and pulling down his hose, he was shocked to be confronted by a mob of the woman's angry friends, whom she had made 'aware of it', clamouring for his arrest.

In imposing morality, gangs of women were not, though, always so supportive of their female neighbours. It was a group of 'honest wives' of Windsor and Eton who became suspicious of their unmarried neighbour, Alice Riding, in 1517. Taking it upon them-

selves to strip her and examine both her belly and breasts, they determined that she had recently given birth.[38] It was soon discovered that she had borne a child by a priest before killing the baby and burying it in her father's orchard. In 1584, poor Emma Nash found herself in a very unfortunate position when the vicar of Churchill in Oxfordshire complained to his flock that she had given him a venereal disease. Accordingly, 'divers honest women of Churchill' accosted her in order to examine her to see whether 'she had burned him or not', as well as checking her for the signs of other diseases. It was humiliating for both parties. The vicar evidently hoped that matters could remain within his parish, which proved impossible when the archdeacon's court heard the matter in Oxford. In spite of the pair's denials, both were required to publicly confess and do penance. Somewhat bizarrely, it was the vicar in question – Richard Bagley – who supervised and certified Emma's penance.[39]

In short, as King Henry attempted, all too publicly, to slough off his first wife, 'that goggle-eyed whore Nan Bullen' became widely unpopular; her mother and her father, too, were bearing the brunt of rumours and innuendo.[40] One Mistress Amadas, wife of a London goldsmith, was arrested for saying that Anne was a 'harlot' and her father 'was bawd both to his wife and his two daughters'.[41] A Friar Peto made similar claims in 1532. Sir George Throckmorton went so far as to repeat the rumours to the king, advising him not to marry Anne, since 'it is thought you have meddled both with the mother and sister'.[42] Henry VIII denied the accusation on that occasion, bluntly replying 'never with the mother'; yet many believed the worst of both Anne and Elizabeth Boleyn. By the late sixteenth century claims were published that Anne was actually Henry VIII's daughter,[43] although no evidence actually exists of a relationship between Elizabeth and Henry. The rumours are really a testament to the close relationship between mother and daughter, and to Elizabeth's importance in Anne's rise.[44] Anne relied upon her mother in these years, once writing candidly to a friend that Elizabeth was the woman that she loved best in the world.[45]

∞

Although often at court, Elizabeth and Anne would sometimes take a step back from the politicking and hostility and return home to Hever. They were in Kent during the first week of October 1528.[46] So, too, was Elizabeth Barton, still immured in her nunnery. On 1 October 1528, Archbishop Warham carefully composed a letter to Cardinal Wolsey, England's papal legate and the man in charge of attempting to secure Henry VIII's divorce. He wrote on behalf of the religious woman 'which had all the visions at Our Lady of Court-of-Street'.[47] She had asked for an audience with the cardinal. Warham, impressed with everything he had seen in her, was happy to facilitate it. With the stroke of a pen, Elizabeth Barton was released onto the wider political stage.

11

OF POLITICS AND PROPHECIES

Elizabeth Barton and Anne Boleyn

I t was the late 1520s, or perhaps early in the following decade, when a woman named Helen began to experience trances and revelations at her home near Tottenham, close to London. She was alarmed by her experience, but knew where to go for aid. This was not to the local priest, nor even the bishop of her diocese; instead she sought out Elizabeth Barton, by then almost universally known as the 'Holy Maid of Kent'. Barton listened as her visitor spoke to her of what she had seen, before dismissing the events: 'They were no revelations, but plain illusions of the devil', and Helen should 'cast them out of her mind'.[1]

Helen did just that, later informing Sir Thomas More that the Holy Maid's words and actions seemed like a miracle. Barton, however, was modest, later batting away the eminent gentleman's praise: 'forsooth, sir, there is in this point no praise unto me, but the goodness of God, as it appeareth, hath wrought much meekness in her soul, which hath taken my rude warning so well and not grutched [i.e. complained] to hear her spirit and her visions reproved'. The noted humanist approved of this answer, as he did of her comments that those visited by such visions must always 'take heed and prove well of what spirit they come of'. She herself claimed many encounters with the Devil, who appeared in her nunnery in the form of 'a strange

ugly fashioned bird'[2] or, at other times, like a 'goodly man'[3] or
even a 'jolly gallant' wooing her as his bride.[4] It all contributed
to her mystique and reputation – even if, as investigators later
alleged, these devilish visitings were really the result of noxious
chemicals, including brimstone, hidden in the straw of her bed.[5]

For the most part, the Holy Maid seems to have lived quietly
at her nunnery, appearing, according to Archbishop Warham
himself, as a well-disposed and virtuous woman.[6] Many of her
visions were entirely innocuous, consisting of companies of
angels, martyrs, confessors and virgins.[7] She also played a role in
helping the bereaved, offering them her assistance and speaking
to the spirits of the recently dead.[8]

Under duress later, she said that 'she had never in her whole
life any revelation from God but that they were of her own
feigning, wherein she used much craft to make and devise them
consonant and agreeable to the minds of them who were resort-
ing unto her, with the help of Dr Bocking, her ghostly father'.[9]
Whatever the truth of her revelations as they seemed to the Holy
Maid, it was their effect that made her a woman of international
political importance. She was certainly not motivated by financial gain, as an inventory of her meagre possessions in 1534
makes clear. She had a simple room, furnished only with two
ancient cushions, as well as two small rugs, one of which was cut
into pieces.[10] For her bed, she lay on an old mattress, covered
with seven coarse sheets and two blankets, and had two pillows
and a bolster. For eating, she had two plates, four dishes and
two saucers. Only her 'little basin', weighing 12 pounds, was
worth anything; the prioress coveted the item enough to later
pay 4 shillings for it. Elizabeth Barton also had two candlesticks
with which to have light, a plank of wood for a table and a little
wooden chest.

What she did receive, she gave away. Two new cushions,
which could have replaced her worn ones, were donated to
the nunnery's church, while she gave her old clothes to the

youngest nun. Even her Irish mantle, a cupboard and two stools were given over to the use of the prioress. When one man – Mr White – fell dangerously sick and asked Elizabeth to 'make meekly petition to God' for his deliverance, he supplied her with the sum of 4 nobles.[11] He had given her the same sum before, only to be dismayed to hear that she had kept only 6s 8d back for herself, using the rest charitably.

Dr Bocking came to Elizabeth Barton's nunnery daily, counselling her on the stories of St Bridget and St Catherine of Siena, both of whom were holy prophetesses.[12] The pressure to please Bocking was intense, as the monk goaded her when she failed to supply him with new revelations for the great book that he was writing. He would ask: 'How do you live now? Virtuously? Meseemeth God hath withdrawn His grace from you, that ye have no revelations this season.'[13]

She still felt the need to return to Court-at-Street if a revelation was required.[14] The little chapel had become a place of pilgrimage, with worshippers flocking there.[15] In front of adoring audiences, Elizabeth, in her trances, would see the Virgin, showing her sanctity by:

> ... *lighting candles without fire, moistening women's breasts that before were dry and wanted milk, restoring all sorts of sick to perfect health, reducing the dead to life again, and finally doing all good, to all such as were measured and vowed (as the popish manner was) unto her at Court of Street.*[16]

While she confined herself to these kinds of miracles and revelations, the authorities were more than happy to allow her to continue unmolested. But Elizabeth Barton's interest in Cardinal Wolsey, in 1528, was a sign of her increasing ambitions. The wily son of an Ipswich butcher had risen to the pinnacle of power, even eyeing the papacy from his palatial residence of

Hampton Court. By the late 1520s, he was supreme over all others under the king – so much so that John Skelton, Elizabeth Boleyn's old acquaintance, would write satirically: 'Why come ye not to court?/To which court?/To the king's court,/Or to Hampton Court?' To Skelton, it was Hampton Court that 'hath the pre-eminence'. He was not alone in thinking this way.

It was the cardinal who had been trusted with securing the king his divorce and, thus, enabling his marriage to Anne Boleyn. But the latter had always blamed Wolsey for the breaking of her relationship with Henry Percy, while he considered Anne his 'serpentine enemy' and the 'night crow', whispering in the ear of the king. Nonetheless, at first the pair were prepared to work together. Anne and her mother were both with the court at Windsor in March 1528, where an air of jollity prevailed. King Henry was out hawking every day when the weather was fair, or taking a walk in the park.[17]

On 3 March 1528, Thomas Hennege, a servant of Wolsey, came upon Anne and her mother at dinner. Calling him over, Anne informed the man that she was afraid that the cardinal had forgotten her, since he had not sent her a token recently. This was not so, Hennege assured her, Wolsey had simply forgotten to send one. Elizabeth Boleyn then stepped in. She had spoken to Wolsey's previous messenger when he had been at court and asked him to request 'a morsel of tuna' from the cardinal when next he saw him, but she had not received it yet. Could Hennege obtain this delicacy for her?

Anne, too, was interested in what Wolsey could supply for her table, asking Hennege to request carps, shrimps or other good meat from him. Hennege was rather embarrassed, but did as he was bid, writing to his master: 'I beseech Your Grace, pardon me that I am so bold to write unto Your Grace hereof; it is the conceit and mind of a woman.' But in requesting these delicacies from the all-powerful cardinal, Anne and her mother were making a political point. They had the power now to ask

– and he would be wise not to cross them; he should not forget to favour them with tokens again.

Cardinal Wolsey must have felt himself beset on all sides by women, since Catherine of Aragon, too, despised and distrusted him. By 1528, he was in his fifties, obese and in poor health, but still anxious to retain his power. No full account of his first meeting with the Holy Maid survives, although she was evidently as bold in her dealings as ever, informing the papal legate that she had seen a vision of three swords, all pressed by God into his hands.[18] He must keep them well ordered, she told him, since they represented his earthly responsibilities. The first symbolized his spiritual power as legate and the second his temporal power under the king. Finally, the third sword represented the 'meddling he was put in trust with by the king, concerning the great matter of his marriage'.

This was the first time that Elizabeth Barton had spoken out openly against Henry's attempts to remarry. Her words were effective, since Thomas Cranmer, who would replace Warham as archbishop, believed privately that both his predecessor and Wolsey were afraid of her. In Cranmer's view, 'with her feigned visions and godly threatenings, she stayed them very much in the matter'.[19] She went more than once to the cardinal – and, through him, obtained access to the king himself.[20]

Angels' food and holy maids

Elizabeth Barton was far from being England's only prophetess. In the previous century, Margery Kempe had declared that she spoke to God, earning herself an examination for heresy.[21] Prophecy was, for women, a route to political influence, and there were a few other scattered examples, such as Joan the Meatless, who lived in Norfolk in the fifteenth century and was sustained only by the bread of the sacrament.[22]

Not all prophetesses earned a positive reception, particularly from the 1530s onwards, as the Reformation began to progress. Thomas Cranmer, archbishop under both Henry VIII and Edward VI, firmly believed that such women did the work of the Devil. He based his faith on the scriptures, not on the utterings or claims of supposed visionaries. Even the visions of angels were not 'sufficient to make any one new article of our faith, or establish any thing in religion without the express word of God'.[23]

Cranmer was not alone in his scepticism. Many could recall the Holy Maid of Leominster, who had proved to be anything but pious when she had moved into a cell in Leominster's parish church in the early years of the sixteenth century, cut off from the congregation by a 'grate of iron'.[24] There, she impressed pilgrims by existing only on 'angels' food'; on many occasions, the bread of the sacrament was witnessed flying across the church and into her mouth. When Lord Abergavenny came

to investigate, his dogs rushed straight under her bed, pulling out animal bones and the debris of other hearty meals. Hidden, too, was 'a privy door, whereby the prior made resort to her and she to him, at their pleasures'. When questioned, the Holy Maid admitted that she had plucked some of her fair hairs from her head, before knotting them together, and attaching them to the sacrament bread. A sharp tug was all that was needed to perform a miracle.

Another example known to Cranmer was a young woman healed at St Albans when she came 'creeping upon her knees, and leaning upon two short staves, inquiring after St Alban's bones'.[25] She produced a key – reportedly given to her by an angel – which unlocked the saint's shrine. Rising to her feet before the gawping crowds, the woman gave praise to God and St Alban, for 'giving her strength to walk, which was born lame'. Thankfully, the monks there were persuaded to carry out investigations before ringing their bells for a miracle. Everyone in the woman's home village was very surprised to hear her claims that she had been lame since birth. She had recently left there perfectly able to walk.

A woman with rather better claims to sanctity was Anne Wentworth, a young gentlewoman from Suffolk, who began to fall into trances and have visions, during which she 'told many men the secrets of their hearts, which they thought no man could have told, but God only'.[26] She, too, could perform miracles, sending those that doubted her 'stark mad'. She was never proved to be a fraud; but there were those that doubted the source of her powers. Cranmer, for one, thought they were devilish.

Henry was circumspect in his dealings with Elizabeth Barton, but he met with her on several occasions. Every time, she spoke out against his proposed marriage.[27] She was able to be outspoken partly because of the fact that she was a woman. Certainly, at the time the fact that she spoke for God appears to have been largely unquestioned. The elderly but highly learned John Fisher, Bishop of Rochester, never doubted that she was holy. She appeared as an angel of Heaven to him when she first decided to visit him when riding from London home towards Kent, having been with the king.[28]

Fisher was not just a believer in the Holy Maid; he was already an outspoken critic of the king's attempt at divorce, and Elizabeth Barton's words gave him courage. On hearing her reprove the king for his sins, he wept for joy, giving the girl all the more credence for having said the same to Henry himself.[29] She was, he believed, 'the person that by many probable and likely conjectures, I then reputed to be right honest, religious, and very good and virtuous'.[30] He was almost childlike in his failure to question her credentials. Then, and on two further visits, Elizabeth Barton informed Fisher that she had heard 'threats of God' that Henry would not live seven months if he married Anne Boleyn.[31] She told others that if Henry married Anne, 'he should not be king a month after'.[32]

Anne Boleyn was widely known to be unconcerned by prophecy, declaring on one occasion that she had heard a queen should be burned, but that she intended to press on regardless. There had, initially, been some good news for Henry's divorce plans, with the pope agreeing to send the absentee Bishop of Salisbury, Cardinal Campeggio, to hear the case in April 1528. Campeggio's progress towards England was, though, painfully slow, while neither Henry nor Anne can have been aware that he had secret papal instructions to 'persuade the queen to a divorce; and dissuade the king from it, as having either way the end he proposed'.[33] He failed at both, finding Henry so intractable that 'if an angel was to descend from Heaven he would not be able to persuade him to the contrary'.[34] Since Elizabeth Barton claimed that it was an angel that had first commanded her to go to 'that infidel prince of England' and command him to amend his life, he had arguably already ignored such heavenly warnings.[35]

Later, Elizabeth Barton would claim that the angel had appeared again and bid her return to Henry to complain that 'he hath more highly studied to bring his purpose to pass'.[36] She informed the king that she had seen him standing with Anne and her father in a garden, with the three discussing 'how to bring the matter to pass, and by no means it would not be'.[37] Then, a little devil whispered in Anne's ear, pushing her to say: 'you shall send my father unto the emperor, and let him show the emperor your mind and conscience, and give him these many thousand ducats to have his good will, and thus it will be brought to pass'. Barton was also, she recounted, told to bid the king to 'take his old wife again, or else'.

Henry, though, would listen to none of Barton's warnings nor to Campeggio's persuasions. There was nothing for it but to take the case to a legatine court, at which the two cardinals, Campeggio and Wolsey, presided on the opening day at Blackfriars on 18 June 1529. To everyone's surprise, Catherine heeded the summons and came to court; but, as proceedings opened, she got to her feet and walked over to Henry, kneeling before him as she made an impassioned speech, before leaving the chamber.

The case continued in her absence. Although Henry pushed Campeggio to give judgement, the cardinal had no authority to do so. When Campeggio finally stood up to revoke the case to Rome, Henry's brother-in-law, the Duke of Suffolk, was heard to exclaim that 'cardinals never did good in England'. Anne Boleyn agreed. She was soon speaking negatively about Wolsey to Henry, declaring one day at dinner: 'Is it not a marvellous thing to consider what debt and danger the cardinal hath brought you in with all your subjects?' Although Henry weakly tried to defend him, saying that he perceived she was 'not the cardinal's friend', Anne merely agreed: 'I have no cause to be. Nor hath any other man that loves Your Grace. No more has Your Grace, if ye consider well his doings.'

Henry was, in truth, as furious as Anne at Wolsey's failure to secure his divorce. It spelled the end of Wolsey's pre-eminence in the land. On 9 October 1529, the cardinal was formally charged with taking orders from a foreign power – meaning the pope – and compelled to surrender his chancellorship. He was later told to go north to his diocese of York. Wolsey was staying at Cawood in November 1530 when Anne's 'ancient suitor', Henry Percy, arrived to arrest him. It was Anne Boleyn's final revenge. The broken cardinal endured the indignity of being tied to his horse as he was taken southwards. He did not reach his destination, dying at Leicester before he had to experience the shame of a trial in London.

It was Wolsey's death that Elizabeth Barton, at home in St Sepulchre's, claimed to have foreseen. But it was premature – he had died fifteen years before God's appointed time, she complained, leaving his soul in limbo since 'Almighty God hath given no sentence upon him, but will defer it till those years be expired which it was the will of God he should have lived in the world'.[38] Nevertheless, she later credited herself with saving his soul, after seeing devils fighting over him in Purgatory.[39] She was widely believed.[40]

By 1530, Elizabeth Barton was a political force to be reckoned with. Her influence extended even outside England, thanks to her meetings with two of the pope's ambassadors and her own correspondence with the pontiff.[41] There would, she warned, be plagues on a biblical scale if the pope gave sentence against Catherine of Aragon, while he himself would be destroyed 'if he did not his duty' in the matter.[42] Timid Pope Clement feared her direct line to his heavenly master. The Holy Maid's warnings further strengthened his resolve to deny the king his divorce.[43] Elizabeth Barton was wildly convincing on the matter; she even exhibited a letter supposedly written in Heaven by Mary Magdalene herself.[44] Few seem to have seen any reason to doubt her: she lived so virtuously in her nunnery.[45]

The king's old friend, Sir Thomas More, had been chancellor since 1529. He initially had had little time for Barton's prophesies, declaring that 'some were very strange and some were very childish', but was not prepared to dismiss them out of hand. He conceded to one of Elizabeth's associates, Father Rich, an Observant friar of Richmond, that 'many of them might be true, and she a very virtuous woman too'. At around Christmas 1532, Father Risby, an Observant friar of Canterbury, stayed a night at More's house and, after supper, spoke favourably of the nun, which More 'was very glad to hear'. He heard further praise of Barton a few months later, when Father Rich – a mutual friend of his and Risby's – also visited his residence. Sensibly, though, he refused to hear anything that she had spoken about the king – even though More himself was an opponent of the divorce.

Thomas More finally had the opportunity to meet Elizabeth in person when he came across her during a visit to Syon Abbey.[46] The pair went to a little chapel, where they could be alone together. He assured her, he said, that he had not come out of curiosity about her revelations, 'but for the great virtue that I had heard for so many years, every day more and more spoken and reported'. He hoped, he said, 'that she might have somewhat the more occasion to remember me to God in her devotion and prayers'. Barton appeared as virtuous as More had been led to believe, answering humbly that she would pray for him, although she was but a 'poor wretch' who was unworthy. Sir Thomas 'heartily thanked her'.

He was satisfied enough to later sit down and write to her, offering her advice that she cease to speak of anything concerning the king or his matters.[47] Did she not recall the late Duke of Buckingham, he asked? He had come to grief when he was 'moved with the fame of one that was reported for an holy monk and had such talking with him as after was a great part of his destruction and disinheriting of his blood, and great slander and infamy of religion'. It was a brief letter – one of caution – but also one of friendship, signed 'your hearty loving Brother and Beadsman'. As he later assured the monks at Syon, 'I liked her very well in her talking.' The lord chancellor was, by now, convinced that Elizabeth Barton spoke for God.

More always insisted that he had refused to hear her words concerning the king; but this was not the story she told. Under close questioning later in the year, Elizabeth admitted that although More had initially given her revelations in this respect little regard, he soon rejoiced to hear God's words from her mouth.[48] She spoke on similar subjects with Henry's kinswoman, the Marchioness of Exeter, who invited her to visit in the summer of 1533.[49] Then, the conversation turned dangerously to the possibility of civil war.

∽

It was unsurprising that Elizabeth Barton should talk of war in 1533, for there was much murmuring throughout the kingdom. Her religious faith was entirely traditional, and her visions were increasingly speaking out against the heresies and schisms that she saw besetting the realm.[50] Once, she claimed to have miraculously stopped the ships of two monks journeying to join the exiled Bible-translator William Tyndale, while she told another monk to burn his English New Testament.[51] She had no time for the religious reform movement that was then sweeping Europe, and which encouraged the publication of the scriptures in vernacular languages. Others, however, including Anne Boleyn and her family, showed the new religious thinking rather more interest.

Anne and her father were thought by some to be 'more Lutheran than Luther himself', although this was a considerable exaggeration. Elizabeth Boleyn's daughter did, however, own a number of anti-papal works, including Tyndale's *Obedience of a Christian Man* and Simon Fish's *The Supplication of Beggars*, both of which she showed to Henry.[52] Fish went so far as to argue that the pope's laws should not be enforced above the king's, a view that Henry was also starting to take. In 1531, he made his first move against the pope, insisting that the English clergy recognize him, the king, as the sole protector and Supreme Head of the Church of England.[53] This proved to be the first step towards the break with Rome, which was further assisted in August 1532 by the death of the aged Archbishop Warham. The way was cleared for a new – more reform-minded – appointee at Canterbury.

By 1532, the Boleyn family were riding high at court. Elizabeth Boleyn and her half-sister, Lady Bryan, were particularly prominent in Henry VIII's New Year's gift list.[54] Meanwhile, Elizabeth Barton had, for some time, been doing all she could to 'marvellously stop the going forward of the king's marriage by reason of her visions'. [55] By the summer of 1532, that marriage looked imminent to many, but Barton denied that it was so when asked by her friends.[56] No, she said, the marriage would not happen so soon, but that when it did, Henry would not live for more than six months afterwards. At other times, she said that Henry's post-marital bliss would be limited to one month.[57]

That October, the king and his fiancée travelled to Canterbury, *en route* to Calais, where they had arranged an interview with the King of France.[58] Both Henry and Anne had been alarmed by Barton's most recent prophecy; in fact, they had decided to make overtures towards her to ensure that she was more compliant. Calling Barton to his presence in Canterbury, Henry asked her whether he could make her an abbess as payment for her silence.[59] He was furious when she refused.

At the same time, Elizabeth Boleyn sent a message personally to Barton, asking that she come 'to wait upon her daughter'. The nun was informed that she was to be asked to remain with Anne in court and, therefore, on her payroll.[60] These were flattering offers, but she would not accept. She had already told Father Rich, after he informed her that the king did not visit the monasteries at either Christ Church or St Augustine's, that Henry 'was so abominable in the sight of God, that he was not worthy to tread on hallowed ground'. The final break came when she claimed that while the king was at Calais she was magically transported to his chapel. As she watched – invisible – the king reached out for the bread of the host, only for it to be carried by an angel for Barton to take herself, before she was suddenly returned to her nunnery.[61]

Elizabeth Barton was confident that this revelation had prevented the king from marrying Anne in France.[62] But, true or not, it was just a delay. Early in the morning of 25 January 1533, a small group assembled in private at Whitehall Palace.

As Elizabeth Boleyn, her husband and her son watched, Anne Boleyn was discreetly married to the king. The ceremony was over in minutes, yet it set the clock ticking on Elizabeth Barton's prophecies. Would Henry indeed die one, six or even seven months after his marriage, as she had foreseen?

OF INQUISITIONS AND TREASONS

Elizabeth Barton and Anne Boleyn

For Anne's mother, the fulfilment of all the family's hopes must have seemed like a dream. The wedding was initially kept a secret, while the king continued to extricate himself formally from his first marriage. As a precursor to this effort, Thomas Cranmer, who had been a Boleyn family chaplain and had strong reformist leanings, was appointed as Archbishop of Canterbury early in 1533. After repudiating his oath of loyalty to the pope and sealing the break with Rome, he convened a Church court, which declared Henry and Catherine's marriage invalid. He then hurried back to London to crown the new queen.

Elizabeth Boleyn appeared proudly in her daughter's coronation procession, in a chariot covered with cloth of gold, while Anne sat in a litter of white satin. Although the day went without a hitch, the new queen could not help but notice 'a great many caps on heads', while some of the crowds called out 'HA HA' in mockery of the royal couple's displayed initials.[1] Anne was crowned on 1 June 1533 – five months and six days after her secret wedding. Everyone who had heard Elizabeth Barton's prophecies waited with baited breath.

Elizabeth Barton had, at various times, prophesied that Henry would die one, six or even seven months after his second marriage. But, as these deadlines came and went, the king continued in conspicuous 'good health, honour, and prosperity'.[2] Barton now offered a reinterpretation: instead of death, she declared, 'it was revealed unto her that the King's Grace should not be king one month, nay, one hour, in the acceptation or reputation of God, after that he married'.[3] That summer, Dr Bocking wrote in his great book celebrating Barton, which was almost ready for the printers, 'that God was highly displeased with our said Sovereign Lord for the same matter', for it had been revealed to Elizabeth that if he married he would no longer be king in the eyes of God and that 'he should die a villain's death'.[4]

Elizabeth Barton's credit survived Henry VIII's failure to die. As late as 15 July 1533, one of her supporters, Henry Man, was writing from the Charterhouse at Sheen to Dr Bocking to praise the 'holy virgin', who had 'raised a fire in some hearts that you would think like the operation of the Holy Spirit in the Primitive Church'. As he said, 'I rejoice that I have lived to see this day.'[5] Bocking's book, too, was finally ready. The canny churchman had come to an arrangement with the printer whereby he could offset the cost of printing 500 copies by allowing the printer to make and sell for himself a further run of 200 copies.[6] This was a sizeable print run, and as the press began to clack into action, both men confidently predicted that they had a bestseller on their hands. Unfortunately for historians today, all 700 copies later fell victim to the censor's fires; but a Latin draft of Bocking's Prologue has been identified. Elizabeth Barton was presented to Bocking's readers as a 'spiritual virgin', provided to mankind as part of the 'benignity and kindness of God'.[7]

In reality, her time was running out. Barton had once claimed that she would 'receive the crown of martyrdom' thanks to the message of an angel, claiming to know the time and place when this would occur.[8] If she did, she took no steps to prevent her fall – which was both brutal and efficient.

Aware by July 1533 that he had survived all of Barton's doom-laden prophecies, Henry VIII was ruminating on the vexatious prophetess. His fury was building against the 'hypocrite nun', who had so tried to thwart him and had threatened his throne. That month, he summoned his chief minister, Thomas Cromwell, telling him to instruct Archbishop Cranmer to begin an investigation.[9] Malleable Cranmer was rather less credulous than his predecessor had been, and had his own strong doubts over the nun's claims. He wrote a brief note to Elizabeth's prioress, bidding her to come to him at his manor of Otford. She was, he said, to 'bring with you your nun which was some time at Court up Street'. He ended, warning her to ensure that 'ye fail not herein in any wise'.[10]

Elizabeth Barton had already been fêted by a pope, a king, a cardinal and an archbishop – and the prospect of a meeting with Cranmer held no fear for her, as she rode beside her prioress. On her arrival, she was surprised to find herself subjected to an interrogation, the questions written by Cromwell himself, whose servants were present, alongside the somewhat more benign Cranmer.[11] Her visions were all true, she insisted, although they were difficult to interpret. Why, she said, 'at Whitsuntide last, she, being in a trance, had partly an answer of the King's Highness and of the Queen's Grace; but it was no certain answer what end they should have in the matter'. Instead, her voices had told her that without fail at the next trance she would have 'a determinate answer'. Would Cranmer give her licence to go back to Court-at-Street for her answer? She would then know what God intended for the king and his new queen.[12]

Cranmer was still not ready to show his true face and played along. Of course she could go, but she was to return straight to him. As far as Elizabeth Barton was concerned, the interview had gone well. She was unaware that Cranmer was – as Cromwell was informed by his agent – being but 'dainty with her, as [if] he did believe her every word'. As soon as he had gleaned everything he could from her, he intended to send her to Cromwell.

∞

That summer, as Elizabeth Barton's star was beginning to fall, Anne Boleyn's was still riding high. She had already been in the early stages of pregnancy at the time of her marriage, and was soon boasting of cravings for apples; she had also added an extra panel to the front of her gowns. Anne ceremonially took to her chamber at Greenwich Palace on 26 August 1533, in order to await the birth of her child. With her mother most likely present, Anne gave birth at 3pm on 7 September to a baby that was healthy, but which, to the 'great regret' of both parents, was a girl.[13] The king immediately cancelled the grand tournament he had planned for the birth of a son.

After years of stillbirths and miscarriages with Catherine of Aragon, a daughter was at least something, and the restoration of royal fertility held promise for the future. The baby was named Elizabeth, after her paternal grandmother, Elizabeth of York. This was the name also, by happy coincidence, of her other grandmother – and of the princess's nearly forgotten aunt, the first Elizabeth Tudor. Once the christening was over, the baby was taken to be raised in her own household, with her great-aunt, Margaret Bourchier, Lady Bryan, presiding. It was naturally hoped that baby Elizabeth's arrival would soon be followed by brothers.

A princess's household

When Princess Elizabeth was born in September 1533, she was almost immediately provided with her own household of women to attend her, away from court, with younger siblings expected to join her – as and when they were born. Elizabeth's own half-sister, Princess Mary, now declared illegitimate by her father, arrived there, to serve the king's then only legitimate child.

By 1536, Elizabeth would also find herself declared illegitimate, but her household still remained substantial. At the age of three she was served by thirty-two people, all employed to ensure her comfort.[14] Amid the political dramas of the time, they provided stability to her early life, since many of the people serving her then were still employed by the princess in 1546, when a second census was taken of her household.

During Elizabeth's childhood, her household was dominated by her lady mistress, Lady Troy, a Welsh gentlewoman. And, even from the age of three, Elizabeth was attended by five gentlewomen to provide female company and support – Katherine Champernowne, Elizabeth Garrett, Mary Hill, Elizabeth Candish and Mary Norris. Inferior in rank were two female chamberers, both of whom remained with her for at least a decade, as well as gentlemen ushers and grooms of the chamber. The infant Elizabeth employed a chaplain, too, who may have carried out some of her early lessons. Agnes Hilton – the laundress – held the lowliest post in the household throughout the princess's childhood. The numbers of her household population were increased by the fact that many of her servants had servants of their own.

Although stable, the household was not always free of internal disputes and quarrels. Blanche Parry, who had originally been employed to rock Elizabeth's cradle and who had remained with her throughout her childhood, was always assumed by her aunt and godmother – Lady Troy – to be the natural eventual replacement as lady mistress.[15] But Katherine Champernowne, who would soon marry and take the name of Ashley, coveted the appointment herself. Henry VIII had heard good reports of Katherine's learning and the 'distinguished teaching' she could provide, and personally appointed her as Elizabeth's governess in 1536. By 1544, however, Elizabeth's curriculum had advanced beyond what the gentlewoman could teach her, and thus the scholar William Grindal arrived as the girl's tutor to introduce a rigorous curriculum of Plato and other classical heavyweights, leaving Katherine Ashley without a role.[16] When the elderly Lady Troy did retire, in late 1546, Katherine, who was a rather more forceful character than the quiet, dutiful Blanche Parry, was soon able to secure Henry VIII's support for her own appointment as lady mistress.[17] She was, in any event, a woman to whom Elizabeth was devoted.

Elizabeth's household was far from unusual in its habits, since members of the royal family were expected to maintain significant establishments. Like all great landowners, the princess and her household moved regularly, packing up their belongings into chests and loading them onto wagons. As princess, Elizabeth spent much time at Hatfield in Hertfordshire, but also regularly used Enfield and Hertford as residences, among other houses. Her servants were instantly recognizable as her own by the livery that they wore. In later life, she would choose stylish black satin for her staff. During her brother's reign, she provided her gentlemen with fine velvet coats, each identical in colour and style.[18] Despite the label of illegitimacy still attached to her, Princess Elizabeth lived in the style of royalty, particularly after her father's death in 1547, since she had been left well provided for in his will.

Elizabeth Barton was rather hoping the opposite. She had already sent a message to the close-confined Catherine of Aragon, via one of her supporters, Henry Gold. He had informed the former queen that God had revealed she 'should prosper and do well, and that her issue the Lady Mary the king's daughter should prosper and reign in this realm, and have many friends to sustain and maintain her'.[19] According to the charges that would later be laid against her, Barton also asked God 'to know when several wars should come whether any should take my Lady Mary's part arms', and obtained a favourable answer for the girl's cause.[20] Barton was effectively the voice of those who were disaffected by the king's religious and marital changes;[21] it is no surprise that she made known her prayers of guidance concerning the former queen and her daughter.[22]

Catherine, very wisely, refused to have any dealings with Elizabeth Barton. Nonetheless, her chaplain, Thomas Abel, was less cautious – he would later be attainted for misprision of treason for his dealings with Elizabeth, which included the charge that he had 'animated the said Lady Catherine obstinately to persist in her wilful opinion against the same divorce and separation'.[23] Although Cromwell was reported to be particularly anxious to obtain a confession from Elizabeth Barton of her dealings with the ex-queen, she said nothing.[24] There was little to confess – and even Cromwell praised Catherine for her circumspection in relation to the Holy Maid.[25]

∞

Once Thomas Cranmer had exhausted his questions for Elizabeth Barton, he sent her under guard to the Tower of London. This ancient fortress, which stood square and mighty against the Thames, loomed ominously in front of those who approached either by land or by boat. Perhaps Elizabeth was taken in through the grim water entrance, later known as

Traitor's Gate. More terrifying still, she might have entered by land, crossing the bridge over the moat to pass through the Lion Gate, so named for its proximity to the royal menagerie. Day and night, prisoners were alarmed to hear the growling of bears and the roaring of lions, kept close by in cages.[26] Cromwell still hoped to extract information from Barton, and so he gave orders that she be well kept, 'as a high-born lady' would be.[27] Nevertheless, conditions were still far from comfortable.

Imprisonment and everything that went with it took its toll – and the Holy Maid seemed to start cracking. Under increasing interrogation that autumn, Elizabeth Barton confessed to Cromwell 'that she never had visions in all her life, but all that ever she said was feigned of her own imagination, only to satisfy the minds of them the which resorted unto her, and to obtain worldly praise'.[28] She had still not quite given in, however, telling her supporter Thomas Gold, when he was permitted to visit her, that:

> ... she had confessed to divers of the King's Grace's Council that she had never any revelation from God, but the cause why she had so confessed was by reason of a vision and revelation, which she feigned herself to have had in the Tower. In which God willed her by His Heavenly messenger that she should say that she never had revelation from God.[29]

Gold was instructed to relay this to her supporters. Gold's brother, Henry, then wrote to Dr Bocking to inform him that 'he should stick sure to her revelations, for certain causes which he would show them when they met'.[30] Elizabeth was not going to give up being the Holy Maid of Kent quite so readily.

The net, though, was closing. Following her arrest, those that believed in her and had helped her were also quickly rounded up. On Cromwell's orders, Bocking and his monastic colleague Mr Hadley, who had first examined Elizabeth, were arrested on 25 September 1533.[31] Their chambers were immediately searched, and while nothing of importance was found in Hadley's room, incriminating papers were found in Bocking's. Both the men and Bocking's papers were sent up to Cromwell in London; on the following day, Richard Masters was also apprehended. Cromwell himself intended to conduct the examination of Bocking and the unfortunate Hadley.[32] Poor Edward Thwaites, who had excitedly written his pamphlet of the miracles he had witnessed at Court-at-Street, was arrested too by the end of September.[33] At the same time, copies of his pamphlet and Bocking's book were collected together and burned.

In November 1533, the king called together his Council, along with the principal judges in England and many of the prelates and the nobility. This eminent group met for three consecutive full days.[34] According to the ambassador from the Holy Roman Empire, Eustace Chapuys – a man who had a nose for information – it was the judges who dominated proceedings. There was no proof of treason, nor even of a conspiracy to commit treason, they said, since the Holy Maid had actually told King Henry to his face everything she was accused of disseminating.[35] Ironically, therefore, Barton's audacity held the possibility of saving her life. It certainly did save her from conviction at a trial, for the king resolved to proceed by other means.[36]

At the end of the third day, Elizabeth Barton was brought into the room. The authorities had only recently discovered her apparent duplicity in telling Thomas Gold that her confession was feigned. Accordingly, Bocking and Henry Gold were brought in too, to hear Elizabeth confirm that even this last 'revelation' had been false.[37] The two men were astounded, declaring loudly that she was 'the falsest woman that ever God gave life unto'. In the face of her friends' anger, she broke down into tears.[38]

With Elizabeth still standing tearfully by, Cromwell stood before everyone assembled and asserted that 'every Englishman was greatly bound to return thanks to the Almighty, who, by His divine goodness and mercy, had permitted the damnable abuses and wicked deeds of the said nun, her adherents and accomplices, to be discovered and made manifest'. He spoke for a long time on the nun's doings and her treachery, claiming that Elizabeth Barton had meant to induce the English to rebel against the king – words that prompted from his audience cries of 'To the stake! To the stake!' According to Chapuys, the Holy Maid showed no fear; but the words must have terrified her. Her ordeal was still far from over.

The edifice constructed around Elizabeth Barton now began to fall apart, as people flocked to disassociate themselves from her. The monks of Bocking's own monastery, as a whole body, felt it politic to write to the king seeking his forgiveness for the actions of their 'miserable brother'.[39] After speaking to Cranmer, they also offered money – £200 or £300 – to Henry, which they hoped might help him see his way to forgiving them.[40] On 25 November 1533, the Marchioness of Exeter also wrote an abject letter to the king, entirely condemning the 'most unworthy, subtle, and deceivable' Barton.[41] By 16 November 1533, it was being reported in London that Barton had 'confessed herself not only a traitoress but also an heretic'.[42] She had 'mocked all Kent' with her 'marvellous hypocrisy'.[43]

Elizabeth Barton was led out of the Tower on Sunday 23 November 1533, to do public penance. She climbed onto a scaffold at Paul's Cross beside Dr Bocking and eight other of their associates.[44] This 'comedy', as the imperial ambassador considered it, was intended finally to blot out any lingering belief in Barton's sanctity from the minds of the king's subjects. Before the hostile crowd and Dr Capon, Bishop-elect of Bangor, Barton stepped forward to read a short confession.[45] She was, she said, a 'most miserable and wretched person', who had 'been the original of all this mischief, and by my falsehood have deceived all these persons here and many now present'. Suddenly humble, Elizabeth Barton continued by saying that 'I have most grievously offended Almighty God and my most dread Sovereign the King's Grace. Wherefore I humbly and with heart most sorrowful desire you to pray to Almighty God for my miserable sins.' She concluded by considering that it 'may do me good to make supplication to my most Sovereign Lord for me for His Grace's mercy and pardon', before falling silent.

'Uncomely speeches'

In circumstances that touched less on weighty affairs of state, the crimes of feigning revelations or spreading slander would ordinarily be dealt with in Tudor times by the Church courts, which handled matters of religion and morality in England. And within that orbit, women's verbal excesses – as they were seen – appear fairly frequently in the records.

In 1584, the archdeacon's court of Oxfordshire interrogated Anne Wrigglesworth of Islip, accusing her of making up a slanderous rhyme. It was not true, she said. Around Christmas time, she claimed, she had come to the market at Oxford, where she met with a neighbour, Richard Neville.[46] He had sung to her: 'if I had as fair a face as John Williams his daughter Elizabeth has, then would I were a tawdry lass as goodman Bolt's daughter Mary does, and if I had as much money in my purse as Cadman's daughter Margaret has, then would I have a bastard less than Butler's maid Helen has'. Wrigglesworth defended herself, swearing that she had reported it to Goodwife Williams and her daughter, as well as Goodwife Cadman and her daughter, 'because she thought it was made to their discredit'. She proved convincing, for the court agreed with her version of events, and the case was dismissed.

In another case concerning speaking out of turn, it was reported of one Emma Comber that 'on May Day last she used in the church any disordered behaviour or uncomely speeches or unquiet in the disturbing of the minister or parishioners'.[47]

She was lucky that witnesses were instead able to lay the blame on another woman, Elizabeth Robinson, who had actually spoken the words. For those found guilty of such crimes, penance – in which the accused individual was made to publicly confess – was the most usual punishment.

The group then stood mute, as their crimes and all that had occurred was rehearsed in the most lurid terms possible. 'The original ground,' declared Dr Capon, 'of this ungracious conspiracy is this nun here present.'[48] At the end of his long sermon, the prisoners were bundled into wagons and taken home to Kent to repeat the same 'comedy' two weeks later in the churchyard of the Holy Trinity in Canterbury.[49] It was all too much for bookish Richard Masters, who fell so ill following the second sermon that Cromwell's commissioners feared that he would 'miscarry by the way, or soon after' if he attempted the journey back to London.[50] He was, instead, sent home 'on sufficient security', as were Richard Deryng and Father Lawrence – although the danger had not yet passed for any of them.[51]

Parliament opened on 15 January 1534, and amid business concerning the paving of Holborn, the regulation of pewterers and the destruction of wildfowl, the Lords and Commons considered the more weighty matter of attainders against the Holy Maid and her associates, a process by which someone could be condemned without trial. Sir Thomas More, who hurriedly wrote to try to clear himself 'concerning my communication with the Nun of Canterbury' was lucky to escape censure.[52] Bishop John Fisher, who also wrote indignantly to the House of Lords, was less fortunate and was named in the document.[53] So, too, was his chaplain, along with many of Barton's other associates, including Dr Bocking, Richard Masters and Edward Thwaites. All were convicted either of treason, or the concealment of treason, thanks to their 'wilful and perverse opinions grounded of malice corruption and affection' in looking to hinder the king's marriage.[54] Elizabeth Barton and six of her most important associates were sentenced to death.[55]

The 20th of April 1534 was the last day of Elizabeth Barton's life. Just over eight years after she was first carried to Court-at-Street for a miracle, she found herself the centre of an entirely different procession. Leaving the Tower with her were her associates Dr Bocking, John Deryng, Hugh Rich, Richard Risby and Henry Gold; Richard Masters, though attainted, was lucky to escape with his life – and pardoned later that year.[56] The group was strapped to hurdles before being drawn through the dusty streets.[57] Their 5-mile journey, bumping along the rutted roads and attended by hostile crowds, was an ordeal in itself; but all six knew that worse was to come. When they reached Tyburn, they mounted a scaffold in turn, uncomfortably aware of the gallows behind them and the nooses, already prepared.

According to the contemporary chronicler, Edward Hall, Elizabeth Barton stepped out bravely onto the scaffold. In a clear voice, she admitted everything, saying: 'Hither am I come to die, and I have not been the only cause of mine own death which most justly I have deserved, but also I am the cause of the death of all these persons which at this time here suffer'.[58] Nonetheless, she also knew that she, an uneducated country girl, had evolved into a useful tool for others, pleading:

... and yet to say the truth, I am not so much to be blamed considering it was well known unto these learned men that I was a poor wench without learning and therefore they

might have easily perceived that the things that were done by me could not proceed in no such sort.

They should have judged, she considered, that her visions 'were altogether feigned'; but in her words, as the chronicler Hall reported them:

> ... *because the things which I feigned was [sic] profitable unto them, therefore they much praised me and bare me in hand that it was the Holy Ghost and not I that did them, and then I being puffed up with their praises fell into a certain pride and foolish fantasy with my self and thought I might feign what I would, which thing hath brought me to this case.*

She begged mercy of God, and the king, before asking those assembled to pray for her. Whether Elizabeth ever uttered these final contrite words is impossible to tell – so much of her story is clouded by censorship.

After stepping onto the scaffold, a noose was tied around Elizabeth's neck. She then suffered the agony of hanging, before her broken body was finally cut down. Even then, she was not left in peace. She and her five associates were decapitated; two of the heads were mounted on London Bridge, and the other four at the gates of the city.[59] As a small mercy, Elizabeth's headless body was permitted burial, along with those of Risby and Rich, in the church of the Grey Friars in London.[60]

Whether Elizabeth Barton was guilty of feigning her revelations, or whether she truly believed that she spoke to God, can never be conclusively known. Not everyone believed that she was a fraud. The later sixteenth-century Jesuit, Nicholas Sander, for example, was on the fence. Thomas More had, he reasoned, been 'unable to discover in it any trace of that fanaticism which was maliciously laid to her charge at the time'.

Also, he considered, 'what is certain is this, that she said that in due time things would come to pass which were at that time regarded as impossible; for Mary, who then was made to give way to Elizabeth, came afterwards to the throne before her, and in her own right'.[61]

What is clear and remarkable for a Tudor woman of such inauspicious beginnings is what might be called her 'political agency' – the manner in which she thrust herself onto the national stage and into matters of the highest contemporary concern. To the government, her connections with many of the most disaffected in the kingdom, coupled with the way that she spread her message, made her a dangerous opponent. Elizabeth had inspired great love and devotion among her adherents, creating a bond between them. To one of them, Elizabeth was, as he said, 'my lover, my sister, my earthly comfort'.[62] She seemed that, and much more, to many others. It was no wonder that, as the king sought to impose on his kingdom the novelties of his break with Rome, his supremacy over the Church and his second marriage, it was regarded as essential to destroy Elizabeth Barton and to break that bond between her and her supporters.

∽

For a time, it was another Elizabeth – Elizabeth Boleyn – and her daughter Anne who were triumphant. On the day of Barton's execution, royal commissioners were out in London, busily taking oaths 'in most parts of this city' by which people swore to support Henry and his legitimate issue by Anne Boleyn.[63]

Yet, any sense of victory did not last long. The birth of Princess Elizabeth failed to presage sons for Anne; by April 1536, the king was certain that he would have 'no more boys by her'. Instead, his thoughts were turning to a new love – Jane Seymour, who was the daughter of Elizabeth Boleyn's cousin, the meek Margery Wentworth. It was soon clear to many that the king was intent on ending his second marriage.

On 30 April 1536, Mark Smeaton, a young musician in Anne's household, was arrested by Cromwell and questioned. Amid rumours that he had been placed on the rack or subjected to some other torture, he confessed to an adulterous affair with the queen. The following day, she too was arrested, joining Smeaton and her friend Henry Norris in the Tower of London. Other accused men soon followed them there, including Anne's brother, George, with whom she was accused of incest. As Anne awaited her fate, her thoughts turned to her mother, lamenting to William Kingston, Lieutenant of the Tower, 'O my mother, thou will die of sorrow.'[64]

That April, Elizabeth Boleyn was suffering from a bad cough, 'which grieves her sore', although she was still at court.[65] Sorrowful and ill, she took no part in the events attending the fall of her daughter or the execution – on 17 May – of her only son. Two days later, it was Anne Boleyn's turn to die, stepping out onto a scaffold just as Elizabeth Barton had done. 'Good Christian people,' she called to the crowd of invited guests, which had assembled in the privacy of the Tower, 'I am come hither to die, for according to the law and by the law I am judged to die, and therefore I will speak nothing against it.'[66] She would, she said, 'accuse no man,' nor would she 'speak anything of that whereof I am accused and condemned to die'. The fallen queen had a daughter to think of, as well as the fate of her parents, and it was politically wise for her to ask that 'God save the king and send him long to reign over you,' before adding 'for a gentler nor more merciful prince was there never: and to me he was ever a good, a gentle, and sovereign lord'. Yet, she added, 'if any person will meddle of my cause, I require them to judge the best': she was not guilty.

Standing on the straw of the scaffold, Anne began to pray, as her ladies stepped forward to blindfold her. Kneeling, she cried out: 'O lord have mercy on me, to God I commend my soul', as the specially commissioned French headsman stepped up behind her and severed her head with a sword. It was a bloody end to a career that – like Elizabeth Barton's – had once been filled with promise. At both ends of the social spectrum, life could be dangerous for those Tudor women who raised their heads above the parapet.

Hurrying home to Hever Castle, Elizabeth and Thomas Boleyn found themselves cast adrift from court for a time.[67] But despite their tragedies, it remained a powerful lure, and by the following June Elizabeth is recorded as being again at court.[68] She was in London, too, in April 1538 – when she breathed her last.[69] Fittingly, Elizabeth Boleyn was buried in Lambeth's Church of St Mary, among the tombs of her Howard ancestors. The world she had been born into, and which those ancestors represented, was already radically changing – thanks in no small part to the influence and actions of her daughter.

'A most grievous and lingering death'

Hanging and beheading were among the more merciful forms of execution on offer in Tudor England. The most horrifying, contemporaries agreed, was a form of death that was a Tudor legal innovation: boiling alive. This punishment was so gruesome that, at one execution, when the condemned man 'roared mighty loud' a number of pregnant women in the crowd fell sick or swooned at the sight.[70] Other members of the crowd considered heartily that they 'would prefer to see the headsman at his work'. It was an understandable feeling of revulsion.

That particular case involved the condemned being locked in chains before being attached to a gibbet and repeatedly dunked into a cauldron of boiling water.[71] It was a painfully slow end, was 'a most grievous and lingering death',[72] especially since the method left no chance of a merciful drowning. The heat of repeated dunkings would shear off the skin, leaving the victim red raw and in agony as they were dragged back up on their chains.

At least the punishment was rare. Four examples are known from Henry VIII's reign. But women were equally, if not more, at risk of being on the receiving end, for the form of execution was reserved for certain crimes of poisoning – a crime that was most liable to be carried out by those charged with preparing food and drink. Women's victims were often their husbands or employers, making the crime of poisoning seem akin to treason in the eyes of contemporaries. For example, in Essex in the period, among four cases of poisoning, three involved women perpetrators: a serving maid who poisoned her mistress, and two cases of women poisoning their husbands.

The punishment was laid down in law when, in 1531, a male cook in the household of John Fisher, Bishop of Rochester, was condemned for trying to poison the household.[73] The king and Parliament were outraged at this crafty and secretive means of committing mass murder and came down heavy in legislation. In the Act of Parliament condemning the cook, it was declared that 'from henceforth every wilful murder of any person or persons by any whatsoever person or persons hereafter to be committed and done by mean or way of poisoning shall be reputed, deemed, and judged in the law to be high treason'; and for added deterrence, the punishment laid down by statute was boiling.[74] Before then, boiling alive was not totally unknown; it had already been meted out in London's Smithfield in 1523, when the victim was chained over a bubbling cauldron, before being 'let up and down divers time till he was dead' – in that particular case, for the crime of counterfeiting.[75] But the new legislation formalized the grim procedure.

Two of the recorded victims of boiling alive during Henry's reign were convicted female poisoners.[76] The first died at around the same time as John Fisher's cook; she was a maidservant, boiled in the market place at King's Lynn, Norfolk, for poisoning her mistress.[77] More famously, Margaret Davy was boiled at Smithfield on 17 March 1542, for multiple murders.[78] This maidservant had been caught red-handed poisoning members of three households in which she had served.[79] Her last victim had been her most recent mistress, who died from her ministrations. On discovering this crime, the authorities turned to Davy's past life, noting the suspicious deaths of a Mr and Mrs Darington, who had passed away while she was a servant in their house in Coleman Street in London. Farther back, too, she had been employed by a Mrs Tinley, who had also died in suspicious circumstances.[80]

Investigating Margaret Davy was detective work of some

sophistication for the rudimentary Tudor justice system. But even her egregious murders of four people were not considered sufficient justification to convince contemporaries of the need for boiling alive. Henry VIII's Act was repealed soon after his death, and instead the more merciful death of hanging was ordered for poisoners. The Elizabethan justice Sir Edward Coke voiced most people's sentiments when he said that the punishment of boiling alive was 'too severe to live long'.[81]

But there was one exception, again targeting women. Wives who poisoned their husbands were to burn, as Margery Mills of Charlwood, Surrey, discovered after she had slipped poison into her husband's food on 25 September 1599.[82]

The Fifth Age

OF PILGRIMAGES AND PUNISHMENTS

Margaret Cheyne, Lady Bulmer

For William Shakespeare, the fifth age of Man was that of 'the justice', an official heading towards comfortable retirement. For men, it was the time to reap the rewards of a life well spent: the age of contentment and middle-aged spread. It was in this phase of life that male office-holders were at the height of their power and prestige, patronizing the youths that they once had been.

There was little equivalent for Tudor women. No women entered the Tudor 'establishment' to serve as justices of the peace, judges or Church officials. But the nature of the establishment was becoming less stable, and the consequences affected women too. For women wanting to preserve the lives they'd built around them, the times were not necessarily sympathetic.

Traditionally, the Church, while not offering official positions to women, had provided other ways in which they could carve out roles and define hierarchies in their communities, as well as offering a framework of belief and personal behaviour. The local church was central to Tudor life, and everyone believed in God – the word 'atheism' would only emerge during the period – and traditional elements of religious belief and practice were still popular and vibrant.[1] But the Reformation, which swept onto the people of England in the 1530s and

1540s, wrought changes that rocked the very foundations of what men and women had known and been taught.[2]

King Henry's break with Rome was a shocking development, even though it had little immediate or overt effect on worship in the country's parish churches. It was to be some years before the nation's official religious orthodoxy could be described as 'Protestant'. But, rejecting the pope's authority encouraged a receptivity to new ideas. At first, there were whisperings of religious reform and of greater access to the scriptures (and other texts) in English. They soon began to increase in volume. Equally, there was counter-reaction from those who feared where innovation might lead. From the 1530s, doctrine and the Church became the sites of controversy – and ones in which women, too, sometimes felt they had to take sides. It was so for Margaret Cheyne.

'The better hand in the seat'

Tucked away in the medieval church in Skenfrith, Monmouthshire, is a family pew, which once belonged to the locally prominent Morgan family. This box pew, dating from 1564 and carved in sturdy, dark oak, could have contained a family in some privacy. And that was important, for churches were not merely for the veneration of God and the dissemination of religious teaching; they were contested locations for status in the community's hierarchy. The humble pew was the cause of gender division, infighting and social turbulence in Tudor England.

Church seating was usually divided along gender lines, with women commonly assigned the north – inferior – side of the building.[3] Within this arrangement, pews had their own internal hierarchies. It was, for example, socially advantageous to be seen in a prominent seat close to the altar, a prize that could be fought over.

Pews could also be big business for churches, for the rights to occupy individual pews, or half-pews, were sold off. One unanticipated side-effect of the Reformation was an increase in this form of Church revenue, as chantry chapels were removed from churches, making way for more seats.[4] In addition, pews could revert to the church for resale, making the practice even more profitable, although the new owner could not take their seat until the death of the old.[5]

Women often owned their own pews. One Alice Lane held a desirable one in Ludlow, which was quickly resold by the church bailiffs following her death in 1540, earning more than eight shillings[6] – and generating a dispute.[7] Another woman, Margery Hoods, held a pew in the church for the duration of her life, until, in 1549, the reversion was sold.[8] The purchaser – who could take up occupation only on Margery's death – must have eyed her enviously. Not everyone was content to wait.

In 1584, tensions boiled over in the parish of St Ebbe,

Oxfordshire, when Margery Hopkins and Barbara Nichols 'fell at words together in the church for their seats'.[9] As they quarrelled, the churchwardens arrived to break up the fight, ordering the women to share the wooden seat. Tellingly, however, they awarded Hopkins – a freeman's wife – 'the better hand in the seat'. But the lowlier Nichols was not ready to give in. When Margery Hopkins attempted to sit, her neighbour 'jostled further into the seat and would not let her come into her own place there'. 'If you will not let me come into my own seat I will sit upon your lap the next day', Hopkins retorted furiously. They pushed and shoved, and matters became even more heated as they traded insults of 'whore and bastard & such like'. It was with difficulty that the churchwardens again broke them up.

Earlier that year there had been another fight in the same church, when Emma Cumbre had 'cast out' Elizabeth Robins' mat from a pew that she had occupied since long before her marriage.[10] Soon, 'disordered behaviour' and 'uncomely speeches' were passing between the pair in church, before they were hauled before the archdeacon's court to account for their conduct.

Anne Cripps of Ambrosden, Oxfordshire, was rather more restrained when, a few years later, she arrived in church for a service. She had acquired her own pew from the previous owner of her house and had sat in it every week for thirteen years. She was therefore horrified to find a neighbour, Margaret Smithe, resolutely sitting in it one day.[11] Rather than causing a scene, on that occasion Cripps 'departed the church & used no words'. But if she had hoped Smithe had made a mistake, she was to be quickly disabused. Soon, the two women were brawling in the church, and the dispute was still not settled when the local archdeacon became involved.[12]

For these women and others, there was more at stake than just a comfortable seat from which to watch the service. A woman who ceded her pew in church also ceded something of her place in village society.

∽

Margaret Cheyne was an unlikely martyr. Her fame – and notoriety – rests squarely on the events of spring 1537.[13] Her origins are almost entirely obscure. She may have been an illegitimate daughter of Edward Stafford, Duke of Buckingham, the overmighty subject who famously displeased Henry VIII and lost his head.[14] Years later, a son who could not have remembered her claimed that she was instead the bastard daughter of Buckingham's cousin, Henry Stafford.[15] While the circumstances of her birth were murky, she was accounted 'a very fair creature' and 'beautiful'.[16] Her charms recommended her to a London merchant named William Cheyne. They wed, but at some point thereafter she moved northwards – alone.

In Cleveland, Yorkshire, Margaret encountered Sir John Bulmer, a local gentleman and friend of the Stafford family, who was born some time around 1490.[17] He was nervous, timid and clumsy in his affairs, but also kindly. Soon, the couple – both of whom were probably still married – fell in love. This was scandalous, but they made no attempt to conceal the relationship, or the births of two, or possibly three, daughters. Theirs was a passion that would endure to the ends of their lives, and their friends and neighbours accepted and recognized the relationship.[18]

Probably on the death of his wife, Sir John finally married Margaret in around 1534, although the legitimacy of their union was doubtful.[19] Margaret's first husband might still have been alive, or at least there was the suspicion that he was, which would later play into their enemies' hands.[20] Margaret was portrayed as a scarlet woman, Sir John's 'paramour'.[21] Events would quickly overtake them when they became embroiled in the Pilgrimage of Grace, that expression of discontent against the upheavals being ushered in on the coat-tails of the break with Rome.

∞

Despite King Henry's assertions – set out in the August 1536 publication of his 'Ten Articles' – that the Church of which he was now supreme head was a conservative one, a major pillar of the old Church's institutions was on the verge of destruction. In 1535, Cromwell had, among his manifold duties, been appointed as Henry's 'Vicar-General', empowered to conduct visitations of the religious houses in England. The reformist administrator was searching for sin, and he found it – while passing over the good.[22] He soon let it be known that 'all the clergy were found to be clean out of order'.

The purpose became all too clear at Easter 1536, when Parliament passed the first Act for the Dissolution of the Monasteries, granting the king ownership of all religious houses worth less than £200 per year. Elizabeth Barton's old home, St Sepulchre's, was just one of the estimated 400 casualties.

Some surrendered quietly; others put up a fight. To the local communities, which had been dominated by their monasteries, it was alarming. At Hexham in Northumberland, on 28 September 1536, the monks began to ring their bells in alarm as Cromwell's commissioners approached, before assembling armed at the gates. Worse – for Henry – was to follow.

The Vicar of Louth, in Lincolnshire, was informed that he could expect government commissioners to arrive on 2 October 1536 to enquire into the fitness of the clergy. The vicar – and others – recognized the parallel with the earlier visitations. From his pulpit on 1 October, he called on the support of the people of the small market town, and following the service townspeople assembled outside their large parish church. They moved to walk in procession behind the church's three silver crosses. The situation grew more tense as a local shoemaker, Nicholas Melton, who would soon go by the name of 'Captain Cobbler', took charge of the crowd. After evensong, the townspeople took the church keys from the churchwardens, declaring that they did so 'for saving of the church jewels'. The next day, crowds assembled, the church bells rang, and the spark of rebellion was lit.

This 'Pilgrimage of Grace' soon spread through Lincolnshire, Yorkshire and the other northern counties. The occupants of those regions – whether male or female, highborn or lowly – all found themselves caught up in the turmoil. On 3 October, the rebels swarmed out of Louth towards Caistor, where the commissioners for the king's tax subsidy were due to sit; one of the commissioners, Lord Burgh, whose sympathies lay with the religious reformers rather than the rebels, hurriedly rode off on a fast horse having heard that 20,000 rebels were descending. In fact, only 3,000 had taken up arms, but it was still a formidable host that now turned its attentions towards Sir William Askew, another commissioner.[23] He, along with his fellows, had attempted to ride for home, but they were soon captured.

Aware that even the servants with whom he was riding supported the rebels, Askew had little choice but to comply.

At home, Askew's fifteen-year-old daughter, Anne, was reluctantly preparing for her wedding. She was a clever girl and had been given a very good home education, particularly in religious matters.[24] She probably already had strong theological doubts about the cause that the rebels espoused. News of her father's capture threw the household into disarray; they now waited to hear what would become of him. Anne's brothers, too, were quickly rounded up by rebels, and the house was placed under watch.

It was Sir William Askew and his fellows who were given the unenviable task of informing the king of what had happened. Writing under obvious duress, they complained to Henry that 'the common voice and fame was that all the jewels and goods of the churches of the country should be taken from them and brought to Your Grace's Council, and also that your said loving and faithful subjects should be put off new enhancements and other importunate charges'.[25]

With one voice, the rebels demanded that no more changes be made to their Church.[26] By 6 October, 40,000 of them had assembled at Lincoln under the banner of the Five Wounds of Christ, while fires, fuelled by heretical books, burned in the towns through which they passed. Give us Thomas Cromwell, they demanded of the king; they demanded, too, the most openly reformist bishops, including Thomas Cranmer and Hugh Latimer. The king was furious, responding to the demands dismissively from the relative safety of Windsor. With no clear leadership, the Lincolnshire rebels soon dispersed; but, ominously, warning beacons had been lit along the south side of the River Humber during the first week of October. They could clearly be seen from neighbouring Yorkshire.

On 7 October, the town of Beverley in Yorkshire rose in support of the Lincolnshire rebels. Robert Aske, a one-eyed lawyer from a good family, soon took control.[27] He organized his 'pilgrims' in military fashion, decked out in their badges and banners of the cross and wounds of Christ.[28] Infantry troops need captains, and Aske knew where to find them. In the early days of October, a group of rebels surrounded Snape Castle in Yorkshire and carried off Lord Latimer into the night, leaving his wife, Catherine – the future sixth wife of Henry VIII – behind as a hostage to his good behaviour.

They came, too, to Wilton Castle in Cleveland, where Sir John Bulmer was staying. Like Latimer, he did not go willingly. After ordering the gates barred against the rabble, Bulmer was alarmed when they threatened to burn them; in any case, the rebels forced their way in and ransacked the place.[29] Amid the chaos, Bulmer was, like Latimer, forced to swear the rebels' oath. He rode away as both their captive and their leader.

Margaret, Lady Bulmer, was in the later stages of pregnancy when she watched her husband carried off into the night. She had been raised in the traditional faith, as had her entire generation, and she probably sympathized with the rebels.[30] No evidence suggests that either she or her husband were more than conventionally pious; but, for most of the people of England, Henry VIII's church reforms had been unwelcome and unlooked for.[31] This was probably true for Margaret and her husband.

The Pilgrimage of Grace touched the lives of women the length and breadth of the country. Safe inside Windsor Castle's stout walls, Queen Jane Seymour discovered this to her cost. Henry VIII's third wife, whom Martin Luther considered 'an enemy of the gospel', had already made attempts to preserve the nunnery at Catesby in Northamptonshire.[32] While the manner in which the king should respond to the rebellion was debated and argued at court, the queen took more direct action. The usually mousy Jane threw herself on her knees before Henry and publicly begged him to restore the abbeys. Might the Pilgrimage not, after all, be God's response to Henry 'ruining so many churches'. The king thought not and ordered her to her feet, since 'he had often told her not to meddle with his affairs'. She was silenced by a pointed reminder of the fate of her predecessor as queen, which an onlooker considered 'enough to frighten a woman who is not very secure'.[33]

∽

As news of the rebellion spread, it struck terror into the hearts of some; but for others in Henry's kingdom, it raised hopes. Aske's rebels met with widespread sympathy and support in the North. They quickly took York, and by 20 October they were in control of much of Yorkshire. The following day, between 34,000 and 35,000 men were assembled at Pomfret Castle, a hitherto royal fortress which had been surrendered hastily by the sympathetic Lord Darcy. At the same time, the king had a much smaller army of only around 8,000 men under the command of the Duke of Norfolk at Doncaster. Norfolk, who was the son of the long dead Countess of Surrey, was on familiar turf in the North, yet the odds seemed overwhelming. He agreed to meet with the rebels and soon agreed terms with them. With a general pardon granted by a reluctant Henry and following a promise of a Parliament to further consider the Commons' demands, the rebels dispersed in December 1537 – and Sir John Bulmer returned home.

He rather hoped that the king would show mercy and take the uprising 'but for a dream'.[34] This was to prove impossible, when, on 16 January, parts of the North rose once again under the leadership of Sir John's nephew, Sir Francis Bigod. Bigod proved a poor commander; within days he had fled into the forest, heading in the direction of Cleveland. This was Bulmer's moment, in the eyes of his son-in-law Matthew Boynton, who wrote to spur him into action.[35] Might Bulmer not, he wrote, keep the people quiet in his own neighbourhood while, at the same time, search for the elusive rebel? If he managed this feat, Boynton was sure that Bulmer 'should have the greatest thanks of the king's highness that ever ye had in your life'. But it was advice that Bulmer did not follow.[36]

Sir John was naturally nervous and indecisive. The letter threw him into a quandary. Family loyalty pushed him towards Bigod, while good sense pressed him to serve the king. Both Margaret and the trusted family chaplain, William Stainhus, listened to Sir John's troubles. He should join with his nephew, they agreed, and raise the Commons once more if it looked as though rebellion was again to break out.[37] Margaret was days from giving birth and she was frightened for the future of her husband and family. She told him to flee England if the Commons would not rise, for she was sure that they would otherwise be parted. This was a prospect that neither could bear to contemplate. Yet, for the moment, Sir John followed his own counsel. As the people once again began to stir, he took steps to quell them, still hoping that way to secure the king's favour.[38] At the same time, he made a lacklustre attempt to track his nephew, quietly glad 'that matter was past help before word came to me'.[39] In the end, Bigod was arrested in February 1536.[40]

Margaret gave birth some time around 25 January, at Lastingham, Yorkshire.[41] It was the couple's first son together, and the event gave them a brief respite from the drama that was engulfing them. Towards the end of 1537, Bulmer's eldest son, Ralph, had gone to London on behalf of his father and step-mother to find out how matters were being handled there. His servant, Thomas Fulthorpe, came hurrying up to Lastingham as Margaret was lying in, having ridden fast from London. His news was terrifying. Ralph had discovered, he said, that 'the king hath rigged forth 30 ships with men and ordinance to come upon us and that my Lord of Norfolk is coming down'.[42]

Bigod's rebellion had been the excuse that Henry VIII needed to move against the rebels that he had previously pardoned. With Robert Aske and others imprisoned, rumours were flying around the capital. Aske had, reported Ralph to his timid father, 'accused diverse gentlemen', while Sir George Darcy had even 'accused his own father'. Do not 'stir out of the country for no fair letters nor words,' advised Ralph, for 'all is falsehood that then deal with'. Sir John took heed of his son's advice, writing frantically to his brother, Sir William Bulmer, to advise him to 'see that watch be laid along the sea coast with you and that beacons be in readiness and watch set through the country, for I fear me it is high time'. Sir John's trepidations were compounded when he – alone among his neighbours – was pointedly not invited to receive the Duke of Norfolk at Doncaster in February.[43]

As the weeks passed and Margaret recovered her strength following the birth, Sir John was still engaged in trying to keep the people around Lastingham quiet. They were far from happy with the king's lack of action over their demands and their leaders' attempts to clear themselves. This was a county-wide problem. Soon after Christmas, Lord Latimer, who had captained the rebels alongside Bulmer, decided to hurry south in a bid to clear his name. On the road, he received a message from the King's Council, ordering him to remain in the North until he was summoned. He soon had reason to be grateful for this command, when he learned at Stamford that the Commons, 'grieved at my coming up' (to London), had risen and broken into Snape Castle, taking his wife and children hostage and pilfering his goods.[44] It was only Latimer's rapid return northwards that saw the interlopers leave Snape. But soon he was forced to hurry away again, to meet the Duke of Norfolk at Doncaster.

The countryside must suddenly have seemed terrifying to a gentry anxious now to display their loyalty to the king. At Lastingham, the Bulmers were worried to find a number of treasonable documents circulating in the area. One proposed to kidnap both Sir John Bulmer and his brother, in a bid to force

Norfolk to keep his promises.[45] On all sides, they seemed to be beset by enemies. There was nothing that they could do but wait and pray that their activities during Bigod's rebellion went unnoticed.

In mid-March, a messenger arrived at the Bulmers' gates, carrying a summons for the couple to go to the king.[46] Immediately, the house was in uproar. Ralph – Bulmer's eyes at court – had just sent a message telling him that he 'should look well to himself, for, as far as he could perceive, all was falsehood that they were dealt withal'. The moment of their separation had surely come. No one who had been summoned to court that winter had returned home safely. They had all been put on trial. Matters were confirmed when, on 27 March 1538, twelve leaders of the Lincolnshire rebellion were sentenced to death.[47] Heeding his son's advice, Bulmer obtained permission from Norfolk to put off his journey, having been granted a deferment until Easter Saturday.[48]

The evidence of what happened next is reliant on a neighbouring parson's hearsay about hearsay from the Bulmers' servants, via a Rosedale farmer named Hugh Cramer. Supposedly, Margaret's husband declared furiously that 'he had leave be racked than to part from his wife'.[49] From this, the parson of Essington, John Watts, conceived a very negative picture of Margaret. He told the Bulmers' family chaplain, Stainhus, that he believed that Sir John was led by the 'counsel of a strong and arrant whore', who tempted him to treason because 'she is feared, that she should be departed him forever'. Putting words into Margaret's mouth during his conversation with Stainhus, Watts imagined her saying: 'Mr Bulmer, for my sake break a spear'. 'Like a doe,' Watts imagined Bulmer assuring her: 'Pretty Peg, I will never forsake thee.'

In order to encourage Bulmer, Watts believed, Margaret showed him 'things and trifles and makes him believe that he may do that thing that is impossible'. She was dangerous, he was sure. The parson warned Stainhus to 'take heed of yourself, and ye are a wanton priest, beware you fall not in love with her, for if ye do you will be made as wise as your master and both will be hanged then'. Stainhus replied that he did not think that she loved him much.

In Parson Watts's view, Margaret's beauty and the love and esteem in which her husband held her were dangerous – almost treasonous. Better evidence, in the shape of Bulmer's own testimony, suggests that Margaret initially counselled him to flee on hearing of the summons. In Palm Sunday week, with Norfolk's deadline looming, she begged him again to take ship with her to Scotland. Bulmer refused – and instead took the first steps towards rebellion.

Not long after this conversation, Sir John sent the loyal Stainhus to John, Lord Lumley, who lived nearby, before visiting him himself on Wednesday 28 March 1537.[50] Lumley was the obvious choice of ally for the desperate Bulmers. He was an old soldier, having served heroically at Flodden Field in 1513, and his house too had been invaded by the October rebels, who were seeking out the peer and his son, George, as their captains.[51] By March, George Lumley, who had become a commander in Bigod's rebellion, was imprisoned in the Tower of London.

Initial reports from Stainhus were certainly encouraging. He confirmed that Lumley had said that 'if he were commanded to come up he would bring 10,000 at his tail'.[52] During his own visit, Sir John offered an alliance with Lumley, even suggesting that they take up residence together 'till they might provide some way for themselves'. He may also have suggested that the pair capture the Duke of Norfolk.[53]

Sir John Bulmer was content with the way the interview went. On arriving back home, he informed his wife of his rebellious plans; as far as he was concerned, 'he was as good be slain and die in the field as be martyred as many was above at London'.[54]

This development was both troubling and hopeful for Margaret, who sought out Stainhus the following day. Did he, she asked, think that the people would rise again? When he did not answer, she declared boldly that she would rather be torn to pieces than go to London. She enquired, too, about other potential allies, asking whether the priest thought that 'Bartholomew Coteham or Parson Franke would raise any because he [Bulmer] was a captain [of the rebels] before'. She told Stainhus several times that if Norfolk's head were off, then the rebels could go where they would. The priest, for one, believed that Margaret enticed her husband into raising the commons again. From Thursday 29 March, it was a joint enterprise.

With only two days to go until their journey to London, the Bulmers had to act quickly. Although they were more likely motivated by fear of death, in planning a new rebellion they embraced the religious and social aims of the Pilgrimage: their cause was now that of traditional religion. But almost immediately, they suffered a setback when word reached them that Lord Lumley had fled. Anxious to acquire more allies, Sir John sent Stainhus to canvas the neighbouring clergy.[55] Margaret had originally suggested Parson Franke, who held a living in nearby Loftus. He had been one of Robert Aske's leading captains but was now lying low in his benefice until the trouble calmed down.[56] Stainhus met with both him and John Watts, the Essington parson, on Good Friday, in the hope that they could tell him of their parishioners' willingness to rise. They must surely have knowledge of this, believed the desperate Bulmers, by virtue of 'men's confessions'.

The interview did not go well. Franke appeared 'very angry' on being told that the Bulmers had sent a message.[57] 'He would hear none', he declared, before furiously denouncing his visitor to the town's rather lacklustre bailiff. Watts, too, was troubled, informing the chaplain: 'Sir, you are a priest, counsel your master to take heed of himself, and also take you heed, for surely you must be first hanged; for surely Sir William there is not one man in all England will take your master's part.'[58] The people were not about to rise for the Bulmers, and on the next morning Franke denounced them to the Duke of Norfolk.[59]

Margaret and Sir John's 'rebellion' failed even more emphatically than that of Sir Francis Bigod. They, and their lukewarm but loyal chaplain, were the only ones to actually rise. They were soon apprehended. On 8 April 1537, Norfolk wrote to King Henry from Newcastle, enclosing 'certain such confessions' that he had gathered concerning Sir John Bulmer and 'his pretended wife'.[60] He sent these to London, along with the persons of Margaret and Stainhus. The couple's worst fear had been realized: they were already parted. Sir John was sent separately to the Tower later that month.[61] It is not known whether Margaret, too, was then sent to the Tower; she may have been taken with Stainhus to the bleak Marshalsea prison.

Once in London, both Margaret and Sir John were interrogated. The knight held up well under questioning, doing little to implicate his wife. Her involvement had, in any event, been marginal. Nonetheless, as a female traitor, she was particularly notorious. When the pair were brought to trial, along with other rebels on 16 May, they pleaded guilty.[62] They may have done so to save Ralph Bulmer, who was arraigned with them but not convicted; but they failed to save themselves.

On Friday 25 May, Sir John Bulmer, along with a number of other gentlemen and churchmen who had been unwise enough to involve themselves in the Pilgrimage, were taken to their deaths at Tyburn. Sir John and Sir Stephen Hamilton were relatively fortunate, since their sentences were commuted to hanging and post-mortem decapitation. The others were disembowelled and cut to pieces. The heads of all the men were set on London Bridge and the other gates of the city.[63]

For Margaret, a far worse fate awaited later that day. She, like the men before her, was strapped to a low hurdle and dragged through the streets of the city to Smithfield, amid the jeering throng. As she was untied and staggered to her feet, she could see that a pyre of wood had already been erected. Once there, she was tied to a stake at the centre and burnt.[64] It was an agonizingly slow death and one that reflected the king's rage at her actions.

∞

Margaret Cheyne's life, from her colourful extra-marital relationship to eventual rebellion against her king, defied the orthodoxies for women of the time. It was not a life propelled by religiosity. Yet, in the end her cause became that of defending traditional religion against – as she saw it – the damage being done to it and to its place in the social fabric of communities, in the aftermath of Henry's break with Rome. Her sense of dislocation was shared by many.

She would not be the only woman in Tudor England to die in the flames for her faith. But not all of them wanted to defend tradition; there were those who wished for a much more thoroughgoing turn away from the Church of Rome, and who threatened Henry's regime and religious settlement from another flank. And they included Anne Askew.[65]

14

OF BIBLES AND BURNINGS

Joan Bocher, Anne Askew and Catherine Parr

The idea of the scriptures being available in English had always made Henry VIII nervous. That they should be read and mediated by anyone other than an educated elite, conversant with Latin, was dangerous, since it opened the way to challenges and questions. William Tyndale, who had in exile prepared an English translation of the New Testament, was burned for his efforts. Yet, among the raft of changes sweeping the country in the 1530s, an official English Bible did emerge in 1539 – ironically drawing heavily on Tyndale.

But, Henry's worries proved correct. A Bible, in English, fostered debate – and people kept reading and questioning. Opinions proliferated, too many for a monarch who was now officially head of the Church. It seemed wise to rein things in. Among the other items on the agenda during the Parliament of 1543 was an important Bill, close to the king's own heart. The Act for the Advancement of True Religion passed easily on 12 May 1543.[1] Among its terms, henceforth no woman below the rank of noblewoman or gentlewoman was to read the Bible in English; and those permitted to continue, should do it only in private. Great swathes of Englishwomen were suddenly criminalized; but many kept on reading either at home or in public. Anne Askew was one. Joan Bocher was another.

Religious reformers during Henry VIII's reign strongly promoted the publication of the scriptures in English, since they wanted to strip away the centuries of Church interpretation that, in their eyes, had come between the Word of God and their faith. For women in particular, who were rarely taught Latin and almost never Greek, an English Bible shone a light into hitherto dark areas. For the first time, a woman with a reasonable level of learning could read and understand the scriptures in which she was raised, and some revelled in the experience. Joan Bocher was one such woman.

∞

Vain, at times, but single-minded, on reading the Bible for herself, Joan Bocher was entirely persuaded that her interpretation was correct.[2] With the fervour of a missionary, she set to work in a hostile land to spread her faith. Joan trod a dangerous, uncertain path, at times using aliases as she travelled from place to place, reliant on the goodwill and financial support of the people to whom she preached. Although mostly recorded as 'Joan Bocher',[3] sometimes she was 'Joan Baron',[4] sometimes 'Joan Knell'.[5] She was sometimes even 'Joan of Kent'.

Joan appears suddenly in the records in the 1540s, when she was already in trouble for her fervent beliefs. Her early life is obscure.[6] She had a husband at one time, living with him in the tiny hamlet of Westbere, which lay a few miles from Canterbury.[7] Even then, thanks to her reading of the Bible and the contact that she had with others who held reformist beliefs, she had become convinced of the new ways.[8] She was certainly well travelled. Perhaps her husband was a merchant, which would account for why she was able to move around more widely in England than others of her class. She was no gentlewoman, but she could read and write and had a good understanding.

Joan did not have to wait for Henry's Great Bible of 1539. Merchant contacts could also explain how she was earlier able to obtain a copy of the 'heretical' Tyndale English New Testament. She became noted as 'a great reader of Scriptures', and soon was a great disseminator too.[9] Bocher was later charged with being 'the principal instrument' by which Tyndale's Bibles were distributed when they arrived in England, smuggled in bales of cloth. Her new faith brought her connections to some of the more influential and religiously radical women of the court, and she made herself useful to them: taking up several New Testaments at once, she carefully bound them with string beneath the layers of her dress, before boldly walking into court with her hidden wares, where they were hurriedly distributed.

Joan was right to be covert. The growth in the reform move-ment, which would ultimately develop into Protestantism, was an unexpected side-effect of Henry VIII's break with Rome. England, in the 1530s, was led by a king still largely traditional in his beliefs; he was a schismatic rather than a heretic. Once, at Colchester, Joan was required to publicly abjure her faith, returning to the traditional church of her youth.[10] Perhaps she was influenced in this by her husband, who took care to inform the parson at Westbere and their neighbours of what had occurred.[11] He died soon afterwards, and his widow abjured her abjuration.

By late 1540 or early 1541, Joan Bocher was living in Frittenden, close to her former parish. She was as bluntly out-spoken as ever, declaring on one occasion that 'matins and evensong was no better than rumbling of tubs'. These tradi-tional ceremonies were not in the scriptures as she understood them, and so she had little respect for them. Even the reform-ist Archbishop Cranmer – who had, himself, broken Church rules with a secret marriage – found Bocher's behaviour 'offen-sive'.[12] Unsurprisingly, there were soon mutterings of heresy against her. On being evicted by her landlord, she packed up her belongings and made for Canterbury.

The walled city of Canterbury seemed a metropolis to the people of the countryside around it, drawing them in. It had always been the centre of the English Church, and Joan, too, was attracted by the place's spirituality. She went at once to the house of John Toftes in Westgate, close to an imposing and castle-like gateway into the city. It was a crowded neighbourhood and one in which she was right at home.

Gossip in the city was that Toftes was 'a common maintainer and harbourer of persons accused of heresies, and of persons who have made themselves priests and were none'. Certainly, his house was well frequented by religious radicals and subversives. One, Giles Barham, had been a monk of Dover, but now he presented himself improperly as a priest. He had recently heard confessions in Lent and taken the service in the church at Northgate.[13] Another character was the parson of Hothfield, who claimed that the Virgin was neither the queen of Heaven nor more important than any other woman, being only the 'bag' in which Christ grew.[14] Such an offbeat belief resonated with Joan, who found her own ways to show her contempt for the established Church. On Easter morning, she and another radical, John Clerk, prepared a calf's head for their breakfast in Toftes' house – feasting when they should have been fasting. They wanted to provoke. For Joan, true religion was only what she could read in the scriptures; and in Toftes' house she found an environment in which she was able to experiment, and to learn and display her faith as the equal of the men around her.

Joan's conduct could not be ignored indefinitely by the authorities. Heresy had long been a capital offence in England, with such trials always high-level matters.[15] Since the early fifteenth century, the prescribed punishment was burning, if the heretic did not abjure their beliefs. It was on the charge of heresy that Joan was arrested and imprisoned in late 1540 or early 1541. She did not deny it, when questioned. Showing her contempt 'with many slanderous words', she signed her own confession, declaring that she refuted the miracle of transubstantiation: the bread and wine of the sacrament were not, she asserted, transformed into the body and blood of Christ.[16] Such a view was, and always would be, heresy in the church under Henry VIII. Joan held steadfastly to her beliefs for two long, miserable years in her gaol cell.

Finally, early in 1543, Joan Bocher was taken to trial in a criminal court. Surprisingly, no evidence was offered against her, in spite of the existence of her own proud confession.[17] But this was not the end of the matter, and Joan was then taken before the Church commissary court for the diocese of Canterbury. This was the archbishop's own court, with the power of life and death over those that were sentenced there.

All was, perhaps, not lost, because Joan had already made strong connections among Canterbury's reformist circles, which extended right to the very top of the Church. Indeed, she may already have been acquainted with Cranmer's personally appointed commissary, Christopher Nevinson, before whom she was now brought. He was a Cambridge-educated lawyer, married to Cranmer's niece; he was also as reformist in his sympathies as his patron and determined to use his office to benefit his co-religionists.[18]

Joan's defence rested on a royal proclamation, issued on 26 February 1539, in which the king showed remarkable restraint towards those 'who have been seduced by Anabaptists and Sacramentaries coming from abroad and mean to return to the Catholic Church'.[19] She, in her denial of the transubstantiation, was certainly a Sacramentary. She also associated with Anabaptists and may already have come round to their unorthodox views on the role of the Virgin Mary in Christ's divinity. Had she been willing to express herself desirous of returning to the traditional Church, then the proclamation should have been enough to save her. Reviewing his prisoner, but without similarly appraising the evidence, Nevinson immediately declared her 'guiltless'. She was free to go – almost.

John Milles, one of the cathedral canons, was watching proceedings and was not best pleased with Nevinson's loose approach to the law.[20] He knew, as did everyone there, that Joan had not abandoned her heretical beliefs. Stepping forward, he declared loudly: 'Mr Commissioner ye do not well to deliver her by proclamation, for her own confession hath condemned her.'[21] This was an unexpected intervention, and Nevinson asked: 'Be you all able to prove that you have spoken?' Milles could, pointing out: 'Sir, her own confession is in your registry.' Nevinson, however, had thought of that: 'I have enquired for them, but I cannot find them. But I will look them out, for shorting of the matter.' With that, he was forced to adjourn proceedings. Joan Bocher, who kept quiet throughout, was still in danger.

Shortly afterwards, Nevinson summoned Milles to him. He could not find Joan's confession, he said, implying that the matter should be dropped. Milles was not about to let a heretic go free, and he searched for the conveniently mislaid document himself; on finding it, he returned triumphant to the commissary. They read it together, Nevinson – presumably – with a sinking heart.

The next time the court sat, Nevinson reluctantly declared Joan a heretic, both by her confession and witnesses. Boldly, she 'utterly denied' this to the court. 'You cannot deny it', said the commissary. He had read the evidence himself. John Toftes had, by then, arrived to speak in Joan's defence, although it is less than clear how valuable the support of a well-known heretic was to her. He was himself under investigation for complaining that it was idolatry to kneel before the host as he went to church that Easter. But Joan was not about to go down without a fight. From her clothing, she produced a copy of the king's proclamation, offering to abjure and return to the official Church in accordance with its terms.

Again, this concession should have been enough to save her; but Milles had been carrying out his own investigations. He produced the parson of Westbere, as well as two of his parishioners, and all three gave evidence that they had heard Joan's husband say that she was abjured at Colchester.[22] As the king's proclamation applied only once, Nevinson must have been wringing his hands by this stage. 'Do you know it for truth that she was abjured?' he asked the witnesses sharply. 'No,' they all agreed, 'but thus said her husband.' He was grasping at straws, but this uncertainty was just enough for Nevinson to order that no further witnesses be heard, before releasing Joan on the authority of the proclamation.

It was a farce of a proceeding, after which the religious conservatives in Canterbury grumbled. The order that Joan be acquitted had probably come from Cranmer himself, who shared some of her views. Her name featured repeatedly in depositions relating to the so-called Prebendaries' Plot against Cranmer which erupted in 1543 – an attempt by the conservatives in Canterbury to bring down the archbishop and have him declared a heretic.[23] So, too, did Christopher Nevinson's, with his failure to prosecute Joan held up as particularly lamentable. Cranmer survived, but afterwards he was rather more careful. Joan, too, laid low for a time. She did, however, continue to maintain strong links with other religious radicals – and her 'nearest friendship' was with Anne Askew.[24]

Church courts

Tucked away in the south-west corner of Chester Cathedral is a small room, which, in the early seventeenth century, was furnished and fitted out as a court. The bishop's consistory court, which had jurisdiction over matrimonial and probate disputes, sat there until the early twentieth century. It survives today as the oldest English church courtroom.

On a throne, looking down at the assembly, would have sat the judge, while the accused would have stood before a wooden table, in a space enclosed by wooden panels.[25] As an institution, the consistory court of Chester is older still, its cases heard by the bishop in the sixteenth century. Similar bodies sat in other jurisdictions throughout the period.

The Church courts existed alongside their civil counterparts.[26] As well as regulating the clergy, they were given powers to enquire into the bedchambers of the people of Tudor England, with authority to deal with a wide range of moral and religious improprieties. Even those who lived far from the courtrooms were not immune to their gaze, since the court could – and did – go on circuit, with cases heard in churches and other spaces within the parish.[27] Women were called before the courts in similar numbers to men; indeed, many people in Tudor England at some stage found themselves before a church court.

Church attendance was a major concern for the courts. In Colchester in 1542, William Makyn and his wife Katherine were accused of keeping 'a common ale-house', to which 'light persons' of the parish would come to play bowling or skittles at times when they should have been in church.[28] They were warned many times by the parish constables but did not amend their behaviour. The couple were hauled before the bishop's court in London, where Katherine was named as the ringleader of the offenders. She was subject to the additional charge of failing to attend divine service more than four times a year, because of her need to be in her ale-house.

Allowances could be made for necessity. Margery Alexander of Waterstock, in Oxfordshire, would – her son assured the archdeacon's court in 1584 – love to come to church more regularly. But, as he lamented, his mother was 'a very old woman and not able at all times to come to the church, but doth as orderly come to the church as orderly as any other doth when her body will serve her'.[29] The outcome of her case is not recorded.

The Church courts frequently dealt with matters of

public morality. It was, for example, a matter for the Church courts if a wife refused to live with her husband, as was the case with Margaret Alanson of Coppingford, Huntingdonshire, who was recorded as leaving her spouse to move to nearby Stanground in 1514.[30] And Church courts also monitored the chastity of both men and women.

In a 1584 example, again from the archdeacon's court in Oxfordshire, reports were investigated that Richard Beckley of Newton Purcell and Elizabeth Wilkins of Heath were lovers. Beckley strenuously denied it; He had never known Wilkins carnally nor 'attempted her honesty', he assured the court.[31] Nonetheless, they required him to do penance in front of some of his neighbours within a fortnight. One John King, of Duns Tew, Oxfordshire, caused a local scandal that same year with his amorous attentions towards a neighbour, Ursula Saule. In this case, he was at least able to assure the archdeacon's court that 'he doth owe goodwill unto Ursula Saule in the ways of marriage and intendeth to marry her at Michaelmas next

when he hath provided a living for her'.[32] He achieved a happier outcome than Richard Beckley had done: King's protestations that he saw Ursula only in public and that the relationship was not yet consummated satisfied the court.

On 7 October 1558, Thomas Hoghton brought a matrimonial case before the consistory court of Chester, alleging his wife's adultery with a man named Guy Holland.[33] Katherine Hoghton strongly disputed her husband's version of events, declaring that the witnesses he had brought to support his case were his own illegitimate half-sisters and thus far from impartial. Was this true, the court asked one John Osboston of Blackburn, who arrived as a witness and had known the couple for decades? He agreed that the first witness – Anne Procter – was indeed a 'near friend to Thomas Hoghton articulate & bastard sister to the said Thomas as she is commonly named & taken'. As for the other witness, Alice Singleton, he agreed that 'by the common name and fame of the country' she was indeed Thomas's sister, although 'whether she be enemy to Katherine Hoghton or what she has deposed in the matter his deponent knows not'. Osboston himself seemed anxious to keep his involvement in the whole unhappy business to a minimum. He was, however, sure that he had never heard rumours that Katherine was guilty of 'breaking her wedlock'. On the contrary, he believed her to be a woman of much honesty and good condition'.

Katherine was evidently furious to hear the accusations against her. She took her own actions, bringing a case of defamation against her husband in January 1559 for his use of his sisters as witnesses against her.[34] One of her own witnesses, one Christopher Walmsley of Blackburn, who had known her for fourteen years and her husband since his childhood, fully supported her, considering that 'he thinks and

credibly believes that the said Katherine Hoghton is not culpable of the crime that is now here laid against her and further things that the said Katherine with a pure conscience may make her lawful purgation thereof'. The Sheriff of Chester, too, who was a family friend, also told the court that 'she was honest and virtuous as ever he saw woman'.[35]

Katherine Hoghton was lucky, in that she was able to produce a number of influential witnesses to support her position. While the Church courts could not order imprisonment, they could refer individuals to the criminal courts to be punished; and they had the power to require public penance to be made, something which was particularly shameful to women, whose social position was tied up with perceptions of their moral character.

∞

Anne Askew's family had survived the ructions of the Pilgrimage of Grace. They were upstanding members of Tudor society; one of Anne's brothers served as Sheriff of Lincolnshire in 1544,

1. *The Family of Henry VII with St George and the Dragon*, c.1505.
Tudor parents often took steps to memorialize their deceased children.
Here, the children of Henry VII and Elizabeth of York are shown as
adults, even those who died in infancy.

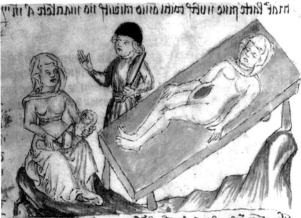

2. A late fifteenth-century image of a woman undergoing a caesarean section. Inevitably fatal, caesarean sections were only carried out on deceased mothers in the Tudor period in the hope of preserving the child for baptism.

3. Death stalked the nurseries of Tudor England, as shown here in a depiction of Death snatching away a wetnurse and a baby in the *The Danse Macabre of Women*.

4. Late sixteenth-century swaddling bands. Many children possessed a 'best' set of swaddling bands for special occasions, such as this example, which once belonged to a high-status child.

5. Peter Bruegel's famous *Children's Games*, 1560. The painting depicts scores of games, including hide-and-seek, leap frog, stilt-walking, handstands and a mock wedding.

6. Arbella Stuart, great-great-granddaughter of Henry VII, depicted as a toddler with her doll.

7. A stained glass window depicting Elizabeth Tylney, Countess of Surrey, from Long Melford, Suffolk. The Countess oversaw the education and upbringing of a number of noble girls entrusted to her care.

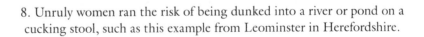

8. Unruly women ran the risk of being dunked into a river or pond on a cucking stool, such as this example from Leominster in Herefordshire.

9. For Tudor girls, embroidery and sewing were essential parts of their early education. Girls such as Jane Bostocke, who created this work, would produce a sampler to practise their stitching.

10. Upper-class Tudor women wore layers of elaborate and restrictive clothing. This corset, from Elizabeth I's funeral effigy at Westminster Abbey, probably belonged to the queen and dates to around 1600.

11. Many early Tudor women took vows of perpetual widowhood, putting on a black gown and white veil. Here, Henry VII's mother, Margaret Beaufort, is shown as a vowess.

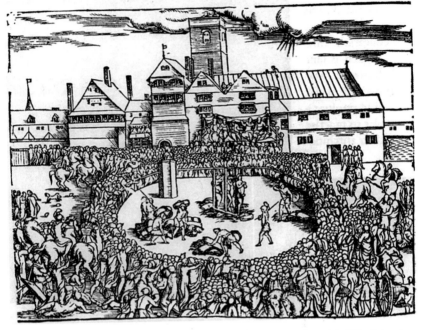

12. The burning of Anne Askew at Smithfield from John Foxe's *Acts and Monuments*. Askew was not the only woman to die for her faith in Tudor England.

13. The Protestant Rose Hickman, a merchant's wife, chose exile rather than martyrdom when the Catholic Mary I acceded to the throne. Rose spent the years of Mary's reign in Antwerp, returning to England following Mary's death.

14. The recusant Margaret Clitherow, a young butcher's wife from York, was pressed to death in March 1586 for harbouring Catholic priests. Clitherow was canonized as a Catholic martyr in 1870.

The most wonderfull

and true storie, of a certaine Witch named *Alse Gooderige* of Stapen hill, who was arraigned and conuicted at Darbie at the *Assises* there.

As also a true report of the strange torments of Thomas Darling, *a boy of thirteene yeres of age, that was possessed by the Deuill, with his horrible fittes and terrible Apparitions by him vttered at* Burton vpon Trent *in the Countie of* Stafford, *and of his maruellous deliuerance.*

Printed at London for I. O. 1597.

BIBLIOTHECA

15. The title page of *The Most Wonderfull and True Storie, of a certaine Witch named Alse Gooderidge*, 1597. The bewitching of Thomas Darling in Derbyshire in 1596 caused a sensation, with the 'witch of Stapenhill' and her daughter, Alice Gooderidge, soon apprehended and imprisoned.

16. A commanding image of Elizabeth I, known as the Darnley portrait. It was painted in *c*.1575, when she was in her early forties, around the time of her marriage negotiations with the Duke of Alençon.

17. A posthumous image of Elizabeth I. Time sleeps on her right-hand side, whilst Death looks over her left shoulder. In her left hand she holds a copy of the Prayer Book.

while her other brother, Edward, was employed in Archbishop Cranmer's household.[36]

When Anne was still a child, her father had arranged a marriage for her older sister with Thomas Kyme, the son and heir of a wealthy neighbour.[37] Money exchanged hands, and Sir William Askew was unwilling to abandon the match on his daughter's sudden death; rather, he simply substituted his second daughter for his first. Anne Askew had no wish to wed Thomas Kyme, later declaring that she was 'compelled against her will or free consent to marry with him'. What pressure was brought to bear on her is unknown, but it was sufficient for her to succumb, and she would duly bear her husband two children.

Like Joan Bocher, Anne Askew was inspired by the changes around her. She acquired an English Bible and, in her spare moments, would often sit and read. Being a gentlewoman, and thus a cut above Joan Bocher socially, Anne was legally permitted to continue reading the Bible in English, following the 1543 Act, so long as she did so in private. It had a profound effect on her. As she later confessed, she 'fell clearly from all old superstition of papistry, to a perfect belief in Jesus Christ'.[38] It was an epiphany, and she was vocal about it. Soon, she had so offended the priests in the neighbourhood that they complained to her husband, who was embarrassed and angry about his upstart wife. He turned on her, violently driving her out of the house.

Anne's marriage had long been unhappy, and her dissatisfaction with her husband was wrapped up in her faith, for, as she later admitted, she 'could not think him worthy of her marriage which so spitefully hated God the chief author of marriage'.[39] Now, having lost her home, her children and her status, she turned all her energies towards God.

On being warned that, as she recalled, 'there was bent against me, three score priests at Lincoln', she nevertheless resolved to go there.[40] She spent six days in the county town, looking for confrontation. She found it when, on going to the cathedral to read the Bible, she was surrounded by angry priests. She was probably reading aloud the text and adding her own interpretative gloss. It was unacceptable that a woman should so take it upon herself to teach in church; but she got away with it, for the priests merely 'went they their ways again without words speaking'. Anne was brim-full of confidence, later declaring to the Bishop of London that 'I would wish, that all men knew my conversation and living in all points, for I am so sure of myself this hour, that there are none able to prove any dishonesty by me.'[41] She resolved to find a bigger stage – and to go to London.

Anne travelled the long road towards the capital in the company of her loyal maidservant.[42] The pair took lodgings in a house close to the Temple, the legal centre of London, where Anne was even able to impress her neighbour, one Mr Wadloe, 'a great papist'.[43] Peeking at her through the window, he was surprised to see a woman, whom he suspected of heresy rising at midnight to pray for hours. Why, he later admitted, she was 'the devoutest and godliest woman' that he had ever known.[44] Others thought so too.

London in the 1540s, rather than Canterbury, was the centre of the religious reform movement in England. While most parts of the country still remained – largely – traditional in their thought and practice, the capital was filled with radicals, such as the family of Rose Hickman. In around 1610, the eighty-five-year-old Rose sat down to write her memoirs, 'to be perused by her children and posterity'.[45] She was a twice-widowed merchant's daughter, raised against a backdrop of London trade and religious controversy. Her father, the London merchant William Locke, had won a small measure of lasting fame – and his daughter's eternal pride – when he braved a papal curse at Dunkirk in around 1534 in order to tear down a paper against Henry VIII and his divorce.[46]

It was Locke who sent reformist texts to his wife from across the sea, allowing Rose's mother to (as her daughter recalled) 'call me with my 2 sisters into her chamber to read to us out of the same good books very privately for fear of trouble because those good books were then accounted heretical'. The danger was very real. Only a few streets away, one Paginton, 'who used to bring English Bibles from beyond sea', was shot dead as he walked close to his home.[47] On hearing of this, Rose's mother hurriedly hid the books a little better, telling her daughters 'to say nothing of her reading to us for fear of trouble'. Women such as Rose Hickman's mother were at the forefront of the revolution in faith that was happening in Henry VIII's capital city.

Anne Askew may have drawn spiritual sustenance from the English Bible, but she had no means of material support. To improve her circumstances, she sent her maid out among the London apprentices to beg funds.[48] She also made use of her own connections, in particular seeking out her younger sister, who had married George St Paul, an official in the household of the Duke of Suffolk.[49] Catherine Willoughby, Duchess of Suffolk, was in her mid-twenties and thus only a year or so older than Anne. She was also well-known to be interested in religious reform, and may well have been one of the court ladies who gratefully received Joan Bocher's smuggled Bibles.

Soon 'diverse gentlewomen' were supplying Anne with money. On at least one occasion, a man with a blue coat arrived with 10 shillings and a message from the Countess of Hertford. Another visitor – this time in a violet coat – brought money from Lady Denny, wife of Sir Anthony Denny.[50] Anne, who had re-adopted her maiden name of Askew and was seeking a divorce (for which there was little chance of success), found herself accepted into the very highest circles in the land.[51] These ladies were the intimate friends of Henry VIII's new wife: the former Lady Latimer, Catherine Parr.

Following the Pilgrimage of Grace, Lord Latimer had settled with his wife on 'such small lands' as he had in the south.[52] He died in London early in 1543, but his attractive and intelligent young widow had already caught the king's eye. Catherine had been raised at court and she knew Henry well.[53] And the king, since the execution of his adulterous fifth wife, Catherine Howard, in 1542, was unattached. Henry's attentions could not be denied.

Catherine Parr was a reluctant bride, later writing of her marriage that 'God withstood my will therein most vehemently for a time, and through his grace and goodness, made that possible which seemed to me most impossible; that was, made me renounce utterly mine own will, and to follow his will most willingly.' She viewed her queenship as the will of God.

Catherine's sympathies were with the reformers. In 1545, she became the first Englishwoman to publish under her own name, releasing her *Prayers; or, Meditations*. She was also involved in the translation of Erasmus's *Paraphrases upon the New Testament*, a work that would later be considered heretical. Zealous in her faith, she wrote that she would gladly abandon her 'life, honour, riches' or anything else that she possessed 'to win any man to Christ, of what degree, or sort soever he were'.[54] Inadvertently, it seemed, Henry VIII had married a religious radical. The conservatives at court, who were in the ascendancy in the mid-1540s, were outraged.

'To live chaste from this time forward'

When Catherine Parr married Henry VIII, she was still relatively young but had already been widowed twice; and shortly after Henry's death in 1547, she would marry one last time. It was a sign of the times, for things had not always been so. Such a proliferation of marriages was not encouraged in the pre-Reformation Church. Rather, the idea of the chaste widow was held up as something morally superior to the status of the married woman – although still lagging behind the purity of the virgin.[55] As a result, widows were coaxed by their bishops and local clergy to forsake a new husband and instead take a vow of widowhood.

On the appointed day, dressed in her usual clothes, the prospective vowess made her way to church, where she attended a service given by the diocesan bishop. Then, in front of all assembled, she made her vow.[56] The wording was usually very similar for each vowess. Joan Plumpton, a widow in 1480, promised before one of the suffragan bishops in the diocese of York 'to live chaste from this time forward', making the sign of the cross with her hands.[57] Six years later, another widow, Agnes Hunt, promised the Archbishop of York that she would 'be chaste of my body and truly and devoutly shall keep me chaste from this time forward as long as my life lasteth after the rule of St Paul'.[58]

The vowess brought a bundle of clothes with her to church, which she then presented to the bishop to be blessed and sprinkled with holy water. That done, she changed into her black gown and her white veil and mantle, which entirely obscured her hair and neck. She put on a ring, too, as a mark of her new status. The widows taking these vows were not nuns, and they were not required to shut themselves away from the world; but their vows were demonstrations of their new commitment to God. Taking the vow was a popular choice for early Tudor widows, at all levels of society.[59]

Very occasionally, if a woman had the right contacts, it was not necessary to actually wait to be widowed to take such a vow of chastity. Portraits of Henry VII's formidable mother, Margaret Beaufort, Countess of Richmond, show her in the garb of a vowess, kneeling at prayer or reading from a religious text.[60] Margaret, who died in 1509, had been a driving force behind Henry VII's successful claim to the throne. As such, she always remained one of his closest advisers, being officially made a *femme sole* by Act of Parliament early in the reign.[61] She gained the consent of her husband, Thomas Stanley, Earl of Derby, to take a vow before

John Fisher, Bishop of Rochester, to 'with all my heart promise from henceforth the chastity of my body. That is never to use my body having actual knowledge of man after the common usage in matrimony.'[62] She reaffirmed the vow when she was actually widowed, in 1504.

Unlike Margaret, some women later came to regret an over-hasty decision to take this binding vow – a promise from which only the pope could release them.[63] Given the long widowhoods that some women endured, a decision made in a moment of grief could seem a much less good idea years later. Jane, Lady Barantine, would find this in 1542, when her marriage to Sir William Barantine was called into question.[64]

She had, she admitted, taken a vow before a bishop when she was 'almost besides herself with sorrow' over the death of her earlier husband, Sir Arthur Pole. The choice of a vow had been strongly encouraged by her brother-in-law, Lord Montague, who wanted to ensure that her inheritance from her father passed only to her children by Pole. Montague had taken her to the church at Bisham, outside her own diocese. But she was, she later claimed, already having doubts, telling the Bishop of St Asaph, who was officiating: 'If I may take it upon me for a season and leave it at my pleasure I am content to take it upon me, or else not.' On being assured 'God forbid else, Madam, for all religious persons have a time of probation', she duly took the vow. She had changed her mind within two days, returning to her secular garb. Nevertheless, she was later subject to an enquiry into her children's legitimacy thanks to her over-hasty promise.

∽

It was not long before Anne Askew, now in London, came to the attention of the authorities.[65] In March 1545, she was taken to be examined at Saddler's Hall, to be charged with violating

Henry VIII's Act of the Six Articles (1539), which had been passed in order to make deviation from the official tenets of the English Church a civil offence.[66] The primary accusation against Anne – that she denied the miracle of the sacrament – was also one of heresy; but it was before the civil rather than religious authorities that she was first examined, being brought before a royal commissioner who was tasked with examining her beliefs.[67]

Although still only twenty-four years of age, Anne was fearless.[68] When asked whether, as she said, 'I did not believe that the sacrament hanging over the altar was the very body of Christ really', she turned the interrogation around, enquiring: 'Wherefore St Stephen was stoned to death?' When her interrogator admitted 'he could not tell', she said that 'no more would I assoil his vain question'. She was cocky, self-assured, bold – and this was not how a woman was supposed to behave. She readily quoted the scriptures, and evaded anything too incriminating.[69] When asked whether she had the spirit of God within her, she answered: 'If I had not, I was but a reprobate or cast away.' When questioned again on the sacrament, she begged only that her interviewers would 'hold me excused concerning that matter'.[70]

Anne was then taken to Sir Martin Bowes, Lord Mayor of London.[71] Tell me, he asked, trying a different tack, 'whether a mouse eating the host, received God or no?' Anne said nothing, 'but smiled'.[72] The Bishop of London's chancellor, who was also present, was annoyed. She was, he said, 'much to blame for uttering the scriptures'. Her sex counted against her, 'for St Paul,' he said, 'forbade women to speak or to talk of the word of God'. She dismissed this comment: 'I knew Paul's meaning so well as he' – the Bible only barred women from instructing a congregation. She then used her sex to her advantage, commenting that 'he ought to find no fault in poor women, except they have offended the law'. The men who examined her found her infuriating, with the result that the lord mayor abruptly ordered her imprisonment – and refused to accept her sureties for her release.[73]

Anne spent the next twelve days in prison, permitted to speak only to the priest who visited her daily.[74] He had been sent by Edmund Bonner, Bishop of London, a notable conservative. The priest, although mild in his questioning, could get nothing from her. Finally, on 23 March 1545, she was permitted to receive a visit from a cousin, who was attempting to bail her.[75] Thanks to his efforts, it was agreed that she would be examined again on 25 March, before the bishop himself. Everyone hoped that she would abjure and thus secure her release.

Bonner came armed with a declaration of orthodox faith for her to sign.[76] When asked whether she agreed with it, Anne confirmed that 'I believe so much thereof, as the holy scripture doth agree to', and she asked him to add that as a line. Furious, the bishop retorted, as Anne recalled, 'that I should not teach him what he should write'. She then took the paper and wrote 'I Anne Askew do believe all manner of things contained in the faith of the Catholic Church', throwing Bishop Bonner into such a fury that it was all Anne's cousin could do to persuade him she acted only from her 'weak woman's wit'. She was then sent back to prison for a night, before being released the next day. The authorities claimed that she had abjured; she denied it. Regardless, she was soon busy in London promoting her faith.

Anne also continued to seek her divorce, with such a suit unusual enough for the Privy Council to become involved. On 24 May 1546, they issued letters to both Anne and Thomas Kyme, ordering them to appear before them within ten days of receipt.[77] Kyme duly came, making the long journey from Lincolnshire to the Council chamber at Greenwich.[78] Anne was brought in too, to face 'Master Kyme'. The Council began to question them on their relationship. Anne replied tartly that 'my lord chancellor knew already my mind in that matter'. When her co-operation was insisted upon – on the king's own authority

– she said she would speak only to the king. After all, she said, King Solomon had taken the time to hear the suit of two poor women. Eventually, though, she relented. Master Kyme was not her husband, she insisted, although she, as they recorded, could not give any 'honest allegation' to justify the separation.

The questioning then turned to the real reason that she had been summoned. Pitted against Stephen Gardiner, the wily but very learned Bishop of Winchester, Anne was questioned on the sacrament. 'Make a direct answer', he insisted, in a tense exchange that lasted more than five hours.[79] 'I would not sing a new song to the lord in a strange land', she replied, only to be told that she spoke in parables by Gardiner, the leader of the court conservatives. You are a parrot, he declared when she continued to evade him. She replied that she was 'ready to suffer all things at his hands'. Weary of her intransigence, her interrogators committed her to Newgate prison.

Anne arrived at a gaol already centuries old and creaking with years of deterioration and neglect. Venerable, dilapidated Newgate was a harrowing place. It was crammed with souls, a perilous hive of disease, in which criminals, debtors and religious prisoners like Anne were stuffed into fetid corridors and filthy cells. Sometimes, prisoners were fettered in irons; bars connected their wrists and ankles, which were in turn attached to a collar around their necks. They were then pinned back to the wall. Being locked in this awkward pose for any length of time was agonizing. The road from Newgate led directly to Smithfield's execution site, which was enough to strike fear into the hearts of the condemned. There was little light or fresh air in the stinking conditions, and prisoners depended on friends on the outside for their food and clothing.[80]

Anne was ordered back before the Council the next day. Once again, she was examined by Bishop Gardiner, who declared to her that she would be burnt.[81] 'I had searched all the scriptures,' said Anne, 'yet could I never find there that either Christ or his

Apostles put any creature to death.' It was an uncomfortable meeting, since she recognized John Dudley (Lord Lisle) and William Parr (Earl of Essex), brother of the queen, who accompanied the bishop. Turning to them, Anne pointed out 'that it was great shame for them to counsel contrary to their knowledge'. They merely muttered 'that they would gladly all things were well'. She had suddenly become very dangerous to Queen Catherine and her reform-minded circle. The examinations continued over several days, until Anne fell sick in the unhealthy Newgate air. She still would not give a straight answer.

∽

On 18 June 1546, Anne came to trial at London's Guildhall, alongside Dr Shaxton, the former Bishop of Salisbury, a London gentleman named Nicholas White, who had been caught printing heretical books, and an Essex tailor called John Adams.[82] Sir Martin Bowes headed a panel of noblemen, churchmen and justices, who surveyed their four prisoners. Did they 'deny the sacrament to be Christ's body and blood'? The three men confessed that they did. Anne, too, had resolved finally to be direct about her faith, answering 'yea'. Christ is in Heaven, she declared, provocatively, 'and as for that ye call your God, is but a piece of bread. For a more proof thereof (mark it when ye list) let it lie in the box but three months, and it will be mould, and so turn to nothing that is good. Whereupon I am persuaded, that it cannot be God.' She was sentenced to burn. The following day, the Privy Council sent a message to Thomas Kyme, who had been cooling his heels in London. He should return home: he was no longer needed.[83]

Back in Newgate, Anne began to make preparations for death. She was surprised, on the Tuesday after her trial, to be bundled into a litter. Carried hurriedly in the quiet of the early morning, she was taken to an inn marked with the sign of a crown over its door. There, she found Sir Richard Rich, one of the king's Council, and Bishop Bonner. Tucked away from prying eyes, the two men tried 'with all their power and flattering words' to persuade her to recant.[84] At some point, the newly condemned Nicholas Shaxton arrived too. She should abjure, he counselled her, as he had done the night that he was sentenced to burn. Nicholas White, too, who had also been condemned to die with them, had now returned to orthodoxy. It was the only way Anne could save her life.[85] She refused.

Anne remained defiant. With an air of finality, Rich ordered her to be sent to the Tower. She was taken there at once, being kept in the foreboding fortress alone until 3pm, when Rich and one of his fellows on the Council arrived. The questioning began immediately. Did she, Rich asked, know others of her 'sect'?[86] 'I knew none', replied Anne. They were more specific. Did she know the Duchess of Suffolk, the countesses of Sussex and Hertford and ladies Denny and Fitzwilliam, all great friends of the queen? The king had been informed that she could provide a great many names, Rich said; but Anne replied only that he was 'deceived in that behalf'. He then demanded to know who maintained her, but all that she would admit was that she had once received sums from men purporting to be sent from the ladies Hertford and Denny.[87] This was not good enough.

Torture was not common in Henry VIII's reign, and it was rarely admitted to have taken place. But the Tower contained a selection of implements designed to elicit information from even the most reluctant of tongues. Strapping her onto the fearsome rack, Lord Chancellor Wriothesley and Rich turned the handles with their own hands, cranking the mechanism to stretch and break their prisoner's bones. It was brutal, but she 'lay still and did not cry', in spite of the agony inflicted. She was 'nigh dead' by the time she was finally released, swooning to the floor.[88] Even then, the ordeal was not over. When she regained consciousness, Wriothesley sat with her on the bare floor to continue the examination. Finally, with 'weary and painful bones', she was taken to a house and laid in a bed. The torture was initially kept secret. It was at first claimed that she had merely been shown the implements to frighten her. Anne herself believed that the authorities were 'ashamed of their uncomely doings'.

Wriothesley now sent her a message, telling her, as she recorded, that 'if I would leave my opinion, I should want nothing. If I would not, I should forth to Newgate, and so be burned.' She replied: 'I would rather die, than to break my faith.' Her body had already been broken.[89]

Not far away, in the gilded cage of the court, Catherine Parr and her ladies were aware of Anne's arrest and condemnation. The queen would hold religious meetings in her own household, at which those interested in reading and studying the scriptures could attend. Catherine had been encouraged by Henry's ostensible acceptance of this arrangement, and she had begun to speak more boldly of her beliefs to her ageing husband, encouraging him to take the religious changes that he had unleashed further. In her zeal, she had failed to notice that Henry was furious with her. On one occasion, after she had left his chamber, he commented in Bishop Gardiner's presence that 'a good hearing, it is, when women become such clerks; and a thing much to my comfort, to come in mine old days to be taught by my wife'.

So offended was Henry that he agreed to Catherine's arrest for heresy, and a warrant was immediately drawn up. She was fortunate that the document was conveniently dropped outside her chamber and brought to her. After overcoming her terror, the queen composed herself enough to go to Henry and abase herself before him. She was, she insisted, 'ignorant' and 'inferior' to him. She had only presumed to debate with him in the hope of distracting him from his sickness, as well as improving herself, since, as she said, 'I, hearing Your Majesty's learned discourse, might receive to myself some profit thereby.' It was a masterful response and saved both Catherine and her circle of ladies. 'And is it even so, sweet heart!, and tended your arguments to no worse end?' asked a king who had been facing the end of his sixth marriage. 'Then, perfect friends we are now again, as ever at any time heretofore.'[90] With an embrace, all was suddenly sunny for Catherine Parr. But no one dared speak up for Anne Askew, who had said nothing even as her bones cracked on the rack.

On 16 July 1546, Anne left Newgate for the last time, her body so broken that she could not stand.[91] Instead, she was carried on a dung cart, held up between two sergeants, as she sat on a chair.[92] With her came her co-condemned John Adams, as well as two other men. The four were tied to stakes in the same pyre.[93] 'By the king's commandment,' Dr Shaxton then preached to the prisoners and the large crowd that had assembled, 'declaring his error that he had been in of the said sacrament'. There was still time for Anne Askew to abjure.

Many of the king's Council were there, some of them watching from a window of the Hospital of St Bartholomew, which stood close by.[94] With the sermon ended, they observed as the officers set fire to the reeds around the pyre.[95] The four condemned looked intently at the flames, as they faced this most 'painful and doleful kind of death'. Taking comfort in each other, they were observed 'confirming one another with mutual exhortations'.[96] As the fire 'consumed their blessed bodies', many of those looking on considered them holy martyrs. There was, as more than one eyewitness observed, 'a pleasant cracking from Heaven' as Anne Askew died.[97]

To Joan Bocher, her friend was burned 'for a piece of bread'.[98] She would soon suffer in her turn for 'a piece of flesh'.

'Prayers' and a Lamentation'

On 2 June 1545, a short book entitled *Prayers Stirring the Mind unto Heavenly Meditations* appeared in print for the first time. It was soon a bestseller, with two further editions printed that same year – the latter versions under the more succinct title *Prayers; or, Meditations*. What was remarkable about this volume of conventional piety was that its author, who was named in all editions, was Queen Catherine Parr. Henry VIII's sixth wife was the first Englishwoman to publish a book under her own name.[99]

Catherine was an evangelical in her piety, determined to use her exalted position to further her reformist faith, even as far as attempting to influence the religious beliefs of her husband. Although *Prayers; or, Meditations* was unobjectionable in its theology, a further work, which the queen was writing during the last months of Henry's life, went rather further. She did not dare publish it in his lifetime, but on 5 November 1547

Catherine's *Lamentation of a Sinner* appeared in print.

Lamentation of a Sinner was about as radical a work as Catherine could have produced. It looked inwardly at her own soul, laying herself bare for all to see as a sinner and a 'dung-hill of wickedness'. She emphasized the reformist belief in justification by faith alone, and identified the reading of the scriptures as a route to God. Those that did not follow scripture, she considered, 'build upon the sand' and grounded their faith on 'a weak foundation'. It was a very personal account of her own conversion to evangelicalism, acknowledging that she had once 'loved darkness better than light: yea, darkness seemed to me, light'. The queen, who had been born a member of the gentry, had embraced the religious reform movement and the access to religious texts in the vernacular that it brought.

She was not the only member of her evangelical circle to write and publish in the period.

Catherine's friend Elizabeth, Lady Tyrwhit, also became a published author when she released her *Morning and Evening Prayers* in 1574.[100] It was a work written in a similar vein to Catherine's *Lamentation*, with Lady Tyrwhit acknowledging 'mine often and grievous offences that I have committed against thy Divine Majesty, from my youth hitherto'.[101] In a period when religion was so central to everyday life, it is no surprise that the published female writers of the period focussed on faith and spirituality.

OF CONSCIENCE AND CATHOLICS

Joan Bocher, Princess Mary and Jane Grey

The death of Henry VIII in January 1547 saw the accession of his nine-year-old son. Almost immediately, his uncle, Edward Seymour, Earl of Hertford, who promoted himself to the title of Duke of Somerset, took power as 'Lord Protector'. Somerset was, himself, a religious reformer, whose wife had been one of the women accused of financially supporting Anne Askew. He ushered in a series of changes designed to turn England into a Protestant country, including the repeal of the heresy legislation.[1]

Joan Bocher – who had remained quiet during Henry VIII's last years – should have been overjoyed. Yet, things turned out quite differently. While, under the new religious direction, the ornaments and vestments of traditional ceremony were being cleared out of parish churches, and the walls whitewashed to obliterate frescoes, Joan found herself in considerable difficulties. She was arrested for heresy early in 1549. In the years following her acquittal in Canterbury in the early 1540s, her faith had progressed substantially. She had come to believe, as Archbishop Cranmer would put it, 'that the Word was made flesh in the Virgin's belly; but that Christ took flesh of the Virgin you believe not, because the flesh of the Virgin, being the outward man, was sinfully gotten, and born in sin. But the Word, by the consent of the inward man of the Virgin, was made flesh'.[2]

In other words, she denied the common creed that professed Christ 'born of the Virgin Mary', as well as the words of St Paul. This was the view of Mary associated with Anabaptism, and was highly unorthodox. To Bishop Hugh Latimer, who would later denounce Joan in the pulpit, it was a 'foolish opinion', since it implied that Christ 'was not very man'.[3] At her examination, Joan attempted to justify her belief, considering that 'The Son of God' (as she said) 'penetrated through her [Mary], as through a glass, taking no substance of her'. To Latimer, this 'foolish woman' could 'show no reason why she should believe so'. Joan was, however, adamant. She had read the scriptures and considered them. To her, this was the natural interpretation, and she would never waver from it.[4]

On 12 April 1549, Cranmer excommunicated Joan, before passing her to the secular authorities.[5] On being hauled before the court, she was outspoken as ever – and condemned to die. In reaction, she spoke 'very scornfully', reminding her judges that they had once burned Anne Askew for denying the sacrament – a belief that they now held. Referring to her own beliefs, she considered that 'in the end you will come to believe this also, when you have read the scriptures and understand them'.[6] They doubted it. As far as the Protestant rulers of the Edwardian state were concerned, Joan was a heretic.

Although she was sentenced to death, strenuous efforts were made to convert her in her prison, as a steady stream of learned men visited to dispute with her. One was Roger Hutchinson, who had attended Oxford with the generation of great men who passed through its doors in the latter years of Henry VIII.[7] He was known as a religious thinker of some gravitas, and arrived with another eminent scholar, Thomas Lever.

What is your opinion of Genesis 3:15?, asked Hutchinson and Lever – referring to 'the seed of the woman shall grind or break the serpent's head', a passage usually interpreted as foretelling the birth of Christ and his redemption of mankind.[8]

Joan had read the scriptures as many times as they had, and she refuted their interpretation. 'I deny not that Christ is Mary's seed' she said, 'or the woman's seed; nor I deny him not to be a man; but Mary had two seeds, one seed of her faith, and another seed of her flesh and in her body.' Christ was, she maintained, formed from Mary's 'spiritual' or 'heavenly seed', rather than 'a natural and a corpor[e]al seed'. In their battle of wills, in which each side quoted scriptural authority at the other, Joan – a woman with no access to the universities – held her own. Here was solid evidence that the publication of the scriptures in English had opened the way for women to become 'doctresses', just as Henry VIII had feared.[9] Clinging to her own scriptural interpretations, Joan remained in prison for over a year, while the authorities still remained in 'hope of conversion'.[10]

Joan Bocher was far from the only woman in Edward VI's England to consider herself persecuted for her faith. The Protestant regime's disfavour also fell much nearer home, on the young king's eldest half-sister.

As a child, Princess Mary had been very promising, but her life had been blighted by the end of her parents' marriage. Although declared illegitimate by her father, she was grudgingly reinstated in the line of succession by Henry in 1545, after his five subsequent marriages had failed to produce more than one son. By 1550 and the minority of her half-brother, she was heir to the throne and a figure of major political importance.

Mary was already thirty-four years old, but no one had troubled to arrange a marriage for her. On the Continent, her powerful cousin, Holy Roman Emperor Charles V, was growing increasingly concerned about her treatment in England. On 22 April 1550, shortly before the final sentence was passed on Joan Bocher, the Imperial ambassador, Francis Van der Delft, wrote to his master. He had, he said, spoken to the English Council concerning the princess's marriage to the Prince of Portugal, a match promoted by the Emperor, who had always taken a fatherly interest in his kinswoman.[11] Matters had, as usual, stalled. In the climate of the times, she was too dangerous to the Protestant cause in England to be permitted to leave the country.

Mary had been raised in the traditional faith, and was staunch in her beliefs, being particularly devoted to the mass; and this was widely known. The Duke of Somerset, who was the most powerful man in the kingdom during his lord protectorship of 1547–9, had considered her beliefs nothing but superstition; but he was prepared to turn a blind eye to the royal heir's private worship. So, too, was the young king, whom the Council always protested 'dearly loved his sister'.[12] She could hear mass, the Lord Protector agreed verbally, but only in the company of two or three women of her household and then in the privacy of her personal chambers.

Mary, who watched with alarm the changes to the Church inaugurated by Somerset, wanted more freedom. The mass should not be furtive; Mary threw open her doors, as the Council would later complain, to 'all and sundry', with both her household and neighbours accustomed to hearing mass within her chapel. Perhaps Somerset had not been clear? Van der Delft claimed in April 1550 that Mary's 'whole establishment and household' had been permitted to worship with her. That might have once been true, but the pace of the Edwardian reformation was increasing. The political situation was also changing. In late 1549, Protector Somerset fell from his pre-eminence and, although he had returned to the Council early in 1550, real power now lay with John Dudley, the new Duke of Northumberland, who was less inclined to treat the princess gently.

Mary's religion was an issue of international importance. On 21 April 1550, Ambassador Van der Delft arrived at court for a tense interview with the King's Council. His master required, he said, that letters patent be granted to permit Mary to continue with her Catholic worship without government interference.[13]

That would never happen, cunning Sir William Paget informed him. Paget was the man who had almost single-handedly secured the protectorship for Somerset; he had also managed to weather the storm of the Lord Protector's fall. Why, he continued, the king and his Council had, in Parliament, determined the way that religion was to be observed in England, 'without exception of persons'.[14] Mary, as the king's subject, was to follow the laws in the same way as anyone. She would never be granted any exemption.

Van der Delft professed himself baffled. She already had such a verbal exemption for all her servants, he insisted. William Parr, now Marquess of Northampton, interjected: 'I have never heard anything said except that she alone might be privileged to do so, with but two or three of her women.' This was untrue, the ambassador retorted, before pointing out just how difficult it would be to have two different religions observed in the same house.

Her devotion to the old religion was a sign of the princess's stupidity, considered the Council, who were, to a man, of a reformist bent. William Parr had been shifty and evasive when drawn into the examination of Anne Askew; but now he was adamant. The best they would promise, the Council declared with one voice, was that 'the king will permit her to keep the mass for herself, in the hope that God will grant her grace that she may be enlightened and conform with us'. His master would be 'greatly displeased', Van der Delft countered, if he heard that his cousin had changed her faith – an obvious threat. But the Council ignored him. All the ambassador could obtain was the verbal agreement that Mary would be left alone provided that she caused no scandal.

When he once again protested that he could see that 'they had no intention of keeping to what they had once promised, and that they wished the Lady Mary to act against her con-science', Van der Delft was met with fury. Northampton once interjected: 'You talk a great deal about the Lady Mary's conscience; you should consider that the king's conscience would receive a stain if he allowed her to live in error.' He spoke so sharply that the Council were forced to interrupt him; but the ambassador knew they shared his views.

The ambassador was left with the distinct impression that the Council wished to wipe out Catholicism in England. He could not even take the princess's case to the king, since the boy was being raised as an ardent Protestant. Van der Delft had heard that the monarch took 'pleasure in disputing on and upholding the said doctrines,' and concluded, as he noted, 'there is no hope therefore that I may obtain anything from him. He would more likely pride himself on overthrowing my arguments.' In an era when tolerance of religious diversity was an alien concept, it was accepted that it was a duty to God to ensure conformity in practice and belief.[15]

While Van der Delft was pleading Mary's case, she was at Woodham Walter, 30 miles from the capital.[16] She was staying in a smart brick house only a few decades old, close to the Essex coast,[17] and borrowed from the Catholic Fitzwalter family, who probably availed themselves of the unofficial freedom to worship in the princess's chapel. True, the moated residence was uncomfortably near the parish church, in which the princess would have seen the villagers dutifully going to their newly Protestant services.[18] But it was otherwise an isolated spot – only a few scattered farmsteads, in a settlement more than 2 miles away from the larger town of Maldon – which suited a princess who had spent the past few years sunk in a deep depression. There were pleasant gardens to walk in, and the countryside around was wooded and tranquil. On 23 April 1550, Van der Delft arrived there for an appointment, to discuss with Mary the outcome of his negotiations.[19]

He found her agitated. She had been informed by some of her friends, she said, that the Council intended to deprive her of the mass.[20] Was it true? She knew that Van der Delft had already spoken to the Council on the subject. And what did her cousin, the Emperor, think? Without Charles's aid, she insisted, 'she could hardly hope to escape from the danger that threatened her, which went on increasing as time passed'. He reassured her, saying that the Emperor intended to preserve her against any danger or threat to her person. This was not enough, Mary contended. She surprised the ambassador with a sudden desire to flee England.

This was a shocking proposal. Van der Delft cautioned her to 'temporise', since she still had good hopes of the throne if she remained in England. Accident or illness could strike down the healthiest of men, let alone a child king. But, were Edward to die while she was abroad, he said, then 'her absence would deprive her of the crown, and religion would be set aside for good without any hope of mending it'. The hopes of the Catholic Church in England rested on Mary sitting tight.

She was unconvinced, answering that 'if my brother were to die, I should be far better out of the kingdom; because as soon as he were dead, before the people knew it, they would despatch me too'. 'There is no doubt,' she insisted, that her brother's Council 'would kill me by some means or other.' More positively, she knew that she was a popular figure, telling Van der Delft that 'I feel certain that the whole country would be favourable to me and would set no one in my place in violation of my rights, if I were safe myself in a place of safety.' Besides, she insisted (piously declaring 'may God have my brother in His keeping'), she had no lust for the crown: 'I desire nothing else except to live in peace without burdening my conscience. But as I see clearly that I shall not be allowed to do so if I remain here, I am quite resolved to withdraw elsewhere, and I hope the Emperor's Majesty and my friends will not fail me.' She must leave England in order to continue to practice her religion, otherwise the Council would send orders to 'crush me completely'.

She would, she insisted, 'rather suffer death than stain my conscience'. Her cause was 'so righteous in God's sight' that she could not possibly fail. With these outpourings of her woes, on this day an 'extremely distressed' Princess Mary made the decision to escape England.

∞

Although she feared murder, Mary knew at least that the Council would never be so bold as to risk the Emperor's wrath and judicially execute her for her faith. But, for Joan Bocher, whose transgressions of faith came from a very different direction, there were no such protections. Nevertheless, it remained embarrassing to Cranmer and the other Church leaders that they could not bring someone who had once been one of their number round to their way of thinking. A final attempt was made in late April 1550 by the bishops of London and Ely, and the results of their work were fed back directly to the boy king. He noted bluntly that 'she withstood them'. Edward himself was none too keen to burn Joan, so that it was left to Archbishop Cranmer to step in to persuade him.[21] On 27 April 1550, the Privy Council ordered the Sheriff of London to proceed with Joan's burning for the 'certain detestable opinion of heresy'.[22]

To the famous martyrologist, John Foxe, the idea that his co-religionists should burn someone was horrifying. On hearing that the sentence was due to be carried out against Joan, he went to his friend, John Rogers, who was a royal chaplain.[23] Could he use his influence with Cranmer to spare 'the life of the wretched woman', he begged? She was not dangerous, he said, since they could keep her locked away, 'far removed from intercourse with weak persons'. But Rogers was having none of this, answering curtly 'that death must be inflicted'. If that were the case, Foxe continued, why inflict the 'torments of this dreadful death' when a milder method of execution would do just as well. To Foxe's chagrin, Rogers told him that 'to burn men alive was the least agonising of all punishments and sufficiently mild'. Foxe scoffed at these words, 'which breathed so little care and respect for the agonies of wretched men'. Grasping for his friend's hand and beating it, he replied 'well, maybe the day will come when you yourself will have your hands full of this gentle burning'.[24] He had done all he could.

There was one final chance for Joan Bocher. After the Council confirmed her sentence, she was sent to lodge in the house of Sir Richard Rich, who was now both lord chancellor and a confessed Protestant.[25] She was a troublesome houseguest, appearing entirely unrepentant to Rich, who daily admitted Cranmer and Bishop Ridley to try to convert her. Yet, during the days that she lodged with him Rich observed her 'so high in the spirit, that they could do nothing with her for all their learning'. Years later, he recalled that she 'went wilfully into the fire'.

One who did not want to go wilfully to the flames or any other sort of death, if it could be avoided, was Princess Mary. She was still waiting – anxiously – at Woodham Walter. Although initially reluctant about Mary's desire to flee, Van der Delft was quickly convinced in its wisdom and that haste was required.[26] He wrote to his master on 2 May 1550 with details of the plan. Sir Robert Rochester, comptroller of her household, was, according to Mary, able to find a ship. Then, escorted by three Imperial warships to 'frighten away the pirates who up to the present have always come up to us', Mary and four of her ladies would be able to make their way to Flanders. The princess could bring nothing but her rings and jewels, the ambassador noted, but about this Mary was not bothered. To Mary, life outside England meant freedom of conscience.

There would be no such freedom for Joan Bocher. On that same day of 2 May 1550, she was brought to Smithfield. As she waited on the pyre, John Scory, a former chaplain to Archbishop Cranmer and a well-known Protestant firebrand, stepped forward to preach. He was interrupted by Joan herself, who shouted over him, insulting him even as he opened his mouth.[27] 'He lied like a rogue,'[28] she declared, as he began to attack her beliefs before warning 'all men to beware of them'.[29] 'Go, read the scriptures', she called out dismissively, as Scory finally gave up.[30]

Joan's death was not inevitable. The very day after she had been condemned, a tanner of Colchester, who was also an Anabaptist, was apprehended. Unlike Joan, he recanted, carrying a faggot to Paul's Cross to give public penance.[31] But Joan Bocher had read the scriptures and decided, unswervingly, for herself. As the fire was lit and the crowd watched her being engulfed, she died because she chose to do so for her beliefs – one of only two heretics, and the only woman, to be burned at the stake under Edward VI.[32] For good or ill, it was not a death soon forgotten. The Protestant John Philpott, who would face the flames in Queen Mary's reign, considered Joan 'a heretic indeed, well worthy to be burnt because she stood against one of the manifest articles of our faith, contrary to the scriptures'.[33] And not long after her death a verse pamphlet was published, denouncing Joan as 'the devil's eldest daughter'.[34] Nevertheless, the burning of Joan Bocher was one of the most controversial events in Cranmer's career, and would later be compared with his own demise.[35]

'To Muddy Death'

In steadfastly adhering to her own Biblical interpretations, Joan Bocher knew the ultimate retribution that lay in wait, and so she quite consciously sought out death. But this was not quite the same as suicide, or 'self-murder' as contemporaries described it, which was a shocking act in the Tudor era.

When Shakespeare's Ophelia, driven mad by Hamlet's rejection of her, meets a 'muddy death' after she 'fell in the weeping brook. Her clothes spread wide', the two grave-diggers later question whether someone who 'wilfully seeks her own salvation' can receive Christian burial.[36] In Ophelia's case, it is only the evidence of her madness that compensates for her actions and allows her body to be so honoured. In reality, to the Tudor Church suicide was a sin, leading only to damnation, and under English law it was a crime.[37] The punishment was confiscation of the deceased's goods and the denial of a Christian burial.

Few questioned this state of affairs. In the late sixteenth century, Elizabeth I's godson, Sir John Harington, turned his attention in a short handwritten treatise to whether suicide should always lead to damnation.[38] In his work, which was written as a dialogue between the Biblical Saul, Samuel and Solomon, he failed to reach a conclusion, ending with Solomon leaving it to the 'secret judgment of God'. There was a possibility of salvation, but no guarantee. His idea did not, though, catch on. As in the case of Ophelia, the only valid excuse for suicide

was evidence of madness.[39] But in a world where all suicides were considered to be carried out at the instigation of the Devil, proving mental illness was a challenge.

Given the legal and spiritual prohibitions, it is perhaps surprising that as many as 12 per cent of violent deaths in the Tudor period may have been the result of suicide.[40] The rates were worryingly high, and in one period, between May and November 1590, 20 per cent of violent deaths in London were accounted self-murder.

Women took their lives in the same numbers and manners as men. In August 1563, Margaret Chaunte of Brantford in Middlesex, 'at the instigation of the Devil', cut her own throat with a knife, dying later that day. Nearly thirty years later, on 7 July 1590, Agnes Mitchell drank 'rat's bane' (white arsenic) with her breakfast in her house in Bell Alley, near London's Holborn Viaduct. She lingered, painfully, before dying twelve hours later. She was a poor woman; indeed, the coroner's jury that assembled on the following day was unable to confirm whether she owned any property at all. Anything she did possess, however, would have been confiscated.

By far the majority of male and female suicides hanged themselves in various ways, usually in their own homes. On 8 July 1554 a spinster named Elizabeth Avery was found hanging by a piece of rope in Poplar, Middlesex, and was accorded by the inquest a verdict of suicide. In November 1563, Margaret Yeoghen hanged herself in the parish of St Martin's in the Fields, London; she used her girdle strung onto a beam in the house in which she was employed. The following August, a spinster named Alice Emery in Enfield, north of London, hanged herself with a halter. Women used whatever they had to hand. A prisoner named Mary Keys, alias Beck, rose from her gaol bed between 1am and 2am on 2 September 1585, and, moving quietly, bound her girdle around her neck before attaching it to a post.[41] She was found dead the next morning.

Late summer 1590 saw two married women commit suicide in London. Agnes Hinderwell,

the wife of a cooper, was home alone at 4pm on 31 August when she hanged herself from a post.[42] Just a week later, on 7 September, sixty-year-old Amy Stokes, a sawyer's wife, was in her house at 9am when, not 'having the fear of God before her eyes', she went into her chamber and knotted a cord around her neck. Then, balancing on a three-legged stool, she tied the cord to a beam, before kicking the stool away. The rope had only just been short enough to strangle her, since she was discovered with the tips of her toes touching the floor. She was buried at night at a crossroads, with a 'stake driven through her breast'.[43] It was a shallow grave. The tip of the stake was left to poke through the ground as her 'memorial', and thus warn others against undertaking a similar desperate action.

The manner of Amy Stokes's burial was not unusual, since suicides were commonly believed to walk abroad after their deaths. Crossroads could therefore confuse a wandering spirit, while a stake through the heart would pin them into their graves.[44] The Church took a hardline approach on the matter. When Alison Hopton of Shrawardine, Shropshire, drowned herself in 1521, her friends and neighbours decided that she had been lured into the water by an evil spirit. With this conclusion, the parish priest permitted her to receive the full funeral rites of the Church and consecrated burial.[45] But when word of this concession reached the Bishop of Hereford, he issued a prohibition against divine service in the church until Alison Hopton's body had been removed from the churchyard.

Such an attitude was far from unusual. Given the peril that self-murder posed to the immortal soul, the relatively high rates of suicide in Tudor times are testament to the desperation in which people must have found themselves.

∞

As the flames flickered around Joan Bocher, Princess Mary's plans to preserve her conscience through flight proceeded apace. But around her, changes were under way. On 13 May 1550, the Emperor wrote personally to Edward VI to officially recall his ambassador, who had been resident at the English court since the last years of Henry VIII.[46] For a while, the elderly Van der Delft had been desiring a recall; he was greatly troubled with gout and was ready to retire. His departure had the added advantage that his successor – Jehan Scheyfve – could be kept entirely innocent of the escape plot. The younger man arrived in London on 19 May, filled with enthusiasm.[47] He was only mildly nonplussed when his predecessor insisted on going without him to say farewell to the princess.[48]

Van der Delft found Mary deeply troubled when he arrived in Essex with his secretary, Jehan Dubois. The pair were admitted at once. With Mary's comptroller present, once again they rehearsed the dangers in fleeing. The risk of losing the crown remained, considered Van der Delft, but Mary was unperturbed: 'I am like a little ignorant girl,' she said, 'and I care neither for my goods nor for the world, but only for God's service and my conscience.' She continued: 'I know not what to say; but if there is peril in going and peril in staying, I must choose the lesser of two evils.' She would 'willingly stay,' if only she could 'be able to live and serve God as I have done in the past; which is what I have always said'. She ended plaintively, referring to the alterations in the hierarchy of power that had already occurred in her brother's reign: 'but these men are so changeable that I know not what to say. What say you, Mr Ambassador?'[49] Van der Delft merely repeated all that he had previously said: he did not know what the future held, but he 'must believe they would eventually go so far as to forbid My Lady the observance of the old religion'. Her very soul was at stake.

Mary had been unable to source a local vessel, so the four sat down to consider a new plan.[50] Van der Delft considered it best for a ship to be sent over, under cover of selling corn to the household. He was sure that a suitable craft could be hired at Ostend; and the loyal and shrewd Dubois could disguise himself as a merchant. After slipping past, or overpowering, the night's watch, Mary could be smuggled aboard. Once escorted across the sea by a fleet of Imperial warships, she would be safely in Flanders before word even reached London that she had gone. The presence on that day of the familiar Van der Delft gave her strength, and she seemed, he thought, 'to cling to me', begging that he should be on the vessel to receive her. She informed him that she would put her trust in providence.

Van der Delft returned to the Netherlands by 6 June, on which day he wrote to his master from Turnhout, setting out details of the plan. Charles was 'very anxious' about the whole business, as he confided in a letter to his sister, the Queen Dowager of Hungary, two days later.[51] He had always played a fatherly role in his English cousin's life and was genuinely fearful for her safety in a business that he was sure 'cannot possibly be kept secret much longer'. He considered that 'if the matter is discovered, she will certainly be in danger'. He would have liked to have abandoned the whole hazardous business, but he feared that Mary would then take matters into her own hands. And so, he ordered his fleet to be prepared, under the command of the experienced Admiral Cornelius Scepperus. The Emperor's nerves were further frayed on 14 June when Van der Delft died, after a brief sickness.[52] The ambassador never did achieve his comfortable retirement.

Jehan Dubois inherited his master's role in the plot, as well as responsibility for sorting through Van der Delft's papers and forwarding on Mary's increasingly anxious letters.[53] Matters were proceeding apace. Under the pretence of seeking Scottish pirates, Scepperus put to sea with eight warships in the last week of July, sailing out into a strong headwind.

The fleet reached the English coast on Sunday 29 June, before steering away from the mouth of the Thames and travelling northwards that night.[54] A dense fog hampered progress, and the Imperial admiral took the decision to split his fleet, so that some vessels remained out to sea while others stayed in the port of Harwich. Scepperus took the eighth ship to lie close to Maldon, where he remained on the Tuesday, Wednesday and Thursday. As he later told the Queen of Hungary – rather pointedly – it was Dubois who 'managed everything except the navigation'.[55] Van der Delft's loyal secretary, in his hired merchant vessel, had travelled with Scepperus's fleet as far as Harwich, before leaving for Maldon before him.[56]

When Dubois landed at Maldon, he was surprised to find no one there to meet him. Pulling out his inkwell and pen, he quickly composed a letter to Sir Robert Rochester, warning Mary's comptroller that there was danger in delay. While he was writing, Dubois's brother-in-law, who had gone ashore earlier, arrived with one of Mary's servants. They took him to the churchyard, where he found Rochester pacing up and down with a friend from the village. The comptroller, a fifty-year-old Essex man, had served Mary for at least three years, and he showed every sign of being trustworthy, loyal and devoted to her.[57] But he was nervous. The plot may have seemed sensible and exciting in the planning, but, when faced with Dubois, Rochester lost his nerve. After carrying out a mock bargain for the corn, the pair withdrew to the house of the comptroller's friend.

Once away from prying eyes, they walked in the garden, speaking earnestly. 'There was no earthly possibility,' Rochester asserted, 'of bringing My Lady down to the waterside without running grave risks'. To Dubois, he seemed frightened, troubled by both the danger of the watch posted every night and the suspicions of some members of the household, 'which was not so free of enemies to her religion as she imagined'. Rochester had been consulting astrologers, too, who had assured him that the king would die the following year. Why, he asked Dubois, amid the garden's summer greenness, should she leave when she was still free to worship? He believed that flight would certainly cost her the succession. 'This is not a matter to hurried', he considered.

This was a very considerable difference in opinion at a moment when, to Dubois, time was very much of the essence. That afternoon, on returning to his ship, he found himself harassed by customs officials, who had noted Scepperus's ships out to sea and made the connection between them.

Against his better judgement, Dubois was forced to go in person to Mary. Riding secretly to Woodham Walter, where he feared being recognized at any moment, he found a household in uproar. Mary and her ladies were attempting to stuff her possessions into long hop sacks, in a bid to bring them down to the ship. Once again, Dubois spoke with Rochester, who was visibly agitated. While waiting to be received by the princess, the secretary commented that if Mary did not go, it would be impossible to keep the attempt secret. 'For the love of God,' hissed the comptroller, 'do not say that to My Lady! She is a good woman and really wants to go; but neither she nor you see what I see and know. Great danger threatens us!' Rochester had no stomach for flight.

He was not alone. In the end, neither did Mary, who, under Rochester's persuasions, was beginning to waver. On summoning Dubois to her, she pointed to the chaos, declaring that 'I am as yet ill-prepared, and it seems you wish to be for tonight.' Dubois did indeed want to leave that night, but he assured her that he was at her disposal. After speaking quietly with the comptroller and one of her ladies, the princess suggested that the secretary come back in two days. She could then leave the house at 4am, on the pretext of going for a swim in the sea, as some of her ladies did. On being informed that the tide would still serve, Mary seemed to Dubois to be relieved, commenting that 'it is more than time I was hence, for things are going worse than ever. A short time ago they took down the altars in the very house my brother lives in.'

This was a greater delay than Dubois thought prudent, but he dared not contradict the Emperor's cousin. Worse was to follow. While they were speaking, there was a knock at the door. Rochester went to open it, disappearing outside for a time. On returning, he told the company that it was his friend from Maldon, who had ridden hard to warn him that the bailiff and townsmen were planning to arrest Dubois and his crew, suspecting them, as Rochester related, 'of having some understanding' with Scepperus's fleet. It was really very serious, the comptroller assured them. He expected warning beacons to be lit by the next evening, while the watch would be doubled, with men stationed on the church tower to survey the darkened countryside. On hearing this, Mary entirely lost her nerve, anxiously repeating: 'What shall we do? What is to become of me?'

Rochester offered no suggestion. He merely restated that it was very dangerous and advised the secretary to depart at once. If matters were really as bad as suggested, asked Dubois, should he not take Mary to his ship right now? That was impossible, Rochester answered, for they would never escape the watch. With the princess continuing to ask plaintively 'But what is to become of me?', Dubois reluctantly agreed to make a new attempt in ten or twelve days. The pressure was suddenly relieved, and Mary turned to Rochester, declaring: 'You see, that it is not our fault now.' The comptroller nodded, pointing towards Dubois. 'No,' he said, 'but his for not bringing more corn'.

Dubois rode back to his ship, easily slipping past the watch and noting, angrily, that there was no lookout on top of Maldon's church tower. He had been defeated by Sir Robert Rochester, whom he suspected 'had made out the situation at Maldon to be more dangerous than it was in reality'.

There would be no second attempt. On 13 July, the Council sent an army into Essex in order, as the boy king himself wrote, 'to stop Lady Mary going away because it was credibly informed that Scepperus was to steal her away to Antwerp'.[58] Three days later, a further 800 men were sent to patrol the Essex coast, while word was sent to Mary to move inland.[59]

The princess's fears were soon realized, for later that month two of her chaplains were indicted for saying mass in her household.[60] Perhaps she regretted staying; perhaps not. When speaking to Van der Delft for the last time, she had raised concerns that, in leaving, her household might 'become lost sheep, and even follow these new opinions'.[61] Might she then 'incur God's censure'? That 'would be a heavy grief to me'. Mary's conscience told her to stay.

It would be very nearly three years before the pressure on the princess was relieved. On the other hand, a throne awaited her.

'Queen for only nine days'

Mary's path to the throne of England was by no means an unchallenged one. Evidence of that lies in the British Library, where there is a tiny book of prayers written in English.[62] It is a colourful, beautifully produced little volume, written by hand. Exquisite though the book is, the real treasures lie tucked away in the margins of the work. The observer who looks closely will see two handwritten messages. One is to the Lieutenant of the Tower of London, who received the book as a present from a prisoner on the scaffold. The other is addressed to Henry Grey, Duke of Suffolk, assuring him that the writer 'by leaving this mortal life, have won an immortal life'.[63] The writer in question was his daughter Jane – Lady Jane Grey – who was the first woman to be proclaimed as a reigning Queen of England.[64]

The fourteen-year-old Edward VI fell ill at Easter 1552 and failed to fully recover; by the summer of 1553, those around him were despairing of his health. Apart from the seven-year-old son of his cousin Margaret Douglas, Countess of Lennox, he was the only legitimate male descendant of Henry VII. It was inevitable that England would have its first reigning queen. Indeed, Henry VIII had provided for this eventuality in his will, by the terms of which the crown – should Edward have no issue – would pass to his daughters Mary and Elizabeth in turn.

However, Edward, as a fanatical Protestant, had no wish to be succeeded by his defiantly Catholic half-sister. Instead, his chief minister John Dudley, Duke of Northumberland – who was the effective ruler of England – persuaded the boy to leave his crown to Jane Grey. She was the daughter of Frances Brandon, Duchess of Suffolk, who was in turn the daughter of Henry VIII's younger sister, Mary. She also now happened to be Northumberland's new daughter-in-law.

After Edward's death on 6 July 1553, Jane was proclaimed

queen. She was brought to the Tower of London on 10 July in a great procession, in which her own royal mother held her train.[65] As cannons were shot to welcome her, 'Queen' Jane was ushered into the royal apartments, at one point receiving the crown of England, as she recalled, 'to try whether it really became me well or no'.[66]

The teenaged Jane was a reluctant monarch, surprised by her elevation. But, on asking God whether 'what was given to me was rightfully and lawfully mine', she had been brought to accept the honour – and showed she was determined to rule in her own right.[67] When she was informed that another crown 'should be made to crown my husband with me', Jane refused, declaring that 'if the crown belongs to me, I should be content to make my husband a duke, but would never consent to make him king'. She was later forced to lock the doors to the Tower to stop him from leaving and publicly shaming her by refusing to support her.

Jane's 'rule' was but a brief one, and she would never see a coronation. Proclamations declared her royal challenger Mary to have been 'unlawfully begotten', but this was not how most people in England saw matters.[68] On the evening that Jane arrived in the Tower, a letter arrived from Henry VIII's eldest daughter, declaring herself Queen of England. The population flocked to Mary, who was at large in East Anglia. When Northumberland left the Tower to raise an army and confront the princess, he was alarmed that, as he said, 'the people press to see us, but not one sayeth God speed us'.[69] He was met with stony faces all the way to Cambridge, where, on hearing of the overwhelming response to Mary's call to arms, he succumbed to the inevitable and himself proclaimed her queen in the marketplace.

Jane Grey was dining in the Tower on the evening of 19 July, when her father entered the room and tore down the canopy of estate from above her head. By nightfall, she was a prisoner. Almost eight months later, on the morning of 12 February 1554, Jane was brought to Tower Green, where a scaffold had been erected. After making a short speech, in which she declared her innocence of involvement in recent plotting against Mary, she was beheaded. She was sixteen years old. As one contemporary observed, she was 'queen for only nine days, and those most turbulent ones'.[70]

16

OF PROTESTANTS AND PYRES

Queen Mary, Rose Hickman, the Marian martyrs,
Margaret Clitherow and the new Queen Elizabeth

Edward VI's life indeed proved as fragile as Van der Delft had suggested, and after the boy's and the Duke of Northumberland's attempt to disinherit his Catholic half-sister came to nought, Mary swept to power in July 1553, on a wave of popular support. In her own version of Shakespeare's fifth age, this woman in her late thirties settled herself on the throne and was now in a position to dispense her own sort of justice. Her accession was, in her eyes, God's doing – and she must now do His work. This meant turning back the clock on the Reformation.[1]

Mary faced an uphill struggle in trying to rebuild her Church. Much of the ritual fabric of the buildings, from rood screens to crucifixes and chalices, had been removed and sold. As late as 1557 the church of Thurnham in Kent, for example, was still badly in need of reinstatement, with such items as 'a convenient box or a purse to carry the sacrament in to the sick' urgently required.[2] To one local woman, the return to the old ways was a chance to turn a profit. Thurnham's canopy cloth, which usually hung over the altar, was found in the house of a widow named Joanna Wood. When challenged, she insisted that her husband had purchased it during the previous reign. She was happy to return it – providing that an appropriate cash payment was made to compensate her for the loss.[3]

The new queen also had to deal with the fact that some of the clergy had married. These priests' wives suddenly found themselves as concubines. Father Howe, who had been serving as vicar of Newington in Kent before Mary's reign, went on the run with his 'pretensed wife', only for the pair to be located and summoned before Church commissioners.[4]

Rose Hickman was living in London at the time of Mary's accession, with her first husband, Anthony. He was, like her father, a merchant. The Protestant couple were alarmed at the 'public profession of popery' and 'cruel persecution of those good Christians that in a good conscience refused to yield themselves to that idolatry'.[5] They were brave, setting up a secret prayer room in their house, into which anyone who would come was welcome. 'Keeping the doors close shut', the group would read the gospel.[6] Such congregations, particularly in London, were well known to exist; but they soon proved to be too much for the authorities.

A proclamation issued on 4 March 1554 required that all should attend the parish church and receive the sacrament there. Rose and Anthony Hickman – in common with most people – had no stomach for martyrdom, and they immediately closed down their covert prayer group. But they remained busy, with Anthony arranging for the preachers and other Protestants to escape across the sea, as well as giving them money for the journey. He did not escape official notice and was soon imprisoned in the Fleet prison for his pains, where he inhabited a dank cell alongside Rose's brother, Thomas Locke. The two men were later held captive in the more salubrious house of the Marquess of Winchester, before finally securing their freedom by means of a large bribe of 'chests of sugar and pieces of velvet to the value of £200 or thereabouts'.[7] Anthony then fled to Antwerp, joining a growing community of exiles in a city that was conveniently situated for his business.

Rose was pregnant when her husband fled.[8] She, too, judged it advisable to leave the capital, travelling to Chilswell in

Oxfordshire. There, she took lodging in a house that 'stood far from any church or town', so that she could be delivered away from the prying eyes of the authorities. The birth of a child in this religious climate created a terrible dilemma for Rose. She secretly sent a message to bishops Cranmer, Latimer and Ridley, who were by then imprisoned at Oxford on charges of heresy. Might she, she asked, 'suffer my child to be baptised after the popish manner'? She could, they agreed, since 'the sacrament of baptism, as it was used by the papists, was the least corrupted'. With this permission, Rose duly handed her child over to a Catholic priest. Making a secret show of disobedience, as she later recalled, she 'did not put salt into the handkerchief that was to be delivered to the priest at the baptism, but put sugar in it instead of salt'. She could not bear the thought of baptizing any subsequent children in the Catholic faith.

Rose then made plans to abandon her 'fair house' in London and her country mansion in Romford in Essex, 'both of them well furnished with household stuff'. She professed herself happy to forget all worldly goods in return for 'liberty of conscience for the profession of Christ', although she did take the time to hide the finest items in the houses of her friends. She also shipped out her favourite featherbed, laid flat in the bottom of the ship's hold that carried her over the sea. The five days and nights of the voyage, in a vessel that was alarmingly leaky, would haunt her for the rest of her life. The captain's own announcement during the turbulent crossing that 'if it pleased God to speed us well in that voyage, it [the ship] should never go to sea again', calmed no-one's nerves.

The alternative was to conform to England's new Church, a thought that filled Rose with dread. Shortly before she left, she had complained to her sister-in-law, who refused to leave England for the sake of her faith, 'sister, you stay here for covetousness and love of your husband's lands and goods: but I fear the Lord's hand will be upon you for it'. As far as Rose was concerned, God did indeed have his vengeance. She later recorded that her brother, Thomas Locke, was so grieved by his need to conform to Catholicism that he, and seven of his children, shortly died.

Most people in England did conform throughout the changes and counter-changes of the English Reformation. For many people, the return to Catholicism was a return to a form of belief, practice and routine that had much deeper roots than Protestantism. But sometimes compliance was made under duress. One Margaret Geoffrey of Ashford, Kent, denied the sacrament and was sentenced to come to church during mass. Once there, she was to sit in the midst of the chancel, holding her rosary beads and 'devoutly behaving herself' before taking the sacrament before the eyes of the parish.[9] Another Kent resident, Elizabeth Poste, was ordered in 1557 to go to church and make a public declaration 'that in the sacrament of the altar there is the very body and blood of Christ really'. She was also to affirm the truth of all the sacraments and that 'all the ceremony now used in the church be good and godly'.[10]

Now in power, 'Bloody' Mary, who had once been persecuted for her faith, was as disinclined to offer tolerance as her brother's Council had been. England was returned to the embrace of Rome, and Mary took, as a husband, a staunchly Catholic monarch, King Philip of Spain. But the queen's dark historical reputation rests less on her doctrinal and ceremonial revivals, and rather more on the burning of more than 280 Protestants during the final four years of her short reign, a tally that included 50 women.[11] This was an enormous number, mostly concentrated in the major cities, with London particularly hard hit.[12] To the queen and her advisers, such measures were justified, although, as the damage to Mary's reputation became apparent, she was increasingly counselled against it. The campaign, though, was beginning to have an effect by the time that the queen died in November 1558.[13] Apart from churchmen such as Cranmer – who had sought in vain to save his life by recanting, before finally withdrawing his recantation – the vast majority of people burned were of much lower status, without the resources to flee. The state also made stringent efforts to persuade those arrested to recant; as during the reigns of Henry VIII and Edward VI, only the most doggedly committed to their views were sent to the pyre.[14]

∞

One such individual was the former serving maid Elizabeth Cooper, Protestant wife of a Norwich pewterer.[15] Following Mary's accession, she had gone with her family and neighbours to the parish church of St Andrews, where she had, at first, recanted her faith. This was the sensible option; but she was soon 'unquiet for the same, and greatly troubled inwardly'. Like Anne Askew, Joan Bocher and Queen Mary before her, she was absolutely persuaded of the rightness of her own beliefs. Unable to bear the inner turmoil any longer, she entered her parish church as a service was under way. Standing, as everyone stared, she declared that 'she revoked her recantation before made in that place, and was heartily sorry that ever she did it'.

As the church erupted into uproar, she continued to speak, 'willing the people not to be deceived'. 'Master sheriff!' cried out one of the assembled worshipers, 'Will you suffer this?' Elizabeth's conduct was outrageous – far outside the socially acceptable norms of female behaviour. She hurriedly left the church to return home, knowing that arrest was imminent. The sheriff was a personal friend of Elizabeth's and 'very loath to do it'.[16] Nonetheless, at the repeated urging of his fellows, he was persuaded to go to her house. At his knocking at the door, she came down the stairs and meekly allowed herself to be taken to prison.

Having already recanted once, there could be no second chance for Elizabeth Cooper. She was condemned on 13 July

1557. Five days later, she was led out of the city to a place called the 'Lollard's Pit', where heretics had been burned since the fifteenth century. With her was one Simon Miller, who had travelled to the city from King's Lynn in order to make a public show of his Protestant faith. The pair were tied to the stake back to back. As the fire was lit and the flames approached Elizabeth, her resolution wavered and she cried out – and Miller reached out behind him to hold her hand, willing her to be 'strong and of good cheer', 'for, good sister, we shall have a joyful and a sweet supper'. To the crowd that gathered, this seemed to strengthen Elizabeth and she 'stood as still and as quiet as one most glad to finish that good work which before most happily she had begun'. It was a gruesome, painful death, but the pair bore it bravely.

The deaths of Elizabeth Cooper and Simon Miller had drawn a big crowd, with people pressing as close as they dared to the pyre. One among them was Cicely Ormes, the thirty-two-year-old wife of a worsted-weaver, who also lived in Norwich.[17] She was a tailor's daughter and generally considered 'a very simple woman', who could not even write her name. Like Elizabeth Cooper, she had recanted, but she remained troubled. She was carrying a letter when she went to watch the executions, which she had paid a scribe to write for her. In it, she 'repented her recantation from the bottom of her heart, and would never do the like again while she lived'.

As Cicely watched the burning, she suddenly cried out that 'she would pledge them of the same cup that they drank on'. This was scandalous, prompting one Master Corbet, standing close to her in the pressing throng, to grab her and send her to Michael Dunning, the chancellor of the diocese of Norwich. Like Anne Askew and Joan Bocher before her, she was questioned as to her belief regarding the sacrament. 'What is that that the priest holdeth over his head?', her interrogator asked testily when she had attempted to evade the question. Boldly,

Cicely declared: 'It is bread: and if you make it any better, it is worse.' She was sent to the bishop's prison, where she suffered 'many threatening and hot words' from the keeper of the gaol.

On 23 July 1557, Cicely Ormes was brought once again before Dunning, who offered to spare her life if she would only go to church 'and keep her tongue'. She refused, saying that 'she would not consent to his wicked desire therein, do with her what he would; for if she should, she said, God would surely plague her'. The chancellor, in offering her the chance to recant for a second time, had already shown her considerable favour, for he believed her to be 'an ignorant, unlearned and foolish woman'.

Cicely Ormes rejected his offer – and he sentenced her to burn. On the morning of 23 September 1557, she was led out to the Lollard's Pit. As she reached the stake, she kneeled and prayed to God, before rising to her feet to address the crowd. 'Good people! I believe in God the Father, God the Son, and God the Holy Ghost, three persons and one God', she declared. 'This do I not, nor will I recant: but I recant utterly from the bottom of my heart the doings of the pope of Rome, and all his popish priests and shavelings. I utterly refuse and never will have and do with them again, by God's grace.' She was an unlikely preacher – and it was unusual for a woman to be permitted to speak as she did – but she continued: 'And good people! I would you should not report of me that I believe to be saved in that I offer myself here unto the death for the lord's cause, but I believe to be saved by the death and passion of Christ; and this my death is and shall be a witness of my faith unto you all here present.' She ended by asking: 'Good people! As many of you as believe as I believe, pray for me.' Cicely then turned to the stake, which was still black with soot from the deaths of Elizabeth Cooper and Simon Miller. She touched it lovingly, to 'welcome the cross of Christ', before looking down and seeing that her own hand was blackened. She wiped it on the smock that she wore, before kissing the stake. She did not struggle as she was bound to the stake and the fire was kindled around her. 'My soul doth magnify the lord, and my spirit rejoiceth in God my saviour', she declared, as she raised her hands up towards her breasts and tilted her head upwards. As the fire licked up around her, she made no sound, but raised her hands higher and higher until her arms were burnt away. In yielding up a life 'as quietly as if she had been in a slumber' or 'as one feeling no pain', simple, ordinary Cicely Ormes became a mighty piece of Protestant propaganda in the ongoing religious struggles of the Reformation.

∞

Unlike these women of Norwich, Rose Hickman had the financial means to keep herself safe. Antwerp, which was then the greatest trading centre in Europe, was not a Protestant city. But the churches there were so large that absences were rarely noticed, and the Hickmans were able to carry out their religion and their trading business without too many difficulties. They were far from the only Protestants to flee England. Another woman, Catherine Knollys, a niece of Anne Boleyn, escaped to the German states with her husband during the period. When she left, Catherine's cousin, Princess Elizabeth, who was beset with her own difficulties, wrote her a sympathetic letter. Rather like Rose Hickman's sister-in-law, Elizabeth chose to conform outwardly, going regularly to mass, where she would complain that her stomach hurt as a means of disrupting the service.

In Antwerp, Rose Hickman gave birth to a further child. She was adamant that this baby – unlike her previous one – would not be baptized in a Catholic church. With the help of her female attendants, she conceived an elaborate subterfuge. It was the custom in Antwerp that a mother would hang a little piece of cloth over the door of her house when a child was taken out for baptism. Conveniently, the house in which she lived occupied a corner plot, so Rose simply hung cloth over two doors, which faced different streets. When her neighbours noticed this, but had not seen the procession leave the house, they assumed that she had simply garbled the custom by decorating both doors, and that she had left by the other exit. No one thought any more of the matter, assuming that the child had been properly baptized. This allowed Rose to have her child 'secretly carried' later to one of the hidden Protestant congregations, where a minister performed the service. The ceremony was so secret that she did not even know the names of the child's godparents.[18]

The Hickmans were still in Antwerp when they heard the 'not a little joyful' news that Queen Mary had died on 17 November 1558, at the age of forty-two. To Rose, God had answered her prayers, since she 'had often prayed earnestly to God to take either her or me forth of the world'. She could later proudly record that, during the reign, she had never once attended any 'popish masses, or any other of their idolatrous service'.[19]

Unlike Edward VI, the dying Mary reluctantly accepted that she could not divert the succession, even though her heir – Anne Boleyn's daughter – would put the Catholic restoration under dire threat. Although the new queen, Elizabeth I, had been attending Catholic services, her true beliefs were well known.[20] In March 1559, during an interview with the Spanish ambassador, she made this quite clear. She could not possibly marry the widowed Philip of Spain, who had been angling for a marriage, for in his eyes 'she was a heretic'.[21] That same year, Elizabeth's Act of Supremacy was passed, breaking with Rome again and making the queen the head of the English Church. The Act of Uniformity, also of 1559, made regular attendance at Protestant services mandatory. A decade later, in 1570, when the papal bull 'Regnans in excelsis' confirmed Elizabeth as a heretic and gave Catholics – both English and foreign – justification for overthrowing her, the very survival of Elizabethan England came to be bound up with battling the perceived Catholic threat.

The changes wrought by Elizabeth's religious settlement were to be the final great alteration in English religion under the Tudors; but without crystal balls, people could not know the latest changes would stand. Although it was said of Elizabeth that she turned a blind eye to people's beliefs – in her words, that she did not wish to make windows into men's souls – Catholic *worship* was always illegal under her rule. The vast majority of Catholics became 'church papists' who conformed by attending the parish church.[22] But some, including women, took a more active stand. A room in a house could easily be converted into a makeshift chapel, while a priest could hide as a servant or distant member of the family.[23] For Catholics living and worshipping this way, there was always danger. At the Croydon Assizes on 18 July 1561, a priest, Thomas Langdon, was indicted for celebrating a private mass at Southwark three months before. Three of his flock – John and Joan Hoskins, and their son John – were also arrested.[24] Some Catholics, 'recusants', refused to come to church at all, and they faced stiff penalties for their disobedience. Others, including a number of women, went further still, suffering under Elizabeth every bit as cruelly as the Protestant martyrs did under Mary I.

Alice Elton, recusant

In Elizabeth's England, 'recusants' would come to risk both imprisonment and crippling financial penalties for failing to turn up at church. And one family who knew this only too well were the Eltons of Ledbury, in Herefordshire.

They were an old gentry's family, well established in the rolling hills of their Welsh borders home.[25] In 1569, the head of the family, Anthony, made an excellent and happy marriage to Alice Scudamore, the daughter of the wealthy

John Scudamore of nearby Kentchurch, producing thirteen children.[26]

Alice's family was staunchly Catholic. Both her parents and her eldest brother, Thomas, refused to attend their local parish church.[27] This was already a serious business when, in 1581, the punishments for recusancy were dramatically increased.[28] Where once it had been an easy matter to pay a small fine, from 1581, the financial penalties were set at the crippling sum of £20 a month. Those who were unable to pay were imprisoned; and there was mandatory incarceration for those caught attending mass.[29]

Alice Elton at first attended her local parish church, in spite of the Protestant services. At least twice in 1574, she made her way there to stand as godmother to two local children, while her own offspring were also baptized there.[30] This was far from unusual, the vast majority of Catholics in England being 'church papists' at least some of the time. Perhaps she covered her ears, or recited her prayers in Latin, as others did, to avoid listening to a heretical service.

In 1577, though, both Anthony and Alice were named in an official survey of those 'as refuse to come to church' in Herefordshire, with the result that their lands and chattels were valued, with a view to confiscation.[31] In April 1582, Alice's father's lands were seized by the Crown and let out. He continued to be convicted of recusancy throughout the 1580s – and was soon gaoled.[32]

At the same time, Anthony Elton, along with his brother-in-law Thomas Scudamore, appeared ominously on an official list of recusants 'remaining at liberty'.[33] Under considerable pressure, Anthony was reconciled with the Church of England in 1586.[34] This concession saved the family's wealth and status, while Alice continued to safeguard their spiritual welfare, later being convicted of recusancy between September 1586 and March 1588.[35] She was still refusing to go to church in 1587, when her husband, in his early forties, died.[36]

Now a widow with young children, Alice Elton returned to her home parish of Kentchurch, where she continued to be regularly convicted of recusancy.[37] She had chosen a dangerous path through her adherence to a Catholic teaching that maintained it was a sin to attend heretical church services. She was just one of many women to keep the faith in this way, and to suffer arrest and imprisonment for recusancy.

Margaret Clitherow was among those martyrs, and she endured a particularly gruesome death. This young woman, who was graced 'with comely face and beauty', as well as a good wit, was born in York during the reign of Mary I. Her family were prosperous – her father once served as sheriff. At fifteen, she married John Clitherow, a widower twice her age, who made a good living as a butcher in the city. Only two or three years after their marriage, her husband, who remained a Protestant, was surprised to discover that she had converted to Catholicism, becoming 'a lively member of the Church'.[38]

To Margaret, the initiative for her conversion was entirely her own. She threw herself into her faith, declaring that she was prepared to 'forsake husband, life, and all'. Margaret had a mantra, enduring all hardships with the words:

> *I will not be afraid to serve God, and do well. This is a war and trial in God's Church, and therefore if I cannot do my duty without peril and dangers, yet by God's grace I will not be slacker for them. If God's priests dare venture themselves to my house, I will never refuse them.*[39]

She spent much of her time at prayer and took the sacrament twice a week.[40] When she had leisure time, she would read a translation of the New Testament, as well as other spiritual books, while she also learned the service for matins in Latin.[41] She was busy with day-to-day routines too, running her household, raising her children and organizing her servants, who diligently kept secret the priests hidden in her house. Most people in York knew that the butcher's pretty young wife was a Catholic. But so, too, did the authorities – and as a result she endured many spells of imprisonment.

Margaret had been free from prison for nearly eighteen months when, in March 1586, she received word that her husband had been summoned before the Council at York.[42] She was frightened, commenting that 'they pick quarrels at me, and they will never cease until they have me again, but God's will be done'. She was ready when commissioners arrived to search her house; she had already sent her priest to hide with a neighbour, and his books and chapel furnishings were hurriedly concealed. The authorities found Margaret busy at her household work, feigning innocence. But the priest was soon located, and Margaret was arrested and taken to York's castle prison to await her fate.

On 14 March, Margaret was arraigned before the judges on the charge of harbouring priests in her house. 'Margaret Clitherow, how say you? Are you guilty of this indictment or no?', asked one of the judges, anxious to arrange her trial before a jury. Margaret stood still: 'I know no offence whereof I should confess myself guilty'. 'Yes,' replied the judge, 'you have harboured and maintained Jesuits and priests, enemies of Her Majesty'. No, said Margaret, 'I never knew nor have harboured any such persons, or maintained those which are not the queen's friends. God defend I should.' When asked: 'How will you be tried?', she declared: 'Having made no offence, I need no trial.' She maintained this position throughout the trial, to the judges' exasperation: they could not try her if she would not plead. As she continued to maintain her silence, there was uproar. She was mad, some of the judges declared furiously. Others used her sex against her, declaring that 'it is not for religion that thou harbourest priests, but for harlotry'. Still silent, she was sent back to prison.

The following morning, when she was once again arraigned, a judge declared that 'if you will not put yourself to the country, this must be your judgement'. In a case where the prisoner refused to plead, there was only one sentence to be pronounced. She would be taken out of her prison before being stripped naked and laid on her back on the ground. Then, there would be 'as much weight laid upon you as you are able to bear'. This torture would continue for three days, with Margaret to be offered nothing but 'a little barley bread and puddle water' to sustain herself. On the third day, if she still refused to plead, she would 'be pressed to death, your hands and feet tied to posts, and a sharp stone under your back'. It was a devastating sentence. She kept her face calm and expressionless, merely saying: 'If this judgement be according to your own conscience, I pray God send you better judgement before Him. I thank God heartily for this.' She was then taken back to prison.

Margaret Clitherow had looked for martyrdom, but nevertheless the prospect of the sentence was alarming. On the night before she died, she asked for a maid to stay with her, hastening to add that this was 'not for any fear of death, for it is my comfort, but the flesh is frail'.[43] She spent much of the night at prayer, finally lying down at 3am for three hours of rest.

They came for her at 8am on 25 March 1586.[44] She went 'cheerfully to her marriage, as she called it', giving alms to the throng of people who pressed along the streets to see her. She was barefooted and barelegged, wearing only a loose gown to cover herself. When told to hurry, she replied: 'Good master sheriff, let me deal my poor alms before I now go, for my time is but short.'

For modesty's sake, Margaret asked if she could die wearing her smock, a request that was denied. She was, however, able to persuade the men that had gathered to turn their faces away as women undressed her and laid her on the ground, covering her in a long linen habit. She was shown a small mercy, since the sharp stone that would kill her was placed on her back that first day, rather than on the third day as her sentence had stipulated. Once in place, a door was laid upon her and her hands bound. She prayed, wishing that the queen would become a Catholic. As weights were laid upon the door, she cried out: 'Jesu! Jesu! Jesu! Have mercy upon me!' These were her last words. In the quarter of an hour that it took her to die, she suffered greatly, with the pressure breaking her ribs and causing them to protrude through her skin. Her body was then left in the press for six hours. It was a cruel and barbarous death.

Margaret Clitherow – like Anne Askew, Joan Bocher, Elizabeth Cooper and Cecily Ormes – came to her own conclusions about religion. After her death, she became an example to other Catholic women. One of those, a gentlewoman named Margaret Ward, was hanged at Tyburn in 1588 for supplying a rope with which a priest made his escape from prison.[45] This was, contemporaries asserted, 'a noble proof of constancy despite her sex'. She, too, had suffered torture before her death, being hung up in prison by her wrists, with only the very tips of her toes touching the floor. Stretched in this way, she was then whipped, only being released when she was so 'crippled' with pain that she could no longer stand.[46] In 1601, a former Puritan named Anne Line was also hanged at Tyburn, for harbouring priests. This unlikely martyr had seen a vision inspiring her to act.[47] She was too weak to walk to her trial and execution, but, as she stood on the gallows, she found the strength to make the sign of the cross on her body before she died.[48]

A few years earlier, a widow named Jane Wiseman had been lucky not to share the same fate as Margaret Clitherow when she was sentenced 'to be crushed' for aiding a Catholic priest.[49] With the queen anxious to avoid another public spectacle, her sentence was quietly commuted to imprisonment; she was eventually released, after Elizabeth's death. She was fortunate, although she failed to obtain her martyr's crown.

∞

England's Reformation ushered in much that was good for the advancement of women. It was inextricable from the Tudor novelty of not one, but two reigning queens (even three, if one admits Jane Grey) – women reaching the pinnacle of power in a way unknown in English history. For many more women, the increasing educational opportunities and the publication of religious texts in English allowed them to think about their faith in a way inaccessible to them before. It was also a brutal time, with all sides of the religious debate proffering death to those that opposed them.

Ironically, the very turbulence that stemmed from the battle between tradition and reform, interwoven with the needs of very different Tudor monarchs to demand obedience from their subjects, created conditions that gave women who transgressed a platform. In an age where women had little scope for agency outside the home, their involvement in speaking out against the religious and political orthodoxies was truly remarkable. In their trials and examinations, and from their pyres and scaffolds, they could argue their cases and even preach and inspire. And in the retellings of martyrologists, they acquired an enduring imaginative power.

The Sixth Age

17

OF SETTLEMENTS AND PROPOSALS

Queen Elizabeth and Rose Hickman

When Elizabeth I was young, her hair was golden-red, her skin fair and smooth, while her eyes – which had been her mother's best feature – were 'lively and sweet, but short-sighted'.[1] She was more handsome than beautiful. But the crown that Elizabeth Tudor first put on in November 1558 was a powerful aphrodisiac. As the years passed, there were many around her who continued to 'admire her beauty'. They began to pretend, growing more and more exuberant in their praise.[2] She seemed, to observers, to be 'strangely pleased to hear the beauty of her face, the sweetness of her voice' and her other virtues so admired by others.

In darker moments, she knew it was a fiction, as courtiers rushed to rid rooms of mirrors as the queen strode through her palaces. If she happened – by accident – to glance into a forgotten looking-glass, 'she would be strangely transported and offended, because it did not still show her what she had been'.[3] Youth was wasted on the young, believed the ageing queen. She remembered, when she was in her fifties, a time 'when I was fair and young, and favour graced me'. There were many then, who sought her love, but, as she recalled, 'I did scorn them all, and said to them therefore,/ 'Go, go, go seek some otherwhere; importune me no more.'[4] She regretted that she had once been so dismissive.

Old age seemed a poor reward for survival in Tudor England. Times had changed, said some, looking back to a gilded past when the old had once been treated with more respect.[5] A good number of the elderly found no place in the homes of their children and other relatives. With no prospect of retirement, many lower down the social scale only had hard work, physical degeneration and hardship to look forward to as they took their final steps towards the grave.[6] Yet, old age has always been poorly defined, and the aged were then, as now, no homogenous mass.[7] With short generations, a mother and her daughter could both be old women, and there could still be a world of difference between the two.

The sixth age of life was the start of old age, believed contemporaries. For some it could be active, even liberating. More commonly, it was regarded, as by Shakespeare, as the time when a man was shifting 'into the lean and slippered pantaloon,/With spectacles on nose and pouch on side'. Clothes once filled by muscle had become too large; the once 'big manly voice' had turned 'again toward childish treble, pipes/And whistles in his sound'. This sixth age – that of the young-old – was often portrayed as a sad one, of decline and loss, but carrying with it a sense of the ridiculous, too, as 'pantaloon' suggests. It could be this way, too, for women; perhaps it was so, in some respects, for the ageing Elizabeth in her vanities.

There has never been any agreement about exactly when 'old age' starts.[8] In the medieval period, it was sometimes considered to be forty, sometimes forty-five, sometimes nearer fifty-eight or sixty.[9] One writer considered it to be the surprisingly young thirty-five.[10] For women, it was often associated with the menopause and the end of fertility around the age of fifty.[11] Intensified by poor diets and physically demanding lives, the bodily changes wrought by the menopause could be very obvious: age spots, facial hair, a stooped posture likely, and teeth missing as a result of repeated pregnancies.[12] Such changes did not happen overnight, but they were enough to signal a woman's entry into old age.

Contemporaries also attributed psychological changes to the onset of old age. Medieval works, such as Andreas Capellanus's twelfth-century *The Art of Courtly Love*, considered post-menopausal women incapable of romance and love. Ideas of a post-menopausal woman's undesirability were tied up with the Church's teaching that sex was for procreation only. If there was no prospect of bearing a child, then there was no Christian reason to remarry. But many widows did so anyway.

Rose Hickman was one of those. She had returned to England from her self-imposed exile following Elizabeth I's jubilant accession. She and her husband spent the next few years concentrating on their business and raising their family. Anthony Hickman did not survive to old age, dying in 1573 and leaving a widow in her late forties, either approaching the menopause or perhaps already beyond it. Nonetheless, at some point after her husband's death, her attention was caught by a gentleman named Simon Throckmorton. He was of good gentry stock – cousin of the prominent Throckmortons of Coughton.[13]

The scion of a large family of brothers and cousins, Simon was forced to shift for himself, inheriting little more material than a family name.[14] He proved an enterprising man, securing his election to Parliament for Huntingdon, which helped him make his name. He also purchased the manor of Brampton in 1550, where he made his home as a country squire.[15] This widower, with adult children of his own, was a cut above Anthony Hickman socially, possessing connections at court.[16]

The relationship between Rose and Simon was probably a love match, driven by affection in a way that Rose's first marriage, to a man selected by her father, never could be. Both Rose and Simon were independently wealthy; and they knew there could be no children. Elderly, by the standards of the time, the couple set up home in the fair brick manor house at Brampton that Simon had built.[17] They had only a few years together before Simon's death on 27 March 1585, just before

Rose turned sixty.[18] His widow did not marry again, but it was by no means the dusk of her own life. She lived quietly for many more years, close to a family that included 'her children's children'.[19] Rose, who would outlive the Tudor dynasty and most of her generation, wrote her autobiography at the age of eighty-five. She died, two years later, on 21 November 1613.[20]

Late second marriages were by no means uncommon. In Norwich in the 1570s, there were disproportionate numbers of widows thanks to women's tendency to outlive their spouses.[21] The majority of aged men, however – even the most undesirable of specimens – were able to find a new bride.[22] The social advantages of marriage evidently outweighed the disadvantage of having another mouth to feed and support for the women of Tudor Norwich. It was the same in other towns and villages in Tudor England, with many men and women outliving multiple spouses during their lifetimes. Not all these relationships were characterized by tender care. In January 1569, one Joan Emery was berated by the Board of St Bartholomew's Hospital for having taken 6s 8d from them to pay for the care of her elderly husband's 'sore leg', but once in possession of the funds, she had spent them before abandoning her husband at the hospital gates to become (as the board complained) 'one of the poor of this house'.[23] The Board furiously ordered her to at least pay a contribution towards his upkeep.

Lives recorded and remembered

On Friday 24 August 1599, Margaret, Lady Hoby of Hackness in Yorkshire, rose from her bed and dressed.[24] As always, she then said her prayers, before joining her husband for breakfast. That done, she rode to church, to hear a sermon, before taking dinner mid-morning – as was customary at the time. She then 'passed the time in talk with some friends', before once again attending to her private devotions. She and her husband 'took the air in the coach' in the late afternoon, after which she returned to walk in the garden and meditate 'on the points of the sermon' and her own private prayers. All too soon, it was supper. Prayers with her household preceded retirement to bed.

It was a typical day for this pious noblewoman. We know about Rose Hickman, because in her eighties she did the rare thing of recording her life in her autobiography, and we know the daily routines of Lady Hoby because she was one of a handful of Tudor women diarists whose work has survived.

Lady Hoby kept her journal from 1599 until 1605, tracking her life and religious devotions. It was intended as a private record, a toll that might assist her in her own religious self-assessment.[25] She included details of her health and other activities too, but it is clear that there was a rhythm to Lady Hoby's daily life, of work and other household activities, punctuated by religious routine.

The aristocratic Lady Anne Clifford kept diaries for many decades of her long life, with the first beginning at the Tudor dynasty's end in 1603, as Elizabeth I's life concluded. She was an eyewitness to the last Tudor queen's funeral, although not an official mourner. Nonetheless, Anne took her place in Westminster Abbey 'to see the solemnities performed'. In the days following Queen Elizabeth's death, Anne recorded that 'we used very much to go to Whitehall and walked in the garden which was frequented by Lords and Ladies'.[26] Although a child, she could see that everyone there was 'full of hopes every man expecting mountains & finding molehills', although she also noted a frostiness in the relations between her mother and the chief minister, Sir Robert Cecil.

Diary writing was not, of course, restricted to women, but such records are particularly useful when they relate to women, whose lives were typically less visible than men. In them, we learn, for example, about household management and women's relationships with their tenants and neighbours, as well as gaining a glimpse of the routines and concerns of the individual writers – for the most part, women from the higher echelons of society.

∞

The most prominent Tudor woman of them all had, at least so far, always resisted marriage. Elizabeth I had swept to the throne at the age of twenty-five amid public celebration, having passed through much danger. She was determined to maintain her position, adeptly batting away offers of marriage that would have reduced her authority. In February 1559, Parliament formally petitioned her to marry and provide England with a king to share her rule. Her response, although courteous, was surprising. She intended, she said, to remain 'a virgin pure until her death'. No one believed her: the queen must have a husband.

She seemed to do well enough without one. She had inherited a kingdom at war with France, divided as to religion and nearly bankrupt. Beset by serious challenges on all sides, she handled her affairs carefully and made her kingdom great. While side-stepping marriage, as a young queen she flirted with her male favourites as she presided over a cultured, glittering court. She also resisted all attempts by disease, accident or foul play to kill her – no mean feat in sixteenth-century England. The reward for this longevity was grey hair, which was soon covered by red wigs, and a wrinkled face disguised beneath layers of toxic white make-up. Her smile was a largely toothless one, causing puckered and sunken lips. A queen who assiduously propagated her regal image, she attempted strategic deception. By the end of her life she owned 3,000 gowns, being firmly of the belief 'that the eyes of her people, being dazzled with the glittering aspect of those accidental ornaments would not so easily discern the marks of age and decay of natural beauty'.[27] It worked – to some extent. A visitor to her court in 1602 was impressed by a glimpse of her 'snow-white skin'.[28] 'Even in her old age,' he considered, 'she did not look ugly, when seen from a distance'.

Whatever her looks, Elizabeth's crown ensured her continuing desirability to foreign princes. There were few unmarried men in Europe who would have refused her, although the future Henry III of France caused offence by calling her 'an old creature with a sore leg'. His younger brother, Francis, Duke of Alençon, was less particular, offering marriage in 1571 when he was sixteen. Elizabeth, who was by then approaching thirty-eight – mature if not yet onto old age – baulked at the idea of marrying a teenager. But Alençon proved persistent, writing to her in August 1573 that he was nearly dead for her love, before sending her a ring as proof of his affection.[29] This had little effect. Elizabeth refused, absolutely, to allow him to make a public visit. Indeed, she had heard such mixed reports of him that, as she confided to her favourite, Robert Dudley, Earl of Leicester, she did not want even to see him in private.[30]

Alençon, who was the fourth surviving son of Henry II of France and Catherine de'Medici, became heir to the French crown following the deaths of his elder brothers Francis II and Charles IX and the accession of Henry III. He was, accordingly, promoted, acquiring also the title of 'Duke of Anjou' in 1576. But he had a poor relationship with his brother and mother, thanks to his support for the Protestant Huguenots in France and his involvement in the rebellion against Spanish – and Catholic – rule in the Netherlands. Although prepared to flirt with Protestantism, he remained a Catholic. He was opportunistic and ambitious, and the idea of becoming King of England appealed. In 1578, he took up the challenge once more – and proposed marriage again.

On 5 January 1579, Alençon's 'chief darling' and Master of the Wardrobe, Jean de Simier, arrived in England to woo

Elizabeth on his master's behalf.[31] There was merit in this delegated courtship, since Alençon was widely considered an unpromising physical specimen.[32] He had originally been christened 'Hercules', which was somewhat ironic given his notably tiny stature. Disease, too, had been unkind. While Elizabeth herself had survived a serious bout of smallpox largely unscathed, in 1562, Alençon's own brush with the disease had left him seriously pock-marked. The true extent of his pitted skin became an issue of some diplomatic importance, for the English were determined to learn the extent of his deformity. The pock-marks were, one report decided sagely, 'no great disfigurement in the rest of his face because they are rather thick than deep or great'. Except, of course the reports continued, those at the end of his nose, which were unmissable. It was to be hoped that the right woman could see past all this, with the assistance of God moving 'the heart of the beholder'.[33]

While Alençon's chief weapon could not be his physical appearance, in Simier he had 'a man thoroughly versed in love fancies, pleasant conceits and court dalliances'.[34] The forty-five-year-old Elizabeth, with her wigs, lost teeth and painted face, was utterly charmed by him. She nicknamed him her 'monkey' and even forgave his playful theft of her nightcap right out of her bedchamber. Wooing by proxy had its advantages.

'To transform human creatures'

Elizabeth I famously attempted to turn back time with the ample use of cosmetics. Later portraits, such as the anonymous 'Darnley portrait', which may have been painted from life, show a white, wax-like face which may not have been entirely the result of artistic flattery.[35] (In the years since it was painted, pigment fading has further increased the effect of paleness.) A pale, line-free skin was much admired at the time, and many women, both young and old, would go to some lengths to achieve it.

But this use of cosmetics was widely mocked in the period, too, with one work – published in 1616 – calling the practice 'paintings laid one upon another, in such sort that a man might easily cut off a curd or cheese cake from either of their cheeks'.[36] Some women, the author added, had applied so many concoctions that 'they have made their faces of a thousand colours'. It was irreligious, since by covering 'her natural face', a woman was defying God. Although this *Discourse Against Painting and Tincturing of Women* was written by a man, its transmission was aided and abetted by a woman named Elizabeth Arnold, who translated it from the Spanish.

In spite of this sort of disapproval, many women continued to use make-up to improve their appearance, particularly as they aged. To achieve a smooth white complexion,

such potions as bacon grease mixed with egg whites and a little powder were applied.[37] Another recipe used ground-up pig bones.

For the wealthiest members of society, there was the mixture of white lead and vinegar, which was known as 'ceruse'. This highly toxic compound gave the skin the desired lustre when applied, but also caused considerable skin problems. After a time, the skin could become grey and wrinkled, further exacerbating the need for cosmetics. One early seventeenth-century writer, Thomas Tuke, considered that 'white lead, wherewith women use to paint themselves was, without doubt, brought in use by the Devil, the capital enemy of nature, therewith to transform human creatures, of fair, making them ugly, enormous and abominable'.[38] But for Elizabeth I, who, like many women, had some smallpox pits and later wrinkles and other blemishes to cover, the attraction of white lead was perfectly understandable.

The favour that Elizabeth showed to her French monkey was impossible to miss: she kept him constantly at her side.[39] In the face of this French rival, the established favourite, Leicester, was particularly furious. He was probably the source of rumours that the French emissary had employed love potions and sorcery for his wooing.[40] Alençon, too, kept up the romantic pressure, with a steady stream of letters. He would, he promised his hoped-for bride, gladly lay down his life in her service – if only she would set him to work.[41] Elizabeth remained coy, protesting in March 1579 that the French prince was planning 'so disadvantageous a match for him'; but she seemed interested.[42]

That same month, Elizabeth's chief minister, the capable, orderly and hardworking William Cecil, methodically drew up a list of objections that might be made to the queen's marriage, complete with an answer for each of them.[43] The first objection was, appropriately enough, 'Her Majesty's own mislike to marriage, which might breed in her a discontented life hereafter, if she should marry'. Elizabeth had always swatted away suitors, both at home and abroad, sometimes keeping them hanging on for years. Yet, with Alençon she seemed more serious. She should, thought Cecil, take 'council therein only of God and of her own heart' and make her choice.

Another, more tangible objection was 'the peril of Her Majesty's person if at these years she should be delivered of a child'. At forty-five, any such delivery must have seemed unlikely, but Cecil had made discreet enquiries among the queen's physicians and attendants to confirm that she was still menstruating. Childbirth was always a danger to women, but all the more so for a woman undergoing her first confinement on the cusp of old age. She was healthy and a fine physical specimen, so had good chances of survival, considered Cecil; but the risk was immense. Only the prospect of the birth of a child to continue 'in the blood of the body of that famous king Henry the Eighth' made such a risk worthwhile. God, who was 'the author of Her Majesty's marriage' could also perhaps be relied upon to sustain her.

Recognizing the extreme unlikelihood of Elizabeth being able to bear Alençon a child, Cecil then worried lest the Frenchman might be driven to murder her if she proved barren. It was, he considered, 'hard for a Christian man to have such a thought of a Christian prince', but it was possible, particularly if he inherited the French crown. With Elizabeth remaining in her own realm, she would be protected 'both presently and hereafter when she shall be past child bearing and have no child'. There were concerns, too, about maintaining her husband, about protecting the Protestant religion, and about the dangers of the queen making a foreign match. If Alençon should succeed to the throne of France, there was every concern that both Elizabeth and any child might be spirited away, leaving England subject to a viceroy 'to the discontentment of the realm'.

Cecil was not entirely negative. He also identified some benefits to the match, the chief of which was the alliance with France that it would bring. Pertinently, it would also prevent Alençon from taking a Spanish bride and forging an alliance with England's greatest enemy. This was, probably, the driving force behind Elizabeth's own interest in the match; but she also enjoyed the pursuit it entailed, and the proof it provided of her continuing desirability. By 12 April 1579, Simier was feeling rather hopeful, although he resolved to wait 'till the curtain is drawn, the candle out, and Monsieur in bed' before he gave way to boasting.[44] Privately, he professed himself pleased with what he saw in Elizabeth, whom he thought 'the most virtuous and honourable princess in the world; her wit is admirable, and there are so many other parts to remark in her that I should need much ink and paper to catalogue them'. His master would, he was sure, be 'very fortunate if God will further this business'.

At the same time as wooing the queen herself, Simier was also trying to negotiate a marriage treaty; but matters soon became bogged down. Alençon wanted to be crowned king as soon as the marriage ceremony had been celebrated, as well as being given the joint authority with Elizabeth to make grants, and a pension of £60,000 for life.[45] The second demand was, on 3 May 1579, 'utterly denied' by Elizabeth's commissioners, while the other two were considered doubtful and would have to be referred to Parliament. This response was disappointing for the Frenchman, although Elizabeth did agree to permit Alençon to practise his Catholic faith in England – a considerable concession, given the fact that the worship had been banned in her realm for nearly twenty years.[46]

The impasse was only broken when Alençon agreed to do something that few of the queen's suitors had done before: he would come to visit. His cause was also helped immeasurably in July 1579, when the wily Simier, intending 'to remove Leicester out of his place and favour with the queen', revealed that the earl, Elizabeth's greatest and longest-standing love, was secretly married. Hurt and furious, the queen had to be strongly persuaded not to send Leicester to the Tower.[47] She never forgave his bride – her cousin, Lettice Knollys.

∽

Elizabeth's countless offers of marriage received during her twenty years on the throne had begun with the suit of her brother-in-law Philip of Spain, who had reluctantly proposed for the good of Catholicism. Her insistence that she would only wed a man that she had met and liked had always proved a useful tool, since few foreign princes were prepared to risk ridicule if their visit was met with rejection. Elizabeth was therefore now charmed when the heir to the French throne agreed to come. In preparation, she gave the key to her chamber at Greenwich to Simier, directing him on how to enter privately through the door to her private chapel.[48] Her incognito visitor, who had

landed in England with only a handful of attendants, arrived
quietly at Greenwich on 17 August 1579.[49] Alençon went at
once to Simier's apartments, in the waterside palace where
Elizabeth had been born. Greenwich – which had been built as
a pleasure palace on the Thames – made an excellent backdrop
to romance, away from the busy crowding of London's streets.
On hearing of his arrival, the queen slipped into Simier's rooms
herself, with only one lady in attendance, to dine with the duke.

Elizabeth and Alençon were either both extremely tactful,
or pleasantly surprised. They gave every sign of being attracted
to each other. The Spanish ambassador, who knew all about
Alençon's 'boyish trick' in arriving incognito, made no comment
as the apparently smitten queen began to drop hints about her
visitor when he next saw her. Elizabeth was, he surmised:

> ... *delighted with Alençon, and he with her, as she has let
> out to some of her courtiers, saying that she was pleased to
> have known him, was much taken with his good parts, and
> admired him more than any man. She said that, for her
> part, she will not prevent his being her husband. The French
> say the same thing.*[50]

Of course, Elizabeth wanted the Spanish ambassador to fear
an alliance with France. His master, Philip of Spain, still considered the match improbable on both sides. There was, he
thought, no 'great desire for it, but on the contrary a large
amount of pretence'.[51] Others were more concerned. Leicester,
who appeared emotional after a meeting with the queen, was
worried, as was the Earl of Sussex, who was on her Council.[52]
Margaret Clifford, Countess of Derby and great-niece of Henry
VIII, who had hopes of the succession herself, was alarmed
enough to consult a sorcerer to try to discover by witchcraft just
how long the queen would live. She was promptly arrested for
her efforts.

The Duke of Alençon was immediately favoured with one of the queen's bestial nicknames, becoming her 'frog'. At a court ball held on Sunday 23 August, Elizabeth was observed to dance more than usual. Everyone pretended not to see the little signals she directed towards an arras, behind which her covert visitor was hiding. The queen – only weeks away from her forty-sixth birthday – was in her element. She was saddened when, on 27 August, Alençon set out once more for Dover.[53] He was charming to the last, presenting the object of his endeavour with a diamond ring worth (as the French boasted to the Spanish ambassador) 10,000 crowns, as they said their farewells at Cobham, just south of London.[54] Tenderly, Elizabeth bestowed her own jewel on the prince. Both professed the hope that the parting would be but a short one; and Simier remaining behind to continue the wooing. Alençon, for his part, wrote to the queen as soon as he reached Paris to inform her that he was 'dying for want of news from her'.[55]

In his absence, Elizabeth was continually 'dwelling upon Alençon's good qualities', when she met with the Spanish ambassador.[56] She gave all appearance of being serious about a marriage that she had previously 'felt repugnance' for, 'as she was a woman of middle age, and the ardent desire of so young a man as Alençon to marry her must give rise to grave considerations'.[57] But in many ways, she was still younger than her years. Her constitution was something to be marvelled at. The queen kept herself so fit that, even at the very end of her life, she was observed in her gardens 'walking as freely as if she had been only eighteen years old'.[58] Nonetheless, Elizabeth repeatedly brought up the age gap in the negotiations: it concerned her.

Matters seemed to be moving along by October 1579, with the queen declaring confidently 'that she will never any (if she shall marry) but him', as well as the more lukewarm assertion that 'she doth nor mislike him'.[59] Among her ladies, she praised him, speaking favourably of his 'nature and conditions' and professing herself furious if anyone spoke out against her match. This was a quandary for her Council, who were entirely in the dark about her motives. They simply could not reach any agreement as to whether they should promote the marriage or speak against it, even when the queen herself asked them for their opinion. Eventually, they sent to her to ask her to 'show to them any inclination of her mind'.[60] The queen wept to receive this poor advice, complaining that they had failed to ratify her decision to 'marry and have a child of her own body to inherit, and so to continue the line of Henry the Eighth'. She was furious, declaring that she had thought to have had 'a universal request made to her to proceed in this marriage than to have made doubt of it'. On hearing this, 'and the earnest disposition for this marriage they conceived in her', the Council politically confirmed their full support for the match. They were persuaded that the queen did indeed mean to marry.

While Elizabeth gave the impression of being serious about marriage, she would not be rushed to the altar. On 11 February 1580, Alençon wrote to the queen to assure her that recent news of her had 'restored his soul to his body'.[61] But now the momentum stalled, as 1580 drew to an end and 1581 began. To the duke, it was frustrating. He wrote, on 19 April 1581, demanding 'a certain and definite answer as to her wishes for the fulfilment of the marriage so long treated of'.[62] He had done more than any other foreign suitor – but it was apparent to Alençon that it still might not be enough. Elizabeth professed herself troubled. Yet, when Leicester again began to try to persuade her against the marriage that month, she silenced him.[63] Matters had gone so far that she could not turn back, she assured him. She was frightened of war with Spain and worried about alienating the French. She therefore permitted the marriage negotiations to continue.

A marriage treaty was finally agreed in November 1581, confirming that the couple would marry within six weeks of its ratification. Much of the same ground as before was covered, including the confirmation of Alençon's freedom to worship. After the marriage was consummated, he would 'enjoy the title and honour of king, but shall leave the management of affairs wholly and solely to the queen'. Elizabeth promised, too, to ask Parliament to permit her suitor a coronation and the continued title of 'king' during the minority of any children, while letters patent would be issued in both names, as in the time of Philip and Mary. The queen, too, promised Alençon a 'considerable sum of money yearly' if he outlived her, while if she outlived him, she would receive 40,000 crowns a year from his French lands.

Optimistically, given the fact that Elizabeth was forty-eight years old, it was agreed that if they had two sons, the eldest would inherit France and the second England, while a sole son would take both realms, on the promise that he lived in England for a third of the time. Alençon would have the guardianship of any sons under eighteen and daughters under fifteen if he outlived Elizabeth, providing that he did not meddle with the law and customs of England. He promised, too, that he would 'not convey the queen nor her children out of the realm of England, but by her own consent and the consent of the peers of the realm'. Finally, and importantly, the French prince would have no claim to England. It was confirmed that 'the queen alone shall bear the superiority'. It looked to all the world as though Elizabeth had finally decided to embark on matrimony, although there were still certain – unspecified – points to be addressed before she was 'bound to consummate the marriage'.

Alençon, who had pushed for the marriage for so many years, was overjoyed. He hurried to England, hoping to marry at once, or at least secure financial support for his expedition to the Netherlands. Coming, ostensibly, as the queen's fiancé, he was pleased to find himself respectfully received by Elizabeth, who showed him considerable affection. He was there during the celebrations to mark the anniversary of her accession on 17

November and, seemingly in the heat of the moment, as the couple talked of love, Elizabeth took a ring from her finger and placed it on Alençon's.[64] To those standing by, it looked to all the world as though the queen had contracted her marriage by promise, binding herself to the Frenchman with or without a religious ceremony. In the Netherlands, the news was met with outpourings of public joy, including bonfires in the streets of Rose Hickman's old home of Antwerp and guns discharged in jubilation.

In England, celebrations were rather more muted. Some at court were joyful, but most were dismayed. Even before the gossip crossed the Channel, Elizabeth, too, was having doubts. On the night of 17 November, her gentlewoman began to lament and bewail the engagement, speaking of the perils of childbirth. William Camden, Elizabeth's earliest biographer, believed that this 'did so terrify and vex her mind, that she spent the night in doubts and cares without sleep amongst those weeping and wailing females'. The next day, Elizabeth sent for Alençon and, shooing away everyone around them, they spoke privately for some time. Finally, the duke stalked away. Returning to his chamber, he threw Elizabeth's ring from him, before finally placing it back on his finger again. Complaining of the 'lightness of women' and 'the inconstancy of islanders', he made plans to return to the Netherlands, his journey funded by the queen. He had reluctantly agreed to a perpetual betrothal.

Alençon was still, to the world, the queen's fiancé; but no one can have truly believed that the marriage would occur. Elizabeth flirted seriously with marriage as she approached the menopause and old age, but, ultimately, she pulled back. Perhaps she had genuinely considered marrying the young Frenchman, who had surprised her by coming to woo in person; perhaps – more likely – she had indulged his advances for political reasons. Nonetheless, she seems to have genuinely cared for her 'frog', even if she never could bring herself to become his wife.

∽

At the time of 'Monsieur's departure', Elizabeth wrote a poem, seemingly opening up the heart of a woman grieving and forced to dissemble.[65] Her care was, she recorded, 'like my shadow in the sun'. At the same time:

> *I grieve and dare not show my discontent;*
> *I love, and yet am forced to seem to hate;*
> *I do, yet dare not say I ever meant;*
> *I seem stark mute, but inwardly do prate.*
> *I am, and not; I freeze and yet am burned,*
> *Since from myself another self I turned.*

She ended: 'Let me float or sink, be high or low;/Or let me live with some more sweet content,/Or die, and so forget what love e'er meant.'

The couple continued to write regularly for years. Often, she addressed him as 'dearest', but the topics were usually political, focussed on the Netherlands and France.[66] Yet, it was in the guise of a fiancée that she wrote to Catherine de'Medici on learning of Alençon's early death in 1584, considering that the mother's grief 'cannot be greater than my own. For inasmuch as you are his mother, so it is that there remain in you several other children. But for me, I find no consolation except death, which I hope will soon reunite us.'[67] If Catherine could only look into her heart, Elizabeth assured her, she 'would see the portrait of a body without a soul'.

The Duke of Alençon was to be Elizabeth's last suitor. With his death ended the fiction of the queen's betrothal and the mock display of her maidenly youth. She was, in 1584, fifty-one – in contemporary terms already old, and quite securely in the sixth age of life.

The Seventh Age

OF WIGS AND WITCHCRAFT

Queen Elizabeth in her sixties, and the
witches of England

T o William Shakespeare, the final, seventh, stage of life
was the 'last scene of all, that ends this strange eventful
history', characterized by 'second childishness and mere
oblivion/Sans teeth, sans eyes, sans taste, sans everything'.
While everyone had their final scene, most people in Tudor
England never lived long enough to clock up the kind of years
associated with Shakespeare's description. To many that did, it
must have seemed a scant prize for their endurance. In medieval
literature, too, the image of a 'second childhood' was a common
one – if not descending into outright senility, then, like children,
contemporaries asserted, the very elderly were foolish and
lacking judgement.[1]

Elizabeth I turned sixty in September 1593 – old by anyone's
standards at the time. No other Tudor monarch had reached that
number. Following this important birthday, she celebrated her
accession day with particular splendour. At Windsor, her thirty-
five years on the throne were marked with 'a great triumph'
of plays, masques and tournaments.[2] There was, of course, no
question that she should retire, although, as one contemporary observed, 'this crown is not like to fall to the ground for
want of heads that claim to wear it'.[3] Soon, her subjects would
proudly boast that she was 'that good old princess the now

queen, the eldest prince in years and reign throughout Europe or our known world'.[4]

In an age when men and women were expected to work until they could not physically do so, Elizabeth was doing nothing unusual in retaining her firm grasp on affairs. At the other end of the social scale, as in the poorest streets of Norwich in 1570, the elderly were also often active, but through necessity.[5] A widow named Elizabeth Menson had lived in the town for forty years by 1570, and claimed to be eighty years old. She was 'a lame woman of one hand', perhaps having suffered a stroke; but she was still able to eke out a living with her spinning. She could also wind wool for money with one hand.

Eighty-year-old Alice Cotton, who was also lame in one hand, similarly spun for a living, as did Katherine Brand, another eighty-year-old widow, who could no longer walk. The even older Janice House, at eighty-five, had lived in the town all her life; she, too, was still spinning wool to support herself. They were lucky that their advanced years and illnesses did not prevent them from making a living. Many were not so fortunate, and had to throw themselves on charity. A widowed contemporary, Eme Stowe, also 'lame in her arm', lived with an eleven-year-old boy, 'a bastard of her daughter's', and the pair went about the town begging for aid. Agnes Durant, who claimed to be eighty-four in 1570, could no longer spin cloth for a living, and in her ill health relied on her daughter and eight-year-old granddaughter, both of whom had taken her place at the spinning wheel. The family were very poor, earning only 2d a week.

For most in Tudor England, old age was synonymous with poverty. In Ipswich, a census of the poor in 1597 revealed that many of the destitute there were elderly. A visitor to the most crowded and impoverished streets of the city, might meet Anne Jackson, a sixty-year-old widow, who lived alone and scratched a living by gathering rushes.[6] There was Joan Browne, aged sixty-five, who survived by picking wool. Widow Carick, who was sixty, eked out a living, as did so many in the area, by spinning wool.

A number of elderly women in Ipswich also had to support their 'impotent' husbands, including the wife of Old Frize, an eighty-year-old ex-cobbler. She spun wool to keep the roof over their heads and food on the table. Cicely Sharpling, at sixty, was already 'impotent' herself, trying to stretch her 8d in poor relief to survive, when she really needed a shilling. Elderly couples could at least pool their resources. Thus, seventy-year-old George Bales still worked as a smith, while his sixty-three-year-old wife mended clothes. Eighty-six-year-old Thomas Smith and his seventy-year-old wife were 'both impotent and lame', but just able to spin and card wool for pennies (while their thirty-year-old child did the same). In their case, the family were considered deserving enough to receive 2 shillings a week towards their living from the charitable will trust of Henry Tooley, a wealthy town merchant.

∞

Old age could be particularly hard on women. Contemporaries had only to consider the wildly popular *Women's Secrets* to know that old women should be viewed with suspicion.[7] Best keep these crones away from infants, cautioned the learned text, since they could 'poison the eyes of children lying in their cradles by their glance'.[8] All women were 'entirely venomous', readers were told, but in earlier years menstrual blood at least served to dilute these evil humours. With the onset of the menopause, the poison was left to stew fetid in the body, with the worst toxins escaping malignantly through wrinkled eyes. It was advisable to be wary of these spider-like old women,[9] especially the poorer sort, who were worse than the rich thanks to a diet of 'coarse food, which contributes to the poisonous matter'.

It is no surprise that old women, therefore, were disproportionately victims of the charge of witchcraft. In one case, on Sunday 15 August 1574, two young Londoners, Agnes Briggs and Rachel Pinder, were taken to Paul's Cross, where they gave penance and publicly admitted that they had pretended to be bewitched.[10] Rachel, who was eleven years old, had been particularly artful, arching her back and vomiting out hair, feathers and threads. Briggs, who had seen Pinder perform, had aped her, hiding pins and fabric in her cheeks before bringing them forth in feigned fits. Both had named 'Old Joan' as the cause of their affliction – their neighbour, elderly Joan Thornton. She was fortunate that the girls' duplicity was soon uncovered, though Briggs's subsequent remorse and desire 'to ask forgiveness of the said Joan Thornton' can have been little comfort.

A similar story was played out when young Thomas Darling fell ill after getting lost in Winsell Wood, Derbyshire, in 1596.[11] After his urine was examined by a physician, the boy was questioned as to whether he could have been bewitched. It was possible, agreed the boy, who had then been vomiting and falling into fits for some days. He recalled that, while in the woods, he had come into a little coppice where 'I met a little old woman; she had a grey gown with a black fringe about the cape, a broad rimmed hat, and three warts on her face'. He recognized her, he said, since he had seen her begging from door to door in the little town of Stapenhill.[12] He had, he confessed, broken wind as he passed her, to which the old woman angrily responded: 'Gyp with a mischief, and fart with a bell: I will go to Heaven, and thou shalt go to hell', before going about her business. The remark, coupled with her old appearance, was enough to raise suspicions. The woman must be, said those around the boy, Elizabeth Wright, 'the witch of Stapenhill'. No, said others, Elizabeth 'went little abroad'. It was her daughter, Alice Gooderidge, who had hexed the boy.

Alice was herself almost sixty years old and poorly educated, proving unable to recite the Lord's Prayer under stern questioning. She was brought at once to Thomas, who, on seeing her, 'fell suddenly marvellously into a sore fit'. Suspicion was always likely to fall on elderly Alice and her ancient mother, for they had been held four or five times before on suspicion of witchcraft. For good measure, Alice's husband and daughter, too, were arrested.

Elizabeth Wright, 'the Witch of Stapenhill', who must have been at least seventy-five, proved a particularly pitiable prisoner. It was universally believed that only the witch herself could relieve her victim, and thus the ancient woman was brought into Thomas's house. 'Alas that ever I was born, what shall I do', cried Elizabeth at the door, but she was forced inside and induced to pray for him. Both she and her daughter were stripped and searched by a group of duly appointed women, 'to see if they could find any such marks on them. As are usually found on witches.' Elizabeth – on whom blemishes and other scars were unsurprising, given her age – was found to have 'behind her right shoulder a thing much like the udder of a ewe that giveth suck with two teats'. She had, as well, two 'great warts' on her shoulders. She had been born with the 'teats', she insisted. Her daughter had, in desperation, attempted to cut warts from her belly on hearing that she would be searched. They found instead 'a hole of the bigness of two pence, fresh and bloody'.

Under pressure, Alice confessed that on her way to buy eggs, 'I met the boy in the wood, and he called me witch of Stapenhill'. She had then complained to him that 'Every boy does call me witch, but did I ever make your arse to itch?' After being subjected to threats, she confessed to bewitching the boy that day. Immured in Derby gaol, the unfortunate woman died before she could be executed. Thomas Darling underwent an exorcism and was soon quite well.

Elderly women such as Elizabeth Wright and Alice Gooderidge looked the part of witches and could do little to defend themselves against the rumours and accusations. They were far from alone. Witchcraft touched even the family of godly and practical Rose Hickman, when her five great-nieces suddenly gave every appearance of being possessed.[13] These five Throckmorton girls had only recently moved into the manor house at Warboys, in Huntingdonshire, when around 10 November 1589 the second youngest – nine-year-old-Jane – fell ill. Her symptoms were strange, with sneezing fits signalling a fall into a trance.[14] Then, her body would seem to swell and her legs shake violently, before the symptoms affected her arms and head. She stayed like this for two or three days, while curious neighbours came to see the strange sight and commiserate with the family.

One visitor was elderly Alice Samuel, smartly dressed in her black-fringed cap, who lived in the house next door. On entering the parlour, she had only just sat down when the girl cried out: 'Grandmother, look where the old witch sits', before pointing directly at her aged neighbour. 'Did you ever see one more like a witch than she is?' the girl asked. Embarrassed, her mother rebuked her; but it was noted that Alice all the while sat still and silent. She looked 'very rueful'.

Soon, all five of the Throckmorton girls, along with a number of the serving maids, were showing the same symptoms. All cried out against Alice, declaring: 'Take her away. Look where she stands here before us in a black fringed cap', even when she was not present; 'it is she that has bewitched us, and she will kill us if you do not take her away'. At first, Mother Samuel had tried to be helpful, protesting that 'she would come to the said children, whenever it pleased their parents to send for her, and that she would venture her life in water up to her chin, and lose some part of her best blood, to do them any good'.

However, when called for, her courage failed her, and she had to be forced, going 'as willingly as a bear to the stake'. Once in her presence, the girls all predictably fell down, appearing 'strangely tormented', while Alice was forced to place her hand in Jane's, as the girl scratched at it violently. It was, quite literally, a witch hunt, and when another neighbour, Lady Cromwell, fell ill and died after interrogating Alice, it seemed that Alice had added magical murder to her crimes. All Alice could say in her defence was that 'Master Throckmorton and his wife did her great wrong, so to blame her without cause.' To Lady Cromwell, she had protested: 'Madam, why do you use me thus? I never did you any harm as yet.' Nothing she said could have cleared her – she looked like a witch and everything she said seemed, to observers, to confirm her guilt. Finally, Alice, her husband John and daughter Agnes were all imprisoned. In prison, old Mother Samuel appeared so unruly that she was chained to a bedpost. Under these conditions, she made a confession, but it was not enough to save either herself or her family. They were convicted and hanged in 1593. The Throckmorton girls recovered.

Once accused of the nebulous crime of witchcraft, a woman could only with difficulty clear her name. An accusation was therefore a powerful weapon, used to settle local scores and put some of the more marginal members of the community in their place. Elizabeth Wright of Stapenhill was already rumoured to be a witch, while Agnes Samuel looked the part. Perhaps their 'victims' were subject to hysteria, perhaps they acted out of malice, but the effect was the same. The fact was that women and girls played notable roles in denouncing and incriminating witches, acting as witnesses and helping to search for witch marks, as well as frequently playing the role of victims.

'There are a great number of witches here'

Part of the power of witchcraft in the Tudor imagination was that it knew no bounds. It could reach the highest in the land. Queen Elizabeth's cousin, Margaret Clifford, Countess of Derby, had been imprisoned in 1579 for asking a sorcerer to predict the queen's death. Such a charge had not surprised the Spanish ambassador to England since, as he considered, 'there are a great number of witches here'.[15] It was, indeed, no great leap from pulling children sharply away from the poisonous eyes of their grandmothers to considering elderly women capable of black magic.

Henry VIII had made witchcraft a felony in 1542, punishable by death, and Elizabeth I's Parliament restated much of this legislation in 1563. In an age of great religious faith, it was unsurprising that many people believed in the power of the Devil to possess the unfortunate, or of witches to do them harm.[16] Some men were tried and convicted in the period, but the vast majority of those accused were women.[17] Like poisoning, witchcraft was seen as an indirect – pernicious – crime. As a result, many women were dragged before the courts of Tudor England, with elderly widows being particularly vulnerable to accusations.

In one county – tranquil, leafy Surrey – approximately thirty accused women were rounded up and dragged before the assize judges during Elizabeth's reign. The crimes of which they were accused were serious. Joan Gowse of Banstead had, the judges were assured, magicked an ox to death in 1564. The following year, her neighbour, Rose Borow, had 'bewitched Alice Lambert, wife of Geoffrey Lambert, so that she died'. Both were convicted at Croydon on 7 August 1565 and thrown into gaol. Borow was still there four years later.[18]

In 1582, a veritable coven was uncovered in the pleasant market town of Godalming, in the Surrey hills. The apprehended townswomen filled the assize courtroom at Kingston on 26 July. Elizabeth Coxe and her daughter, Joan, were supposedly the ringleaders, having committed four murders by sorcery over a period of more than two years.[19] Their neighbour, Agnes Waters (alias Stevens), had at the same time bewitched ten bullocks and a cow, causing their deaths.[20] Juliana Page, another Godalming matron, had used spells to murder a five-week-old baby.[21] Under questioning, Waters confessed, but the others staunchly denied the charges.

They were fortunate, since the court that day displayed a healthy degree of scepticism. Only the unfortunate Waters was convicted.

There had evidently been a rounding up of witches in the area, since one Elizabeth Cowper of Shalford was also brought before the judges that day. She had, they were told, bewitched Joan Lambert 'so that she became lame'.[22] She, too, was found not guilty. Joan Marlowe, who was accused at the same time of murdering William Haydon, at Egham, by witchcraft, had not seen fit to trust her fate to the jury, fleeing before she could be indicted.[23]

The unfortunate Agnes Waters of Godalming was released under a general pardon not long afterwards; but she was soon back before the Croydon Assizes on 12 July 1585. She was still practising her devilish arts, the judges were told, but now on people. First there was six-year-old Margaret Roker, who had clung onto life for nine months after being hexed in March 1583; then, three months later, there was Richard Charman, who lasted for a little over a month after being bewitched, and finally Catherine Hamond, who survived nine months after a magical attack by Agnes Waters on 26 June 1583.[24] With such long periods between the reported crime and the eventual deaths, it would have been hard to bring any 'evidence' to bear. But Waters, already a convicted witch, was found guilty and imprisoned. She was lucky not to face the death penalty; many others accused of witchcraft did.

∽

A world away from either the impecunious old spinners of East Anglia or the unfortunate witches of Surrey, Elizabeth I's queenship was exhibiting an increasing divergence between image and fleshly reality. By the late 1590s her post-menopausal body was visibly ageing; and yet, in the years following the abandonment of the Alençon marriage, she had become 'Gloriana', reaching the height of her political powers. The 1587 execution of her chief rival, Mary, Queen of Scots, who had been under house arrest in England for years, had shored up her throne against home-grown treason. Of direct descent from Henry VII, the several-times married Mary had been raised a Catholic in France. Nearly everyone had recognized that she was the next hereditary claimant to the English throne, but her complicity in plotting to assert herself prematurely proved her undoing. With a master-stroke of political manoeuvring, Elizabeth managed to distance herself enough from the circumstances of the death that Mary's son, the Scottish King James, was pacified.

England's former king, Philip of Spain, was less convinced, launching his Armada the following year, but it was merely to prove the English queen's greatest victory. To most of her subjects, she had become an icon: the armour-clad queen sur-veying her troops at Tilbury, while the Armada was destroyed at sea, whose 'body but of a weak and feeble woman' was just the exterior of 'the heart and stomach of a king'. To those who flocked around her, and to the poet Edmund Spenser, the woman who had presided over the defeat of the Spanish had become England's 'fairy queen'– an eternally youthful personi-fication of her country.[25]

It was a triumph of the image, in portraits, poems and paeans, but with it went an ever sharper contrast with the realities of old age. Elderly women were frequently referred to as 'Mother', 'Goodwife' or simply 'Old' in sixteenth-century England.[26] No exception was made even for Elizabeth who, in her fifties and sixties, was being called 'the old queen' or, more impertinently, 'Old Bess'.[27] She was aware of time passing too, frequently referring to herself as 'foolish and old' when speaking to the new French ambassador at the end of 1597.[28] She was, by then, sixty-four – although she told the ambassador she was still only sixty.[29] Nonetheless, this 'haughty woman', as he considered her, had no wish to conceal the forty years during which she had reigned. She had, she assured him, been 'intended for affairs of state, even from her cradle'.[30]

The ambassador, Monsieur de Maisse, was surprised to find a queen willing to reflect on approaching death. She was, she assured him at one meeting, 'on the edge of the grave and ought to bethink herself of death', before suddenly stopping and declaring that 'I think not to die so soon, Master Ambassador, and am not so old as they think.'[31] She did, however, look it, considered the Frenchman. She had a 'somewhat wrinkled' appearance, and while he noted some parts of her skin to be still 'exceeding white and delicate', her face was yet 'very aged'. Her teeth, too, betrayed her years, being 'very yellow and unequal'. Thanks to the popularity of sugar amongst the Tudor upper classes, many of Elizabeth's peers suffered from missing teeth. She was no exception, with so many of her teeth missing that it was difficult for de Maisse to understand her. She had, though, retained her graceful, slender figure and remained 'a woman of so fine and vigorous disposition both in mind and in body'. But she was suffering from gout in her hands – once her best feature.[32]

Elizabeth's prestige was not in doubt. She remained queen and retained admirers and flatterers until her dying day. She could, if she chose, believe that those around her were fooled by her majesty and increasingly elaborate clothing, as she played at love with her male favourites, of which Robert Devereux, Earl of Essex, would be the last. On 28 September 1599, the foolish, impetuous Essex, who had left his military command in Ireland without the queen's consent, suddenly appeared at Nonsuch Palace and burst into her chamber as she dressed. There, to his surprise, he found Elizabeth 'newly up, the hair about her face'. Her red wig, which covered sparse grey wisps, was not yet in place, and her visage was not yet swathed in layers of white lead. She looked every year of her age, and more. Essex appeared unperturbed, kneeling to kiss his sovereign's hand, while she too was gracious, given the circumstances. But Essex's intrusion had stepped behind the illusion. Later – when the queen was ready – he would discover the true extent of her fury.[33]

Elizabeth was not ready to be confronted with the realities of time, as was evident in an incident three years earlier, at Lent 1596, when she took her place in the chapel at Richmond to hear a sermon by the Bishop of St David's.[34] On flatteringly being asked to preach before the elderly queen, it must have seemed to the bishop an inspiring idea to take as the central theme Psalm 90: 'teach us so to number our days, that we may apply our hearts unto wisdom'. 'Let me now come,' he began, warming to his theme, 'to the most reverend age of my most dear and dread sovereign, who hath (I doubt not) learned to number her years, that she may apply her heart unto wisdom.'[35] The queen, he imagined, recalled 'the thirty-seven years past of my reign', while she prayed to God: 'O Lord, I am now entered a good way into the climacterical year of mine age, which mine enemies wish and hope to be fatal unto me.' She had, he considered, 'grey hairs' and her strength had 'failed'. In the bishop's fantasy, his queen asked God whether she would have fifteen, or even thirty, years more of life.

It was a remarkably tactless message to a queen rumoured to have such an aversion to mirrors that she had not looked in one for nearly twenty years.[36] On hearing the bishop's words in her chapel, the queen was livid. Finally, unable to contain herself, she cried out loudly that he should 'keep his arithmetic for himself'.[37] The cowed bishop was placed under house arrest until he apologized, three days later. The queen had, by then, calmed down, complaining only that 'the good bishop was deceived in supposing she was so decayed in her limbs and senses as himself perhaps and other of that age were wont to be'.[38] She, by contrast, was a marvel and 'she thanked God that neither her stomach nor strength, nor her voice for singing nor fingering instruments, nor lastly, her sight was any wit decayed'.

To prove this was so, she produced a little jewel, with an inscription in very small letters. She offered it to the Earl of Worcester and Sir James Crofts, both of whom protested, diplomatically, that they were unable to read it. She then read it herself to those around, to general applause.

She would also have been able to see that, with no children of her own, nor younger siblings or half-siblings, the Tudor dynasty itself had reached its seventh age.

The centenarians of East Anglia

Surprisingly, it was not all that rare for elderly Tudor women to claim to be centenarians although, in the absence of reliable birth records, it is difficult to either refute or prove such claims. Given the fact that women tended to live longer than men anyway, many more women than men claimed to have passed their 100th birthday.

Joan Forcet was 100 years old, she was proud to tell commissioners who visited her house in Norwich in 1570.[39] She could still support herself with spinning work, too. Her neighbour, Cicely Amis, who also assured her visitors that she was 100, was no longer able to work, however. In Ipswich in 1597, commissioners for a charitable foundation came across one William Wast, a sixty-year-old weaver, who supported a lame wife claiming to be a hundred:[40] if true, it would have been an unusually large age gap in a marriage. One Alice Taylor was admitted to the town's Christ's Hospital, a charitable foundation, on 8 April 1570 when she was ninety-four; she survived there for almost eight years, dying when she would (by her calculations) have been 101 or 102.[41]

It was not, of course, impossible for someone to reach 100, but to find such individuals among the poorest section of crowded, disease-ridden Norwich or Ipswich would have been unlikely. These women, who had all lived in the local area all their lives, must indeed have been ancient, but they may well have inflated their ages in a bid to attract sympathy and charitable support.

19

OF FRAILTIES AND FINALITIES

*Jane Dormer, 'Gloriana', and the poor
women of England*

In late January 1603, a royal party set out from Westminster in driving rain, carrying chests of finery, carefully stowed. It was the middle of dark winter, and a change in the wind made the air piercingly cold.[1] The queen wrapped herself up, as the cavalcade made its way towards Richmond 'in very foul and wet weather'.[2] It was to be Elizabeth's last journey.

She may, as one contemporary considered, have been 'thinking on her death' when in conversation with the Earl of Nottingham. Perhaps she did, as reported, inform him that 'my throne hath been the throne of kings, neither ought any other than he that is my next heir to succeed me'; but the remark seems too pointed – too specific – for a queen who always shied away from thinking on the succession.[3] She passed into Richmond Palace, the building her grandfather had intended to symbolize the might of his new dynasty. The red-brick walls would soon witness the dynasty's end.

Across the Continent was a woman of similar age who would shed no tear for the end of Elizabeth's reign. Jane Dormer, who was almost Elizabeth's contemporary, had been accounted 'the fairest and the sweetest woman in the world' when she had served Queen Mary in the 1550s.[4] The young gentlewoman, who had been so carefully educated, despised her mistress's half-sister and successor. Jane, already engaged to the Spanish ambassador, the Count (later Duke) of Feria before Mary's death, had left England with him in 1559, accompanied by her grandmother, Lady Dormer, who had raised her. Neither woman had plans to return to Elizabethan England.

The elder woman was already aged, having been widowed in 1552 after forty years of marriage.[5] Being 'disburdened of the obligations of a wife', as a servant of her granddaughter's put it, Lady Dormer turned to religion, spending much of her time in 'prayer and devotion'. Instead of continuing on to Spain, she went to Louvain, 'there to keep a house and settle herself; where resided many worthy and learned English priests'. She had around twelve more years of life, in which she occupied herself with 'virtue, piety, charity, and other Christian works'. She was known for making coats and garments for widows and the poor, particularly making a point of clothing poor soldiers. In Holy Week, she would wash the feet of twelve poor widows, giving each of them a new gown, a smock and a little purse of money and dinner for two days. Such charity was entirely proper for an elderly woman in the sixteenth century. Jane Dormer would herself strive to emulate her grandmother, who lived to around eighty, in her own old age.

Jane endured a long widowhood when her own husband died on 8 September 1571, after only twelve years of marriage. While raising her family, running her estates and becoming Spanish in all but birth, she also showed considerable political ability, maintaining contact with English Catholics following Elizabeth's Protestant settlement. By the start of the seventeenth century, she was in her sixties and the years were beginning to show. Although her 'health passeth reasonable well,' wrote her servant Henry Clifford from Madrid in late

1605, she was 'troubled often with such infirm and diseaseful accidents as her age is subject unto'.[6] Poor health was to be expected of the old, even though – as Clifford hoped – she was not yet at death's door.

He wrote on 14 December 1605 that 'Her Grace passeth with her health in reasonable sort; and I hope by God His preservation I shall serve her yet very many years'.[7] Three months later, he could assure Jane's English family that 'Her Grace passeth with indifferent health and beareth her age reasonably well, for on Twelfth day last she made fully seventy-one years of age, and yet hath her discretion, judgment and memory as mature as ever'. She could still remember her native tongue, although she had – by then – little reason to use it, and she maintained a 'modest and matron-like carriage'.[8]

She kept herself busy. Even after her seventy-first birthday, she would rise at daybreak, going to her chapel where she would remain for two hours.[9] Her chaplain would then say mass. If it was a Feast Day, Jane would attend the local church, going every day in Holy Week. She would dine in the English fashion at 11am, eating only sparingly. Then, in the afternoon she would visit or receive visits from ladies, before further religious services and an early bed.

Few of her contemporaries were then still alive, and their passing must have brought the shadow of death nearer. She was getting more frail, with her bones fragile and aching. By August 1609, she had begun to carry her left arm in a scarf, 'by reason of a pain she had in her breast on that side'. The Duchess of Infantado, who was herself an elderly woman, was oblivious to this makeshift sling when she visited Jane on 20 August that year. Insisting that her English friend take the place of honour through a doorway, the visiting duchess attempted to propel Jane forwards with her left arm, jarring it above the elbow. Groaning in pain, Jane cried out: 'my arm is broken', as her servant Clifford hurried forward. He was, as he later admitted, 'astonished at the sudden cry and complaint, not imagining it could be broken with so small a violence'.

He called for her women to attend her, and, aware that she was in 'extreme' pain, summoned a bone-setter. Elderly Jane suffered this local man's 'rude handling'. Her grandson, who had by then been called too, and her physician eventually forced the man to desist from his ministrations due to 'the extreme pain he put her to'. Discussing what next to do, the family sent for the king's own bone-setter, but even his skill was not good and 'she remained still with extremity of pain and without rest, still complaining that the bone was not well set'.[10] It was only seven or eight days later, when a third man was sent for, that it was discovered that a splinter of cracked bone had been left unset, and her wound was finally appropriately attended to.

Clifford watched with considerable sympathy for his elderly mistress and 'the great pain she passed, in so delicate and aged a body of seventy-two years'. With such treatment, it was a wonder that she survived at all. The old duchess took to her bed for forty days, where she lay still 'in one posture, without turning her; for if she stirred, the pain of her arm would force her to lie still on her back'. She was quiet, often at prayer. When finally able to leave her house in late October, she went on a pilgrimage to pray for her recovery. But her friend's rough handling of her and the two bone-setters' poor skills were the beginning of her drawn-out decline.

In the time following her injury, those around Jane observed her growing daily weaker.[11] Sometimes she would be fevered, her physicians, alarmed at 'that great age and feebleness of body', ordering that her blood be let. She was already thinking of death and making ready. After fastening the image of a little skull to her rosary beads, she would sit and meditate on it, aware that her remaining days were short. She made her will, as well as taking steps to dispose of her estates.

For a time, Jane recovered some mobility; but, one day, on picking up her little granddaughter in her arms, she pulled her broken arm once more, falling into a faint. As Clifford observed sadly, 'after that it put her to such trouble and affliction as she could not lift it to her head, nor pluck out a pin with that hand, but carried it always in a scarf'. With the pain seeming to spread throughout her body, she took to bed early in 1612. She could pray and eat and sit up in bed, but everyone knew that it could not be long. She remained lucid until almost the end, when, surrounded by family, she died on 23 January 1612, at the advanced age of eighty-four. At least she had outlived the monarch she so heartily disliked.

∽

By the turn of the seventeenth century, Elizabeth I could not be described as ancient, even by the standards of her times, but she was certainly elderly. By 1600 too, her kingdom was much changed from that which her grandfather had won on the field at Bosworth.[12] Although there had been decades of war in Ireland and trouble with Spain, it was now a largely peaceful place. Indeed, as one contemporary assured his readers, 'in England there is no great reckoning made of castles and fortresses, for they do willingly let them go to ruin and instead thereof build them stately pleasant houses and palaces'.[13] Elizabeth had, nonetheless, one more rebellion to see out, when her last favourite, the Earl of Essex, rose up against her early in 1601. She had done much for him, but now she was faced with ordering his execution; he was replaced by no successor in her affections.

Elizabeth personified the age like no Englishwoman before her. The anniversary of her accession day on 17 November 1602 was greeted – as her chief minister, Robert Cecil, was gratified to write – 'with as great an applause of multitudes as if they had never seen her before'.[14] It was then just over a year since she had come to the Parliament house to make what would be known as her Golden Speech. As she sat on her throne before her assembled representatives, she promised that 'I have ever used to set the Last Judgement Day before my eyes and so to rule as I shall be judged, to answer before a higher Judge'. She was mortal – she knew she would die. Yet, 'there will never queen sit in my seat with more zeal to my country, care to my subjects, and that will sooner with willingness venture her life for your good and safety, than myself'. She continued: 'for it is not my desire to live nor reign longer than my life and reign shall be for your good. And though you have had and may have many princes more mighty and wise sitting in this seat, yet you never had or shall have any that will be more careful and loving.'[15] Even then, at her greatest hour, she made a reference to her 'sexly weakness', but it was of small importance at that moment. It was to be her final Parliament.

Despite the fact that Elizabeth had generally enjoyed robust health,[16] she was still anxiously watched. A pain in her face, caused by the cold October wind, was breathlessly reported to Robert Cecil in late 1602.[17] Despite this, she was in good spirits at the Christmas celebrations.[18] There were niggles, of course; the queen was certainly 'sensible of some weakness and indisposition both of health and old age'.[19] But, this was to be expected in a woman so venerable.

The queen considered this year, her seventieth annum, to be 'her climacterical year'. So it proved. At Richmond in January 1603, she began to pray and attend services with more frequency. She also finally gave in to the pain in her hands, ordering her now too-small coronation ring, which had never before been removed, to be filed off. This 'was taken as a sad omen, as if it portended that her marriage with the kingdom, contracted by that ring, would now be dissolved'.

Richmond Palace had been the height of modernity when Henry VII built it to replace Sheen Palace at the turn of the sixteenth century, with its fine brick courts and beautiful gardens. Less labyrinthine than many of the larger palaces that would follow, it had soon been superseded. But it enjoyed a reputation as a winter palace, warm and comfortable, and it was now a suitable location for an ageing queen as she looked forward to the warmth of spring.[20]

At Richmond, Elizabeth was initially 'in excellent health' and 'in perfect possession of all her senses', something which the recently arrived Venetian ambassador, Giovanni Carlo Scaramelli, attributed to the fact that 'she neither eats nor sleeps except at the call of nature'.[21] As he heard, while he was in London, 'everyone hopes and believes that her life is much further from its close than is reported elsewhere'. He finally secured an audience with the queen for the afternoon of Sunday 16 February 1603, making his way over to Richmond punctually.[22] It was still raining hard as he travelled through the winter gloom.

Scaramelli was taken straight into the queen's Presence Chamber, which was crowded with many of the ladies and gentlemen of the court. At its centre, he found Elizabeth, resplendent in silver and white taffeta, trimmed with gold. Her dress was open at the front to reveal multiple necklaces of pearls and rubies, while 'great pearls like pears' covered her forehead. Her hair, which was 'of a light colour never made by nature', betrayed her age – an obvious wig. Her skirts, which were voluminous, began too far down her waist to be fashionable; as was common with the elderly, she was a little behind the times. But she glittered gorgeously, swathed in jewels. He was so dazzled by the image, that he almost failed to notice the elderly woman at its centre. She had, he reflected later, 'never quite lost beauty'.[23]

Scaramelli met with a queen who remained at the height of her powers. She rose when he entered, offering him her hand to kiss. 'Welcome to England, Mr Secretary,' she declared, before adding: 'It was high time that the Republic sent to visit a queen who has always honoured it on every possible occasion.' He returned her words with praise, before congratulating her 'on the excellent health in which, by the grace of God, I found her'. She read a letter passed to her, before 'her countenance, which had hitherto been placid and almost smiling, assumed a graver aspect'.

'I cannot help feeling,' she said, 'that the Republic of Venice, during the forty-four years of my reign, has never made herself heard by me except to ask for something, nor for the rest, prosperous or adverse as my affairs may have been, never has she given a sign of holding me or my kingdom in that esteem which other princes and other potentates have not refused.' It could not be her gender that had brought her this discourtesy, she considered, 'for my sex cannot diminish my prestige nor offend those who treat me as other Princes are treated, to whom the Signory of Venice sends its ambassadors'. She would not, however, be discourteous.

The ambassador had some work to do. He assured her that he was glad 'to learn that Your Majesty has reigned, and worthily, for forty-four years over your ample dominions, for this makes it certain that Your Majesty is no novice in the affairs of this world, and will therefore know that princes must govern according to circumstances'. She was formidable, serious, but also playful, ending by saying: 'I do not know if I have spoken Italian well, still I think so, for I learnt it when a child, and I believe I have not forgotten it.' He kissed her hand and left, noting that she had stood throughout the entire interview.

∽

Elizabeth's display before the Venetian ambassador was an impressive performance, belying the fact that her capacity for work was diminishing. She did not, though, need to worry at the end of her working life about the possibility of descending into destitution, as did the elderly poor, and especially the elderly women, of Tudor England. When no longer able to work, the elderly were supported by their families – if possible. In 1570, for example, the extremely old Alice Cotes, at ninety-two, was living in Norwich with her eighteen-year-old granddaughter, who maintained both of them by knitting hose for a meagre sum. Alice was lucky that her granddaughter was willing, and able, to provide for her in this way. Without family, many of the oldest women found themselves reliant on the charity of the parish.

However, the Reformation, among its many other consequences, had an impact on the nature of charity in Tudor England. Medieval theology had considered that a deceased person's time in Purgatory, that liminal place between Heaven and Hell, could be reduced both by pre- and post-mortem charity and intercessory prayers. Accordingly, before the Reformation it was very common for people to include charitable bequests in their wills and for their surviving family members to ensure that they were carried out. The prayers of the destitute were considered particularly worthy, and many testators specified charitable bequests to poor people who could be brought to pray for them at their funeral.[24] The Reformation stripped away official support for Purgatory in England, removing the theological motivation for charity.[25]

But the poor and the elderly remained a demonstrable presence, which society had to deal with. In the case of poor, blind Cicely Reeves, who was living in Norwich in 1570 and could no longer knit for a living, she was permitted to live in the church house and receive 2d a week in alms. This was the future that awaited many Tudor women who survived to their seventh age.

'Honest, aged poor women'

Whether motivated by lingering fears of Purgatory, or impelled by social conscience, charitable foundations proliferated in Tudor England, and elderly women were often reliant on them. Almshouses, which provided the elderly with a home and, usually, also a pension, were particularly attractive. They were often established in the wills of the wealthy dead.[26] Tudor almshouses, some of which continue to fulfil their original purpose as retirement homes, can still be seen in some places in England; they include the charming Lord Leycester's Hospital building in Warwick, or the almshouses on Church Street in Stratford-upon-Avon.

In 1542, Alderman William Dauntsey of London directed in his will (dated 10 March) that his executors should purchase the vacant ground of the parish church of Allhallows, West Lavington, Wiltshire, and there build a church house, a school house and eight chambers. The school, which was to educate poor children 'forever', would be presided over by a schoolmaster who lived in one of the eight rooms. Five would be given over to 'poor aged and impotent men' and the remaining two to 'honest aged poor women'. They would be called the beadmen and beadwomen of West Lavington.[27] In October 1553, the executors made the necessary land purchase and built the required structures, and the first poor men and women were soon in residence.

There are many other examples. In 1584, a woman named Elizabeth Harrison left funds for the foundation of almshouses in Holborn for thirteen poor men and thirteen poor women;[28] by his will of 1592, a London lawyer named John Fuller left funds for the building of two almshouses – one in Stepney for twelve aged men, and one in Shoreditch for twelve women of good repute.[29] Fuller's widow carried out the bequest, although it took her some years to do so. Such matters took time, both in obtaining probate of the estate and in purchasing the necessary lands on which to build the houses.

Such institutions multiplied, particularly in London. Anne, Lady Dacre, who had served at court, left funds in her will of 1595 to build a hospital in Westminster for twenty poor and aged persons, as well as for the training of twenty poor children.[30] The next year, a Spaniard named Balthazar Sanchez founded an almshouse in Tottenham for eight poor widows and widowers from the local area.[31] There were at least thirty-seven almshouses founded in London and the surrounding areas between 1541 and 1600, with the endowments totalling more than £25,000.[32] These housed more than 300 people.

The London livery companies, too, administered a number of charitable bequests. The Mercers' Company oversaw the gift of Sir Lionel Duckett, who died in 1585. He left £200 to be lent out, with the interest applied to the relief of certain poor and aged people.[33] Sir Thomas Bennett, a London alderman, left £20 to be paid to 'the most poor and aged sort of men and women' in Wallingford when he died in 1615.[34] The Mercers' Company took on the responsibility for administering this bequest too.

Much of the charitable provision in Tudor England came from will trusts and other bequests made in wills. Henry Tooley, the wealthy merchant who had died in 1551, left money for almshouses to be erected in Ipswich.[35] In 1568, the town burgesses agreed to establish a poorhouse to complement the Tooley Foundation's work, and thus the Christ's Hospital was granted its charter in 1572. Together, these institutions provided free accommodation, an allocation of fuel and a uniform to those in need. The old folks who benefitted from Henry Tooley's generosity were a common enough sight in the town, wearing their red and blue badges to mark them out as the charitable cases that they had become. Few would have objected to being identified in this way.

In general, charity was not given lightly. Christ's Hospital was founded to provide for 'the aged, the orphans, the widows, the sick, and others that are in want', as well as those considered less deserving, such as 'the vagrants and vagabonds begging without real necessity'. Those who were able-bodied were required to work while resident in the hospital, keeping house and educating the children. If they refused to work, they received no food. Elderly women were frequently admitted to the hospital, including, for example, seventy-six-year-old Agnes Davy, a single woman, who arrived there on 23 December 1569.[36] She was allowed 12d a week from the Tooley Foundation, and she remained there for eighteen months until her death. Her place was in such demand that, the day after her burial, sixty-year-old Agnes Foster was given her bed. She, too, received a pension, remaining there until her own death on 5 May 1579.[37] Occupants of the foundation's almshouses and recipients of its pensions were mainly women; in fact, women comprised nearly 90 per cent of those receiving support in 1588-9, a testament to the fact that more women than men tended to live long enough to reach elderly infirmity.[38]

With limited funds available, the decision to offer charity to a petitioner was a serious matter. On 21 December 1588, the Tooley Foundation wardens resolved that 'Alice Taylor, an aged and impotent wench of this town, in respect of her poverty, age, and lameness, shall be admitted and allowed of the said Foundation, and that she shall have allowed unto her 6d a week for her relief, to be paid by the renter-warden'.[39] Even in her old age and infirmity, she was expected to earn something towards her keep, since 6d was not enough to live on. It quickly became apparent just how infirm she was, however, and only a month after she was admitted, she received an increase of 2d a week. At the same time, Helen Hadnam, 'an old poor woman of the said Foundation', received an increase of 2d a week as she had gone blind and could now earn nothing towards her own support.[40]

Alice Taylor burdened the Foundation for some years, with steady increases to her pension as she became more infirm. The Foundation's charity extended to her burial, in February 1598, after nearly a decade of support, while they had also funded her medical treatment during her last sickness.[41] The Foundation was of vital support to old men and women of the town; on one day alone, 26 February 1589, three 'poor, aged and impotent women' were admitted.[42]

Most towns made some charitable provision for the aged poor. Norwich also contained a charitable hospital, to which sixty-year-old Margaret Fen was taken in 1570 when she was found to be lame and unable to work.[43] The town authorities, who complained that she was 'an unruly woman' who walked about the streets causing trouble, did not consider her particularly worthy of their charity. Nonetheless, she was in need. This attitude reflected a religious duty to help the poor.[44]

Elizabethans tended to divide the poor into three types, so that:

> ... *some are poor by impotence, as the fatherless child, the aged, blind, and lame, and the diseased person that is judged to be incurable; the second are poor by casualty, as the wounded soldier, the decayed householder, and the sick person visited with grievous and painful diseases; the third consisteth of thriftless poor, as the rioter that hath consumed all, the vagabond that will abide nowhere, but runneth up and down from place to place (as it were seeking work and finding none), and finally the rogue and the strumpet.*[45]

The elderly fell firmly into the first two categories of the deserving poor, being second only to orphans in terms of attracting public sympathy.[46] Every parish in the kingdom would make a weekly collection to help support the poorer residents, and some places went further still.

∾

London, to which so many people gravitated, had been particularly badly affected by the impact of the Reformation on traditional charitable bequests, so much so that one contemporary lamented of the late 1540s: 'Was there ever in any age the like number of poor people as there are at this present begging in the streets of the city and wandering in the fields so idly, being ready to attempt any mischief upon any light occasion'?[47] The streets and lanes of the city seemed almost 'to swarm with beggars and rogues'.[48] Everyone agreed that something must be done, and the mayor and aldermen organized a committee to investigate.[49] There were, they reported back, 2,160 destitute people in the city.[50] That figure included 300 orphans, 20 'sore and sick persons', 330 'poor men overburdened with their children', 400 'aged persons', 650 'decayed householders' and 200 'idle vagabonds'. It was agreed that some provision had to be made for them.

Fortunately, although the dissolution of the monasteries had stripped away much of the provision for the poor, it had at least left the buildings, decaying but still solid. All the orphans and other poor children that could be gathered were brought to the dissolved house of the Grey Friars, later renamed Christ's Hospital, to be provided with food, lodging and learning.[51] Once, of course, that they had cleared out the 'whores and rogues harboured therein all night'.[52]

For the 'lame and aged people such as had not any place to go unto', there would be the Hospital of St Thomas in Southwark, which had been dissolved by Henry VIII a few years before. There, they would be provided with 'meat, drink, and lodging, surgeons and other officers to attend upon them'.[53] The hospital building had stood 'void and empty a long time', and there was much to be done to ensure that it was 'made sweet and ready to receive the poor'.[54] For this project, an early version of an old people's home, the City had ambitious plans. As a major fundraising drive got underway, the authorities ordered 500 featherbeds and 500 straw mattresses for their two establishments, as well as enough blankets and sheets to cover them, at a cost of 1,000 marks.[55] With the intention that St Thomas's would open its doors to 300 of the oldest and poorest people in London, the authorities also purchased land worth £150 a year from the king, to provide it with an endowment.[56] In 1551, the hospital began by admitting 260 of the 'aged and lame' of London.

Not every resident was entirely happy to be there. Porters were obliged to keep a strict watch on the gates and administer 'sharp' punishments, before all 'could be brought to abide within the bounds of their houses'.[57] These unwilling patients were a minority, however. For most of London's elderly poor, both men and women, the hospital must have seemed like a godsend. Although discipline was strict, they were assured of a reasonable standard of comfort in their old age.[58] Indeed, some families were so desperate to secure admission for their relatives to the oversubscribed hospital that they smuggled them into the building.[59] The authorities had every reason to be pleased with themselves. As one contemporary wrote of the foundations, 'there two worthy houses are perfectly performed: the children which are the roots of beggary are provided for, the lame and aged are removed'.[60]

St Thomas's was soon followed by a second hospital to house the elderly, as St Bartholomew's Hospital in Smithfield was refounded around the same time.[61] Both hospitals were hugely successful.[62] By the start of the seventeenth century, at least 200 of London's oldest and poorest lived in each establishment at any one time, seeking not only to be 'lodged and cured, but also fed and nourished'.[63] They would attend chapel, work if they could, and at least know that they had a bed to return to at night and a meal of bread and, sometimes, beef, mutton, butter and cheese.[64] This was washed down with three pints of beer a day. For the elderly still scratching out a living on the streets or in crowded tenements, it must have seemed like the good life. Unsurprisingly, queues rapidly built up outside the hospitals on days that they took in patients.[65]

The London hospitals not only took in women; they were staffed, in many respects, by women. Elizabeth Collston, possibly the wife of St Bartholomew's hospital porter, was employed for more than twenty-five years as its matron, from 1597.[66] She held a position of some authority, being in charge of all the women and children, as well as overseeing most of the female staff. The matron also took delivery of necessaries brought to the hospital, such as blankets and clothing for the inmates.[67]

The role of matron seems to have attracted capable, dedicated women. The first known matron was a widow named Rose Fisher, first appointed as a 'sister' of the hospital in 1551.[68] The sisters, eleven in number, served under the matron, each in charge of a hospital ward.[69] Sister Fisher, however, was soon promoted. She was a no-nonsense woman, prepared to get her hands dirty. In 1552, for example, an order was given that all the 'very feeble and sick' inmates should eat in her presence, ensuring that she could monitor their sustenance.[70] She also supervised the making of bed coverings for patients and the interrogating of pregnant inmates as to the fathers of their children,[71] as well as being entrusted with money, collecting in bequests from charitable benefactors.[72]

In April 1554, Matron Fisher surprised the hospital authorities by tendering her resignation, although agreeing to stay until Michaelmas, when pushed to do so.[73] She promised to find and train her replacement 'in the affairs of this hospital' and to render her all assistance. Rose Fisher's reasons for leaving are not recorded, but in the end, when her replacement proved unsuitable and after a payment of £10 in 1554, Rose agreed to stay on, presiding over her post for several more years.[74]

Ward sisters were expected to remain unmarried, and the position therefore commonly attracted widows.[75] One such was

Elizabeth Clarke, who was serving the hospital by at least March 1553, when she was granted funds for her livery.[76] She was still at her post on 27 March 1556.[77] On 4 November 1570, she personally appeared before the hospital board. She was, she said, 'an old impotent woman', no longer able to fulfil her duties as sister.[78] Could she, she asked, remain in the hospital as a patient? But her years of service apparently counted for little, as the board promised only that she could apply for admission. Whether or not she was successful is not recorded.

Some forms of paid work could be a form of charity in themselves, and in this respect elderly women were often employed by their parishes to undertake work such as nursing care. One Mistress Peirson was paid by the parish of St Botolph's in London to oversee the maid's gallery in the church; she remained in office for at least twenty years and even after she had become blind.[79] In similar semi-charitable employments, one 'Loades' wife' was employed in washing and mending the furnishings in the London church of St Nicholas in 1534, while the same church also rented out a small shop under the church wall to 'Lothar's wife'.[80]

In August 1576, St Bartholomew's Hospital reluctantly granted their consent to a widow named Elizabeth Faxley, who was staying in the churchyard of Little St Bartholomew's.[81] She was someone whose previous conduct suggested that she could not 'behave herself honestly', but she informed the hospital authorities that she was engaged to be married. She could stay there until then, ruled the hospital, providing that she then 'quietly' left both the church precincts and the ward of Farringdon once she was wed.

Old women, too, could find employment in the parish as 'searchers', who were deputed by the parish clerk to view the bodies of the newly dead and make an appraisal of the cause.[82] These 'old-women searchers' as one contemporary described them, were readily known to be susceptible to bribery and induced with ale, making their judgements often hazy.

Influencing their decisions could save family members from being quarantined for the plague. At the same time, however, the 'ancient women' of the parish were considered most fit to judge on the cause of death, given their life experience.

The practisers of 'physick'

When St Thomas's Hospital was founded, the City Authorities recruited a hospitaller, clerk, steward, butler, cook and six surgeons to make up the senior staff. Surprisingly, some of the surgeons might well have been women.

Surgeons, in medieval and Tudor England, carried out a wide range of responsibilities, including caring for wounds and carrying out operations, including amputations. There had always been female surgeons, even after Henry VIII – concerned about standards – ordered that all practitioners should be licensed.[83] Cecily Baldrye of Great Yarmouth went before the Bishop of Norwich in 1568 to secure her licence to practice surgery. She is not the only example.

Since women were expected to have some medical knowledge, it remained the case that large numbers practised surgery without seeking a licence. 'Physic' was commonly on the educational curriculum for aristocratic girls, who would go on to minister to the people of their neighbourhood as adults. Lady Margaret Hoby recorded in her diary on 16 September 1599 that, after attending the sermon in church, she 'looked upon a poor man's leg'.[84] It was evidently a serious enough matter, and the next day she arranged for the leg to be dressed.

On another occasion, she made a desperate attempt to save the life of a baby born without an anal passage. It proved futile. As Lady Hoby recorded, 'although I cut deep and searched, there was none to be found'.[85] Other, lower-status women also professed some medical knowledge, such as the 'old quacksalver' Margaret Mott, who was the wife of a silkweaver in Hatchet Alley in London's Aldgate.[86] She was described by the parish authorities as 'a counterfeit physician and surgeon' at the time of her death in 1617.

As at St Thomas's, female surgeons could also take paid employment. In 1576, a Mrs Cook was employed as the resident surgeon-apothecary at Christ's Hospital, London, with responsibility for the care of the orphans there.[87] St Bartholomew's Hospital, too, regularly called in Elizabeth Hall to treat 'scald head' (probably ringworm) among its patients in the 1550s. She would receive 3 shillings a time for her trouble; she may have also been the 'Mother Hall' called in during 1555 to assist in a patient's child-bed.[88] Another surgeon, Alice Gordon, was regularly employed at the hospital during 1598.[89] A Mother Edwin treated a boy's hernia at St Thomas's Hospital in 1563.[90] She charged 13s 4d, plus 1 shilling for the materials, with 6s 8d up front, and the remainder payable when he was cured.[91]

The idea of female surgeons did not sit well with some of the male members of their profession. In 1561, the barber-surgeons of Norwich drew up a set of rules for their association, complaining of the 'sundry women' who were practising medicine and surgery.[92] Thomas Gale, who served as master of the Barber-Surgeons' Company in London, was equally scathing. He complained, on a visit to St Thomas's and St Bartholomew's hospitals in 1562, that the patients were in a poor state thanks to their treatment 'by witches, by women, by counterfeit juviels [rascals] that took upon them to use the art of surgery' [93] (An accusation of witchcraft was always a risk for a woman involved in surgery in the Tudor period.) He took a dim view of female surgeons, remarking: 'it was said that carpenters, women, weavers, cobblers, and tinkers, did cure more people than the surgeons'.[94]

∞

Those that managed to reach advanced old age in Tudor England were true survivors who, like Jane Dormer, found that most of their peers had fallen away. Yet, it was universally acknowledged that in reaching these years they were stalked by death. The slightest chill could be the beginning of the end for them.

By the turn of the century, Elizabeth, who had always refused to name her successor, had become the focus of her Council's anxious glances as she grew increasingly venerable. She was, as one member of her court admitted, the woman 'upon whose health our happiness consisteth'.[95] Capable, slippery Robert Cecil was as anxious as the rest. Early in 1603, his brother wrote to him, concernedly pointing out that 'Her Majesty's years can bear no violent nor long sickness'.[96] She had always seemed so healthy, promoting the myth of youthful unchangedness, such that in Cecil's view up until the last days of February 1603 he had 'never beheld other show of sickness in the queen than such as is proper to age'.[97]

Within days of her encounter with the Venetian ambassador at Richmond in February, Elizabeth fell ill with a sore throat. It seemed relatively minor. She continued to eat well, did not cough, and had no fever.[98] Still, she complained of 'a heat in her breasts and a dryness in her mouth and tongue', something which – to her distress – prevented her from sleeping. Unable to keep still, she refused to go to bed, instead walking in her garden in the first week of March. By 9 March, the swelling in her throat had abated and the court let out a collective breath.[99] She was, however, 'melancholy', seeming 'to be much troubled with a peculiar grief'.[100] She suddenly lost her appetite, even as her health appeared to improve.

When Elizabeth's well-beloved cousin, Robert Carey, arrived at court that month, he found her much diminished.[101] She was, he was informed, 'ill disposed' and inclined to keep to her private chambers. Nonetheless, on hearing of his arrival she invited him in. She was sitting in one of her withdrawing chambers, supported by a pile of cushions on the floor. Elizabeth called him over and he kissed her hand. It was, he assured her, 'my chiefest happiness to see her in safety, and in health, which I wished might long continue'. Taking his hand, Elizabeth squeezed it hard. 'No, Robin, I am not well.' Her heart, she assured him dolefully, 'had been sad and heavy for ten or twelve days'. She then sighed heavily, forty or fifty times. He sought to reassure her, using, as he later recalled, 'the best words I could, to persuade her from this melancholy humour'. This proved impossible, for 'it was too deep-rooted in her heart'.

He cheered the queen enough, at least, that in the evening she sent word that she would attend the palace chapel the next morning. Everyone duly assembled, but Elizabeth failed to appear. At 11am, one of the grooms of the chamber appeared to shoo those present away and to ask her chaplains to prepare her private chapel, for 'she would not go to the great'. Carey along with a small number of favoured courtiers made their way to the smaller room. Eventually, Elizabeth arrived to sit on cushions in her Privy Chamber, close to the chapel door. She would not enter to face even the small crowd that had gathered. As Carey observed, 'from that day forwards, she grew worse and worse'.

Elizabeth's illness may have taken those around her by surprise. It was widely considered that she failed to help herself. She would consult no doctors, she said, nor would she come to bed, fearing that once there 'she should never rise'.[102] Instead, she spent a week on her cushions on the floor.[103] She had soon entirely stopped eating, too.

Already those around her were looking towards the future even as they haunted the wintry palace. Elizabeth would later be accused of paranoia in refusing to name a successor, since, as one contemporary put it, 'the female sex and old age are apt to be suspicious'.[104] She was right to be concerned about her court flocking towards the rising – Scottish – sun. Already, in March

1603, there were some hoping for 'novelty and change'.[105] Even Robert Carey, who was such a favourite of hers, was in terror of losing his livelihood, since the queen had given him everything he had. Fearing that 'her death would soon ensue', he secretly wrote to the King of Scots, acknowledging his claim to the English throne and promising that he would bring news of Elizabeth's death immediately. Everyone was waiting for the elderly queen to die.

Elizabeth was finally persuaded to take to her bed by the recently widowed Earl of Nottingham, who had been dragged out of his own mourning to return to court. He took the queen in hand, 'what by fair means, what by force', his brother-in-law Robert Carey knew not, but he 'got her to bed'. She was already almost gone, when, on Wednesday 23 March, she 'grew speechless',[106] appearing 'very pensive and silent' to those who crowded around her bed.[107] Sometimes her eye would fix upon an object for hours; but she had not lost her senses. That afternoon, on being asked again about the succession, Elizabeth put her hand to her head. This was enough for her Council to declare that she had named her cousin James VI, interpreting the gesture as the sign of a crown.[108] He was, by that stage, the only plausible candidate anyway: Elizabeth had outlived the debate.

At around 6pm on 23 March, Elizabeth made signs with her hands for the Archbishop of Canterbury and her chaplains to come to her.[109] She had always had a sincere and deep faith in God and required comfort now. The churchmen gathered around her, 'full of tears to see that heavy sight'. She lay amid her cushions and the bedsheet on her back, one hand tucked in the bed, the other hanging out, which the elderly Archbishop John Whitgift took this in his own hand.

Kneeling beside the queen, Whitgift examined her on her faith. She answered everything 'by lifting up her eyes, and holding up her hand, as it was a comfort to all the beholders'. She would, the old man said, die shortly and must prepare herself. He then began to pray, at which the queen was observed to take 'great delight', lifting up her hands and eyes to Heaven as he spoke. It seemed, to everyone, to give Elizabeth comfort. She continued to squeeze her old friend's hand 'when he prayed or spake of Heaven'.[110]

Whitgift remained at prayer for some time, until – his own bones creaking and his knees weary – he blessed his sovereign and moved to rise and leave. A silent, dying Elizabeth was still the queen and she still expected to be obeyed. Making a sign with her hand, she asked him to continue, which he did for another 'long half an hour'. She made the sign again, to the archbishop's dismay, so he remained on aching knees, making 'earnest cries to God for her soul's health'. Elizabeth seemed to 'much rejoice thereat' – and she eventually released Whitgift from his labours. She was left alone for the night, with her ladies continuing their vigil.

The second Elizabeth Tudor had been blessed with time. Death – the dancing master that had led away her infant aunt of the same name – had failed to find her in her own childhood or steal her away in the perils that could strike at any stage of life, and which attended the dangers of her particular life and reign. It was a dance that could be postponed, but not avoided.

At around 3am on the morning of 24 March 1603, as her people were sleeping, Elizabeth I's own last scene concluded. She died 'mildly like a lamb, easily like a ripe apple from the tree', and with her went the 118-year-old dynasty.[111] As Venetian Ambassador Scaramelli recorded, 'she died a queen who had lived for long, both gloriously and happily in this world. With her dies the family of Tudor.'[112]

A dynasty that had been founded in the masculine heat of battle found its greatest glory in the reign of its most illustrious daughter. Never before had a period of English history been personified by the life of one, remarkable woman.

EPILOGUE

STUART WOMEN

When the last breath left Elizabeth's body, the spell was broken. Gloriana had not proved to be immortal and, as the court began to react, a new reign – and a new dynasty – had already begun.

Some had feared that her death – without a direct heir of her body, or even of Henry VIII's body – would lead to 'commotions'; but that proved not to be the case.[1] Even before sunrise on 24 March 1603, Robert Carey had saddled his horse and set out hard for Scotland to greet England's new king. He was carrying one of Elizabeth I's rings as proof that she was dead.[2] By the morning, James VI of Scotland had been proclaimed in London. It was a welcome surprise to many, since 'this peaceable coming in of the king was unexpected of all parts of the people'.[3]

James, who owed his claim to the English crown to women, moved south unopposed.[4] He was the rising sun. At Richmond, in the darkness of the former queen's chamber, a body that had lived for nearly seventy years was hurriedly prepared for burial. To murmurs of disapproval, she was wrapped only in sear cloth rather than embalmed, and the fabric used was meagre and poor. She was, one contemporary claimed, 'defrauded' of her 'allowance of cloth'.[5]

Once ready, Elizabeth was taken out to her barge and brought to Whitehall, where a solemn vigil was kept. One of those attending, the mother of thirteen-year-old Anne Clifford, sat with the corpse for two or three nights, but she would not allow her daughter to join her. As the girl lamented, 'I was held too young'.

She was also 'not high enough' to walk in Elizabeth's funeral procession alongside her mother and aunt, something which 'did trouble me then'; but she was permitted into Westminster Abbey to watch the ceremonies on 28 April 1603.

The funeral itself was magnificent, as befitted a woman who had ruled for more than forty years, nearly nine times as long as her half-sister, England's only other effective reigning queen. Elizabeth's cousin, Arbella Stuart, who disliked her, had initially been chosen as chief mourner. She declined the honour, and it fell instead to the Marchioness of Northampton.[6] There were places in the procession for Elizabeth's other ladies and gentle-women, while 260 of her poorer female subjects also appeared, dressed in black with their heads covered in linen. The funeral procession itself, as it snaked through the streets from Whitehall to Westminster, represented all levels of Tudor women.

This, the last royal Tudor funeral, also recalled the first – that of another Elizabeth Tudor, who had died so long ago. It was a comparison few would have made, but, for all the religious and social changes in the intervening century and more, much remained the same for women. Even the long, stable and peace-ful rule of a queen failed to change many minds about the desirability of a female monarchy. Most people, in 1603, looked forward to the coming of a king.

The new James I had left his wife, Anne of Denmark, behind in Scotland, but he soon sent word to her to join him. News of her approach caused excitement among the aristocracy of her new realm, with women flocking to meet her on the route. Among them was little Anne Clifford and her mother, who had ridden so hard that they killed three horses under them.[7] England's new queen – not a ruler but a consort – kissed those who arrived to see her and, as Anne Clifford recalled, 'used us kindly'. A new dynasty had begun, and Anne and her mother, like the queen that she hoped to serve, were now Stuart women.

ENDNOTES

Chapter 1

1 J. Guillimeau, *Child-Bed or, the Happy Delivery of Women Wherein is Set Downe the Government of Women* (1635), p. 3.

2 Ibid. p. 3 points out the embarrassment to a physician in misdiagnosing pregnancy and so prejudicing 'their knowledge and discretion, by judging rashly hereof'. Nonetheless, it was a common occurrence. Mary I endured a phantom pregnancy in 1554. A few years earlier, Lady Lisle had also mistakenly believed that she was pregnant for some months.

3 Bartholomew, *De Proprietatibus Rerum* (1535), Book IV.

4 E Roesslin, *The Birth of Mankind* (1572), Book I, ch. 5.

5 Ibid. As Eccles points out, this theory of two seeds meant that 'the man was also obliged to ensure the woman's satisfaction'. See *Obstetrics and Gynaecology in Tudor and Stuart England* (Kent, 1982), p. 36.

6 Bartholomew, op. cit., Book VI.

7 Roesslin, op. cit., Book 1 CVI. *The Birth of Mankind* ran to thirteen editions before it was superseded in 1654. See Eccles, op. cit., p. 12.

8 N. Orme, *Medieval Children* (New Haven, 2003), p. 14. This was not a universally held belief, however; Bartholomew Book VI considered that life began at 46

days for both sexes.

9 Guillimeau, op. cit., p. 8.

10 Ibid.

11 Ibid., p. 10.

12 All quotations, ibid

13 Bartholomew, op. cit., Book VI.

14 Guillimeau, op. cit., p. 19.

15 Chapuys noted of Anne Boleyn in 1533 that her dresses were 'unlaced with placard having put in a piece to enlarge her gown as ladies do when in the family way'.

16 See E. James, *Women's Voices in Tudor Wills, 1485–1603* (Farnham, 2015), p. 275.

17 Ibid.

18 P. L. Hughes and J. F. Larkin (eds.), *Tudor Royal Proclamations*, Vol. I (New Haven, 1964), no. 5, p. 6.

19 K. K. Kesselring, *Mercy and Authority in the Tudor State* (Cambridge, 2003), p. 212; K. Jones, *Gender and Petty Crime in Late Medieval England* (Woodbridge, 2006), p. 35; J. C. Oldham, 'On Pleading the Belly: A History of the Jury of Matrons' in *Criminal Justice History 6* (1985), pp. 1–64.

20 Judges did not always abide by the law, however. When Margaret Clitherow was condemned in York of harbouring Catholic priests in 1586, she was asked 'if she thought in her conscience that she were with child'. When she answered that she might be, she was examined by a panel of

women who declared that she was. This left the judges with a dilemma, with one pointing out that 'God defend she should die, if she be with child; although she hath offended, yet hath not the infant in her womb'. Yet, she was such a high-profile Catholic, she was executed anyway, with one judge declaring he would 'take it upon my conscience that she is not with child'. See J. Mush, 'A True Report of the Life and Martyrdom of Mrs Margaret Clitherow' in Morris, J. (ed.), *The Troubles of our Catholic Forefathers Related by Themselves*, Vol. 3 (1877)

21 MCR p. 55.

22 CAR Surrey nos. 1016 and 1021.

23 *Ibid.* 1090

24 *Ibid.* 1064, 1099, 1137 and 1180

25 MCR, p. 42.

26 Kesselring, op. cit., p. 212, notes that approximately 25 per cent of Elizabethan women convicted in the Essex Assizes proved to be pregnant. In Surrey, more than 60 per cent made a successful plea.

27 P. C. Almond (ed.), *Demonic Possession and Exorcism in Early Modern England: Contemporary Texts and Their Cultural Contexts* (Cambridge, 2004), p. 147.

28 Roesslin, op. cit, f.48; Bartholomew, op. cit., Book VI.

29 Details of Arthur's birth can be found in *Collectanea Topographica and Genealogica* I, p. 279.

30 TNA E404/81/1. The couple were at Greenwich on 6 April 1492. By 21 April they had moved to Sheen, where they remained at least until 22 July. Henry VII's privy purse

expenses also show that he was at Sheen from April until after Elizabeth's birth. See Bentley (ed.), 'Extracts from the Privy Purse Expenses of King Henry the Seventh, from December Anno 7, 1491, to March Anno 20, 1501' in *Excerpta Historica* (1831), p. 89.

31 Items were ordered by Henry VII on 8 February 1503, following the birth of his youngest daughter, Catherine (TNA E101/415/7 no. 144).

32 Elizabeth of York, Jane Seymour and Catherine Parr died in childbed. Catherine of Aragon and Anne Boleyn survived childbirth.

33 N. H. Nicolas (ed.), *The Privy Purse Expenses of Elizabeth of York and Wardrobe Accounts of Edward the Fourth* (1830), p. 78 notes that a monk of Westminster brought the girdle to the queen in good time for her last confinement.

34 Edward I's daughter borrowed the girdle in the fourteenth century. See C. Peers and L. E. Tanner, *On Some Recent Discoveries in Westminster Abbey* in *Archaeologia* 93 (1945), pp. 151–64.

35 R. Scot, *The Discoverie of Witchcraft*, ed. B. Nicholson (1886), p. 165

36 BL Harleian 642 f. 207–220. There is some confusion over the various sets of ordinances, particularly given the fact that only this set is dated. The account of the birth of Princess Margaret in 1489 (BL Cotton MS Julius B XII) supports the view that the undated ordinances were earlier than those devised in 1495. The two sets (BL Harl 6079 and BL Harl 642) are substantially similar,

but not identical. For example,
BL Harl 6079 (undated) opens
with the words 'Her Highness's
pleasure being understood, in
what chamber she will be
delivered in, the same must be
hanged with rich cloths of arras,
sides, roof, windows and all',
while the 1495 Ordinances in
BL Harleian 642 state: 'As to
the deliverance of a queen, it
must be known what chamber
she will be delivered in by the
Grace of God, and that chamber
must be hanged with arras the
roof side and windows... .'
37 BL Harleian 6079 f. 26, with a
restatement in BL Harleian 642
f.218v.
38 BL Cotton MS Julius B XII
f.58.
39 Ibid.
40 *Privy Purse Expenses Elizabeth of
York*, p. 82. In December 1502
the pregnant Elizabeth of York
paid an embroiderer for work on
her rich bed. She probably
intended this for the birthing
chamber.
41 Guillimeau, op. cit., p. 87.
42 Beds frequently appear in
sixteenth-century wills as
bequests. Shakespeare, very
famously, left his wife his
second-best bed.
43 James, op. cit., p. 275.
44 BL Harleian 6079 f.26.
45 BL Cotton MS Julius B XII f.58.
46 BL Harleian 6079 f.26.
47 S. Bentley (ed.), 'Extracts from
the Privy Purse Expenses of
King Henry the Seventh, from
December Anno 7, 1491, to
March Anno 20, 1501' in
Excerpta Historica (1831), p. 89.
48 J. Stow, *Annales, or a General
Chronicle of England* (1631),
p. 474; C. L. Kingsford,
Chronicles of London (Oxford,
1905), p. 197.

49 N H. Nicholas (ed.),
Testamenta Vetusta, Vol I
(1826), p. 25.
50 BL Arundel MS 26, ff29V–30.
Elizabeth's younger sister, Anne,
took her place as chief mourner.
51 Ibid. The confinement of a
queen was accompanied by
considerable ceremony.
Elizabeth's confinement in 1489
is detailed in BL Cotton MS
Julius B XII f.58. The
Ordinances followed are in BL
Harleian 6079 f.26v.
52 BL Harleian 6079 F.26v.
53 Ibid.
54 BL Cotton MS Julius B XII
f.58v
55 Catherine of Aragon ordered
'three smocks of fine Holland
cloth, whereof two be wrought
about the collars with gold, and
the third wrought about the
collar and at the hands with silk'
for one of her confinements. See
Nichols, J.G. (ed.), *Inventories of
the Wardrobes, Plate, Chapel
Stuff, Etc. of Henry Fitzroy, Duke
of Richmond, and of The
Wardrobe Stuff at Baynard's
Castle of Katharine, Princess
Dowager* (1855), p. 40.
56 Kingsford, op. cit., p. 197.
57 *Privy Purse Expenses of Henry
VII*, p. 90.
58 Roesslin, op. cit., f.47.
59 MCR, p. 81.
60 BL Harleian 6079 f.26v.
61 CPR Henry VII Vol. II 1494–
1509, p. 354 contains a grant
made to Alice Massey, 'late
midwife of the queen consort
Elizabeth', dated 18 April 1594.
Since Princess Elizabeth's had
been the most recent royal birth,
it seems probable that she was
the midwife who attended. She
was then engaged by the queen
in 1503 at the time of her last
labour (see *Privy Purse Expenses*

of Elizabeth of York, p. 102). As a mark of their esteem for Massey's services, the king and queen paid her an annual pension of £5 for the duration of her life (CPR Henry VII Vol. II 1494–1509 p. 354).

62 Guillimeau, op. cit., p. 84.

63 None of Elizabeth's children were stillborn, and later a two-day delay in baptizing her youngest child, Catherine, who died at a week old, suggests that her life was not initially despaired of. See Kingsford, op. cit., p. 258.

64 R. Manning, *Robert of Brunne's 'Handlyng Synne'*, AD 1303, 2 Vols, ed. F. J. Furnivall (1901), lines 9638–9640.

65 Guillimeau, op. cit , p. 97; D. Cressy, *Birth, Marriage, and Death* (Oxford), p. 80; Roesslin, op. cit., f.109.

66 Roesslin, op. cit , f.110.

67 Guillimeau, op. cit., p. 185.

68 R. Blumenfeld-Kosinski, *Not of Woman Born* (Ithaca, 1990), p. 21.

69 Wellcome Library of the History of Medicine, MS 49 (The Wellcome Apocalypse) f.38v.

70 Guillimeau, op. cit., p. 185.

71 Ibid.; Blumenfeld-Kosinski, op. cit., p. 2.

72 Guillimeau, op. cit., p. 185.

73 Ibid., p. 186.

74 M. Leach (ed.), *The Ballad Book* (New York, 1955). Other near contemporary rumours are contained in M. A. S. Hume (ed), *Chronicle of Henry VIII* (1889), p. 72; N. Harpsfield, *A Treatise on the Pretended Divorce Between Henry VIII and Catherine of Aragon* (1878), p. 279 and N. Sander, *Rise and Growth of the Anglican Schism* (1877), p. 138, none of which are reliable sources.

75 Blumenfeld-Kosinski, op. cit., p. 39.

76 Ibid., p. 41.

77 Guillimeau, op. cit., p. 188.

Chapter 2

1 J. Jones, *The Arte and Science of Preserving Bodie and Soule in Al Health, Wisedome, and Catholike Religion Physically, Philiosophically, and Divinely Devised* (1579), p. 5.

2 Elyot 1834:21

3 F. C. Cass, *Monken Hadley* (Westminster, 1880), p. 128; TNA C131/85/2, TNA C241/272/30.

4 CIPM Henry VII, Vol. III, p. 952.

5 VCH, Vol. 3, Cheshunt.

6 Sir Robert Greene was a younger son, although his wife Cecily was an heiress. See Cass, op. cit., p. 128.

7 CIPM Henry VII, Vol. III, p. 952. Ages ranging from 20–35 were considered good. Also see Guillimeau, op. cit., p. 635; J. Jones, *The Arte and Science of Preserving Bodie and Soule in Al Health, Wisedome, and Catholike Religion Physically, Philiosophically, and Divinely Devised* (1579), p. 5; T. Elyot, *The Book Named the Governour*, ed. A. T. Eliot (London, 1834), p. 21.

8 Jones, op. cit., p. 5; Guillimeau, op. cit , p. 2; Cass, op. cit., p. 128. Two of Cecily's three sons lived to adulthood.

9 Guillimeau, op. cit., p. 7.

10 Ibid., p. 2.

11 Ibid., p. 3.

12 Elyot, op. cit., p. 21.

13 J. L. Vives, *The Education of a Christian Woman*, ed. and trans. Fantazzi, C. (Chicago, 2000), p. 54 Since most wetnurses

were engaged before the birth, such a distinction would have rarely been possible.

14 Ibid.

15 Guillimeau, op. cit., p. 18.

16 Ibid., p. 23.

17 TNA E404/81/1 Warrant dated 20 July 1491 shows that Margaret Traughton and Frideswide Puttenham were already engaged eight days before Prince Henry's birth. A similar procedure would have been followed for the next royal birth, a year later.

18 Guillimeau, op. cit., p. 18.

19 Ibid.

20 J. Huggett and N. Mikhaila, *The Tudor Child* (Lightwater, 2013), p. 7.

21 Ibid.; A. Buck, *Clothes and the Child* (Carlton, 1996), p. 17.

22 Buck, op. cit , p. 17

23 Huggett and Mikhaila, op. cit., p. 15

24 Catherine of Aragon possessed swaddling bands of this length.

25 J. Sharp, *The Midwives Book* (1671); Roesslin, op. cit., f.110v.

26 Ibid. f.111

27 V&A Museum reference number B.878-1993.

28 J. G. Nichols, *Inventories of the Wardrobes, Plate, Chapel Stuff, Etc. of Henry Fitzroy, Duke of Richmond, and of The Wardrobe Stuff at Baynard's Castle of Katharine, Princess Dowager* (1855), p. 40, from a list of 'Necessaries provided for the Princesse Dowagier, whatte tyme she laye in child bedde'.

29 *The Cholmondeley Ladies*, Tate T00069.

30 Huggett and Mikhaila, op. cit., p. 17.

31 TNA E101/412/25 no. 18.

32 M. Hayward, *Dress at the Court of King Henry VIII* (Leeds, 2007).

33 At Ribchester, there were seven baptisms in the last two weeks of December 1597 alone (ibid.).

34 TNA E404/81/1 Warrant dated 1 September 149).

35 This account of the christening is based on the ordinances contained in BL Harleian 6079. They were very closely followed in the 1489 baptism of Princess Margaret (BL Cotton MS Julius B XII).

36 BL Harleian 6079 f.29.

37 The bishops' names were not recorded. Princess Margaret, elder sister of Henry VIII, was baptized by the Bishop of Ely and confirmed by the Archbishop of York. See BL Cotton MS Julius B XII f.61v.

38 By contrast, Princess Margaret's godparents are known: her grandmother, Margaret Beaufort, the Archbishop of Canterbury and the Duchess of Norfolk. See BL Cotton MS Julius B XII f.61v.

39 BL Harleian 6079 f.28.

40 D. Cressy (ed.), *Education in Tudor and Stuart England* (1975), p. 82.

41 Ibid., p. 84.

42 Privy Purse Expenses of Henry VII, p. 90.

43 Ibid., p. 91.

44 Ibid.

45 H. Woods, *Excavations at Eltham Palace* (1982), pp. 215–265; R. A Brown, H. M. Colvin and A. J. Taylor (eds), *The History of the King's Works*, Vol. II (1963), p. 930; S. Thurley, *The Royal Palaces of Tudor England* (New Haven, 1993), p. 20.

46 Thurley, op. cit., p. 20.

47 Woods, op. cit., p. 228

48 Brown, op. cit., p. 936; Colvin, op. cit., p. 78.

49 Ibid., p. 234.

50 The palace required little work in Henry VII's time (Colvin, op. cit., p. 79). CPR Henry VII, Vol. I 1485–94, p. 220 notes minor improvement works commencing August 1488. W. Campbell (ed.), *Materials for a History of the Reign of Henry VII, Vol. II* (1877), p. 298 shows that these works were part of a general scheme of repairs, with work ordered to be carried out at Westminster, Greenwich and Sheen Palaces, Windsor Castle and the Tower of London at the same time.

51 Colvin, op. cit., p. 82.

52 CPR Henry VII, Vol. I, p. 152.

53 Campbell, op. cit., p. 157.

54 Ibid., p. 290 and p. 349.

55 H. Ellis (ed.), *The Visitation of the County of Huntingdon, 1613* (1849), II I pp. 171–2.

56 Ibid.

57 Only Margaret Gower is mentioned in the warrant dated 13 March 1495 (TNA E404/81/3), but warrants dated 20 July 1491 and 31 December 1491 (TNA E404/81/1) confirm that Anne Mayland was the second rocker. She appears in a warrant dated 17 September 1495 (TNA E404/81/3), indicating that she had remained in the nursery.

58 TNA E404/81/3 Warrant dated 13 March 1495, showing that they each drew a half yearly salary of 33s 4d.

59 Ibid. Warrant dated 13 March 1495

60 Another lady, Alice Skidmore, was employed in the nursery by at least 1495.

61 Ibid. Warrant dated 16 July 1495. TNA E404/81/4 Warrant dated 3 February 1495 contains a similar statement regarding the women 'attending

upon our right entirely wellbeloved children the Duke of York the ladies Margaret and Elizabeth'.

62 D. Erasmus, *Collected Works of Erasmus, Vol. 39 Colloquies*, ed. C. R. Thompson (1997), p. 606.

63 Privy Purse Expenses Elizabeth of York p. 74. This would have been one of the famous 'Princes in the Tower'.

64 CPR Henry VII, Vol. II 1494–1509, p. 11, p. 46, p 345

65 L&P I, p. 82, p. 132, p. 1221; L&P II, p. 658 and p. 659.

66 L&P III, p. 8.

67 Ms. Fr. 995 of the Bibliothèque nationale de France. The wetnurse is depicted on f.34v

68 A. T. Harrison, *The Danse Macabre of Women: MS FR. 995 of the Bibliotheque Nationale* (Kent, 1994), f.34v. The wetnurse replies: 'I must go to-the dance/As the priests go to Communion/I would like to hang back/But I feel swelling under my clothing,/Between my arms, when I breath/This child is dying of plague./Sudden death is a great pity./One may not have an hour or a half hour.'

69 Vives, op. cit., p. 53; Erasmus, op. cit., p. 605.

70 Ibid.

71 Erasmus, op. cit., p. 605 and p. 606.

72 T. More, *Utopia*, ed. E. Arber (ed.) and trans R. Robinson (1869), p. 93.

73 Privy Purse Expenses of Elizabeth of York. Examples of payments towards her children include pp. 10, 19, 22, 34, 86, 88, 93.

74 J. Guillimeau, *The Nursing of Children, Wherein is Set Downe the Ordering and Government of Them From Their Birth* (1635b), p. 1.

75 Jones, op. cit., p. 4. Bartholomew Book VI also states this.
76 Vives, op. cit., p. 53, Erasmus, op. cit., p. 591.
77 More, op. cit., p. 93.
78 E. Clinton, *The Countesse of Lincolnes Nurserie* (Oxford, 1622).

Chapter 3

1 William Shakespeare, *As You Like It*, Act II, Scene 7.
2 Erasmus, op. cit., p. 605.
3 Vives, op. cit., p. 56. Ideas of medieval and Tudor childhood have been badly coloured by the work of Philippe Aries, who considered that parents were indifferent and emotionally withdrawn due to the high infant mortality rates. There is, however, abundant evidence from the period that childhood existed and that children were often cherished by their parents. Rosenthal and Haas give good critical discussions of Aries' conclusions. See J. T. Rosenthal (ed.), *Essays on Medieval Childhood* (Donington, 2007), pp. 1–11 and pp. 12–28. Very recently Dawson refuted Aries' work as 'biased and lacking in evidence'. See H. Dawson, *Unearthing Late Medieval Children* (BAR British Series 593, 2014), p. 14. Very few historians would now consider Aries' arguments persuasive.
4 Harrison, op. cit., f.34v.
5 Guillimeau, op. cit., p. 22.
6 CPR Henry VII, Vol. I 1485–94, pp. 177, 193.
7 Ibid., p. 193. As a testament to Hart's work, in May 1490, he was given security of tenure, with his appointment made for life. He was also finally paid for his previous three years of hard labour, p. 309.
8 Elyot, op. cit., p. 22
9 Vives 2000:55. Elizabeth of York was raised with her sister, Mary, with their care overseen by their mother. See A. F. Sutton and L. Visser-Fuchs (eds.), *The Royal Burials of the House of York at Windsor: II Princess Mary, May 1483, and Queen Elizabeth Woodville, June 1492 (The Ricardian XI*, no. 144, March 1999), pp. 446–62.
10 T. Astle (ed.), 'Wardrobe Account for 1483' in *The Antiquarian Repertory: A Miscellany, Intended to Preserve and Illustrate Several Valuable Remains of Old Times, II* (1779), p. 270.
11 M. A. E. Green, *The Lives of the Princesses of England,* Vol. IV, p. 2.
12 Ibid.
13 Ibid.
14 For example, carpets are recorded in Astle, op. cit., p. 247.
15 Guillimeau, op. cit., p. 24.
16 Erasmus, op. cit., p 605; Bartholomew Book VI.
17 Erasmus, op. cit., p. 605.
18 Dawson 2014 quotes Michele Savonaraola, a fifteenth-century physician.
19 TNA E404/81/3 Warrant dated 13 March 1495 refers to Anne Oxenbridge as Henry's 'late nurse'. Weaning was a sensitive time. When it was proposed to wean the future Elizabeth I in October 1535, her lady mistress had to seek the consent of both her parents (TNA SP1/97 f.116).
20 G. Cross, *Kid's Stuff: Toys and the Changing World of American Childhood* (Harvard, 1997), p. 18.

21 A. Fraser, *A History of Toys* (1972), p. 63.

22 Ibid., p. 98.

23 Cross, op. cit., p. 16. Aries considered that 'most of the dolls in public and private collections are not children's toys, which are usually crude objects roughly treated by their owners, but fashion dolls. However, it is clear from paintings and manuscript illustrations that children played with often quite sophisticated toys. See. P. Aries, *Centuries of Childhood*, R. Baldick (trans.) (1996), p 67.

24 Cross, op. cit., p. 17.

25 Fraser, op. cit., p. 58. [NB Numbering goes wrong around here and chapter notes finish on 98 rather than 95]

26 S. Gristwood, *Arbella: England's Lost Queen* (2003), p. 46.

27 Cross, op. cit., p. 17.

28 N. Orme, 'Education and Recreation' in R. Radulescu and A. Truelove (eds), *Gentry Culture in Late Medieval England* (Manchester, 2005), pp. 63–83

29 Vives, op. cit., p. 57.

30 J. Stow, *Annales, or a General Chronicle of England* (1631), p. 475; C. L. Kingsford (ed.), *Chronicles of London* (Oxford, 1905), p. 197. J. G. Nichols (ed.), *The Chronicles of Calais* (1846), p. 2.

31 Privy Purse Expenses of Henry VII, p. 98; TNA E404/81/3 Warrant dated 19 Oct 10 Hen VII; TNA E404/81/3 Warrant dated 23 August 7 Hen VII, Privy Purse Expenses of Henry VII, pp. 94–96.

32 TNA E404/81/3. A warrant dated 22 December 1491 places Henry in London The following day he was at Eltham.

He was still there on 26 December.

33 TNA E404/81/1 Warrant dated 31 December 1491.

34 Privy Purse Expenses of Henry VII, p. 95.

35 On 5 April 1493, the one-year-old Prince Henry became Constable of Dover Castle and Warden of the Cinque Ports (CPR Henry VII, Vol 1, 2485-2494 p. 423). The following year he was created Lord Lieutenant of Ireland, Earl Marshall, Warden of the Scottish Marches and Duke of York (Stow, op. cit., p. 477).

36 Kingsford, op. cit., p. 203; R. Fabyan, *The New Chronicles of England and France*, ed. H. Ellis (1811), p. 685.

37 J. Gairdner (ed.), *Letters and Papers Illustrative of the Reigns of Richard III and Henry VII*, Vol. I (1861), pp. 389–91.

38 Kingsford, op. cit., p. 203.

39 Gairdner, op. cit., p. 395–401. A list of those who attended survives, which does not include Elizabeth. However, it is far from complete, with the queen and Princess Margaret, who certainly attended, not named.

40 In another example, Elizabeth's younger sister, Mary, for example, would make a public appearance aged six at the public reception of Catherine of Aragon to England, including attending the tournament. See G. Kipling (ed.), *The Receyt of the Ladie Kateryne* (Oxford, 1990), p. 31, p. 53.

41 TNA E101/413/11 no.27.

42 TNA E404/81/3 Warrant dated 14 November 1491.

43 Gairdner, op. cit., p. 391.

44 CIPM Henry VII Vol. III, p. 952.

45 BL Royal MS 2 A XVIII.

46 Erasmus, op. cit., p. 606.

47 CPR Henry VII, Vol. I, pp. 423–4.

48 Guillimeau, op. cit., p. 28; Palliser 1979:119-120

49 D. M. Palliser, *Tudor York* (Oxford, 1979), p. 119. Nine parishes were surveyed. Two had rates of over 25 per cent.

50 C. Webster, *Health, Medicine, and Mortality in the Sixteenth Century* (Cambridge, 1979), p. 61, pp. 82–4. The death rate has been described as 'extremely high', estimated at between 15 and 20 per cent. See A. Wear, 'Medicine in Early Modern Europe, 1500–1700' in L. I. Conrad, M. Neve, V. Nutton, R. Porter and A. Wear (eds), *The Western Medical Tradition: 800 BC to AD 1800* (Cambridge, 2003), pp. 215–362.

51 Ibid., p. 218.

52 Kipling, op. cit., p. 81.

53 MCR, p. 215.

54 F. G. Emmison, *Elizabethan Life and Disorder* (Chelmsford, 1970), p. 157 notes that in the thirty cases of infanticide preserved in the Elizabethan Essex records, only three were to mothers that were married.

55 MCR, p. 235.

56 CAR Surrey, no. 362.

57 Ibid., nos. 362, 387, 416, 425 and 447. She was still in gaol as late as 27 February 1570.

58 MCR, p. 148.

59 Ibid., pp. 201, 154, 215, 235, 250.

60 Emmison, op. cit., p. 157.

61 MCR, p. 120.

62 Emmison, op. cit., p. 157.

63 CAR Surrey, no. 10.

64 MCR, p. 148.

65 Ibid., p. 176.

66 Ibid., p. 196.

67 Harvard University Library STC 3717.3.

68 E. R. Brinkworth (ed.), *The Archdeacon's Court; Liber Actorum, 1584*, Vol. II (Oxford, 1942–46), p. 209.

69 Harrison, op. cit., f.38v.

70 The Dance applied equally to women as to men, as a surviving manuscript of a Danse Macabre solely relating to women shows (Harrison, op. cit.).

71 Stow, op. cit., p. 477; Privy Purse Expenses Henry VII, p. 96.

72 Privy Purse Expenses Henry VII, p. 103–4.

73 TNA E404/81/3 Warrant dated 17 September 1495.

74 BL Cotton MS Vitellius A.XVI f.156v.

75 The contemporary chronicler in BL Cotton MS Vitellius noted the deaths of both Hussey and Princess Elizabeth together as newsworthy items during that stormy autumn (f.156v).

76 BL Egerton MS 2642 f.201v confirms that Elizabeth died on Holy Rood Day (14 September). John Stow claimed that her tomb gave a date of death of 14 November, but this was probably a transcription error. BL Cotton MS Vitellius A.XVI f.156v also notes her death. William Camden recorded her inscription in 1603, giving a date of 14 September 1495 (W. Camden, *Reges, reginae, nobiles et alii in ecclesia collegiata B. Petri Westmonasterii sepulti*, 1603).

77 Green, op. cit., p. 506, was the first to claim that Elizabeth died of atrophy. A. Weir, *Elizabeth of York* (2014), p. 309 points out that there is no evidence that Elizabeth died from atrophy and that, instead, the reference to the goddess related to her cutting short the thread of life.

The Danse Macabre of Women (Harrison, op. cit., f.26v) makes the same analogy.

78 Privy Purse Expenses Henry VII, p. 105. They arrived in Northampton on 12 September and had reached Banbury, which is approximately 30 miles away, by 16 September.

79 BL Cotton MS Vitellius A.XVI f.156v, A. F. Pollard, *Henry VIII* (1913), p. 83.

80 Privy Purse Expenses Henry VII, p. 105.

81 Green, op. cit., p. 505. The most recent precedent for the burial of a princess was that of Mary, the daughter of Edward IV, who had died suddenly in 1482 (Sutton and Visser-Fuchs, op. cit., p. 446). After Mary's death, she was wrapped in swathes of strong cere-cloth at Greenwich, then carried to the local parish church before being taken in ceremonial procession to Windsor for burial (BL Stowe 1047 f.219r-v).

82 BL Egerton MS 2642 f.201v details Elizabeth's funeral.

83 Ibid. f.202. The children of Henry VII and Elizabeth of York were the living symbols of the union of the Houses of Lancaster and York (CSP Venice I, 506)

84 Ten miles would take most of the day to cover. Coupled with the shorter days of autumn, the funeral service was almost certainly conducted after nightfall.

85 Ibid. f.202 lists 'the women mourners that attended the corpse and offered'. They were the Duchess of Suffolk, Countess of Wiltshire, Viscountess Lisle, Lady Dynham, Lady Daubeney, Lady Berkeley and Mistress South.

Other female mourners were also recorded as present in the church.

86 BL Egerton MS 2642 f 202.

87 BL Cotton MS Vitellius A.XVI f.156v.

88 Green, op. cit., p. 506.

89 Ibid., p. 507.

90 TNA E101/414/8 no.27 (also summarized in Hayward, M. (ed.), *The Great Wardrobe Accounts of Henry VII and Henry VIII* (2012), p. 242.)

91 *Collectanea Topographica and Genealogica Vol. I*, pp. 277–80. The dates were obviously compiled over a number of years. For 27 September the entry referred to Catherine of Aragon ('my lady princess') taking her ship from Spain to England while, for 2 October, the entry referred to her landing in Plymouth. If recorded between 1509 and 1533, she would most probably have been recorded as queen. After 1533 it is unlikely any information about her would have been recorded. Henry VIII's death is included, meaning that some of the entries were compiled as late as 1547.

92 Elizabeth was mentioned in a letter by one of the secretaries of Henry VII in 1501, when he referred to the upcoming marriage between James IV of Scotland and Princess Elizabeth (CSP Spanish I 294). This was probably just a slip of the pen – he meant Margaret.

93 H. Dawson analysed child burials in three medieval sites. They usually received the same grave treatment as their adult contemporaries. See p. 128 for shrouds.

94 E. Norton, *Catherine Parr* (Stroud, 2011).

95 E. Norton, 'The Depiction of Children on the Fifteenth and Sixteenth Century Tombs in Kinlet Church' in *Transactions of the Shropshire Archaeological and Historical Society 87*, pp. 35–46.

Chapter 4

1 *Castellum Hutonicum Some Account of Sheriff Hutton Castle* (York, 1824).
2 N. Orme, *Medieval Children* (New Haven, 2003), p. 7.
3 J. Daybell, *Women Letter-Writers in Tudor England* (Oxford, 2006), p. 1.
4 Ibid., p. 2, p. 12.
5 D. Gardiner, *English Girlhood at School* (Oxford, 1929), p. 158.
6 Richard Hyrde, quoted from D. Cressy, *Education in Tudor and Stuart England* (1975), p. 107.
7 T. Becon, *The Catechism* (1559).
8 R. Mulcaster, *Positions Wherein Those Primitive Circumstances be Examined Which are Necessary for the Training of Children* (1581).
9 Daybell, op. cit., p. 12. Such instruction was often through religious manuscripts handed down through generations of the family See P. Cullum and J. Goldberg, 'How Margaret Blackburn Taught Her Daughters: Reading Devotional Instruction in a Book of Hours' in J. Wogan-Browne (ed.), *Medieval Women: Texts and Contexts in late Medieval Britain* (Turnhout, 2000), p. 217. Examples of women being responsible for the early education of their children date back to the Anglo-Saxon period: Alfred the Great learned to read with his mother using a fine manuscript book of poetry.

10 D. Hickman, 'From Catholic to Protestant: The Changing Meaning of Testamentary Religious Provisions in Elizabethan London' in Tyacke, N. (ed.), *England's Long Reformation 1500–1800* (1998), p. 97.
11 L. Pollock (ed.), *With Faith and Physic: The Life of a Tudor Gentlewoman Lady Grace Mildmay 1552–1620* (1993), p. 28.
12 This is suggested by the fact that the motifs that were unpicked were all badges used by the Bostocke family. The images that remained were for the Lee family (Jane's mother's family and Alice Lee's family).
13 T.190-1960. Information on Jane and her family can be found at http://collections.vam.ac.uk/item/O46183/sampler-jane-bostocke/ (date accessed 18 February 2016).
14 The surname is sometimes transcribed as 'Nebabri', but a close inspection of the sampler suggests that the 'Neeadri' is a better transcription. A modern spelling of the name is probably 'Needry' or 'Nedry'. At present, Susan has not been identified. See Ashton
15 This example is in the Museum of London, A7448.
16 Dorman, T. (ed.), *The Sandwich Book of Orphans* (*Archaeologia Cantiana 16*, 1886), pp. 189–90.
17 She was still making Henry VIII's shirts – at his request – some years into his annulment proceedings.
18 S. E James, *Women's Voices in Tudor Wills, 1485–1603* (Farnham, 2015), p. 75.
19 H. Clifford, *Life of Jane Dormer*, pp. 59–63.

20 C. A. Sneyd (ed.), *A Relation, or Rather a True Account, of the Island of England* (1847), pp. 24–6.

21 Gardiner, op. cit., p. 114.

22 A. Clifford, *The Diaries of Lady Anne Clifford*, ed. D. J. H. Clifford, (Stroud, 1992), p. 21.

23 Gairdner, J. (ed.), *The Paston Letters*, Vol. III, (Westminster, 1896), no.886.

24 The Howards were fabulously wealthy. The Countess of Surrey's father-in-law used a 'pissing basin of silver' to answer a call of nature. See John Howard's Accounts 1481–90 in A Crawford (ed.), *The Household Books of John Howard, Duke of Norfolk* (Stroud, 1992), p. 275.

25 John Leland, quoted in *Castellum Huttonicum*, p. 13.

26 The green and red cushions are noted in the first Duke of Norfolk's accounts (1463–72 in Crawford, op. cit., p. 390). The Countess can be expected to have commissioned something similar. An example of wear and tear is contained in a later Howard inventory. In the dining room there was 'an old carpet in the window sore worn'. See J. Ridgard (ed.), *Medieval Framlingham* (Woodbridge, 1985), p. 133.

27 The Countess of Surrey's father-in-law, John Howard, had employed around forty people to serve him long before he became Duke of Norfolk. His son's household was likely considerably larger (Crawford, op. cit., p. xvii).

28 'A Generall Rule to Teche Euery Man that is Willynge for to Lerne to Serve a Lorde or Mayster in Euery Thyng to his Plesure' in R. W. Chambers (ed.), *A Fifteenth Century Courtesy Book* (1914).

29 A. Hanworth, *Home or Away? Some Problems with Daughters* (*The Ricardian XIII*, 2003), p. 243.

30 In the 1524 Framlingham Inventory, Surrey's (by then the Duke of Norfolk) married daughter, Lady Oxford, was the only woman to have her own comfortably furnished chamber. It can be assumed that his married stepdaughter, Lady Dacre, would also have been accorded such an honour when she visited the household in the 1490s.

31 The 1524 Framlingham Inventory includes a young ladies' chamber, close to the chamber of the Duke of Norfolk and his wife.

32 The young ladies' chamber contained some 'very old' red fabric bed-curtains.

33 Surrey's second wife presided over a household in which this occurred (TNA SP1/167 f.138).

34 John Skelton, *Garland of Laurel* (1523).

35 F. Seager, 'The Schoole of Vertue, and Booke of Good Nourture for Chyldren, and Youth to Learne Theyr Dutie By' (from 1557), printed by W. Seares (modern edition in Furnivall).

36 G. de la Tour Landry, *The Book of the Knight of the Tower*, ed. A. Vance (1862), p. 24.

37 Elizabeth's grandfather purchased gowns for his daughters, including a fine green cloth gown and furs. Elizabeth would have been provided with similar clothes (Accounts 1462–71 p286, p. 318).

38 The Young Children's Book (Ashmolean MS 61, c.1500) in Furnivall.

39 John Skelton, *Garland of Laurel* (1523).

40 The children of both her marriages were close. Her eldest son, John Bourchier, Lord Berners, gave a fine gold and sapphire ring to his half-sister, Elizabeth Boleyn (TNA SP1/81 f.156).

41 The Countess of Surrey is depicted in stained glass at Long Melford Church, Suffolk.

42 Skelton's earliest extant biography by John Bale in 1557 states that he was secretly married to a woman he called his concubine. The veracity of this has been disputed – see A. W. Barnes, *Constructing the Sexual Subject of John Skelton* (ELH 71, 2004) – but, given the description of some of the women in his work, most notably in the *Garland of Laurel,* it would appear fair to suggest that he took an interest in women.

43 Skelton described Elizabeth as beautiful, presumably conforming to the contemporary ideal of blond hair and blue eyes (M. Hayward, *Dress at the Court of King Henry VIII* (Leeds, 2007), p. 155.

44 John Skelton, *Garland of Laurel.*

45 She may already have married by May 1495, since it has been suggested that her marriage to Sir John Seymour of Wolf Hall had taken place in 1494. If so, Skelton must have come across her on a previous visit. Margery would become the mother of Henry VIII's third wife, Jane Seymour.

46 John Skelton, *Garland of Laurel.*

47 Paston Letters, Vol. III, p. 692.

48 L&P 2 pt II 3802. Elizabeth Denton had earlier served as mistress of the nursery of Henry VII's children (TNA E101/414/8 no.27).

49 According to Lady Bryan's own account, she was appointed as soon as Mary was born (BL Cotton Otto C/X f.226).

50 TNA SP2/a f.1. In this list of new fees and annuities in 1516, immediately below Margaret was Anne Luke, who received £20. Henry was thinking of his own childhood when he made provision for his daughter's nursery.

51 In a letter dated to 1536, Lady Bryan referred to her service to Princess Mary and 'to the children his grace have had since'. This can only mean Henry Fitzroy and Elizabeth (whom she is known to have served) (BL Cotton Otto C/X f.226).

52 TNA SP1/21 f.60 which relates to 1520, merely refers to her as 'Margaret Bryan'; the earlier payment in SP2/a f.1 gives her the longer title.

53 BL Cotton Vitellius C/I f.19.

54 TNA SP2/r f.14.

55 TNA SP2/r f.15.

56 TNA SP1/85 f.164.

57 J. G. Nichols (ed.), *Literary Remains of King Edward the Sixth* (1857), p. xxxii.

58 *The Book of the Knight of the Tower*, p. 27.

59 Cressy, op. cit., p. 106; Daybell, op. cit., p. 12.

60 M. M. Kay, *The History of Rivington and Blackrod Grammar School* (Manchester, 1931), p. 72.

61 J. Simon, *Education and Society in Tudor England* (Cambridge, 1966), p. 376.

62 N. Orme, *English Schools in the Middle Ages* (1972), p. 54.

63 W. G. Hoskins, *The Midland Peasant: The Economic and Social History of a Leicestershire Village* (1957), pp. 183–4.

64 A. L. Rowse, *The England of Elizabeth* (Madison, 1950), p. 559.

65 J. F. Pound (ed.), *Norwich Census of the Poor, 1570* (Norfolk Record Society 40, 1971).

66 For example, the eldest child of Robert Clerk, cobbler, who was aged 12 years and was recorded as both spinning and going to school.

67 Simon, op. cit., p. 133

68 N. Orme, *Education and Society in Medieval and Renaissance England* (1989), p. 50.

69 Hales 1847, p. 613.

70 Dorman, op. cit.

71 Ibid., p. 185.

72 Ibid., p. 189.

73 Ibid.

74 Ibid., p. 198.

75 E. Power, *Medieval English Nunneries c.1275 to 1535* (Cambridge, 1922), p. 261.

76 Ibid., p. 244, Orme 1973, op. cit., p. 53.

77 TNA SP 1/82 f.69.

78 H. Walpole, *A Catalogue of the Royal and Noble Authors of England, with Lists of their Works* (Edinburgh, 1796), p. 291 lists Margaret's translation works.

79 R. Rex, 'Lady Margaret Beaufort and Her Professorship, 1502–59' in P. Collinson, R. Rex and G. Stanton (eds.), *Lady Margaret Beaufort and her Professors of Divinity at Cambridge 1502 to 1649* (Cambridge, 2003).

80 R. Bayne (ed.), *The Life of Fisher MS. Harleian 6382* (1921), p 10.

81 H. Anstey (ed.), *Epistolae Academicae Oxon, Vol. II* (Oxford, 1898), p. 665.

82 Ibid., p. 667.

83 Ibid , p. 667.

84 J. R. Magrath, *The Queen's College*, Vol. I (Oxford, 1921).

85 A. R. Myers (ed.), *English Historical Documents, Vol. IV* (1969), pp. 894–5.

86 J. Nichols, *The History of the University of Cambridge and of Waltham Abbey* (1840), p. 134.

87 C. H. Cooper, *Memorial of Cambridge*, Vol. II (Cambridge, 1861), p. 24.

88 M. K. Jones and M. G. Underwood, *The King's Mother* (Cambridge, 1995), p. 222.

89 Nichols 1840, op. cit., p. 135

90 'Many sutes and greate troubles which the Bishop of Rochester did undergoe in the behalfe of the colledge'. See J. Fisher, *The Funeral Sermon of Margaret Countess of Richmond and Derby*, ed. J. Hymers (Cambridge, 1840), p. 184.

Chapter 5

1 W. Lambarde, *A Perambulation of Kent* (1826), p. 190 records that, in a trance, she 'often said she would go home, and that she had been at home, whereas (to the understanding of the standers by) she had never been from home, nor from the place where she lay'.

2 A. Neame, *The Holy Maid of Kent* (1971), p. 23, Lambarde, op. cit. p. 189.

3 E. Hall, *Hall's Chronicle Containing the History of England During the Reign of Henry IV and the Succeeding Monarchs to the End of the Reign of Henry VIII* (1809), p. 814.

4 Barton later required an interpreter to speak to papal ambassadors. Whether she could write is unclear – she used a

scribe to produce one of her heavenly letters – but this may have been due to the quality of the calligraphy.

5 C. M. Rousseau and J. T. Rosenthal, *Women, Marriage, and Family in Medieval Christendom* (Studies in Medieval Culture XXXVII, 1998), p. 92; P. Humfrey, *The Experience of Domestic Services for Women in Early Modern London* (Farnham, 2011), p. 7.

6 A. Kussmaul, *Servants in Husbandry* (1981), p. 4.

7 A. M. Froide, *Never Married* (Oxford, 2005), p. 89.

8 Humfrey, op. cit., p. 44.

9 J. Foxe, *The Acts and Monuments of John Foxe* (New York, 1965), VIII, p. 380.

10 Kussmaul, op. cit., p. 4.

11 Ibid., op. cit., p. 32.

12 L. Gowing, *Gender Relations in Early Modern England* (Harrow, 2012), p. 96.

13 Ledger of Thomas Howell, 1519–27. See A. H. Johnson, *The History of the Worshipful Company of the Drapers of London, Vol. II* (1915), p. 255.

14 Ibid. p. 254.

15 The circumstances of this employment are known because Blunte was accused (but found not guilty) of raping the girl on 13 June 1559 (CAR Surrey 24).

16 I. Whitney, *The Copy of a Letter, Lately Written in Meeter, by a Yonge Gentilwoman: To her Vnconstant Louer: With an Admonition to al Yong Gentilwomen, and to all other Mayds in General to Beware of Mennes Flattery* (1567).

17 J. W. W. Bund (ed.), *Worcester County Records: The Quarter Session Rolls Part I* (Worcester, 1899), no.28.

18 W. H. Hale (ed.), *A Series of Precedents and Proceedings in Criminal Causes Extending from the Year 1475 to 1640 Extracted from the Act-Books of Ecclesiastical Courts in the Diocese of London* (London, 1847), p. 588.

19 Kussmaul, op. cit., p. 42.

20 E. R. Brinkworth (ed.), *The Archdeacon's Court; Liber Actorum, 1584*, 2 vols (Oxford, 1942–1946), p. 46.

21 J. R. McKee, *Dame Elizabeth Barton O.S.B The Holy Maid of Kent* (1925), p. 1.

22 A. D. Cheney, 'Richard Masters, Parson of Aldyngton, 1514 to 1558' in *The British Archaeological Association*, New Series, Vol. 10 (1904), pp. 15–28, details taken from a survey made in 1608.

23 Ibid., p. 18.

24 The inventory of Master's goods taken in 1534 (Ibid., p. 25.)

25 J. Fitzherbert, *The Boke of Husbandry* (1540).

26 Ibid; Kussmaul, op. cit., p. 34 notes the work expected of female agricultural servants, which accords with that assigned to the farmer's wife by Fitzherbert.

27 Froide, op. cit., p. 89.

28 Lambarde, op. cit., p 189.

29 L. E. Whatmore (ed.), *Archdeacon Harpsfield's Visitation, 1557*, 2 vols (London, 1950–1951), p. 464.

30 Lambarde, op. cit., p. 189.

31 London Metropolitan Archives X109/127 Repertories of the Court of Aldermen, Repertory I:1495–1504 f.12.

32 CAR Kent, p. 237.

33 Ibid. p. 1351, p. 1369, p. 1371.

34 CAR Essex, p. 64.

35 Ibid., p. 65.

36 Ibid., p. 66.

37 Ibid., p. 323.

38 CAR Kent, p 694.
39 TNA PROB 11/11/669.
40 Whatmore, op. cit., p. 464.
41 Ibid., p. 465.

Chapter 6

1 I. K. Ben-Amos, *Adolescence and Youth in Early Modern England* (New Haven, 1994), p. 13; Vives, op. cit., p. 63.
2 Vives, op. cit., p. 124.
3 Ibid.
4 S. Guazzo, *The Court of Good Counsell* (1607), ch. 6
5 G. R. Corrie, *Adolescence and Youth in Early Modern England* (New Haven, 1994), p. 101.
6 C. Gibbon, *A Work Worth Reading Wherein is Contayned, Fiue Profitable and Pithy Questions, Very Expedient, Aswell for Parents to Perceive Howe to Bestowe their Children in Marriage* (1591) in the section entitled 'Whether the election of the parents is to be preferred before the affection of their children in marriage'.
7 Guazzo, op. cit., chs 1, 3, 5.
8 Statutes of the Realm, IV, I, p. 329.
9 Guazzo, op. cit., ch. 1.
10 Ibid.
11 E. K. M. Jarman (ed.), *Justice and Conciliation in a Tudor Church Court: Depositions from EDC 2/6 Deposition Book of the Consistory Court of Chester September 1558–March 1559* (Record Society of Lancashire and Chester, 2012), f.236.
12 Erasmus, *A Modest Meane to Mariage, Pleasauntly Set Foorth by that Famous Clarke Erasmus Roterdamus*, trans. N.L. Anno (1568)
13 Jarman, op. cit., f.221v. The sharing of the place-name of the locality and the personal name

was not particularly uncommon for gentry families.
14 TNA SP1/167 F.155.
15 J. M. Riddle, *Contraception and Abortion from the Ancient World to the Renaissance* (1992), p. 142.
16 Ibid., p. 140
17 John XXI, *The Treasurie of Health Contayning Many Profitable Medicines, Gathered out of Hipocrates, Galen and Auicen by one Petrus Hyspanus, and Translated into English by Humfry Lloyd* (1560).
18 R. Warnicke, *Wicked Women of Tudor England* (New York, 2012), p. 55.
19 D. Gaimster, P. Boland, S Linnane and C. Cartwright, 'The Archaeology of Private Life: The Dudley Castle Condoms' in *Post-Medieval Archaeology 30* (1996), pp. 129–142.
20 Held by Dudley Metropolitan Borough Council.
21 J. Parisot, *Johnny Come Lately: A Short History of the Condom* (London, 1985), p. 5.
22 On these plant-based contraceptives, see Riddle, op. cit., pp. 135, 145, 153, 155.
23 Ibid., p. 136.
24 L. Pollock (ed.), *With Faith and Physic: The Life of a Tudor Gentlewoman Lady Grace Mildmay 1552–1620* (1993), p. 135.
25 D. O'Hara, *Courtship and Constraint* (Manchester, 2000), p. 30.
26 MCR, Vol. I, pp. 108–9.
27 Jarman, op. cit., f.242v.
28 TNA PROB11/11/300.
29 She had remarried by April 1497. See W. J. Hardy and W. Page (eds), *A Calendar to the Feet of Fines for London and Middlesex, Vol II* (1893), p. 9.
30 Ibid.

31 C. T. Clay (ed.), *Yorkshire Deeds*, Vol. 8 (Cambridge, 2013), p. 127. TNA CP25/1/294/80 no.95.
32 Guazzo, op. cit., ch. 11.
33 Ibid., ch. 5.
34 Surrey acquired the wardship of John Grey, Viscount Lisle in 1499.
35 Harris (2002) p. 44
36 Hickman p. 98
37 After Elizabeth's mother died in 1497, it was her stepmother, Agnes Tylney, who prepared her for marriage.
38 Thomas jousted at royal tournaments and danced in court masques (Samman 1988, Appendix IV).
39 Vokes (1988) p. 30.
40 B. J. Harris, *English Aristocratic Women 1450–1550* (Oxford, 2002), p. 44.
41 *Calendar of the Close Rolls Henry VII*, Vol. 2 (1963), no.179.
42 BL Add MS 24,965 f.231.
43 L&P XI 17.
44 Bedyll v Copwode (J. H. Baker, *Reports of Cases From the Time of King Henry VIII* (2003), p. 11.
45 TNA C1/425/37.
46 VCH Hertford 3; M. K. Jones and M. G. Underwood, *The King's Mother* (Cambridge, 1995), p. 269.
47 Bedell initially served the Stafford family (Jones and Underwood, op. cit., p. 269), although he does not appear to have served Margaret's third husband, Henry Stafford (there is no record of him in household accounts of the period: WAM 12181-90, 5472). He is also not recorded in Margaret's accounts for 1473–4 (WAM 32407). He first appears as treasurer of her household in 1498 (WAM 32364), retaining this position until her death in 1509.
48 TNA PROB 11/19/116. In his will, Bedell asked that his heavy cup of gold and a great gold chain be sold, with the money 'to be distributed and given discreetly unto poor people' for the good of Margaret Beaufort's soul.
49 Tomb inscription quoted in Camden, 1603.
50 Bedell, too, was interested in Cecily's lands, using her local influence to secure an appointment as Bailiff of Cheshunt in 1509. (L&P I i 69.)
51 TNA PROB 11/19/116.
52 Her eldest son, Thomas, married Anne Moncaster, the daughter of a merchant tailor See F. C. Cass, *Monken Hadley* (Westminster, 1880), p. 128.
53 TNA C142/80/11. Details of the Bedells' tomb, which no longer survives, can be found in Camden 1603, which records the inscription: 'Here lieth buried William Bedell Esquier late Treasurer to my Lorde Cardinal Archbishop of York and Chancellor of England, and Cecily his wife, which William deceased the 3 of July 1518'.
54 G. Markham, *Country Contentments, or The English Huswife* (1615), p. 57.
55 Museum of London, A28260
56 A. Sim, *The Tudor Housewife* (Stroud, 2010), p. 64.
57 The bakehouse in Cratfield in Suffolk had at least two ovens, while there was another bakehouse in the neighbouring village of Laxfield. See L. Botelho, *Old Age and the English Poor Law, 1500–1700* (Woodbridge, 2004), p. 34.
58 H. Spurling (ed.), *Elinor Fettiplace's Receipt Book* (1986).

59 Markham, op. cit., p. 66, p. 71, p. 75.

[59 is last note in text]

Chapter 7

1 www.londonroll.org/event/?company=drp&event_id=DRHT1805 and www.londonroll.org/event/?company=drp&event_id=DRHT1806.

2 S. Thrupp, *The Merchant Class of Medieval London* (Michigan, 1962), p. xi. Membership was hugely important and endured after death, as the souls of members were prayed for long after their deaths. See L. Branch, 'Fraternal Commemoration and the London Company of Drapers c.1440–c.1600' in E. C. Tingle and J. Willis (eds), *Dying, Death, Burial and Commemoration in Reformation Europe* (Farnham, 2015), p. 115.

3 S. Rappaport, *Worlds Within Worlds. Structures of Life in Sixteenth Century London* (1989), p. 24. For the most part, the livery companies bumped along quite happily, although a 'great variance and discord' between the Cordwainers and the Cobblers towards the end of Henry VII's reign required arbitration, with both parties agreeing to abide by the mayor's decision (LMA X109/053 f.18). Control of London trade and industry was almost entirely in the hands of the companies. See G. Unwin, *The Gilds and Companies of London* (1908), p. 15; C. Welch, *History of Tower Bridge* (1908), p. iv.

4 Rappaport, op. cit., p. 36.

5 Ibid., p. 37. Freedom of the City and apprenticeship were not the same thing. Freedom allowed an individual to ply their trade in London through one of the livery companies. It was usually obtained through apprenticeship, which was where an individual was bound to a master for a term of years to learn their trade. Freedom could also be obtained through descent or through the paying of a substantial fine.

6 E. M. McInnes, *St Thomas' Hospital* (1963), p. 35.

7 These examples, see Rappaport, op. cit., pp. 3, 4, 37.

8 For example, Elizabeth Knewell in 1557 was apprenticed to Thomas Lawnesdon (E. Ralph, *Calendar of the Bristol Apprentice Book, Part III 1552–1565*, p. 60).

9 *Bristol Apprentice Book: Part II*, p. 1.

10 Ibid., *Book I*, p. 24.

11 Ibid., p. 26.

12 For example, Katherine Apery in 1533, who was apprenticed to Master Richard Saunders, Mercer, and his wife, Agnes (ibid., p. 40)

13 Ibid., p. 47.

14 Ibid., p. 52

15 Ibid., *Book III*, p. 9.

16 Ibid., *Book I*, p. 41

17 Ibid., *Book III*, p. 28. A cardmaker made the implements required for carding wool, which prepared it for spinning.

18 Ibid., p. 35

19 For example, in the advice given by a father in 'How the Wise Man Taught his Son' in J. Ritson (ed.), *Ancient Popular Poetry, Vol. II* (Edinburgh, 1884), p. 19.

20 M Davies, 'Thomasyne Percyvale, "The Maid of Week" (d.1512)' in Barron and Sutton 1994, pp 185–208.

21 His first wife, who died in 1497/8, was also called Katherine (*The Bede Roll of the Fraternity of St Nicholas*, p. 171). It was probably this first Katherine who received a joint bequest of £10 with her husband to pray for the soul of his cousin, Sir John Browne in November 1497. See J. J. Howard (ed.), *Miscellania Genealogica et Heraldica* (1898), pp. 243–5 and *North Country Wills* (Surtees Society, 1908), p. 265.

22 For example, in 1485 and 1494 he served as a City Auditor (*Calendar of Letter Books of the City of London*, Letter Book L f.212, f.311).

23 John's family were strongly connected with trade. His cousin, Sir John Browne, served both as sheriff of London and Lord Mayor (Howard, 1898, p. 243). Browne came from Walcot in Northamptonshire and this may give some clue as to John Fenkyll's background (J. Simpson, *The Brownes of Walcot, in the Parish of Barnack, co. Northampton* (Fenland Notes and Queries, 1891, pp. 316–7). John was active as a draper by 1470 (P. Boyd, *Roll of the Drapers' Company of London* (Croydon, 1934), p. 65).

24 He served as alderman for Aldersgate between 1485 and 1490 and Bridge Ward between 1490 and 1499. See A. P. Beaven (ed.), *The Aldermen of the City of London Temp. Henry IV – 1912* (1908). He regularly attended and voted in the elections for aldermen. Letter Book L f.236b notes his election as sheriff in September 1487. Also, R. Arnold, *The Customs of London, Otherwise Called Arnold's Chronicle* (1811),

p. xxxviii and I. S. Leadam (ed.), *Select Case Before the King's Council in the Star Chamber Commonly Called the Court of Star Chamber AD 1477–1509* (1908), p. 91.

25 In November 1485 he received a royal grant of the custody of the town, port and lordship of Newbiggin, Northumberland. See W. Campbell (ed.), *Materials for a History of the Reign of Henry VII, I* (1873), p. 184. *Select Papers Chiefly Relating to English Antiquities* 1773:155 notes that he attended Elizabeth of York's coronation in 1486. He was listed as the 145th out of 148 knights attending.

26 *A Roll of Arms Belonging to the Society of Antiquaries, Temp. Henry VIII, c.1540*, p. 92 and J. White, *The Names and Armes of Them That Hath Beene Alderman of the Warde of Aldersgate Since the Tyme of King Henry 6* (1878), p. 5. He may have deliberately dodged the expensive appointment of mayor. As an alderman, he was always a potential candidate.

27 LMA CLA/007/EM/02/I/025.

28 For iron: TNA C1/59/249 and TNA C1/257/51. For wine: TNA C1/66/333. In his will of 1499 (TNA PROB 11/11/669) Fenkyll noted an arrangement regarding wine with Thomas Whaplode, a fishmonger.

29 *History of Parliament*, p. 315.

30 Fenkyll owned a ship named *The Peter*, which was seized in 1480–3 as part of his longstanding dispute with the merchant William Folkes who, in 1478 had also been able to persuade the Court of the Admiralty to detain £700 of

Fenkyll's money (CPR 1476-1485 p102 and *History of Parliament*, p. 315).

31 In 1480 he shipped 24 bales of cloths in a vessel belonging to Thomas Grey His brother, Edward, also shipped his own three bales of fabric (Cobb, 1990, p. 77). The two men's wares took up most of the vessel, showing the extent of their interests. The following June, John had a further 218 cloths, stored in 14 sturdy bales to ship, while his brother had four (p. 136). That year, John also shipped 46 cloths with an alternative carrier (p. 194).

32 G. Markham, *Country Contentments, or the English Huswife* (1615), p. 6.

33 Ibid., p. 12.

34 H. T. Riley (ed.), *Liber Albus: The White Book of the City of London Compiled AD 1419* (1861), p. 181. Similar provisions also existed in other cities, such as Lincoln, Hastings and Worcester. See P. Hogrefe, *Tudor Women: Commoners and Queens* (Ames, 1975), p. 39.

35 *Liber Albus*, p. 181–2.

36 TNA C1/201/32. Horne was on friendly terms with Edward IV (White, op. cit., p. 5.)

37 *Calendar of Letter Books: Letter Book L*, f.237b.

38 Sheriff's Tourns, 1 and 2 Philip and Mary in W. Hudson (ed.), *Leet Jurisdiction in the City of Norwich During the XIIIth and XIVth Centuries* (1892), p. 91.

39 For example, in 1392 it was noted in the Leet Roll for the city that 'The wife of Henry Lant is wont to buy fowls, hens, capons and other things in the market on Saturday and sell them on Sundays at the gates of the church of the Holy Trinity, to great heightening and forestalling, and is a common forestaller, wherein great outcry has arisen.' (Ibid., p. 72). Similarly, in 1312/13 Estrilda de Elmham was caught buying cheese, butter and eggs on her way to market before upping the price (ibid., p. 60). There are other examples.

40 J. F. Pound (ed.), *Norwich Census of the Poor, 1570* (Norfolk Record Society 40, 1971).

41 R. Carew (ed), *The Survey of Cornwall*, ed. T. Tonkin (1811), p. 106.

42 Ibid., p. 102.

43 Froide, op. cit.

44 One medieval poem records the lemons, beads, brooches and rings that one such trader brought back from across the sea ('How a Mechande Dyd His Wyfe Betray' in Ritson, op. cit , p. 5).

Chapter 8

1 Drapers' Company Minutes and Records 1515–29, (Rep 7) f.329.

2 Ibid., f.331. Katherine lent a number of items, including a pair of gilt basins and two other basins of parcel gilt. Also two gilt pots, and ten gilt bottles, two with covers. She provided eleven bottles of parcel gilt.

3 Just because a man was a member of a Company did not mean that he carried out the trade from which it took its name. See S. Thrupp, *The Merchant Class of Medieval London* (Michigan, 1962), p. 4. By city custom, a citizen could buy and sell what he pleased, giving many businesses a broad, eclectic feel. The contacts of the Drapers were wide and exotic, with goods bought and sold in

Spain, Portugal, Italy and France. See The Ledger of Thomas Howell, 1519-27 (for example) in A. H. Johnson, *The History of the Worshipful Company of the Drapers of London, Vol. II* (1915), p. 251.

4 *Liber Albus*, p. 338-9.

5 Thomas Cremor's first wife, Jane, was probably John Fenkyll's sister. She was the widow first of a London fishmonger and then William Hariot, who died in 1485 (*History of Parliament 1439-1509*, p 445). Hariot referred to the Fenkyll brothers as his 'brothers' in his will (TNA PROB 11/7/185), while John was co-executor with Jane of her first two husbands' estates (CPR 1476-85 p102).

6 TNA C4/34/26 notes Spence's refusal to act.

7 C. M. Barron, 'Introduction: The Widows' World in Later Medieval London' in C. M. Barron and A. F. Sutton (eds.), *Medieval London Widows 1300-1500* (1994), pp. xiii-xxxiv.

8 Barron and Sutton, op. cit., pp. 209-238.

9 TNA PROB 11/11/669

10 Ibid. St Michael's was destroyed in the Great Fire of London. See H. B. Wheatley, *London Past and Present: Its History, Associations and Traditions,* Vol. II (1891), p. 534.

11 The parish covered a tiny geographical area but in 1548 included 354 adult parishioners, indicating considerable overcrowded. See C. J. Kitching (ed.), *London and Middlesex Chantry Certificate 1548* (1980), p. 22.

12 A. Prockter, R. Taylor, J. Fisher (eds), *The A to Z of Elizabethan London* (1979). The detail is taken from the three maps reproduced here. The Agas Map of 1561-70, the Coppergate Map of c.1587 and the Braun and Hogenberg Map from before 1561.

13 J. Stow, *A Survey of London Written in the Year 1598,* ed. A. Fraser (2009), p. 39.

14 Rappaport, op. cit., p. 5.

15 R. Treswell, *The London Surveys of Ralph Treswell,* ed. J. Schofield (1987).

16 In 1666, of course, a careless baker in Pudding Lane burned down nearly the entire city.

17 For example, at 20 Basing Lane (Ibid., p. 45).

18 House in Fish Street Hill (Ibid., p. 115).

19 Treswell's survey of 7-10 Aldersgate notes two separate tenants in each half of the building.

20 28 Pudding Lane (Ibid., p. 110).

21 Stow (2009), op. cit., p. 45; The Agas Map in Prockter, op. cit.

22 Ibid., p. 70. To further guard the city, the Aldermen passed an order in September 1510 that the aldermen of every ward would keep watch every night with twenty other trustworthy householders, standing at their posts from 9pm until 6am every day and armed for defence (LMA X109/128 Repertories of the Court of Aldermen 2:1506-1515 f.65).

23 References to immigration from I. Scouloudi (ed.), *Returns of Strangers in the Metropolis 1593, 1627, 1635, 1639* (Huguenot Society of London Vol LVII, 1985), pp. 85, 147, 194.

24 Stow (2009), op. cit., p. 86.

25 R. M. Karras, *Common Women: Prostitution and Sexuality in Medieval England* (Oxford, 1996), p. 14.

26 Ibid., p. 35.
27 F. G. Emmison, *Elizabethan Life and Disorder* (Chelmsford, 1970), p. 26
28 *Liber Albus*, pp. 246–7.
29 LMA X109/053.
30 *Liber Albus*, p. 395.
31 LMA X109/053 f.311.
32 *Liber Albus*, p. 395.
33 TNA C131/256/17.
34 TNA C4/34/26. William Fenkyll was admitted to the Drapers' Company in 1501 by patrimony (Johnson (1915), op. cit., p. 54; P. Boyd, *Roll of the Drapers' Company of London* (Croydon, 1934), p. 65.
35 John Fenkyll's namesake cousin also tried to claim the Thames Street house in 1525 (LMA CLC/522/MS20091). The parties came to an agreement, with Katherine transferring the title to John, but retaining her life interest.
36 Rep 7 f.16.
37 LMA X109/053 Petition to the court from John Mychell and others.
38 Thrupp, op. cit., p. 103.
39 Sneyd, op cit., pp. 26–7.
40 TNA WARD 2/65/243/17. There is no further record of her.
41 TNA PROB 11/22/218.
42 Cremor and his first wife were living in her former marital home (TNA WARD 2/65/243/17). Jane's first husband died in 1462, while her second died in 1485, meaning that she was over forty at her third marriage. Her second husband left her very rich (TNA PROB 11/7/185).
43 He is frequently noted in Company Records as being involved in decision making, for example in Rep 7 f 231. He sat on the Company's Council

every year from at least 1515 (when the Company's records begin) until his death in 1526 (Rep 7 f.1, 39, 72, 97, 123, 153, 191, 221. Some estimate of Cremor's wealth can be made in the amount he was assessed to 'lend' the king in 1521–2. Cremor was one of 55 liverymen assessed to pay a total of £950, with his personal contribution £30. In comparison, the six aldermen of the Company were much wealthier, being assessed to pay £1,150 between them. More junior members ('the bachelors') paid only £70 between 17 of them.
44 Cremor was MP for London in 1504, but otherwise held little other official office (Johnson, op. cit., p. 55).
45 For example, TNA C1/508/7, TNA C1/508/6, TNA C1/425/37. In TNA C1/632/39 she describes herself as 'Dame Katherine Fynkell widow, late wife to Sir John Fynkell, knight, and after wife to Thomas Cremor, citizen and draper of the city of London'.
46 TNA WARD 2/65/243/17. 'Garden grabbing' in London was no new phenomena. Thomas Cremor was involved in 1511 in an enterprise to build on a house garden close to the Tower of London, for example (L&P I 857 (14)).
47 TNA WARD 2/65/243/17. It was evidently a desirable house, since, after Thomas and Catherine's deaths, there was a legal claim brought by their nephew, Robert Cremor, for the property, which he claimed as 'nephew and heir of the said Thomas Cremour' (TNA C1/770/46).

48 (Rep 7) f.74, f.25 and f.21, f.32, f.55, f.133 (he paid in instalments).
49 Ibid. f.222
50 Ibid. f. 207, 223. The same source also notes that they went to the king. Cremor had to provide a substantial part of the 20 marks cash, a piece of crimson satin worth more than £20 and a substantial quantity of figs.
51 Ibid. f.251.
52 TNA PROB 11/22/218. The date of his death is given in Rep 7 f.299.
53 Rep 7 f.299.
54 Ibid. f.299, f.300.
55 Ibid. f.300.
56 TNA C1/508/6.
57 TNA C1/508/7, TNA C1/632/39 and TNA C4/32/1.
58 M. Ingram, ' "Scolding Women Cucked or Washed": A Crisis in Gender Relations in Early Modern England?' in J. Kermode and G. Walker (eds), Women, Crime and the Courts in Early Modern England (Chapel Hill, 1994), p. 49; Walker (1994) p. 81.
59 Kermode and Walker, op. cit., p. 87.
60 Emmison, op. cit., p. 259.
61 Ibid.
62 Ibid.
63 CAR Surrey, p 926.
64 Ibid., p. 960.
65 Ibid., p. 1276.
66 Emmison, op. cit., p. 99.
67 Rep 7 f.29.
68 G. Unwin, The Guilds and Companies of London (1908), p. 196; Johnson, op. cit., pp. 4–5.
69 As well as 1527, she was there in 1528 with her plate (Rep 7 f.379).

Chapter 9

1 Daybell, op. cit., p. 1.
2 L. Gowing, Gender Relations in Early Modern England (Harrow, 2012), p 29.
3 B. Capp, 'Separate Domains? Women and Authority in Early Modern England' in P. Griffiths, A. Fox and S. Hindle (eds), The Experience of Authority in Early Modern England (Basingstoke, 1996), p. 118.
4 Corrie, op. cit., p. 253.
5 Capp, op. cit., p. 118.
6 A woman who murdered her husband was also guilty of petty treason and would be sentenced to burn. See J. H. Baker (ed.), Reports of Cases From the Time of King Henry VIII (2003), Vol I, p. 91.
7 Anger, J., 'Her Protection of Women' in Shepherd, S. (ed.), The Women's Sharp Revenge (London, 1985).
8 Ibid., p. 39.
9 An extract from the Homily is printed in Anger (1985) pp. 25–6.
10 Ibid., p. 26.
11 Ibid., p. 638.
12 B. J. Harris, English Aristocratic Women (2002), p. 175; Capp, op. cit., p. 117; B. J. Harris, 'Sisterhood, Friendship and the Power of English Aristocratic Women, 1450–1550' in Daybell, op. cit., p. 21.
13 Legally it was permissible for women to serve as justices of the peace, although none appear to have done so. See B. J. Harris, 'Women and Politics in Early Tudor England' (The Historical Journal 33 (1990), p. 269.
14 Lambarde, op. cit., p. 173 (paraphrasing Thwaites).

15 In the Parliamentary Act of Attainder against all three of them.

16 Writing any account of Elizabeth Barton's life is fraught with difficulty due to the paucity of reliable sources. After her arrest, she was heavily censored with most sources favourable to her destroyed. Instead, we are heavily reliant on four difficult sources. Two were directly produced at the government's behest: the Act of Attainder against Elizabeth and her supporters, and the sermon preached at her public penance. Additionally, Archbishop Cranmer, who considered her a fraud, wrote an account in a private letter. The final source is a paraphrase of a pamphlet produced by Edward Thwaites in her lifetime, which exists in the work of William Lambarde, a late-sixteenth-century antiquary hostile to Barton. All copies of the original pamphlet (which had been a bestseller) were destroyed.

17 The Act claims that he hoped to draw pilgrims to Court-at-Street, but it was not actually in his parish.

18 He later had a financial interest in the manor of Court-at-Street. See A. D. Cheney, 'Richard Masters, Parson of Aldyngton, 1514 to 1558' in *The British Archaeological Association,* New Series, vol. 10 (1904), p. 127).

19 Cranmer says that 'ever since that time hath been commonly sold and gone abroad amongst all people' (letter to Archdeacon Hawkyns p. 274) and Lambarde, op. cit., p. 170.

20 Cranmer to Archdeacon Hawkyns, p. 272.

21 Whatmore, op. cit., p. 465.

22 Ibid., p. 465.

23 Act of Attainder, p 447.

24 Wright VII

25 Lambarde, op. cit., p. 173 (paraphrasing Thwaites).

26 Whatmore, op cit., p. 465.

27 Ibid., p. 469.

28 Act of Attainder, p. 447.

29 R. M. Bell, *Holy Anorexia* (Chicago, 1985). Even the sermon against her admitted that she remained weak from her disease. Whatmore, op. cit., p. 465.

30 Lambarde, op. cit., p. 172 (paraphrasing Thwaites). This account was used in the sermon against her, regarding her early career (see Whatmore).

31 Ibid., p. 169.

32 Ibid., p. 173.

33 Whatmore, op. cit., p. 466. If, of course, the sermon is to be believed, since accounts of Elizabeth's examinations do not survive, and torture cannot be ruled out – as was later applied to Anne Askew.

34 The Act of Attainder claims that both Masters and Bocking counselled Elizabeth to declare that she would be cured at Court-at-Street for reasons of their 'own lucre and advantage'.

35 Wright VI.

36 Whatmore (p. 465) and the Act of Attainder (p. 447) say 2,000 people, Thwaites says 3,000.

37 Lambarde, op. cit., p. 173 (paraphrasing Thwaites).

38 Cranmer to Archdeacon Hawkyns, p. 272 notes that she was carried into the chapel.

39 Whatmore, op. cit., p. 465.

40 Ibid., p. 465.

41 Cranmer to Archdeacon Hawkyns, p 272.

42 Lambarde (paraphrasing Thwaites), p. 174.

43 Cranmer to Archdeacon Hawkyns, p. 272.

44 Whatmore, op. cit., p. 466. The author called these utterances 'feigned'.
45 Cranmer to Archdeacon Hawkyns, p. 272.
46 Ibid., p. 272, p. 274.
47 Act of Attainder, p. 448.
48 Cranmer to Archdeacon Hawkyns, p. 274.
49 Thomas More recalled that he first heard of Barton thanks to Warham's roll, estimating that this was in 1525 or 1526, indicating that the archbishop put it together not long after the miracle at Court-at-Street. See E. F. Rogers (ed.), *The Correspondence of Thomas More* (1947) no.197.
50 Rogers, op. cit., no 197.
51 Ingram, op. cit. (1994) p. 49.
52 Underdown 1985:119
53 Ingram 1994, op. cit., p. 57.
54 *The Cucking of a Scould* (2nd edition, 1630).
55 F. J. C. Hearnshaw and D. M. Hearnshaw (eds), *Southampton Court Leet Records 1603–24*, Vol. I, parts 1–3 (Southampton, 1905–07), I.2, p. 174.
56 Ibid., p. 345
57 Ibid., I.3, p. 381.
58 Ibid., I, p. 401.

Chapter 10

1 Thomas Wyatt – any further information?
2 The future Henry VIII was, for safety reasons, forbidden from jousting. Sources make it clear he was fascinated by tournaments. 'The Justes of the Moneths of May and June' records that, at a tournament in 1507, Prince Henry was an eager spectator, rushing to the combatants 'to speak of arms and of other defence'. See W. C. Hazlitt (ed.), *Remains of the Early Popular Poetry of England*, Vol. II (1866).
3 L&P, Vol. I, p. 81.
4 Ibid., p. 82.
5 The identity of the Lady Boleyn at court early in the reign of Henry VIII is confused by the fact that Thomas had two married younger brothers Norton (2013) pp. 80–97 reviews the evidence and concludes that it was indeed the former Elizabeth Howard that served.
6 Elizabeth received a cup with a gilt cover weighting 16½ ounces (L&P, Vol. I, 1549). It was the fifth-largest gift made to non-royal ladies.
7 TNA SP1/73 f.71. Her half-sister, Lady Bryan, who was then lady mistress to Princess Mary, received a gift weighing only 18 ounces (TNA SP1/73 f.75).
8 L&P, Vol. III, p. 491.
9 E. Casady, Henry Howard, Earl of Surrey (New York, 1975), p. 16. The battle, at which the Scottish king, James IV, was killed, was the greatest military achievement of Henry's reign, occurring while he was absent in France.
10 A. Somerset, *Ladies in Waiting* (London, 1984).
11 E. Norton, *Bessie Blount* (Stroud, 2011), p. 71.
12 L&P. Vol. I, p. 368.
13 N. Samman, *The Henrician Court During Cardinal Wolsey's Ascendancy c.1514–29* (University of Wales unpublished PhD Thesis, 1988), p. 454.
14 E. Hall, *Henry VIII*, ed. Whinley, C. (London, 1904), Vol. I, p. 143.
15 D. Starkey (ed.), *The Inventory of King Henry VIII: Society of Antiquaries MS 129 and British*

Library MS Harley 1419: The Transcript, Vol. I (London, 1998), p. 167–8.

16 L&P, Vol. VI, p. 278.

17 M. St Clare Byrne (ed.), *The Lisle Letters* (Chicago, 1981), Vol. IV, pp. 163–4

18 There are memorial brasses for infant sons Henry at Hever and Thomas at Penshurst.

19 TNA SP1/59, f.98.

20 He paid for two yards and three quarters of black satin 'for a doublet for me', as well as making a substantial payment of £3 6s 8d to his 'broiderer'. There was also a 40s bill due to 'Richard my tailor'.

21 D Gurney (ed) 'Extracts from the Household and Privy Purse Accounts of the Lestranges of Hunstanton, From AD 1519 to AD 1578' in *Archaeologia 25* (1833), p. 483. Anne Shelton had earlier visited Lestrange in 1519 (p. 430).

22 Unfortunately, these are the only known example of Elizabeth Boleyn socializing outside her immediate family circle. An old account of the Berkeley family states that, in 1534, Lord and Lady Berkeley decided to reduce their household charges by lodging with the Countess of Wiltshire in Stone Castle in Kent. See J. Smyth, *The Berkeley Manuscripts* (Gloucester, 1883), p. 257. This Countess of Wiltshire has been mistakenly identified as Elizabeth: see R. Warnicke, *Wicked Women of Tudor England* (New York, 2012), p. 167. It actually refers to Margaret, Lady Wiltshire, the widow of Sir John Wiltshire, who had a life interest in Stone Castle (TNA PROB 11/22/71, TNA C1/596/27; TNA PROB 11/22/51)

23 G. Cavendish, *The Life of Cardinal Wolsey by William Cavendish,* ed. Singer, S.W. (1825), pp. 59–64; R. W. Hoyle, 'Henry Percy. Sixth Earl of Northumberland, and the Fall of the House of Percy', in Bernard, G.W. (ed.), *The Tudor Nobility* (Manchester, 1992).

24 F. A. Munby (ed.), *The Youth of Henry VIII: A Narrative in Contemporary Letters* (Boston, 1913), pp. 126–7.

25 S. Giustinian, *Four Years at the Court of Henry VIII,* 2 vols, ed. Brown, R. (1854), pp. 90–1.

26 Seventeen of Henry's letters to Anne survive (bizarrely) in the Vatican Archives. See E. Norton (ed.), *The Anne Boleyn Papers* (Stroud, 2013b).

27 Bocking's Latin prologue in MacKey p61 [NB can't find this] notes that she was eighteen when she entered her convent.

28 Whatmore, op cit., p 466.

29 Ibid., p. 466. The insinuation is that they spent the night together

30 J. Stevens, *The History of the Antient Abbeys, Monasteries, Hospitals, Cathedral and Collegiate Churches,* Vol. I (1722), p. 518; E. Hasted, *The History and Topographical Survey of the County of Kent,* XII (1850), p. 317; H. Ward, *Ward's Canterbury Guide* (Canterbury, 1843), p. 32.

31 Ward, op cit., p. 30.

32 Roper, W., *The Lyfe of Sir Thomas Moore, Knighte, Written by William Roper, Esquire, Whiche Married Margareat, Daughter of the Sayed Thomas Moore,* ed. Hitchcock, E.V. (1930), p. 60.

33 E. Herbert, *The Life and Raigne of King Henry the Eighth* (1649), p. 226

34 B. Capp, op. cit., p. 132.
35 CSP Venetian, Vol. IV, p. 701.
36 Capp, op. cit., p. 121.
37 H. Machyn, *The Diary of Henry Machyn: Citizen and Merchant-Taylor of London from AD 1550–63*, Nichols, J.G., ed. (1848), p. 310.
38 M. Bowker, *An Episcopal Court Book For the Diocese of Lincoln 1514–1520* (Lincoln, 1967), p. 53.
39 For the Emma Nash story, E. R. Brinkworth (ed.), *The Archdeacon's Court; Liber Actorum, 1584*, 2 vols (Oxford, 1942–46), pp. 52, 64, 78.
40 Not long after Anne's marriage, one Henry Long from Somerset wrote to Cromwell to report one of his son-in-law's servants, who had been overheard speaking 'words against the Queen's Grace and against My Lady her mother My Lady of Wiltshire'. TNA SP1/100 f.64
41 L&P, Vol. VI, p. 923.
42 Elton 1976.
43 N. Sander, *Rise and Grown of Anglican Schism* (1877), p. 24.
44 Norton (2013) discusses the rumours of an affair between Henry and Elizabeth at length.
45 Anne Boleyn to Lady Wingfield. See M. A. E. Wood (ed.), *Letters of Royal and Illustrious Ladies*, Vol II, p. 75.
46 The French ambassador noted on 6 October 1528 that he thought it was unlikely that Anne would yet leave her mother in Kent (L&P, Vol. IV, Appendix, p. 206).
47 Ibid.

Chapter 11

1 E. F. Rogers (eds), *The Correspondence of Thomas More* (1947), no. 197.

2 Ibid.
3 Wright, Vol. IV.
4 Whatmore, op. cit., p. 470.
5 When her cell was later searched, investigators found a paper full of chemicals, including brimstone, which she used 'to make great, stinking smokes ... at such times as she feigned the devil to have been with her in her cell'. Ibid. 469. As always, it is difficult to tell just how much of this was propaganda that was subsequently used against Barton and how much she really confessed.
6 L&P, Vol. IV, Appendix, p. 206.
7 Whatmore, op. cit., p. 470
8 Wright, VII.
9 Whatmore, op. cit., p. 469.
10 BL Cotton Cleopatra E/IV f.97.
11 L&P, Vol. V, 1698 II.
12 Wright VII; D. Watt, *Secretaries of God* (Cambridge, 1997), p. 66.
13 According to the later sermon against her, this pressure would cause her to feign revelations to please Bocking. Whatmore, op. cit., p. 469.
14 Lambarde, op. cit., p. 174 (paraphrasing Thwaites).
15 Cranmer to Archdeacon Hawkyns.
16 Ibid.
17 L&P, Vol. IV, 4005.
18 Rogers, op. cit., no.197.
19 Cranmer to Archdeacon Hawkyns, p. 274.
20 Wright VI.
21 Watt, op. cit., p. 3.
22 Ibid., p. 55.
23 T. Cranmer, 'A Confutation of Unwritten Verities' in J. E. Cox (ed.), *Miscellaenous Writings and Letters of Thomas Cranmer*, p. 64.
24 Ibid.
25 Ibid.

26 Ibid.
27 J. Lewis, *The Life of Dr. John Fisher*, Vol. II (1855), p. 332, no. XXIX, confirms that Elizabeth told Henry to his face what she also told John Fisher, concerning the prophesied loss of his throne.
28 Ibid., p. 335, no.XXX.
29 L&P, Vol. VI, 1468 no.5.
30 Lewis, op. cit., p. 332, no.XXIX.
31 Ibid., p. 335.
32 Whatmore, op. cit., p. 467.
33 Herbert, op. cit., p. 231.
34 St Clare Byrne, op. cit., p. 81.
35 Wright VI.
36 Ibid.
37 Ibid.
38 Whatmore, op. cit., p. 470.
39 Wright VI
40 Thomas More was later informed that Barton saved the cardinal's soul (Rogers, op. cit., no.197).
41 Whatmore, op. cit. p. 468; Wright VI.
42 Wright VII.
43 TNA SP 1/82 f.69.
44 Whatmore, op. cit., p. 470. A monk named Hawkhurst later confessed to writing it.
45 L&P, Vol VI, 1336.
46 More's conversations: Rogers, op. cit., no. 197.
47 Ibid., no.192
48 L&P, Vol. VI, 1468 no.5.
49 Ibid., 1468 no.7.
50 Cranmer to Archdeacon Hawkyns, p. 274.
51 Wright VI.
52 M. Dowling, 'Anne Boleyn and Reform' (*Journal of Ecclesiastical History 35*, 1984), p. 36.
53 J. A. Guy, 'Henry VIII and the Praemunire Manoeuvres of 1530–31' (*English Historical Review 97*, 1982).
54 L&P, Vol. V, p. 686.

55 Cranmer to Archdeacon Hawkyns, p. 274.
56 L&P, Vol. VI, 1468 no.5.
57 Act of Attainder.
58 Privy Purse Accounts of Henry VIII record the king's movements in this period, although there is no reference to his meeting with Barton in the accounts.
59 L&P, Vol. VI, 1468 no.5.
60 Ibid.
61 Wright VII.
62 L&P, Vol. VI, 1468 no 5.

Chapter 12

1 L&P, Vol. VI, p. 266.
2 Whatmore, op. cit., p. 468.
3 Ibid.
4 Act of Attainder, p. 449
5 L&P, Vol. VI, p. 835.
6 Ibid., 1194.
7 The Latin prologue is printed in McKey, pp. 60–3.
8 Wright VI.
9 L&P, Vol. VI, p. 887.
10 Cox, op. cit., p. 252.
11 L&P, Vol. VI, p. 967.
12 Ibid
13 Chapuys to Charles V, 10 September 1533.
14 L&P, Vol. X, p. 1187.
15 R. E. Richardson, *Mistress Blanche: Queen Elizabeth I's Confidante* (Little Logaston, Herefordshire, 2007), p. 4.
16 Ascham to Princess Elizabeth, 1545, in R. Ascham, *Letters of Roger Ascham*, eds M. Hatch and A. Vos (New York, 1989), p. 77.
17 Sir Robert Tyrwhitt to Somerset, 31 January 1549 (SP 10/6/16).
18 Viscount Strangford (ed.), *Household Expenses of the Princess Elizabeth During her Residence at Hatfield, October 1, 1531 to September 30, 1552* (London, 1853), p. 30.

19 Act of Attainder, p. 450.
20 TNA SP 1/82 f.69.
21 Watt, op. cit., p. 53.
22 Wright VI.
23 Act of Attainder, p. 450.
24 CSP Spanish, Vol. IV, p. 1149 notes that they carried out 'diligent searches' for messages that had passed between nun and queen, but found nothing.
25 Ibid., p. 1153.
26 D. Hahn, *The Tower Menagerie* (2003), p. 33, also E. T. Bennett, *The Tower Menagerie* (1829) and D. Henry, *An Historical Description of the Tower of London* (1753).
27 CSP Spanish, Vol. IV, p. 1153.
28 Cranmer to Archdeacon Hawkyns, p. 274. This quote comes from a private letter, written by Cranmer, and therefore does seem accurate.
29 Whatmore, op. cit., p. 474.
30 Ibid. Act of Attainder, p. 450 gives an almost identical version of this.
31 L&P, Vol VI, p. 1149.
32 Ibid., p. 1194.
33 A. D. Cheney, 'Richard Masters, Parson of Aldyngton, 1514 to 1558' in *The British Archaeological Association, New Series, Vol. 10* (1904), p. 112.
34 CSP Spanish IV, p. 1153.
35 Ibid.
36 TNA SP 1/80 f.118 contains a list of who was informed by whom Barton confessed that 'she showed the revelation concerning the king's grace's reign that he shall not be king a month after that he married the queen's grace' to a number of people, including Dr Bocking, John Fisher, his chaplain Dr Adsone, Henry Gold, Edward Thwaites, Richard Masters, Father Rich, Father Risby and Father Lawrence. Hugh Rich then showed these revelations to Catherine of Aragon, Princess Mary, her governess, the Countess of Salisbury, the Marquess of Exeter, the Bishop of Rochester, Thomas Abel and many other members of the nobility and gentry, as well as the nuns at Syon and the prior of Sheen (TNA SP 1/80 f.118).
37 Whatmore, op. cit., p. 474.
38 Ibid.
39 L&P, Vol. VI, p. 1466.
40 Cox, op cit., p 271.
41 L&P, Vol. VI, p. 1464.
42 *Lisle Letters*, Vol. I, p. 77.
43 Chronicle of St Augustine's, Canterbury in J. G. Nichols (ed.), *Narratives of the Days of the Reformation* (1859), p. 280.
44 Whatmore, op. cit., p. 464 and CSP Spanish, Vol. IV, p. 1154.
45 This paper is inserted amongst the charges laid against her and before the sermon at the penance in the State Papers. It is clearly the paper she was required to read on the scaffold (TNA SP 1/82 f.69 pasted in).
46 E. R. Brinkworth (ed.), *The Archdeacon's Court; Liber Actorum, 1584* (Oxford, 1942–46), Vol. II, p. 12.
47 Brinkworth, op. cit., Vol. 1, p. 5.
48 Whatmore, op. cit., p. 464.
49 Ibid.; Cranmer, 'A Confutation of Unwritten Verities' in Cox, op. cit., p. 66.
50 Wright IX
51 Cox, op. cit., p. 272.
52 Rogers, op cit., no.195. More's son-in-law believed that the king used Elizabeth as a means of bringing him down. See W. Roper, *The Lyfe of Sir Thomas Moore*, ed. E. V. Hitchcock (1930), p. 60.
53 Lewis, op. cit., p 332, no. XXIX.

54 Statutes of the Realm 25 Hen VIII c XII, p. 446.

55 Act of Attainder, p. 450.

56 Masters returned to his parsonage, living there until his death in 1558 (Cheney, op. cit., p. 22; L&P, Vol. VI, p. 1666). He was noted as a papist by Cranmer in 1543. At the same time, it was recalled that 'he has been a great setter-forth in his parish of the Maid of Kent, pilgrimages, feigned relics, and other superstitions, and yet never resented nor reproved the same': he did not abandon his belief in Elizabeth (L&P 18 pt II, p. 301).

57 C. Wriothesley, *A Chronicle of England During the Reigns of the Tudors*, ed. Hamilton, D. (1875–8), Vol. I, p. 24; *Lisle Letters*, II, p. 171.

58 Hall, op. cit., p. 814.

59 Wriothesley, op. cit., Vol. I, p 24.

60 J. G. Nichols (ed.), *Chronicle of the Grey Friars of London (1852)*, p. 37. A fanciful account of the deaths of Fathers Rich and Risby survives from later in the sixteenth century. McKey p. 54 recounts this story, which was originally published in Bouchier 1582. As the pair stood on the scaffold, a messenger arrived from the king, offering them their lives in exchange for a public renunciation of the pope's authority. Neither man was prepared to do this, with Risby declaring in Latin that 'I will freely sacrifice to thee, and I will confess to thy name: for it is for their benefit'. He was then executed, before his still beating heart was torn from his body. Next was Rich's turn. Once his heart too was removed, he turned to his executioner, declaring 'what you hold in your hand is consecrated to God'.

61 N. Sander, *The Rise and Growth of the Anglican Schism* (1877), p 112.

62 The words of one of the Gold brothers – it is not known which. Ibid.

63 *Lisle Letters*, II, p. 171.

64 Norton (2011), op. cit., p. 249.

65 *Lisle Letters*, III, p. 673.

66 Hall, op. cit., p. 819.

67 L&P, XI, p. 17.

68 *Lisle Letters*, IV, p. 884.

69 Ibid. V, p. 1137.

70 Burke (1870) p. 240

71 *Grey Friars Chronicle*, p. 35. An earlier example of the punishment from 1523 records a similar procedure (p. 30).

72 E. Coke, *The Third Part of the Institutes of the Laws of England* (1669), p. 48.

73 Stow (1600), op. cit., p. 942.

74 22 Hen VIII c.9.

75 *Grey Friars Chronicle*, p. 30. The punishment had traditionally been associated with those counterfeiters. See W. Andrews, *Old Time Punishments* (Hull, 1980), p. 198

76 Emmison, op. cit., pp. 149–50.

77 W. Richards, *The History of Lynn*, Vol. II (Lynn, 1812), p. 1192. This incident is not mentioned in the contemporary chronicle of King's Lynn. See R. Flenley (ed.), *Six Town Chronicles of England* (Oxford, 1911) Other details of the punishment of boiling can be found in E W. Pettifer, *Punishments of Former Days* (Winchester, 1992), p. 163.

78 *Grey Friars Chronicle*, p. 45; Stow (1600), op. cit., p. 981; Coke, op. cit., p. 48.

79 Stow, op. cit., p. 981.
80 Wriothesley, op. cit., pp. 134–5.
81 Coke, op. cit., p. 48.
82 CAR Surrey, p. 496.

Chapter 13

1 For an extensive study of pre-Reformation piety, see E. Duffy, *The Stripping of the Altars* (New Haven, 2005), p. 4, who contends that 'late medieval Catholicism exerted an enormously strong, diverse, and vigorous hold over the imagination and the loyalty of the people up to the very. moment of the Reformation'.
2 M. Spufford (ed.), *The World of Rural Dissenters, 1420–1725* (Cambridge, 1995), pp. 1–102 questions the importance of religion in sixteenth- and seventeenth-century society, but it is largely accepted.
3 K. L. French, 'The Seat Under Our Lady: Gender and Seating in Late Medieval English Parish Churches' in V. C. Raguin and S. Stanbury (eds), *Women's Space: Patronage, Place and Gender in the Medieval Church* (Albany, 2005), pp. 141–60; C. Schleif 'Men on the Right – Women on the Left: (A) Symmetrical Spaces and Gendered Places' in Raguin and Stanbury, op. cit., pp. 207–49.
4 This can be seen at Ludlow. See P. Klein, 'Ludlow Parish Church and its Clergy at the Reformation' in *Transactions of the Shropshire Archaeological and Historical Society 73* (1998), pp. 20–32.
5 Ibid., p. 19. Half a pew and its reversion were sold in 1544.
6 T. Wright (ed.), *Churchwardens' Accounts of the Town of Ludlow, in Shropshire, from 1540 to the End of the Reign of Queen Elizabeth* (1869).
7 Ibid., p. 13.
8 Ibid., p. 41.
9 Brinkworth, op. cit., Vol. II, p. 171.
10 Ibid., Vol. I, p. 5.
11 Ibid., Vol. II, p. 177.
12 Ibid., p. 186.
13 The only detailed account of her life can be found in S. L. Jansen, *Strange Talk and Dangerous Behaviour* (New York, 1996).
14 Fountains Abbey, pp. 271–2.
15 J. Foster (ed.), *The Visitation of Yorkshire, Made in the Years 1584/5* (1875), Bulmer of Pinchinthorpe.
16 Wriothesley, op. cit., Vol. I, p. 64.
17 M. H. Dodds R. and Dodds, *The Pilgrimage of Grace , 1536–1537, and the Exeter Conspiracy, 1538* (Cambridge, 1915), Vol. 1.
18 Margaret sent her recommendations to her stepdaughter and stepson-in-law when her husband wrote to them in the 1530s (L&P XII.1, p. 304). John and Margaret's son, in later life, insisted that he had been born in 'lawful matrimony' (Foster, Yorkshire Visitation Pedigrees).
19 Jansen, op. cit., p. 7.
20 During her trial, Margaret was referred to doggedly as 'Margaret Cheyne, wife of William Cheyne late of London' (TNA SP1/120 f.78). If she had been a widow, it would have been expected that she would be called 'late the wife of'.
21 Hall, op. cit., p. 825. The chronicler, Charles Wriothesley, called her 'other wife to Bulmer called' (Vol. I, p. 64).
22 Many of the occupants of monastic houses were sincere in their vocations. Sister Katherine

Dodd of the Augustinian priory of Limebrook in Herefordshire, for example, petitioned the Bishop in 1530 for a licence to move to a nearby Cistercian house, since she desired to live by a stricter rule. See A. T. Bannister (ed.), *Registrum Caroli Bothe Episcopi Herefordensis, 1516–1535* (Hereford, 1921), p. 241.

23 G. Moorhouse, *The Pilgrimage of Grace* (2002), p. 47; Dodds, op. cit., Vol. I, p. 97.

24 When she was later in prison she stated that 'I was but a woman, and knew not the course of schools'.

25 L&P, Vol. XI, p. 534.

26 They also wanted to reduce their tax burden.

27 L&P, Vol. XI, p. 1103.

28 Dent, op. cit , p. 26.

29 L&P, Vol. XII.1, p. 1011.

30 Bulmer was appointed by the rebels to take responsibility for the priory of Guisbourne, suggesting an interest in monasticism (TNA SP1/113 f.183). Conservative religious beliefs did not stop him taking a lease of the former monastery of Rastall in Yorkshire (L&P, Vol. XII.1, p. 543).

31 Duffy, op. cit.; C. S. L. Davies, 'Popular Religion and the Pilgrimage of Grace' in A. Fletcher and J. Stevenson, J. (eds), *Order and Disorder in Early Modern England* (Cambridge, 1985).

32 L&P, Vol. XI, p. 188; M A E. Wood (ed.), *Letters of Royal and Illustrious Ladies* (London, 1846), Vol. III, pp. 185–6.

33 L&P, Vol. XI, p. 346.

34 L&P, Vol. XII.1, p. 66.

35 Ibid., p. 164.

36 Dodds, op. cit., p. 76.

37 L&P, Vol. XII.1, p. 1087.

38 Ibid., p. 66.

39 Ibid., p. 304.

40 Ibid., p. 1083.

41 For example, Sir William Bulmer to Sir John Bulmer, 25 January 1537 (TNA SP 1/115 f.67a).

42 TNA SP1/113 f.68.

43 L&P, Vol XII.1, p. 304 and R. W. Hoyle, *The Pilgrimage of Grace and the Politics of the 1530s* (Oxford, 2001), p. 389.

44 Latimer's wife, Catherine Parr, was later a major proponent of religious reform and probably already had little sympathy for the rebels' cause

45 L&P, Vol XII.1, p. 1083.

46 Dodds, op. cit., Vol. II, p. 158.

47 Hoyle, op. cit., p. 397.

48 L&P, Vol. XII.1, p. 1084.

49 Ibid.

50 On Good Friday, Bulmer was said to have visited Lumley two days before (ibid.).

51 E. Milner and E. Benham (eds), *Records of the Lumleys of Lumley Castle* (1904), pp. 26, 30 and 32.

52 L&P, Vol. XII.1, p. 1083.

53 Moorhouse (2002) p. 293.

54 L&P XII.1 1084. It is only from Margaret's conversation with Staynhus on the Thursday before Easter that there is any evidence of treason on her part. This was the day after her husband's visit to Lord Lumley.

55 Moorhouse, op. cit., p 292.

56 L&P, Vol. XII.1, p. 1085.

57 Ibid., p. 1084.

58 Ibid.

59 Moorhouse, op. cit., p. 293. So too did Gregory Conyers, another local man.

60 TNA SP1/118 f.84.

61 Dodds, op. cit., Vol. II, p. 164.

62 Wriothesley, Vol. 1, op. cit., p. 63.

63 Ibid., p. 64.

64 Ibid.l Hall, op. cit., p. 826.
65 Margaret was burned for treason rather than heresy. Henry VIII actually did burn one Catholic for heresy (John Forest in 1538). Following Forest's death, the king tended to reserve executions for heresy for religious reformers, while those who maintained their allegiance to Rome were executed for treason. See P. Marshall, 'Papist as Heretic: The Burning of John Forest, 1538' in *The Historical Journal 41* (1998), pp. 351–74.

Chapter 14

1 34 and 35 Henry VIII c.1.
2 J. Foxe, *The Acts and Monuments of John Foxe* (New York, 1965), p. 621.
3 Sometimes spelled 'Butcher', 'Boucher' or 'Bowcher'.
4 L&P, 18.II, p. 545.
5 J. Strype, *Ecclesiastical Memorials Relating Chiefly to Religion, and the Reformation of it, and the Emergencies of the Church of England under King Henry VIII, King Edward VI and Queen Mary I* (Oxford, 1822), Vol II.ı, p. 334.
6 There is no certain proof to suggest Lollard links as J. Davis, 'Joan of Kent, Lollardy and the English Reformation' in *Journal of Ecclesiastical History 33* (1982), pp. 225–33 suggests.
7 L&P, 18.II, p. 545.
8 Terminology is very difficult in the early Reformation. 'Catholic' was widely fought over and only later became applied to those who maintained traditional beliefs (something which is, in itself, a misnomer, since what would become Catholicism was also undergoing reform and change

in the period). The term 'Protestant' was also not employed until at least the 1550s. Evangelical or reformer are better terms. Here, reformer will be used. See P. Marshall and A. Ryrie (eds), *The Beginnings of English Protestantism* (Cambridge, 2002).
9 R. Parsons, *A Temperate Ward-Word, to the Turbulent and Seditious Wach-Word of Sir Francis Hastinges Knight who Indeuoreth to Slaunder the Whole Catholique Cause, & all Professors Therrof, Both at Home and Abrode* (1599).
10 L&P, 18.II, p. 545.
11 Ibid.
12 Ibid.
13 Ibid.
14 Davis, op. cit., p. 230.
15 G. Gertz, *Heresy Trials and English Women Writers, 1400–1670* (Cambridge, 2012), p. 8.
16 L&P, 18.II, p. 545
17 Ibid.
18 Duffy, op. cit., p. 433.
19 L&P, Vol. XIV.I, p. 374.
20 Strype, op. cit., Vol. I, p. 159.
21 L&P, 18.II, p. 545.
22 Ibid.
23 D. MacCullough, *Thomas Cranmer* (New Haven, 1996), ch. 8.
24 Parsons, op. cit.
25 Ingram, op. cit., p. 1.
26 E. K. M. Jarman (ed.), *Justice and Conciliation in a Tudor Church Court* (Record Society of Lancashire and Chester, 2012), p. xvii.
27 Ingram, op. cit., p. 2.
28 Hale, op. cit., no.365.
29 Brinkworth, op. cit., Vol. 1, p. 116.
30 M. Bowker (ed), *An Episcopal Court Book For the Diocese of Lincoln 1514–20* (Lincoln,

1967), p. 4.

31 Brinkworth, op. cit., Vol. I, p. 4.

32 Brinkworth, op. cit., Vol. II, p. 180.

33 Jarman, op. cit., p. 21.

34 Ibid., p. 25.

35 Ibid., p. 49.

36 J. G. Nichols (ed.), *Narratives of the Days of the Reformation* (1849), p. 39.

37 E. V. Beilin (ed.), *The Examinations of Anne Askew* (Oxford, 1996), p. 92 for later examination. We know very little about Thomas Kyme; even his identification uncertain.

38 Ibid., p. 93.

39 Ibid.

40 Ibid., p. 56 for first examination.

41 Ibid., p. 57.

42 Ibid , p. 124 for later examination, refers to Anne's maid servant

43 Nichols (1849), op. cit., p. 40.

44 Ibid.

45 R. Hickman, 'Religion and Politics in mid Tudor England through the eyes of an English Protestant Woman', in *Bulletin of the Institute of Historical Research 131* (1982), p. 97.

46 Ibid.

47 Ibid.; Foxe, op. cit., v.250.

48 Beilin, op. cit., p. 124 for later examination.

49 P. Zahl, *Five Women of the English Reformation* (Michigan, 2005), p. 28.

50 Beilin, op. cit., p. 121 for later examination.

51 Anne sought a divorce on the grounds of 1 Corinthians: 7, which said that 'if a faithful woman have an unbelieving husband, which will not tarry with her, she may leave him' (later examination p. 93). Such a divorce would have been almost impossible to obtain. In the period, marriages were almost always ended solely by annulment – with the union void from its inception.

52 L&P, Vol. XII, part 2, pp. 74–5.

53 There are a number of biographies of Catherine Parr, including E. Norton, *Catherine Parr* (Stroud, 2010) and S. James, *Catherine Parr* (Stroud, 2008).

54 'The Lamentation of a Sinner' in C. Parr, *Katherine Parr*, ed. J. Mueller (Chicago, 2011).

55 C. McCarthy, *Marriage in Medieval England: Law, Literature and Practice* (Woodbridge, 2004), p. 142

56 J. A. Thomson, *The Early Tudor Church and Society 1485–1529* (1993), p. 337.

57 E. Barker (ed.), *The Register of Thomas Rotherham Archbishop of York 1480–1500, Vol. I* (Torquay, 1976), p. 2.

58 Ibid., p. 214.

59 M. Hayward, *Rich Apparel: Clothing and the Law in Henry VIII's England* (Farnham, 2009), p. 248.

60 For example, National Portrait Gallery, 551.

61 C. Cooper, *Memoir of Margaret, Countess of Richmond and Derby* (Cambridge, 1874), pp. 30–1.

62 Ibid.

63 J. Thomson, *The Early Tudor Church and Society* (1993), p. 337.

64 L&P, Vol. XVIII.1, p. 67 (5, 6).

65 Sources differ on how Anne's religious beliefs were discovered. Her nephew claimed that it was on the grounds of an intercepted letter (Ayscu 1607, op. cit.). She claimed that Thomas Kyme made suit that she be examined (later examination, p. 93), but this might have been a mistake occasioned by her surprise at

finding him in London. Alternatively, John Bale claimed that Anne was first arrested on the testimony of a woman, who had reported her for declaring 'how God was not in temples made with hands' and 'that I had rather to read five lines in the Bible, than to hear five masses in the temple' (Beilin, op. cit., p. 20 for later examination).

66 Anne Askew's own account of her two examinations were first published by the Protestant exile John Bale shortly after her death. The manuscripts do not survive. They are usually accepted as the authentic work of Anne Askew, although some caution must be employed when using them. Stephen Gardiner, who was present at some of the examinations, considered Bale a liar: 'his untruth appeareth evidently in setting forth the examination of Anne Askew, which is utterly misreported'. See Gardiner, 1933, p. 278.

67 Gertz, op. cit., p. 9.

68 Anne's nephew claimed that she was 25 when she died. See Ayscu (1607) op. cit.

69 Beilin, op. cit., p. 23, for first examination.

70 Ibid., p. 24.

71 Not long after this examination, on which Anne was questioned on the doctrine of Purgatory and, thus, the deceased's need for memorial masses and prayers, Bowes would be caught scandalously breaking up and selling the tomb memorials in the Greyfriar's Church in London. He also bought much monastic property. See Mayer, T.F. and Walters, C.B. (eds.), *The Correspondence of Reginald Pole* (Aldershot, 2008), p. 77.

72 Beilin, op. cit., p. 27 for first examination.

73 Ibid., p. 31.

74 Ibid.

75 Ibid., p. 36.

76 Ibid., p. 58.

77 APC I, p. 424.

78 Ibid., p. 462; Beilin, op. cit., p. 92 for later examination.

79 Ibid., p. 93.

80 A. Griffiths, *The Chronicles of Newgate* (1884).

81 Beilin, op. cit., p. 98 for later examination.

82 Wriothesley, op. cit., Vol. I, p. 167; Beilin, op. cit., p. 101 for later examination.

83 APC I, p. 462.

84 Beilin, op. cit., p. 119 for later examination.

85 Wriothesley, op. cit., Vol I, p. 168.

86 Beilin, op. cit., p. 121 for later examination.

87 Ibid.

88 Ibid., p. 127.

89 Ibid., p. 134.

90 There is some debate over the extent of the danger Catherine was actually in. The plot mirrors the earlier Prebendaries Plot against Cranmer, in which the king intervened at the last minute to save his archbishop. The circumstances here, of the arrest warrant being mislaid, along with the fact that Henry had informed his doctor of what was afoot and then sent this man to Catherine, suggests that the king might have intended to scare a disobedient wife rather than actually rid himself of her. That said, had Catherine not submitted, she would have been arrested. See Norton (2010b), op. cit.

91 Nichols (1849), op. cit., p. 43.

92 Ibid., p. 44.

93 Wriothesley, Vol. I, p. 169.

94 Nichols (1849), op. cit., p. 44.
95 Ibid.
96 Foxe, J., 'The Two Examinations of ... Maistris An Askew from John Foxe, Actes and Monuments' in Beilin, op. cit , p. 192.
97 Nichols (1849), op. cit., p. 44
98 Strype, op cit., Vol. II.i, p. 335.
99 A text of this, and Catherine's other works can be found in Mueller, J. (ed.), *Katherine Parr Complete Works and Correspondence* (Chicago, 2011)
100 Felch, S.M. (ed.), *Elizabeth Tyrwhit's Morning and Evening Prayers* (Aldershot, 2008).
101 Ibid., p. 74.

Chapter 15

1 MacCulloch, op cit., p. 474.
2 Strype, op. cit., Vol. II, p. 99.
3 G. Corrie (ed.), *Sermons of Hugh Latimer* (1844), p. 114.
4 That same year a London butcher named Michael Thomb was also arrested for this belief. He recanted (Strype, op. cit., Vol. II, p. 96).
5 Ibid., p. 99.
6 Parsons, op. cit.
7 R. Hutchinson, *The Works of Roger Hutchinson*, ed. Bruce, J. (Cambridge, 1842), p. i.
8 Ibid., p. 146.
9 Henry VIII called Catherine Parr a 'doctress' during the plot against her, for example
10 Edward VI p. 51.
11 CSP Spanish, Vol. X, 22 April 1550.
12 Ibid.
13 Ibid.
14 Ibid.
15 A. Walsham, *A Charitable Hatred* (2009).
16 CSP Spanish, Vol. X, 22 April 1550.
17 *An Inventory of the Historical Monuments in Essex,* vol. 2, no.108.
18 The current church at Woodham Walter was built in the 1560s. The original is also supposed to have stood near the hall.
19 CSP Spanish X 2 May 1550.
20 Ibid.
21 Foxe, op. cit., V, p. 699.
22 APC III, p. 19. Although the statutory provisions against heresy had been repealed, there still remained common-law powers to condemn and burn them (see APC III, p. 475).
23 J. Mozley, *John Foxe and his Book* (1940), p. 35.
24 Rogers was the first Marian martyr, indeed suffering the 'gentle' death of burning.
25 Foxe, op. cit., VII, p. 631.
26 CSP Spanish, Vol. X, 2 May 1550.
27 Edward VI p. 51.
28 Strype, op. cit., Vol. II.i, p. 335.
29 R. Fabyan, *The New Chronicles of England and France* (1811) p. 710.
30 Strype, op. cit., Vol II.i, p 335.
31 Ibid., p. 336.
32 The other person to burn was George van Paris in 1551.
33 Foxe, op. cit., VII, p. 621.
34 E Becke, *A Brefe Confutatacion of this most Detestable, and Anabaptistical Opinion* (1550).
35 MacCulloch, op. cit., p. 475.
36 *Hamlet*, Act V, Scene 1.
37 N. St John-Stevas, *Life, Death, and the Law* (Washington, 1961), p. 233.
38 J. Harington, *Whether it be damnation for a man to kill himself* (BL).
39 T. R. Forbes (ed.), 'London Coroner's Inquests for 1590' in *Journal of the History of Medical and Allied Sciences 28* (1973), p. 378.

40 P E. H. Hair, 'A Note on the Incidence of Tudor Suicide' in *Local Population Studies 5* (1970), pp. 36–43.
41 Ibid., p. 164.
42 All these cases from MCR I, pp. 18, 47, 48, 51, 164, 380, 382.
43 T. R. Forbes (ed.), *Chronicle from Aldgate: Life and Death in Shakespeare's London* (New Haven, 1971), pp. 165–9.
44 C. Daniell, *Death and Burial in Medieval England* (1997), p. 106. St John-Stevas, op. cit., p. 233, notes that burial in this manner continued well into the eighteenth century.
45 A. T. Bannister (ed.), *Registrum Caroli Bothe Episcopi Herefordensis, 1516–35* (Hereford, 1921), p. 119.
46 CSP Spanish, Vol. X, 13 May 1550.
47 Ibid., 23 May 1550.
48 Ibid., 13 June 1550.
49 Ibid., Report of Jehan Duboys, middle of July.
50 Ibid., Van der Delft to Charles V, 6 June 1550.
51 Ibid., 8 June 1550.
52 Ibid., 13 June 1550 Mary of Hungary to Jehan Scheyfve, CSP Spanish X; 13 June 1550 Mary of Hungary to M. d'Eecke.
53 Ibid., 25 June 1550 Charles V to Mary of Hungary.
54 Ibid., 4 July 1550, d'Eecke to Mary of Hungary.
55 Ibid., 14 July 1550, d'Eecke to Mary of Hungary.
56 Ibid., Report of Jehan Duboys, middle of July.
57 History of Parliament, Sir Robert Rochester.
58 Edward VI p. 62.
59 Ibid., pp. 62, 63.
60 CSP Spanish, Vol. X, Scheyfve to Charles V, 26 July 1550 and Scheyfve to Charles V, 3 August 1550.
61 Ibid., Van der Delft to Charles V, 6 June 1550.
62 BL Harleian MS 2342.
63 N. H. Nicolas (ed.), *The Literary Remains of Lady Jane Grey*, pp. 57–8.
64 Before Jane, only the Empress Matilda had claimed the English throne as reigning queen. In 1141 she was declared 'Lady of the English' and journeyed to London for her coronation, but was later forced to flee; her cousin Stephen returned to take the throne (for more information, see Norton, 2010).
65 H. Machyn, *The Diary of Henry Machyn: Citizen and Merchant-Taylor of London*, ed. J. G. Nichols (1848), p. 35.
66 Jane to Mary (Wood)
67 Ibid.
68 Machyn, op. cit., p. 35.
69 J. G. Nichols (ed.), *The Chronicle of Queen Jane and Two Years of Queen Mary* (1850).
70 H. Robinson (ed.), *Original Letters Relative to the English Reformation*, vol. II (Cambridge, 1846), Julius Terentianus to John Ab Ulmis, 20 November 1553

Chapter 16

1 Duffy, op. cit., p. 1 provides an excellent and balanced study of the religious changes of Mary's reign, challenging assumptions that it was 'strong on repression and weak on persuasion'. His views are not accepted by all scholars. A. G. Dickens, 'The Early Expansion of Protestantism in England, 1520–1558' in P. Marshall (ed.), *The Impact of the English Reformation 1500–1640*

(London, 1997), pp. 85–116 argued that Protestantism was a formidable force by 1553.

2 Whatmore, op. cit., pp. 220–1.

3 Church materials very frequently found themselves in lay hands during the changes of the Reformation. In 1584 it was reported to the archdeacon's court that Mrs Stuthberie and Elizabeth Gledwelle had taken into their custody candlesticks, a basin, a crucifix, handbells, banner cloths and cross cloths from the parish church in Shouldham, Oxfordshire, goods for which they had not paid (Brinkworth, op. cit., Vol. II, p. 209).

4 Whatmore, op. cit., p. 249.

5 Hickman, op. cit., p. 98.

6 Ibid., p. 99.

7 Ibid., p. 100.

8 Ibid.

9 Whatmore, op. cit., Vol. I, p. 118.

10 Whatmore, op. cit., Vol. II, p. 207

11 Duffy, op. cit., p. 7.

12 The Diary of Henry Machyn, which was written by a contemporary resident of London, gives some idea of the regularity with which people were burned in the city during this short period.

13 Duffy, op. cit., p. 7 notes that the executions were beginning to tail off by summer 1558.

14 Except, of course, Cranmer, towards whom the queen bore a personal grudge.

15 Foxe, op. cit., VIII, p. 380.

16 Foxe also notes that he was a secret supporter of Protestantism (p. 381). This was hardly surprising, since Norwich had a very large Protestant community and 'only blatant self-incrimination, which accounted for very few martyrs overall, resulted in a death sentence in Norwich' (M. C. McClendon, 'Religious Toleration and the Reformation: Norwich Magistrates in the Sixteenth Century' in N. Tyacke, ed., England's Long Reformation).

17 Foxe, op cit., VIII, p. 429.

18 Hickman, op cit , p. 101.

19 Ibid., p. 102.

20 Elizabeth is often presented as pragmatic in her religious beliefs. However, there is no doubt that she was deeply devoted to Protestantism (Haigh, 1988, p.27). Questier, 2005, pp. 69-94 provides an interesting appraisal of the extent to which Elizabeth's reputation for religious tolerance is justified in relation to her Catholic subjects

21 CSP Spanish (Simancas), Vol. I, 19 March 1559.

22 A Walsham, Church Papists (London, 1993). It is very difficult to identify such individuals, since people rarely left records of their faith. Attempts to use will preambles, which usually contain a statement of faith, are problematic although have been attempted by historians. See, for example, Hickman 1998, op cit., pp. 117–139.

23 Priests could remain undetected for a considerable amount of time. At the Southwark Assizes on 17 February 1592, for example, a gentlewoman named Margaret Gage was convicted, along with her husband, of harbouring a Catholic priest in their house for more than forty days (CAR Surrey, p. 373).

24 CAR Surrey, p. 21.

25 Elton, op. cit.

26 R. Cooke, *The Visitation of Herefordshire in 1569*, ed. F. W. Weaver (Exeter, 1886), p. 26; C. H. Mayo, *A Genealogical Account of the Mayo and Elton Families* (London, 1882), pp. 14–5.

27 P. Ryan (ed.), 'Diocesan Returns of Recusants for England and Wales, 1577' in *Publications of the Catholic Record Society: Miscellanea XII* (1921), p. 77 includes Alice's parents and brother as recusants in 1577. Her father was also listed as a recusant in March 1588. See J. H. Pollen (ed.), *'Recusants and Priests, March 1588'* in *Miscellanea XII*, p. 125.

28 D. Flynn, *John Donne and the Ancient Catholic Nobility* (Bloomington, 1995), p. 99.

29 The increase in sanctions against Catholics was a response to the Jesuit mission to England and the conflict with Spain; see J. Aveling, *The Handle and the Axe* (London, 1976), pp. 52–4. Catholicism was also beginning to be associated – in the eyes of the government – with treason; see P. Holmes, *Resistance and Compromise: The Political Thought of the Elizabethan Catholics* (Cambridge, 1982). The first decade of Elizabeth's reign saw little active persecution of Catholics, although their worship was illegal; see A. Pritchard, *Catholic Loyalism in Elizabethan England* (1979), p. 4.

30 G. Piper and C. Mayo (eds.), *The Registers of Ledbury Co. Hereford* (1899), pp. 77–8 for incidences of Alice standing as godmother and the baptism of her daughter Anne.

31 Ryan, op. cit., p. 77.

32 H. Bowler, H. and T. J. McCann (eds.), *Recusants in the Exchequer Pipe Rolls 1581–92* (1986), pp. 150.

33 *Calendar of the Manuscripts of the Marquis of Salisbury Part IV* (London, 1892), p. 265.

34 Elton, op. cit., p. 3.

35 Bowler and McCann, op. cit., p. 58.

36 *Visitation of Herefordshire*, p. 26.

37 Bowler, op. cit., p. 34.

38 J. Mush, 'A True Report of the Life and Martyrdom of Mrs Margaret Clitherow' in J. Morris (ed.), *The Troubles of our Catholic Forefathers Related by Themselves*, Vol. 3 (1877), pp. 368–9.

39 Ibid., p. 387.

40 Ibid., p. 392.

41 Ibid., p. 393.

42 Ibid., p. 409.

43 Ibid., p. 429.

44 Pollen, op. cit., p. 192

45 Ibid., p. 159. Since large numbers of priests were imprisoned in Elizabeth's reign, the prisons could become important centres of Catholicism, allowing some level of pastoral activity; see P. Lake and M. Questier, 'Prisons, Priests and People' in Tyacke, op. cit., pp. 195–233.

46 Pollen, op. cit., p. 327.

47 *The One Hundred and Five Martyrs of Tyburn* (London, 1917), p. 131.

48 *The Manuscripts of his Grace the Duke of Rutland*, Vol. I (1888), pp. 369–70; *Memoirs of the Missionary Priests, and Other Catholics of Box Sexes, that have Suffered Death in England on Religious Accounts*, vol. I (Philadelphia, 1839), p. 233.

49 Pollen, op. cit., p. 366.

Chapter 17

1 Hayward, op. cit., p. 7.
2 F. Bohun, *The Character of Queen Elizabeth* (1693), pp. 302–3.
3 Ibid.
4 L. S. Marcus, J. Mueller and M Rose, (eds), *Elizabeth I Collected Works* (Chicago, 2002), pp 303–4 Bell 2011 has made a recent attempt to reassess Elizabeth's reputation as a poet. An earlier editor of her work had declined to include 'When I was fair and young' amongst her corpus, considering it too good a work to have been written by her.
5 L. Botelho and P. Thane (eds), *Women and Ageing in British Society Since 1500* (Harlow, 2001), p. 1.
6 Ibid., p. 7; C. S. Schen, 'Strategies of Poor Aged Women and Widows in Sixteenth-Century London' in Botelho and Thane, op. cit., p. 14.
7 M. Pelling and R. Smith (eds), *Life, Death, and the Elderly* (1991), p. 6.
8 Ibid., p. 7.
9 J. Godfrey, *Attitudes Towards Post-Menopausal Women in the High and Late Middle Ages* (2011), p. 10.
10 Ibid.
11 Ibid., p. 11; Botelho, op. cit., p. 43.
12 Ibid., p. 51.
13 *Visitation of Huntingdonshire*, p. 123. It was Simon's uncle, Sir George Throckmorton, who had famously told Henry VIII of rumours that he had 'meddled' with Anne Boleyn's mother and sister.
14 History of Parliament.
15 VCH Huntingdon, Vol. 3, Brampton. His lands in Brampton were evidently reasonably substantial When a tax was raised in 1609, his son (another Simon) was assessed to pay 15s on the value of the Brampton estate, which placed him as a middle-ranking landowner in Huntingdonshire ('Miscellaneous Pieces' in *Liber Niger Scaccarii*, p. 729).
16 History of Parliament.
17 BL Lansdown MS 921.
18 History of Parliament.
19 Rose's epitaph in Hickman, op. cit., p. 96.
20 Ibid.
21 M. Pelling, 'Who Most Needs to Marry? Ageing and Inequality Among Women and Men in Early Modern Norwich' in Botelho and Thane, op. cit., pp. 31–42; Pelling and Smith, op. cit., p. 10.
22 Only 5% of elderly men included in the census lived without a woman, in spite of the fact that Pelling, op. cit., p. 34 points out that 'it would be hard to imagine a less eligible population than the poor, often unemployed, often sick or disabled, elderly men of the Norwich census'.
23 St Bartholomew's Archives Journal, No.2, f.47v.
24 J. Moody (ed.), *The Private Life of an Elizabethan Lady: the Diary of Lady Margaret Hoby 1599–1605* (Stroud, 1998), p. 9.
25 Ibid., p. i.
26 Clifford 1990, op. cit., p. 22.
27 Clapham, op. cit., p. 86.
28 G. von Bulow and W. Powell (eds), 'Diary of the Journey of Philip Julius, Duke of Stettin-Pomerania, Through England in the Year 1602' in *Transactions of the Royal Historical Society 6* (1892), p. 53.
29 *Calendar of Cecil Papers*, Vol.

II, Alencon to Elizabeth, August 1573

30 Ibid., Leicester to the French ambassador, 1 February 1574.

31 T. Wright, *Queen Elizabeth and Her Times* (1838), p. 94.

32 Although, as William Cecil was assured in 1573, he seemed 'daily to grow more handsome than other' (*Cecil Papers*, Vol. II, Dr Valentine Dale to Lord Burghley, February 1573).

33 Ibid.

34 W. Camden, *The History of the Most Renowned and Victorious Princess Elizabeth, Late Queen of England* (1688), p. 227.

35 National Portrait Gallery 2082. It was painted when Elizabeth was in her early to mid forties.

36 T. Tuke, *A Discourse Against Painting and Tincturing of Women* (1616).

37 S. W. Hull, *Women According to Men* (Walnut Creek, 1996), p. 181.

38 Tuke, op. cit.

39 CSP Spain (Simancas), Vol. II, p. 588.

40 Camden 1688:232. Simier was there 'amorously to woo Queen Elizabeth in Anjou's behalf'.

41 *Cecil Papers*, Vol. II, p. 706.

42 *Calendar of State Papers Foreign: Elizabeth I*, Vol. XIII, p. 603.

43 *Cecil Papers*, Vol. II, p. 717

44 *Calendar Foreign*, Vol. XIII, p. 652.

45 *Cecil Papers*, Vol. II, p. 788.

46 Ibid , p. 811.

47 Camden, op. cit., p. 232.

48 CSP Spain (Simancas), Vol. II, p. 590.

49 Camden, op. cit., p. 233.

50 Ibid., p 593.

51 CSP Spain (Simancas), Vol. II, p. 585.

52 Ibid., p. 592.

53 Ibid., p. 595.

54 Ibid., p. 596.

55 *Cecil Papers*, Vol. II, p. 759.

56 Ibid., p. 598.

57 Ibid., p. 88.

58 Bulow and Powell, op. cit., p. 51.

59 *Cecil Papers*, Vol. II, p. 765.

60 Ibid., p. 766.

61 Ibid., p. 817.

62 Ibid., p. 974.

63 CSP Spain (Simancas), Vol. III, p. 82.

64 Camden, op. cit., p. 268.

65 Marcus, Mueller and Rose, op. cit., pp. 302–3.

66 For example, ibid., p. 251.

67 Ibid., p. 261.

Chapter 18

1 J. Godfrey, *Attitudes Towards Post-Menopausal Women in the High and Late Middle Ages, 1100–1400* (2011), p. 27.

2 R. Carey, *Memoirs of Robert Carey* (Edinburgh, 1808), p. 55.

3 T. Wilson, 'The State of England (1600)', ed. F. Fisher (*Camden Miscellany XVI*), p. 5.

4 Ibid., p. 2.

5 *Norwich Census of the Poor, 1570.*

6 'A Census of the Poor, 1597' in J. Webb (ed.), *Poor Relief in Elizabeth Ipswich* (Suffolk, 1966), p. 123.

7 Dating from the medieval period, it went through over seventy printed editions in sixteenth-century Europe.

8 A. Magnus, *Women's Secrets*, ed. H. Lemay (New York, 1992), p. 129. This was no new idea. Aristotle had considered that evil humours could escape through the eyes of crying women (Godfrey, op. cit., p. 30).

9 Commentary B from Magnus, op. cit., p. 131 (taken from a 1508 Venice edition).

10 'The Disclosing of a Late Counterfeited Possession by the Devil in Two Maidens Within the City of London' in P. C. Almond (ed.), *Demonic Possession and Exorcism in Early Modern England: Contemporary Texts and Their Cultural Contexts* (Cambridge, 2004).

11 *The most wonderfull and true storie, of a certaine witch named Alse Gooderige of Stapen* Hill (1597)

12 Currently in Staffordshire but, in the sixteenth century, in Derbyshire.

13 P. C. Almond, *The Witches of Warboys* (2008) recounts the story of the witches of Warboys in considerable detail. The girls were the granddaughters of Gabriel Throckmorton, Simon Throckmorton's brother.

14 'A true and particular observation of a notable piece of witchcraft, practised by John Samuel the Father, Alice Samuel the Mother, and Agnes Samuel their Daughter, of Warboys in the County of Huntingdon, on Five Daughters of Robert Throckmorton of the same town and county, Esquire, and certain other Maidservants to the number of twelve in the whole, all of them being in one house, November 1589' in Almond (2004), op. cit , p. 77.

15 CSP Spain (Simancas), Vol. II, p: 592.

16 Almond (2004), op. cit., p. 1.

17 J. Sharpe, 'Women, Witchcraft and the legal Process' in Kermode and Walker, op. cit., p. 107. K. Jones and M. Zell, 'The Divels Speciall Instruments': Women and Witchcraft Before the 'Great Witch-Hunt', *Social History* 30 (2005), p. 45. It is usually considered that witch persecution reflects the low status of women in the period; see A. Anderson and R Gordon, 'The Uniqueness of English Witchcraft: A Matter of Numbers>' in *The British Journal of Sociology* 30 (1979), for example. Not everyone believed in witchcraft, but enough people did. Elizabeth's successor, James VI of Scotland, certainly did, publishing a work called *Daemonologie* in 1597 in which he spoke of the need for witch hunting.

18 CAR Surrey, p. 253 and p. 254.

19 Ibid., p. 1323

20 Ibid., p. 1324. It is interesting to note that many accusations of sorcery centred on livestock. It has been plausibly suggested that this might, in part, be due to the effects of harmful plants fed to the animals accidentally; see S. Hickey, 'Fatal Feeds?: Plants, Livestock Losses and Witchcraft Accusations in Tudor and Stuart Britain' in *Folklore* 101 (1990).

21 CAR Surrey, p. 1325.

22 Ibid., p. 1326.

23 Ibid., p. 1329.

24 Ibid., p. 1580.

25 Edmund Spenser's *The Faerie Queene* was published in 1590 to Elizabeth's pleasure.

26 For example, Goodwife Toogoode and Goodwife Garland gave sums to the Parish Church of St Nicholas in the Shambles in 1526 for services following the death of their husbands, as did Goodwife Cristell eight years later and Goodwife Brass two years after that (St Bartholomew's Archives No 1, Churchwarden's Accounts, St Nicholas in Shambles 1526–46 f.34v, 59).

27 Bulow and Powell, op. cit., p. 7; *Cecil Papers*, Vol. XII (Richard Hawkins to Edmund Palmer, 23 December 1602).

28 A. H. de Maisse, *A Journal of all that was Accomplished by Monsieur de Maisse, Ambassador in England from King Henri IV to Queen Elizabeth*, G. B. Harrison, G.B. and R. A. Jones, eds. (1931), p. 37.

29 Ibid., p. 2.

30 This was, of course, true, since she had been Henry VIII's heir for the first two and a half years of her life. Her mother, Anne Boleyn, had also had great plans for her education (according to the report of her chaplain, William Latymer), wanting her to learn several languages that would fit her as a potential future monarch. Elizabeth's long dead mother remained in her daughter's thoughts until the very end of her life, with a bed curtain in the queen's chamber at Hampton Court reputedly worked by Anne Boleyn in gold with her own hands, still in place and proudly shown to visitors at the end of 1602 (Burlow and Powell, op. cit., p. 55).

31 Maisse, op. cit., p. 82.

32 J. Clapham, *Elizabeth of England: Certain Observations Concerning the Life and Reign of Queen Elizabeth by John Clapham*, eds. E. P. Read and C. Read (1951), p. 90.

33 A. Collins, *Letters and Memorials of State in the Reigns of Queen Mary, Queen Elizabeth, King James, Charles the First, Part of the Reign King Charles the Second, and Oliver's Usurpation*, Vol. II (1746), p. 127.

34 The text of the sermon was later suppressed by Elizabeth's government, appearing in print for the first time a few weeks after her death; see A. Rudd, *A Sermon Preached at Richmond Before Queene Elizabeth of Famous Memorie* (1603). Unsurprisingly, it had bred much curiosity 'and the sight of it was greatly desired by many'.

35 Ibid., pp. 49–50.

36 BL Cotton MS Juliys F.VI f.121 (printed in Nichols, op. cit., Vol. III, p. 612). The reports were exaggerations, although she did cancel an audience with the French ambassador the following year after 'taking a look into her mirror'. She appeared, she said then, 'too ill' and 'was unwilling for anyone to see her in that state'. Maisse, op. cit., p. 36.

37 J. Chamberlain, *The Letters of John Chamberlain*, ed. N.E. McClure (Philadelphia, 1939), p. 470; J. Harington, *A Briefe View of the State of the Church of England in Queen Elizabeths and King James his Reigne* (1653), p. 162.

38 Harington, op. cit., p. 162.

39 *Norwich Census of the Poor, 1570*.

40 'A Census of the Poor, 1597' in Webb, op. cit., p. 123.

41 Ibid., p. 77.

Chapter 19

1 It was a notably cold winter, being referred to by one contemporary as 'the sharpest season that I have lightly known' (Chamberlain, op. cit., p. 182).

2 Nichols, Vol. III, p. 602. Camden, op. cit., p. 658 refers to the 'badness of the weather'.

3 Camden, op. cit., p. 658.

4 Ibid., p. 68.

5 Clifford, *Life of Jane Dormer*, p. 46.
6 Clifford to Sir Robert Dormer, 8 October 1605 (Ibid., p. xvi).
7 Ibid., p. xvii
8 Ibid., p. xvii–xviii.
9 Ibid., p. xviii–xix.
10 Ibid., p. 155–6.
11 Ibid., p. 181.
12 Wilson, op. cit., p. 10.
13 Ibid., p. 12.
14 *Cecil Papers*, Vol. XII (Cecil to Mr Nicholson, November 1602).
15 Marcus, Mueller and Rose, op. cit., pp. 339–40.
16 Camden, op. cit., p. 658.
17 *Cecil Papers*, Vol. XII (Fulke Grevyll to Robert Cecil, 12 October 1602).
18 Ibid. (Cecil to the Lord President of Wales, 18 January 1602).
19 Camden, op. cit., p. 658.
20 CSP Venetian, Vol. IX, p. 1132.
21 Ibid.
22 Ibid., p. 1135.
23 Ibid., p. 1169.
24 Schen, op. cit., p. 20.
25 Ibid., p. 13.
26 This extended as far as royalty, with Henry VII founding an almshouse in Westminster; see C. M. Fox, *The Royal Almshouse at Westminster c.1500–1600* (Royal Holloway, University of London, 2013).
27 *An Account of the Public Charities of England and Wales* (1828), p. 17.
28 S. E. James, *Women's Voices in Tudor Wills* (Farnham, 2015), p. 49.
29 W. K. Jordan, *The Charities of London 1480–1660, Vol. II* (London, 2006), p. 145.
30 Ibid.
31 Ibid.
32 Ibid.
33 *An Account of the Public Charities of England and Wales*, p. 35.
34 Ibid., p. 24.
35 Webb, op. cit., p. 11.
36 'A Register of the Poor, 1596–83' in Webb, op. cit., p. 76.
37 Ibid., pp. 36, 39, 77.
38 'Tooley Foundation Ordinances, 1588–9' in Webb, op. cit., pp. 22–3.
39 Ibid., p. 23.
40 Ibid., p. 24.
41 Ibid., pp. 43, 47, 49.
42 Ibid., p. 26.
43 Norwich Census of the Poor, 1570.
44 Harrison, op. cit., p 122 considered in 1577 that 'there is no commonwealth at this day in Europe wherein there is not great store of poor people, and those necessarily to be relieved by the wealthier sort, which otherwise would starve and come to utter confusion.
45 Ibid. (Botelho, op. cit., p. 104).
46 Harrison, op. cit., p. 123.
47 J. Howes, *John Howes' MS 1582, Being 'A Brief Note of the Order and Manner of the Proceedings in the First Erection of' The Three Royal Hospitals of Christ, Bridewell & St Thomas the Apostle*, ed. W. Lempriere (London, 1904), p. 1.
48 Ibid., p. 6.
49 Ibid., p. 9.
50 Ibid., p. 21.
51 Ibid., p. 11.
52 Ibid., p. 28.
53 Ibid., p. 11.
54 Ibid., pp. 28, 30.
55 Ibid., p. 31.
56 Ibid., p. 27.
57 Ibid., p. 39.
58 E. M. McInnes, *St Thomas's Hospital* (1963), p. 34.
59 Ibid., p. 33.
60 Howes, op. cit., p. 44.
61 C. K. Manzione, *Christ's*

Hospital of London (London, 1995), p. 37.

62 Although rarely mentioned, it is clear that St Bartholomew's housed female patients. For example, one Margery Bille was admitted in April 1555 (St Bartholomew's Archives No.1 Journal f.275v), while there are references to inmates being in childbed.

63 Harrison, op. cit., p. 123.

64 McInnes, op. cit., pp. 33–4 for St Thomas's. St Bartholomew's showed similar concern for the patients' diets. In February 1550 the hospital authorities 'ordered that because these halfpenny loaves were at that times so small that it suffered not for ii persons at a meal that it was ordered that every ii persons should have bread three farthings at every meal which was for every person all his meal in bread' (St Bartholomew's Archives No.1 Journal f.197).

65 McInnes, op. cit., p. 32. At St Thomas's, this was on Mondays, from 9am in summer and 10am in winter, until 1582 when it was from 8am.

66 S. Mendelson and P. Crawford, *Women in Early Modern England 1550–1720* (Oxford, 1999), p. 339.

67 For example, St Bartholomew's no.1 Journal for 20 June 1551 f.133 notes that 32 yards of cloth were to be given to the matron to make bed coverings.

68 Strype (1882), Vol. II.2, p. 224.

69 We know many of their names, thanks to the sixteenth-century journals of the hospital administration, which periodically named the sisters (for example, St Bartholomew's No.1 Journal f.204v).

70 St Bartholomew's No.1 Journal, f 189v.

71 Ibid., f.205, 206, 235v.

72 Ibid., ff.226, 226v.

73 Ibid., f.205v.

74 Ibid., ff.206, 210v, 224. This was a huge sum. In 17 December 1569 the hospital authorities made an order to pay the then matron 6s for her wages (St Bartholomew's Archives No.2 Journal, f.58v).

75 At St Thomas's Hospital a sister would be dismissed if found to be engaged or, even, 'in suspicion of love', with Margery Thrush and Elizabeth Ockes both removed from their positions on 27 April 1562 (McInnes, op. cit., p. 36). This was serious, given they also lived in the hospital and it was likely their only means of support.

76 St Bartholomew's No.1 Journal, ff.204v, 224.

77 Ibid., f.246.

78 St Bartholomew's No.2 Journal, f.69.

79 Schen, op. cit., p. 21.

80 St Bartholomew's Archives No.1 Journal, f.61, f.81v.

81 St Bartholomew's Archives No.2 Journal, f.65.

82 T. R. Forbes (ed.), *Chronicle from Aldgate: Life and Death in Shakespeare's London* (New Haven, 1971), pp. 96–8.

83 A. L. Wyman, 'The Surgeoness: The Female Practitioner of Surgery 1400–1800' in *Medical History* 28 (1984), pp. 22–41.

84 Moody, op. cit., p. 18.

85 Ibid., p. 161.

86 Forbes, op. cit., p. 93.

87 Wyman, op. cit., p. 29.

88 St Bartholomew's Archives No.1 Journal, f.231v.

89 Mendelson and Crawford, op. cit., p. 318.

90 Wyman, op. cit., p. 30; McInnes, op. cit., p. 39.
91 Wyman, op. cit., p. 30.
92 Ibid., p. 28.
93 Ibid., p. 34; D. Power, 'The Education of a Surgeon Under Thomas Vicary' in *The British Journal of Surgery*, VIII (1921), pp. 254–5.
94 H. Robinson (ed.), *Original Letters Relative to the English Reformation*, Vol. II (Cambridge, 1846), p 416.
95 *Cecil Papers*, Vol. XII (Earl of Cumberland to the Privy Council, 15 March 1603).
96 Ibid. (Lord Burghley to Cecil, 19 March 1603).
97 Ibid. (Cecil to Mr Nicholson, 9 March 1603).
98 Ibid. (Cecil to Mr Nicholson, 9 March 1603).
99 Camden, op. cit., p. 659.
100 Ibid.
101 Carey, op. cit., p. 115. Carey was a grandson of Mary Boleyn.
102 Chamberlain, op. cit., Vol. I, p. 189.
103 Camden, op cit., p 660; Carey, op. cit., p. 117.
104 Camden, op. cit , p 659.
105 Ibid., p. 660.
106 Carey, op cit., p 119
107 Manningham's Diary, p. 145.
108 Carey, op. cit., p. 119. This was likely wishful thinking on their part – Elizabeth was unlikely to break her unwavering refusal to name the person who would supplant her at the moment of crisis. It was, however, enough. Soon the scene had been expanded upon. William Camden later wrote that she said ('with a gasping breath'): 'I said that my throne as a throne of kings, that I would not have any mean person succeed me'. When questioned further by Cecil, Camden claimed that she was more direct: 'I will that a king succeed me: and who should that be but my nearest kinsman, the king of Scots?' (Camden, op. cit., p. 660). Carey, an eyewitness to much of the activity around Elizabeth's deathbed reports none of this.
109 Carey, op. cit., p. 660.
110 Manningham Diary, p. 145.
111 Ibid., p. 146. Loomis (2010) provides an excellent scholarly account of Elizabeth's death.
112 CSP Venetian, Vol. IX, p. 1169.

Epilogue

1 A. Clifford, *The Diaries of Lady Anne Clifford*, ed. D.J.H. Clifford (Stroud, 1992).
2 R. Carey, *Memoirs of Robert Cary, Earl of Monmouth, Written By Himself* (Edinburgh, 1808), p. 128
3 Clifford, op. cit.
4 His great-grandmother, Margaret Tudor, and his mother, Mary, Queen of Scots
5 J. Manningham, *Diary of John Manningham* (1868), p. 159.
6 John Chamberlain to Dudley Carleton, 12 April 1603 (J. Nichols, *The Progresses and Public Processions of Queen Elizabeth*, Vol. III).
7 Clifford, op. cit.

BIBLIOGRAPHY

Place of publication London unless otherwise stated. Abbreviations used in the text are in square brackets. Only works cited have been included.

Manuscript Sources

Bibliothèque nationale de France, Paris
    MS. Fr. 995
The British Library
    Arundel MSS, Cotton MSS, Egerton MSS, Harleian MSS, Lansdowne MSS, Royal MSS, Stowe MSS
Drapers' Hall, London
    Drapers Company Minutes and Records 1515–1529 (Rep 7)
Harvard University Library
    STC 3717.3
London Metropolitan Archives
    CLA/007/EM/02/I/025
    CLC/522/MS20091
    X109/053 Journal of the Court of Common Council, Journal 10:1493–1506
    X109/053 Journal of the Court of Common Council 11: 1505-1519
    X109/127 Repertories of the Court of Aldermen, Repertory 1:1495–1504
    X109/128 Repertories of the Court of Aldermen 2:1506–1515
The National Archives, Kew
    C 1, C 4, C 131, C 142, C 241, CP 25, E 101, E 404, PROB 11, SP 1, SP 2, WARD 2, WARD 4
St Bartholomew's Hospital Archives, West Smithfield
    No.1 Churchwarden's Accounts St Nicholas in Shambles 1526–1546, Christ Church 1546–1548, Persons Healed &c 1549–1550, Journal 1549–1561
    No.2 St Bartholomew's Hospital Journal 1567-1586
Wellcome Library of the History Of Medicine
    MS 49
Westminster Abbey Muniments
    WAM 5472, WAM 12181-90, WAM 32364, WAM 32407

Early Printed Works

Anglicus, Bartholomaeus, *De Proprietatibus Rerum* (1535) [Bartholomew]

Ayscu, E., *A Historie Contayning the Warres, Treaties, Marriages, and Other Occurents Betweene England and Scotland From King William the Conqueror, until the Happy Union of them Both in our Gratious King James* (1607)

Becke, E., *A Brefe Confutatacion of this most Detestable, and Anabaptistical Opinion, that Christ dyd not take hys flesh of the Blessed Vyrgyn Mary nor any Corporal Substaunce of her Body for the Maintenaunce Whereof Ihone Bucher Otherwise Called Ihone of Kent Most Obstinately Suffered and was Burned in Smythfyelde, the ii day of May Anno Domini M.D.L.* (1550)

Becon, T., *The Catechism* (1559)

Bohun, E., *The Character of Queen Elizabeth, or, A Full and Clear Account of her Policies, and the Methods of her Government Both in Church and State Her Virtue and Defects, Together with the Characters of her Principal Ministers of State, and the Greatest Part of the Affairs and Events that Happened in her Times* (1693)

Bouchier, T., *Historia Ecclesiastica de Martyrio Fratrum* (Paris, 1582)

Camden, W., *Reges, reginae, nobiles et alii in ecclesia collegiata B. Petri Westmonasterii sepulti,* 1603)

Camden, W., *The History of the Most Renowned and Victorious Princess Elizabeth, Late Queen of England* (1688, fourth edition)

Clinton, E., *The Countesse of Lincolnes Nurserie* (Oxford, 1622)

Coke, E , *The Third Part of the Institutes of the Laws of England* (1669, fourth edition)

Daybell, J., *Women Letter-Writers in Tudor England* (Oxford, 2006)

Ellis, H., (ed.), *Original Letters Illustrative of English History,* 2nd series vol. II (1827)

Elyot, T., *The Book Boke Named the Governour,* ed. Eliot, A.T. (London, 1834)

Fitzherbert, J., *The Boke of Husbandry* (1540)

Erasmus, *A Modest Meane to Mariage, Pleasauntly Set Foorth by that Famous Clarke Erasmus Roterdamus,* Anno, N.L. (trans.) (1568)

Gibbon, C., *A Work Worth the Reading Wherein is Contayned, Fiue Profitable and Pithy Questions, Very Expedient, Aswell for Parents to Perceive Howe to Bestowe their Children in Marriage, and to Dispose their Goods at Death: As For all Other Persons to Receive Great Profit by the Rest of the Matters Herein Expressed* (1591)

Guazzo, S., *The Court of Good Counsell Wherein is Set Downe the True Rules, How a Man Should Choose a Good Wife from a Bad, and a Woman a good Husband from a Bad, Wherein is also Expressed, the Great Care that Parents Should Have, for the Bestowing of their Children in Marriage: and Likewise how Children Ought to Behave Themselves Towards their Parents: and How Maisters Ought to Gouerne their Servants, and How Servants Ought to be Obedient Towards their Maisters* (1607)

Guillemeau, J., *Child-Bed or, the Happy Delivery of Women Wherein is Set Downe the Government of Women. In the Time of Their Breeding Childe* (1635)

Guillimeau, J., *The Nursing of Children, Wherein is Set Downe the Ordering and Government of Them From Their Birth* (1635b)

Harington, J., *Whether it be dampnation for a man to kill himself* (BL)

Harington, J., *A Briefe View of the State of the Church of England in Queen Elizabeths and King James his Reigne, to the Yeere 1608 being a Character and History of the Bishops of those Times* (1653)

Herbert, E., *The Life and Raigne of King Henry the Eighth* (1649)

John XXI, *The Treasurie of Health Contayning Many Profitable Medicines, Gathered out of Hipocrates, Galen and Auicen by one Petrus Hyspanus, and Translated into English by Humfry Lloyd* (1560)

Jones, J., *The Arte and Science of Preserving Bodie and Soule in Al Health, Wisedome, and Catholike Religion Physically, Philiosophically, and Divinely Devised* (1579)

I.D., *The most wonderfull and true storie, of a certaine witch named Alse Gooderige of Stapen Hill, who was arraigned and conuicted at Darbie at the Assises there as also a true report of the strange torments of Thomas Darling, a boy of thirteene yeres of age, that was possessed by the deill, with his horrible fittes and apparitions by him vttered at Burton vpon Trent in the countie of Stafford, and of his maruellous deliuerance* (1597)

Markham, G., *Country Contentments, or The English Huswife* (1615)

Mulcaster, R., *Positions Wherein Those Primitive Circumstances be Examined Which are Necessary for the Training of Children* (1581)

Parsons, R., *A Temperate Ward-Word, to the Turbulent and Seditious Wach-Word of Sir Francis Hastinges Knight who Indeuoreth to Slaunder the Whole Catholique Cause, & all Professors Therrof, Both at Home and Abrode* (1599)

Roesslin, E., *The Birth of Mankind, Otherwise Called, the Womans Book* (1572)

Rudd, A., *A Sermon Preached at Richmond Before Queene Elizabeth of Famous Memorie, Upon the 28 of March, 1596* (1603)

Sharp, J., *The Midwives Book* (1671)

Stow, J., *Annals of England* (1600)

The Cucking of a Scould (2nd edition, 1630)

Tuke, T., *A Discourse Against Painting and Tincturing of Women* (1616)

Whitney, I., *The Copy of a Letter, Lately Written in Meeter, by a Yonge Gentilwoman: To her Vnconstant Louer: With an Admonition to al Yong Gentilwomen, and to all other Mayds in General to Beware of Mennes Flattery* (1567)

Printed Primary Sources

'A Chronicle and Defence of the English Reformation' in Loades, D. (ed.), *The Papers of George Wyatt Esquire* (1968)

Acts of the Privy Council, vol. I, ed. Dasent, J.R. (1890) [APC I]

Almond, P.C. (ed.), *Demonic Possession and Exorcism in Early Modern England: Contemporary Texts and Their Cultural Contexts* (Cambridge, 2004)

Anger, J., 'Her Protection of Women' in Shepherd, S. (ed.), *The Women's Sharp Revenge* (1985)

Arnold, R., *The Customs of London, Otherwise Called Arnold's Chronicle* (1811)

Arrowsmith, J. (ed.), *The Registers of the Parish Church of Ribchester* (Wigan, 1906)

Astle, T. (ed.), 'Wardrobe Account for 1483' in *The Antiquarian Repertory: A Miscellany, Intended to Preserve and Illustrate Several Valuable Remains of Old Times*, II (1779)

Baker, J.H. (ed.), *Reports of Cases From the Time of King Henry VIII* (2003)

Bannister, A.T. (ed.), *Registrum Caroli Bothe Episcopi Herefordensis, 1516– 1535* (Hereford, 1921)

Barker, E. (ed.), *The Register of Thomas Rotherham Archbishop of York 1480– 1500*, vol. I (Torquay, 1976)

Bayne, R. (ed.), *The Life of Fisher MS. Harleian 6382* (1921)

Beaven, A.P. (ed.), *The Aldermen of the City of London Temp. Henry IV – 1912* (1908)

Beilin, E V. (ed.), *The Examinations of Anne Askew* (Oxford, 1996)

Bentley, S. (ed.), 'Extracts from the Privy Purse Expenses of King Henry the Seventh, from December Anno 7, 1491, to March Anno 20, 1501' in *Excerpta Historica* (1831)

Bowker, M. (ed.), *An Episcopal Court Book For the Diocese of Lincoln 1514– 1520* (Lincoln, 1967)

Bowler, H. (ed.), *Recusant Roll No.3 (1594–1595) and Recusant Roll No.4 (1595–1596)* (1970)

Bowler, H. and McCann, T.J. (eds.), *Recusants in the Exchequer Pipe Rolls 1581–1592* (1986)

Brinkworth, E.R. (ed.), *The Archdeacon's Court; Liber Actorum, 1584*, 2 vols (Oxford, 1942–1946)

Bulow, G., von, and Powell, W. (eds.), 'Diary of the Journey of Philip Julius, Duke of Stettin-Pomerania, Through England in the Year 1602' in *Transactions of the Royal Historical Society 6 (1892):1–67*

Bund, J.W.W. (ed.), *Worcester County Records: The Quarter Session Rolls Part I* (1899)

Calendar of the Cecil Papers in Hatfield House, vols I–XII (1883–1910)

Calendar of the Close Rolls, Henry VII, vol. II (1963)

Calendar of Inquisitions Post Mortem Henry VII, vol. III (1955) [CIPM]

Calendar of Letter Books of the City of London: Letter Book L, Edward IV– Henry VII, ed. Sharpe, R.R (1912)

Calendar of the Manuscripts of the Marquis of Salisbury Part IV (London, 1892)

Calendar of the Patent Rolls Preserved in the Public Record Office: Edward IV, Edward V, Richard III, 1476–1485 (1901) [CPR]

Calendar of the Patent Rolls Preserved in the Public Record Office. Henry VII, 3 vols (1914–16) [CPR]

Calendar of Plea and Memoranda Rolls Preserved Among the Archives of the Corporation of the City of London at the Guildhall AD 1458–1482, ed. Jones, P.E. (Cambridge, 1961)

Calendar of State Papers Domestic: Edward, Mary and Elizabeth, 1547–1580, ed. Lemon, R. (1856)

Calendar of State Papers Foreign: Elizabeth I, vols I–XXIII (1863–1950)

Calendar of State Papers, Spain, vols I–XII, eds. Bergenroth, G.A., De Gayangos, P., and Tyler, R. (1866–1949) [CSP Spanish]

Calendar of State Papers, Spain (Simancas), vols I–IV, Hume, M.A.S. (1892–1899) [CSP Spanish (Simancas)]

Calendar of State Papers Relating to English Affairs in the Archives of Venice, vols I–IX (1864–1897) [CSP Venetian]

Campbell, W. (ed.), *Materials for a History of the Reign of Henry VII*, vol. I (1873)

Campbell, W. (ed.), *Materials for a History of the Reign of Henry VII*, vol. II (1877)

Carew, R., *The Survey of Cornwall*, ed. Tonkin, T (1811)

Carey, R., *Memoirs of Robert Cary, Earl of Monmouth, Written By Himself* (Edinburgh, 1808)

Cavendish, G., *The Life of Cardinal Wolsey by William Cavendish*, ed. Singer, S.W. (1825)

Chamberlain, J., *The Letters of John Chamberlain*, ed. McClure, N.E. (Philadelphia, 1939)

Chambers, R.W. (ed.), *A Fifteenth Century Courtesy Book* (1914)

Clapham, J., *Elizabeth of England: Certain Observations Concerning the Life and Reign of Queen Elizabeth by John Clapham*, eds. Read, E.P. and Read, C. (1951)

Clarke, A.W.H. (ed.), *The Register of St Dunstan in the East London 1558–1654*, Part I (1939)

Clay, C.T. (ed.), *Yorkshire Deeds*, vol. 8 (Cambridge, 2013)

Clifford, A., *The Diaries of Lady Anne Clifford*, ed. Clifford, D.J.H. (Stroud, 1992)

Clifford, H., *The Life of Jane Dormer Duchess of Feria* (1887)

Cobb, H.S. (ed.), *The Overseas Trade of London Exchequer Customs Accounts 1480–1* (1990)

Cockburn, J.S. (ed.), *Calendar of Assize Records Essex Indictments Elizabeth I* (1978) [CAR Essex]

Cockburn, J.S. (ed.), *Calendar of Assize Records Kent Indictments Elizabeth I* (1979) [CAR Kent]

Cockburn, J.S. (ed.), *Calendar of Assize Records: Surrey Indictments Elizabeth I* (1980) [CAR Surry]

Collectanea Topographica and Genealogica, vol. I (1834)

Collins, A. (ed.), *Letters and Memorials of State in the Reigns of Queen Mary, Queen Elizabeth, King James, King Charles the First, Part of the Reign of King Charles the Second, and Oliver's Usurpation*, vol. II (1746)

Cooke, R., *The Visitation of Herefordshire in 1569*, ed. Weaver, F.W. (Exeter, 1886)

Corrie, G.E. (ed.) *Sermons of Hugh Latimer* (Cambridge, 1844)

Cranmer, T., 'A Confutation of Unwritten Verities', chapter 11 in Cox, J.E. (ed.), *Miscellaneous Writings and Letters of Thomas Cranmer, Archbishop of Canterbury, Martyr, 1556* (Cambridge, 1846)

Crawford, A. (ed.), *The Household Books of John Howard, Duke of Norfolk* (Stroud, 1992)

Cressy, D. (ed.), *Education in Tudor and Stuart England* (1975:106)

Dorman, T (ed.), *The Sandwich Book of Orphans* (Archaeologia Cantiana 16 (1886)

Ellis, H. (ed.), *The Visitation of the County of Huntingdon, 1613* (1849)

Erasmus, D., *Collected Works of Erasmus: vol. 39 Colloquies,* ed. Thompson, C.R. (Toronto, 1997)

Fabyan, R., *The New Chronicles of England and France,* ed. Ellis, H. (1811)

Fisher, J., *The Funeral Sermon of Margaret Countess of Richmond and Derby, Mother to King Henry VII, and Foundress of Christ's and St John's College in Cambridge, Preached by Bishop Fisher in 1509,* ed. Hymers, J. (Cambridge, 1840)

Foster, J. (ed.), *The Visitation of Yorkshire, Made in the Years 1584/5* (1875)

Flenley, R. (ed.), *Six Town Chronicles of England* (Oxford, 1911)

Forbes, T.R. (ed.), *Chronicle from Aldgate: Life and Death in Shakespeare's London* (New Haven, 1971)

Forbes, T.R. (ed.), 'London Coroner's Inquests for 1590' in *Journal of the History of Medical and Allied Sciences 28* (1973:376-386)

Foxe, J., *The Acts and Monuments of John Foxe* (New York, 1965)

Furnivall, F.J. (ed.), *Early English Meals and Manners* (1868)

Gairdner, J. (ed.), *Letters and Papers Illustrative of the Reigns of Richard III and Henry VII,* vol. I (1861)

Gairdner, J. (ed), *The Paston Letters,* 3 vols (Westminster, 1896)

Gardiner, S., *The Letters of Stephen Gardiner,* ed. Muller, J A. (Cambridge, 1933)

Giustinian, S., *Four Years at the Court of Henry VIII,* 2 vols, ed. Brown, R. (1854)

Gurney, D. (ed.) 'Extracts from the Household and Privy Purse Accounts of the Lestranges of Hunstanton, From AD 1519 to AD 1578' in *Archaeologia 25* (1833)

Hale, W.H. (ed.), *A Series of Precedents and Proceedings in Criminal Causes Extending from the Year 1475 to 1640 Extracted from the Act-Books of Ecclesiastical Courts in the Diocese of London* (London, 1847)

Hall, E., *Hall's Chronicle Containing the History of England During the Reign of Henry IV and the Succeeding Monarchs to the End of the Reign of Henry VIII* (1809)

Harding, V. and Wright, L. (eds.), *London Bridge: Selected Accounts and Rentals, 1381–1538* (1995)

Hardy, W.J. and Page, W. (eds,), *A Calendar to the Feet of Fines for London and Middlesex,* vol. II (1893)

Harrison, A.T. (ed.), *The Danse Macabre of Women: MS FR. 995 of the Bibliothèque Nationale* (Kent, 1994)

Harrison, W., *Elizabethan England: From 'A Description of England,' by William Harrison (in Holinshed's Chronicles)*, ed. Withington, L. (London, 1577)

Harpsfield, N., *A Treatise on the Pretended Divorce Between Henry VIII and Catherine of Aragon* (1878)

Hayward, J., *Annals of the First Four Years of the Reign of Queen Elizabeth*, ed. Bruce, J. (1840)

Hayward, M. (ed.), *Dress at the Court of King Henry VIII* (Leeds, 2007)

Hayward, M. (ed.), *The Great Wardrobe Accounts of Henry VII and Henry VIII* (2012)

Hazlitt, W.C. (ed.), *Remains of the Early Popular Poetry of England*, vol. II (1866)

Hearnshaw , F.J.C. and Hearnshaw, D.M. (eds.), *Southampton Court Leet Records 1603–1624*, vol. I parts 1–3 (Southampton, 1905–1907)

Hickman, R., 'Religion and Politics in mid Tudor England through the eyes of an English Protestant Woman: the Recollections of Rose Hickman', eds. Dowling, M. and Shakespeare, J., in *Bulletin of the Institute of Historical Research 131* (1982:94–102)

Hollis, D., (ed.), *Calendar of the Bristol Apprentice Book, Part I 1532–1542* (Bristol Record Society)

Howard, J.J. (ed.), *Miscellanea Genealogica et Heraldica* (1898)

Howes, J., *John Howes' MS 1582, Being 'A Brief Note of the Order and Manner of the Proceedings in the First Erection of' The Three Royal Hospitals of Christ, Bridewell & St Thomas the Apostle*, ed. Lempriere, W. (London, 1904)

Hudson, W. (ed.), *Leet Jurisdiction in the City of Norwich During the XIIIth and XIVth Centuries* (1892)

Hughes, P.L. and Larkin, J.F. (eds.), *Tudor Royal Proclamations*, vol. I (New Haven, 1964)

Hume, M.A.S. (ed.), *Chronicle of Henry VIII* (1889)

Hutchinson, R., *The Works of Roger Hutchinson*, ed. Bruce, J. (Cambridge, 1842)

James, N.W. and James, V.A. (ed.), *The Bede Roll of the Fraternity of St Nicholas* (2004)

Jarman, E.K.M. (ed.), *Justice and Conciliation in a Tudor Church Court: Depositions from EDC 2/6 Deposition Book of the Consistory Court of Chester September 1558–March 1559* (Record Society of Lancashire and Chester, 2012)

Jefferson, J.C. (ed.), *Middlesex County Records*, vol. I (Middlesex County Records Society) [MCR]

Jerdan, W., (ed.), *Original Documents Illustrative of the Life and Times of Henry VII and Henry VIII Selected from the Private Archives of his Grace the Duke of Rutland* (1847)

Kingsford, C.L. (ed.), *Chronicles of London* (Oxford, 1905)

Kipling, G. (ed.), *The Receyt of the Ladie Kateryne* (Oxford, 1990)

Kitching, C.J. (ed.), *London and Middlesex Chantry Certificate 1548* (1980)

Lambarde, W., *A Perambulation of Kent* (1826)

Landry, G., de la Tour, *The Book of the Knight of the Tower*, ed. Vance, A. (Dublin, 1868)

Leadam, I.S. (ed.), *Select Cases Before the King's Council in the Star Chamber Commonly Called the Court of Star Chamber AD 1477–1509* (1908)

Letters and Papers, Foreign and Domestic, of the Reign of Henry VIII, vols I–XXI, eds. Brewer, J.S., Gairdner, J., and Brodie, R.H. (1862–1932) [L&P]

Lewis, J., *The Life of Dr John Fisher*, vol. II (1855)

Liber Niger Scaccarii, Nec Non Wilhelmi Worcestrii Annales Rerum Anglicarum, Cum Praefatione et Appendice Thomae Hearnii, vol. II (1774)

Machyn, H., *The Diary of Henry Machyn: Citizen and Merchant-Taylor of London from AD 1550–1563*, ed. Nichols, J.G. (1848)

Magnus, A., *Women's Secrets*, ed. Lemay, H.R. (New York, 1992)

Maisse, A.H., de, *A Journal of all that was Accomplished by Monsieur de Maisse, Ambassador in England from King Henri IV to Queen Elizabeth*, eds. Harrison, G.B. and Jones, R.A (1931)

Manning, R., *Robert of Brunne's 'Handlyng Synne'*, AD 1303, 2 vols, ed. Furnivall, F.J. (1901)

The Manuscripts of his Grace the Duke of Rutland, vol. I (1888)

Manningham, J., *Diary of John Manningham* (1868)

Marcus, L.S., Mueller, J. and Rose, M.B. (eds.), *Elizabeth I Collected Works* (Chicago, 2002)

Mayer, T.F. and Walters, C.B (eds.), *The Correspondence of Reginald Pole* (Aldershot, 2008)

Moody, J. (ed.), *The Private Life of an Elizabethan Lady: the Diary of Lady Margaret Hoby 1599–1605* (Stroud, 1998)

More, T., *Utopia*, ed. Arber, E. and trans. Robinson, R. (1869)

Munby, F.A. (ed.), *The Youth of Henry VIII. A Narrative in Contemporary Letters* (Boston, 1913)

Mush, J., 'A True Report of the Life and Martyrdom of Mrs Margaret Clitherow' in Morris, J. (ed.), *The Troubles of our Catholic Forefathers Related by Themselves*, vol. 3 (1877)

Myers, A.R. (ed.), *English Historical Documents*, vol. IV (1969)

Nichols, J.G. (ed.), *The Chronicle of Calais* (1846)

Nichols, J.G. (ed.), *The Chronicle of Queen Jane and Two Years of Queen Mary* (1850)

Nichols, J.G. (ed.), *Chronicle of the Grey Friars of London* (1852)

Nichols, J.G. (ed.), *Inventories of the Wardrobes, Plate, Chapel Stuff, Etc. of Henry Fitzroy, Duke of Richmond, and of The Wardrobe Stuff at Baynard's Castle of Katharine, Princess Dowager* (1855)

Nichols, J.G. (ed.), *Literary Remains of King Edward the Sixth* (1857)

Nichols, J.G. (ed.), *Narratives of the Days of the Reformation* (1859)

Nicolas, N.H. (ed.), *The Privy Purse Expenses of Elizabeth of York and Wardrobe Accounts of Edward the Fourth* (1830)

Nicolas, N.H. (ed.), *The Literary Remains of Lady Jane Grey* (1537)

North Country Wills: Being Abstracts of Wills Relating to the Counties of York, Nottingham, Northumberland, Cumberland, and Westmorland at Somerset House and Lambeth Palace 1383–1558 (Surtees Society, 1908)

Norton, E. (ed.), *The Anne Boleyn Papers* (Stroud, 2013b)

Parr, C., *Katherine Parr: Complete Works and Correspondence,* ed. Mueller, J. (Chicago, 2011)

Piper, G.H. and Mayo, C.H. (eds.), *The Registers of Ledbury Co. Hereford* (1899)

Pollen, J.H., (ed.), *Unpublished Documents Relating to the English Martyrs,* vol. I 1584–1603 (1908)

Pollen, J.H. (ed.), 'Recusants and Priests, March 1588' in *Miscellanea XII* (1921)

Pollock, L. (ed.), *With Faith and Physic: The Life of a Tudor Gentlewoman Lady Grace Mildmay 1552–1620* (1993)

Pound, J.F. (ed.), *Norwich Census of the Poor, 1570,* Norfolk Record Society 40 (1971)

The Privy Purse Expenses of King Henry the Eighth from November 1529 to December 1532, ed. Nicolas, N.H. (1827)

Prockter, A., Taylor, R. and Fisher, J. (eds.), *The A to Z of Elizabethan London* (1979)

Ralph, E. and Hardwick, N.M. (eds.), *Calendar of the Bristol Apprentice Book, Part II 1542–1552* (Bristol Record Society)

Ralph, E. (ed.), *Calendar of the Bristol Apprentice Book: Part III 1552–1565* (Bristol Record Society, 1992)

Ridgard, J. (ed.), *Medieval Framlingham* (Woodbridge, 1985)

Riley, H.T. (ed.), *Liber Albus: The White Book of the City of London Compiled AD 1419* (1861)

Ritson, J. (ed.), *Ancient Popular Poetry,* vol. II (Edinburgh, 1884)

Robinson, H. (ed.), *Original Letters Relative to the English Reformation,* vol. II (Cambridge, 1846)

Rogers, E.F. (eds.), *The Correspondence of Thomas More* (1947)

Roper, W., *The Lyfe of Sir Thomas Moore, Knighte, Written by William Roper, Esquire, Whiche Married Margareat, Daughter of the Sayed Thomas Moore,* ed. Hitchcock, E.V. (1930)

Ryan, P. (ed.), 'Diocesan Returns of Recusants for England and Wales, 1577' in *Publications of the Catholic Record Society: Miscellanea XII* (1921)

Sander, N., *Rise and Growth of the Anglican Schism* (1877)

Scot, R., *The Discoverie of Witchcraft,* ed. Nicholson, B. (1886)

Scouloudi, I. (ed.), *Returns of Strangers in the Metropolis 1593, 1627, 1635, 1639* (Huguenot Society of London, Vol. LVII, 1985)

Select Papers Chiefly Relating to English Antiquities Published from the Originals, in the Possession of John Ives (1773)

Sharpe, R.R. (ed.), *Calendar of Letter-Books of the City of London: L, Edward IV–Henry VII* (1912)

Sneyd, C.A. (ed.), *A Relation, or Rather a True Account, of the Island of England; With Sundry Particulars of the Customs of these People, and of* the *Royal Revenues under King Henry the Seventh About the Year 1500* (1847)

Spurling, H. (ed.), *Elinor Fettiplace's Receipt Book* (1986)

St Clare Byrne, M (ed.), *The Letters of King Henry VIII* (1968)

St Claire Byrne, M. (ed.), *The Lisle Letters,* 6 vols (1981)

Stephenson, M. and Griffin, R. (ed.), *A Roll of Arms Belonging to the Society of Antiquaries, Temp. Henry VIII, c.1540 (Archaeologia 69,* 1920:61-110)

Stow, J., *Annales, or a General Chronicle of England* (1631)

Stow, J., *A Survey of London Written in the Year 1598,* ed. Fraser, A. (Stroud, 2009)

Testamenta Vetusta, 2 vols, ed. Nicolas, N.H. (1826)

Treswell, R., *The London Surveys of Ralph Treswell,* ed. Schofield, J. (1987)

Vives, J.L., *The Education of a Christian Woman,* ed and trans. Fantazzi, C (Chicago, 2000)

Webb, J. (ed.), *Poor Relief in Elizabethan Ipswich* (Suffolk, 1966)

Welch, C. (ed.), *Register of Freemen of the City of London in the Reigns of Henry VIII and Edward VI* (1908)

Whatmore, L.E. (ed.), *Archdeacon Harpsfield's Visitation, 1557,* 2 vols (London, 1950–1)

White, J., *Fac-Simile of a Heraldic MS Entitled: The Names and Armes of Them That Hath Beene Aldermen of the Warde of Aldersgate Since the Tyme of King Henry 6, Beginninge at the 30 Yeere of his Reigne until this Present Yeere of our Lord 1616,* ed. Price, F.C. (1878)

Wilson, T., 'The State of England (1600)', ed. Fisher, F.J. (*Camden Miscellany XVI 1936:1-47)*

Wood, M.A.E. (ed.), *Letters of Royal and Illustrious Ladies,* 3 vols (London 1846)

Wright, T. (ed.), *Queen Elizabeth and Her Times, A Series of Original Letters Selected from the Private Correspondence of the Lord Treasurer Burghley, the Earl of Leicester, The Secretaries Walsingham and Smith, Sir Christopher Hatton, and Most of the Distinguished Persons of the Period,* vol. II (1838)

Wright, T. (ed.), *Three Chapters of Letters Relating to the Suppression of the Monasteries* (1843)

Wright, T. (ed.), *Churchwardens' Accounts of the Town of Ludlow, in Shropshire, from 1540 to the End of the Reign of Queen Elizabeth* (1869)

Wriothesley, C., *A Chronicle of England During the Reigns of the Tudors,* 2 vols, ed. Hamilton, D. (1875–8)

Secondary Sources

A History of the County of Hertford, vol. 3 (1912) [VCH Hertford]

A History of the County of Huntingdon, vol. 3 (1936) [VCH Huntingdon]

An Account of the Public Charities of England and Wales (London, 1828)

Almond, P.C., *The Witches of Warboys* (2008)

An Inventory of the Historical Monuments in Essex, vol. 2 (London, 1921)

Anderson, A. and Gordon, R., *The Uniqueness of English Witchcraft· A Matter of Numbers?* (The British Journal of Sociology 30 (1979): 359–361)

Andrews, W., *Old Time Punishments* (Hull, 1890)

Anstey, H. (ed.), *Epistolae Academicae Oxon,* vol. II (Oxford, 1898)

Aries, P., *Centuries of Childhood,* trans. Baldick, R. (1996)

Ashton, L., *Samplers Selected and Described* (1926)

Aveling, J.C.H, *The Handle and the Axe* (London, 1976)

Barnes, A.W., *Constructing the Sexual Subject of John Skelton* (ELH 71, 2004)

Barron, C.M., 'Introduction: The Widows' World in Later Medieval London' in Barron, C.M. and Sutton, A.F. (eds.), *Medieval London Widows 1300–1500* (1994:xiii–xxxiv)

Bell, I., 'Elizabeth Tudor: Poet' in Stump, D., Shenk, L. and Levin, C. (eds.), *Elizabeth I and the 'Sovereign Arts'* (Tempe, 2011:105–124)

Bell, R.M., *Holy Anorexia* (Chicago, 1985)

Ben-Amos, I.K., *Adolescence and Youth in Early Modern England* (New Haven, 1994)

Bennett, E.T., *The Tower Menagerie: Comprising the Natural History of the Animals Contained in the Establishment* (1829)

Bernard, G.W., *The Late Medieval English Church* (New Haven, 2012)

Blumenfeld-Kosinski, R., *Not of Woman Born* (Ithaca, 1990)

Botelho, L., 'Old Age and Menopause in Rural Women of Early Modern Suffolk' in Botelho and Thane 2001:43–65

Botelho, L. and Thane, P., 'Introduction' in Botelho, L. and Thane, P. (eds.), *Women and Ageing in British Society Since 1500* (Harlow, 2001:1-12)

Botelho, L., *Old Age and the English Poor Law, 1500–1700* (Woodbridge, 2004)

Boyd, P., *Roll of the Drapers' Company of London* (Croydon, 1934)

Branch, L., 'Fraternal Commemoration and the London Company of Drapers c.1440–c.1600' in Tingle, E.C. and Willis, J. (eds.), *Dying, Death, Burial and Commemoration in Reformation Europe* (Farnham, 2015)

Brown, R.A , Colvin, H.M. and Taylor, A.J. (eds.), *The History of the King's Works,* vol. II (1963)

Buck, A , *Clothes and the Child* (Carlton, 1996)

Burke, S.H., *The Men and Women of the English Reformation* (London, 1870)

Capp, B., 'Separate Domains? Women and Authority in Early Modern England' in Griffiths, P., Fox, A. and Hindle, S. (eds.), *The Experience of Authority in Early Modern England* (Basingstoke, 1996:117-145)

Casady, E., *Henry Howard, Earl of Surrey* (New York, 1975)

Cass, F.C., *Monken Hadley* (Westminster, 1880)

Castellum Hutonicum Some Account of Sheriff Hutton Castle (York, 1824)

Challoner, R., *Memoirs of the Missionary Priests, and Other Catholics of Box Sexes, that have Suffered Death in England on Religious Accounts,* vol. I (Philadelphia, 1839)

Cheney, A.D., 'Richard Masters, Parson of Aldyngton, 1514 to 1558' in
  The British Archaeological Association, New Series, vol. 10 (1904):15-28
Colvin, H.M., Summerson, J., Biddle, M., Hale, J.R. and Merriman, M.
  (eds), *The History of the King's Works,* vol IV, pt II (1982:78)
Cooper, C.H., *Memorial of Cambridge,* vol. II (Cambridge, 1861:24)
Cooper, C.H., *Memoir of Margaret, Countess of Richmond and Derby*
  (Cambridge, 1874)
Cressy, D., *Birth, Marriage, and Death* (Oxford, 1997)
Cross, G., *Kid's Stuff: Toys and the Changing World of American Childhood*
  (Harvard, 1997)
Cullum, P. and Goldberg, J., 'How Margaret Blackburn Taught Her
  Daughters: Reading Devotional Instruction in a Book of Hours' in
  Wogan-Browne, J., Voadem, R., Diamond, A., Hutchison, A., Meale,
  C.M. and Johnson L. (eds.), *Medieval Women: Texts and Contexts in late
  Medieval Britain* (Turnhout, 2000)
Daniell, C., *Death and Burial in Medieval England, 1066–1550* (1997)
Davies, C.S.L., 'Popular Religion and the Pilgrimage of Grace' in Fletcher,
  A. and Stevenson, J. (eds.), *Order and Disorder in Early Modern England*
  (Cambridge, 1985)
Davies, M., 'Thomasyne Percyvale, 'The Maid of Week' (d.1512)' in Barron,
  C.M. and Sutton, A.F. (eds.), *Medieval London Widows, 1300–1500*
  (1994:185-208)
Davis, J., 'Joan of Kent, Lollardy and the English Reformation' in *Journal
  of Ecclesiastical History 33* (1982:225-233)
Dawson, H., *Unearthing Late Medieval Children* (BAR British Series 593,
  2014)
Daybell, J., 'Introduction: Rethinking Women and Politics in Early Modern
  England' in Daybell, J. (ed.), *Women and Politics in Early Modern
  England, 1450–1700* (Aldershot, 2004:1-20)
Dickens, A.G., 'The Early Expansion of Protestantism in England, 1520–
  1558' in Marshall, P. (ed.), *The Impact of the English Reformation
  1500–1640* (London, 1997)
Dowling, M., 'Anne Boleyn and Reform' in *Journal of Ecclesiastical History*
  35 (1984):30-46
Duffy, E., *The Stripping of the Altars* (New Haven, 2005)
Duffy, E., *Fires of Faith: Catholic England Under Mary Tudor* (New Haven,
  2009)
Eccles, A., *Obstetrics and Gynaecology in Tudor and Stuart England* (Kent,
  1982)
Erler, M.C., 'Three Fifteenth-Century Vowesses' in Barron, C.M. and Sutton,
  A.F. (eds.), *Medieval London Widows, 1300–1500* (London, 1994)
Elton, M., *Annals of the Elton Family* (Stroud, 1994)
Emmison, F.G., *Elizabethan Life and Disorder* (Chelmsford, 1970)
Flynn, D., *John Donne and the Ancient Catholic Nobility* (Bloomington, 1995)
Fraser, A., *A History of Toys* (1972)
French, K.L., 'The Seat Under Our Lady: Gender and Seating in Late Medieval
  English Parish Churches' in Raguin, V.C. and Stanbury, S. (eds.), *Women's*

Space: Patronage, Place and Gender in the Medieval Church (Albany, 2005:141-160)

Froide, A.M., *Never Married* (Oxford, 2005)

Gaimster, D., Boland, P., Linnane, S. and Cartwright, C., 'The Archaeology of Private Life: The Dudley Castle Condoms' in *Post-Medieval Archaeology 30 (1996:129-142)*

Gardiner, D., *English Girlhood at School* (Oxford, 1929)

Gaskill, M., 'Witchcraft and Power in Early Modern England: The Case of Margaret Moore' in Kermode, J. and Walker, G. (eds.), *Women, Crime and the Courts in Early Modern England* (Chapel Hill, 1994)

Gertz, G., *Heresy Trials and English Women Writers, 1400-1670* (Cambridge, 2012)

Godfrey, J.E., *Attitudes Towards Post-Menopausal Women in the High and Late Middle Ages, 1100-1400* (2011)

Gowing, L., *Gender Relations in Early Modern England* (Harrow, 2012)

Green, I., *Humanism and Protestantism in Early Modern English Education* (Farnham, 2009)

Green, M.A.E., *The Lives of the Princesses of England*, vol. IV (1852)

Griffiths, A., *The Chronicles of Newgate* (1884)

Gristwood, S., *Arbella: England's Lost Queen* (2003)

Guy, J.A., *Henry VIII and the Praemunire Manoeuvres of 1530-1531* (*English Historical Review* 97, 1982)

Haas, L. and Rosenthal, J.T., 'Historiographical Reflections and the Revolt of the Medievalists' in Rosenthal, J.T. (ed.), *Essays on Medieval Childhood* (Donington, 2007:12-28)

Hahn, D., *The Tower Menagerie: The Amazing True Story of the Royal Collection of Wild Beasts* (2003)

Haigh, C., *Elizabeth I* (London, 1988)

Hair, P.E.H., 'A Note on the Incidence of Tudor Suicide' in *Local Population Studies 5* (1970:36-43)

Hanworth, A., *Home or Away? Some Problems with Daughters* in *The Ricardian* XIII (2003)

Harris, B.J., 'Women and Politics in Early Tudor England' in *The Historical Journal 33* (1990:259-281)

Harris, B.J., *English Aristocratic Women 1450-1550* (Oxford, 2002)

Harris, B.J., 'Sisterhood, Friendship and the Power of English Aristocratic Women, 1450-1550' in Daybell 2004:21-50

Hasted, E., *The History and Topographical Survey of the County of Kent*, XII (1850)

Hayward, M., *Dress at the Court of King Henry VIII* (Leeds, 2007)

Hayward, M., *Rich Apparel: Clothing and the Law in Henry VIII's England* (Farnham, 2009)

Henry, D., *An Historical Description of the Tower of London and Its Curiosities* (1753)

Hickey, S., 'Fatal Feeds?: Plants, Livestock Losses and Witchcraft Accusations in Tudor and Stuart Britain' in *Folklore 101* (1990:131-142)

Hickman, D., 'From Catholic to Protestant: The Changing Meaning of

Testamentary Religious Provisions in Elizabethan London' in Tyacke, N. (ed.), *England's Long Reformation 1500–1800* (1998:117-139)

Hindman, S., 'Peter Bruegel's Children's Games, Folly and Chance' in *The Art Bulletin* 63 (1981:447-475)

Hogrefe, P., *Tudor Women: Commoners and Queens* (Ames, 1975)

Holmes, P., *Resistance and Compromise: The Political Thought of the Elizabethan Catholics* (Cambridge, 1982)

Hoskins, W.G., *The Midland Peasant: The Economic and Social History of a Leicestershire Village* (1957)

Hoyle, R.W., 'Henry Percy Sixth Earl of Northumberland, and the Fall of the House of Percy,' in Bernard, G.W. (ed.), *The Tudor Nobility* (Manchester, 1992)

Hoyle, R W., *The Pilgrimage of Grace and the Politics of the 1530s* (Oxford, 2001)

Huggett, J. and Mikhaila, N., *The Tudor Child*, ed Malcolm-Davies, J. (Lightwater, 2013)

Hull, S.W., *Women According to Men* (Walnut Creek, 1996)

Humfrey. P., *The Experience of Domestic Services for Women in Early Modern London* (Farnham, 2011)

Ingram, M., *Church Courts, Sex and Marriage in England, 1570–1640* (Cambridge, 1987)

Ingram, M., '"Scolding Women Cucked or Washed": A Crisis in Gender Relations in Early Modern England?' in Kermode, J. and Walker, G. (eds.), *Women, Crime and the Courts in Early Modern England* (Chapel Hill, 1994:48-80)

James, S., *Catherine Parr* (Stroud, 2008)

James, S.E., *Women's Voices in Tudor Wills, 1485–1603* (Farnham, 2015)

Jansen, S.L., *Strange Talk and Dangerous Behaviour* (New York, 1996)

Johnson, A.H., *The History of the Worshipful Company of the Drapers of London*, vol. II (1915)

Jones, K. and Zell, M., '"The Divels Speciall Instruments"': Women and Witchcraft Before the 'Great Witch-Hunt' in *Social History 30* (2005:45-63)

Jones, K., *Gender and Petty Crime in Late Medieval England* (Woodbridge, 2006)

Jones, M.K. and Underwood, M.G., *The King's Mother* (Cambridge, 1995)

Jordan, W.K., *The Charities of London 1480–1660*, vol. II (London, 2006)

Karras, R.M., *Common Women: Prostitution and Sexuality in Medieval England* (Oxford, 1996)

Kay, M.M., *The History of Rivington and Blackrod Grammar School* (Manchester, 1931)

Kesselring, K.J., *Mercy and Authority in the Tudor State* (Cambridge, 2003)

Klein, P., 'Ludlow Parish Church and its Clergy at the Reformation' in *Transactions of the Shropshire Archaeological and Historical Society 73* (1998:20-32)

Kussmaul, A., *Servants in Husbandry* (Cambridge, 1981)

Lake, P. and Questier, M., 'Prisons, Priests and People' in Tyacke, N. (ed.), *England's Long Reformation 1500–1800* (1998:195-233)

Leach, M. (ed.), *The Ballad Book* (New York, 1955)

Loomis, C., *The Death of Elizabeth I* (New York, 2010)

MacCullough, D., *Thomas Cranmer* (New Haven, 1996)

Magrath, J.R., *The Queen's College*, vol. I (Oxford, 1921)

Manzione, C.K., *Christ's Hospital of London, 1552–1598 'A Passing Deed of Pity'* (London, 1995)

Marshall, P., 'Papist as Heretic: The Burning of John Forest, 1538' in *The Historical Journal 41* (1998:351-374)

Marshall, P., and Ryrie, A., 'Introduction: Protestantisms and their Beginnings' in Marshall, P. and Ryrie, A. (eds.), *The Beginnings of English Protestantism* (Cambridge, 2002)

Marshall, P., Is the Pope Catholic? Henry VIII and the Semantics of Schism' in Shagan, E. (ed.), *Catholics and the 'Protestant Nation': Religious Politics and Identities in Early Modern England* (Manchester, 2005:22-48)

Mayo, C.H., *A Genealogical Account of the Mayo and Elton Families* (London, 1882)

McCarthy, C., *Marriage in Medieval England: Law, Literature and Practice* (Woodbridge, 2004)

McClendon, M.C., 'Religious Toleration and the Reformation: Norwich Magistrates in the Sixteenth Century' in Tyacke, N., ed., *England's Long Reformation: 1500–1800* (1998)

McInnes, E.M., *St Thomas' Hospital* (1963)

McKee, J.R., *Dame Elizabeth Barton O.S.B. The Holy Maid of Kent* (1925)

Mendelson, S. and Crawford, P., *Women in Early Modern England 1550–1720* (Oxford, 1999)

Milner, E. and Benham, E. (eds.), *Records of the Lumleys of Lumley Castle* (1904)

Moorhouse, G., *The Pilgrimage of Grace* (2002)

Mozley, J.P., *John Foxe and his Book* (1940)

Neame, A., *The Holy Maid of Kent* (1971)

Nichols, J , *The Progresses and Public Processions of Queen Elizabeth*, 3 vols (1823)

Nichols, J., *The History of the University of Cambridge and of Waltham Abbey* (1840)

Norton, E., *England's Queens: The Biography* (Stroud, 2010)

Norton, E., *Catherine Parr* (Stroud, 2010b)

Norton, E., *Bessie Blount* (Stroud, 2011)

Norton, E., 'The Depiction of Children on the Fifteenth and Sixteenth Century Tombs in Kinlet Church' in *Transactions of the Shropshire Archaeological and Historical Society 87* (2012:35-46)

Norton, E., *Boleyn Women* (Stroud, 2013)

The Nuns of Tyburn Convent, *The One Hundred and Five Martyrs of Tyburn* (London, 1917)

O'Grady, P., *Henry VIII and the Conforming Catholics* (Collegeville, 1990)

O'Hara, D., *Courtship and Constraint* (Manchester, 2000)

Okerlund, A., *Elizabeth of York* (New York, 2009)

Oldham, J.C., 'On Pleading the Belly: A History of the Jury of Matrons' in *Criminal Justice History 6* (1985)

Oosterwijk, S., 'Chrysoms, shrouds and infants on English tomb monuments: A question of terminology' in *Church Monuments XV* (2000:59)

Oosterwijk, S., '"I cam but now, and now I go my wai". The Presentation of the Infant in the Medieval Danse Macabre' in Rosenthal, J.T. (ed.), *Essays on Medieval Childhood* (Donington, 2007)

Orme, N., *English Schools in the Middle Ages* (London, 1973)

Orme, N., *Education and Society in Medieval and Renaissance England* (1989)

Orme, N., *Medieval Children* (New Haven, 2003)

Orme, N., 'Education and Recreation' in Radulescu, R. and Truelove, A (eds.), *Gentry Culture in Late Medieval England* (Manchester, 2005:63-83)

Orrock, A., 'Homo Ludens: Peter Bruegel's Children's Games and the Humanist Educators' in *Journal of Historians of Netherlandish Art 4* (2012)

Palliser, D.M., *Tudor York* (Oxford, 1979:119-120)

Parisot, J., *Johnny Come Lately: A Short History of the Condom* (London, 1985)

Peers, C. and Tanner, L.E., 'On Some Recent Discoveries in Westminster Abbey' in *Archaeologia 93* (1945:151-164)

Pelling, M. and Smith, R.M., 'Introduction' in Pelling, M. and Smith, R.M. (eds.), *Life, Death, and the Elderly* (1991:1-38)

Pelling, M., 'Who Most Needs to Marry? Ageing and Inequality Among Women and Men in Early Modern Norwich' in Botelho and Thane 2001:31-42

Pettifer, E.W., *Punishments of Former Days* (Winchester, 1992)

Power, D., 'The Education of a Surgeon Under Thomas Vicary' in *The British Journal of Surgery VIII* (1921:240-258)

Power, E., *Medieval English Nunneries c.1275 to 1535* (Cambridge, 1922)

Pritchard, A., *Catholic Loyalism in Elizabethan England* (1979)

Questier, M.C., 'Elizabeth and the Catholics' in Shagan, E. (ed.), *Catholics and the 'Protestant Nation'* (Manchester, 2005)

Rappaport, S., *Worlds Within Worlds: Structures of Life in Sixteenth Century London* (1989)

Rex, R., 'Lady Margaret Beaufort and Her Professorship, 1502–1559' in Collinson, P , Rex, R. and Stanton, G. (eds.), *Lady Margaret Beaufort and her Professors of Divinity at Cambridge 1502 to 1649* (Cambridge, 2003)

Richards, W., *The History of Lynn*, vol. II (Lynn, 1812)

Riddle, J.M., *Contraception and Abortion from the Ancient World to the Renaissance* (1992)

Robinson, H.B., 'St Thomas's Hospital Surgeons, and the Practice of their Art in the Past' in *Saint Thomas's Hospital Reports New Series XXVIII* (1901:415-448)

Rosenthall, J.T., 'Introduction' in Rosenthal, J.T. (ed.), *Essays on Medieval Childhood* (Donington, 2007:1-11)

Rousseau, C.M. and Rosenthal, J.T., *Women, Marriage, and Family in Medieval Christendom* (Studies in Medieval Culture XXXVII, 1998)

Rowse, A.L., *The England of Elizabeth* (Madison, 1950)

Schen, C.S., 'Strategies of Poor Aged Women and Widows in Sixteenth-Century London' in Botelho and Thane 2001:13-30

Schleif, C., 'Men on the Right – Women on the Left: (A)Symmetrical Spaces and Gendered Places' in Raguin, V.C. and Stanbury, S. (eds.), *Women's Space: Patronage, Place and Gender in the Medieval Church* (Albany, 2005:207-249

Shagan, E., *Popular Politics and the English Reformation* (Cambridge, 2003)

Shagan, E., 'Confronting Compromise: The Schism and its Legacy in Mid-Tudor England' in Shagan, E. (ed.), *Catholics and the 'Protestant Nation': Religious Politics and Identities in Early Modern England* (Manchester, 2005:49-68)

Sharpe, J., 'Women, Witchcraft and the legal Process' in Kermode and Walker 1994:106-124

Sim, A., *The Tudor Housewife* (Stroud, 2010)

Simon, J., *Education and Society in Tudor England* (Cambridge, 1966)

Simpson, J., *The Brownes of Walcot, in the Parish of Barnack, co. Northampton* (Fenland Notes and Queries, 1891)

Smyth, J., *The Berkeley Manuscripts: The Lives of the Berkeleys*, vol. II (Gloucester, 1883)

Spufford, M., 'The Importance of Religion in the Sixteenth and Seventeenth Centuries' in Spufford, M. (ed.), *The World of Rural Dissenters, 1520–1725* (Cambridge, 1995:1-102)

Stevens, J., *The History of the Antient Abbeys, Monasteries, Hospitals, Cathedral and Collegiate Churches*, vol. I (1722)

St John-Stevas, N., *Life, Death, and the Law* (Washington, 1961)

Strype, J., *Ecclesiastical Memorials Relating Chiefly to Religion, and the Reformation of it, and the Emergencies of the Church of England under King Henry VIII, King Edward VI and Queen Mary I*, vol. I.ii, II.i, II.ii (Oxford, 1822)

Strype, J., *Memorials of the Most Reverend Father in God, Thomas Cranmer*, vol. I (Oxford, 1840)

Sutton, A.F., 'Lady Joan Bradbury (d.1530)' in Barron and Sutton 1994:209-238

Sutton, A.F. and Visser-Fuchs, L. (eds.), *The Royal Burials of the House of York at Windsor: II Princess Mary, May 1483, and Queen Elizabeth Woodville, June 1492* (*The Ricardian XI*, no.144, March 1999:446-462)

Swanson, R.N., *Church and Society in Late Medieval England* (Oxford, 1993)

Thomson, J.A., *The Early Tudor Church and Society 1485–1529* (1993)

Thrupp, S., *The Merchant Class of Medieval London* (Michigan, 1962)

Thurley, S., *The Royal Palaces of Tudor England* (New Haven, 1993)

Unwin, G., *The Gilds and Companies of London* (1908)

Walker, G., 'Women, Theft and the World of Stolen Goods' in Kermode and Walker 1994:81-105

Walpole, H., *A Catalogue of the Royal and Noble Authors of England, with Lists of their Works* (Edinburgh, 1796)

Walsham, A., *Church Papists* (London, 1993)

Walsham, A., *Charitable Hatred* (Manchester, 2009)

Ward, H., *Ward's Canterbury Guide* (Canterbury, 1843)

Warnicke, R., *Wicked Women of Tudor England* (New York, 2012)

Watt, D., *Secretaries of God* (Cambridge, 1997)

Wear, A., 'Medicine in Early Modern Europe, 1500-1700' in Conrad, L I., Neve, M., Nutton, V., Porter, R. and Wear, A. (eds.), *The Western Medical Tradition: 800 BC to AD 1800* (Cambridge, 2003:215-362)

Webster, C., *Health, Medicine, and Mortality in the Sixteenth Century* (Cambridge, 1979)

Weir, A., *Elizabeth of York* (2014)

Welch, C., *History of the Tower Bridge* (1908)

Wheatley, H.B., *London Past and Present: Its History, Associations, and Traditions,* vol. II (1891)

Woods, H., *Excavations at Eltham Palace, 1975-9 (Transactions of the London and Middlesex Archaeological Society 33* (1982:215-265)

Wyman, A.L., 'The Surgeoness: The Female Practitioner of Surgery 1400–1800' in *Medical History 28* (1984:22-41)

Zahl, P.F.M, *Five Women of the English Reformation* (Michigan, 2005)

Unpublished PhD Theses

Fox, C.M., *The Royal Almshouse at Westminster c.1500–c.1600* (Royal Holloway, University of London, 2013)

Samman, N., *The Henrician Court During Cardinal Wolsey's Ascendancy c.1514–1529* (University of Wales, 1988)

Vokes, S.E., *The Early Career of Thomas, Lord Howard, Earl of Surrey and Third Duke of Norfolk, 1474–c 1525* (University of Wales, 1988)

ACKNOWLEDGEMENTS

I would like to thank Richard Milbank at Head of Zeus for suggesting the idea for this book and Mark Hawkins-Dady for his work in editing and helping to transform it into its final form. I thank my agent, Andrew Lownie, too for his support.

The staff at the various archive s consulted have been unfailingly helpful, for which I thank them. In particular, I thank the staff at the British Library and the National Archives at Kew for their assistance. Particular thanks must also go to the Drapers' Company of London, for permitting me access to the archives in Draper's Hall, and also to St Bartholomew's Hospital in London for allowing me to use their archives. The staff at the London Metropolitan Archives, the London Guildhall Library, the Westminster Abbey Muniment Room and the other archives consulted were also very knowledgeable and enthusiastic about the project.

Finally, I could not have written *The Lives of Tudor Women* without the support and encouragement of my husband David and my sons, Dominic and Barnaby.

Elizabeth Norton

PICTURE CREDITS

1. *The Family of Henry VII with St George and the Dragon*, c.1505 (Royal Collection Trust © Her Majesty Queen Elizabeth II, 2016 / Bridgeman Images).

2. Fifteenth century image of a woman having a caesarean (Wellcome Trust Library).

3. Scene from *The Danse Macabre of Women* (Bibliothèque nationale de Fránce).

4. Sixteenth century swaddling band (© Victoria and Albert Museum, London).

5. Pieter Breugel, Children's Games, Wikimedia Commons

6. Lady Arbella Stuart, aged twenty-three months (Hardwick Hall, Derbyshire, UK / National Trust Photographic Library / Bridgeman Images).

7. Stained glass window depicting Elizabeth Tilney (Long Melford Church, Suffolk, UK / Bridgeman Images).

8. Cucking stool in Leominster Church, Herefordshire (© Greenshoots Communications / Alamy Stock Photo).

9. Jane Bostocke's Sampler (© Victoria and Albert Museum, London).

10. Elizabeth I's corset (© Dean and Chapter of Westminster).

11. Portrait of Margaret Beaufort (© Active Museum / Alamy Stock Photo).

12. The Burning of Anne Askew (Culture Club/Getty Images).

13. Portrait of Rose Hickman (Private Collection).

14. The Martyrdom of Margaret Clitherow (Wikimedia Commons).

15. *The True Story of a Witch Named Alse Gooderige of Stapenhill*, 1597 (© Lambeth Palace Library, London, UK / Bridgeman Images).

16. Elizabeth I, The Darnley Portrait (Wikimedia Commons).

17. Elizabeth I with Time and Death, *c.*1610, English School (Corsham Court, Wiltshire, UK / Bridgeman Images).

INDEX

abortion, 89, 91–2
adolescence, 53, 73, 85
agriculture, women's roles in, 74,
    77, 78, 103
ale-houses, 110, 214
Alençon, Duke of, 277–88
almshouses, 314–16
ambassadors
    English, 151
    French, 15, 300–1
    Imperial, 178, 179, 234,
        235–9, 240, 244–6
    Spanish, 283, 284, 298, 306
    Venetian, 59, 152, 311–12,
        327
Anabaptists, 211, 233, 241
Anger, Jane, 131–2
Anne of Cleves, 87
anorexia, 135
Antwerp, 254, 260–1
apprentices, 102–6, 123–4
aristocracy. see nobility and
    gentry
arson, 129
Arthur, Prince of Wales, 11, 27,
    89
Ashley, Katherine, 175
Aske, Robert, 197, 199, 201
Askew, Anne, 197, 216–19,
    222–9
Askew, William, 196, 197, 217
Astley, Anne, 49
astrology, 247
authors, female, 31, 131–2, 220,
    230–1, 250

diaries and memoirs, 218–19,
    274–6, 322

Bannister, Elizabeth, 79–80
baptism, 16–17, 21–2, 23, 24–5,
    255, 260–1
Barton, Elizabeth (Holy Maid),
    70, 103, 142
    fall of, 172–3, 176–84
    as maidservant, 73–9, 81–2
    as nun, 150–1, 156–8
    as prophetess, 133–9, 162–3,
        164–9, 171
    and Wolsey, 154, 158, 160
Beaufort, Margaret, 39, 62,
    70–2, 98, 221–2
Becon, Thomas, 54–5
beds, for childbirth, 13
bells, church, 12, 135–6, 138
Bible, English, 207–8, 217, 219,
    234
Bible, on curriculum, 56
birth control, 89–92
Bishop of St David's, 302
Blount, Elizabeth, 144, 145, 148
Blounts, John and Katherine, 49
Bocher, Joan, 208–13, 219, 229,
    232–4, 239–41
Bocking, Edward, 134, 136–7,
    138, 150, 158
    arrest and execution, 177–8,
        179, 182
    book on Barton, 171
Boleyn, Anne, 146–7, 159–60,
    167

birth of Elizabeth, 65, 173, 184
coronation banquet, 145
fall of, 66, 185–6
and Henry, 148–50, 163, 164, 168–9
unpopularity of, 151–2, 154
Boleyn, Elizabeth (earlier Elizabeth Howard), 61–2, 63, 94–6, 130, 167
at court, 142–3, 186
domestic life, 146
as a mother, 149–50, 154, 159–60, 168, 170, 184–5
Boleyn, George, 185
Boleyn, Mary, 145, 148, 149
Boleyn, Thomas, 95, 96, 142, 146
Boleyn, William, 95–6
Bostocke, Jane, 56–7
Bourchier, Anne, 61, 63
Bourchier, Margaret. see Bryan, Margaret
bread, 99–100, 226
breastfeeding, 28–32
breech cloths. see nappies
see also wetnurses
Bristol, female apprentices in, 104, 105
brothel-keepers, 121–2
Bryan, Margaret, 64–6, 167
Bulmer, John, 194–5, 198, 199–206
Bulmer, Margaret, 194–5, 198, 200–6
Burbage, Cecily, 20–2, 33, 34, 38, 39, 44
marriage and widowhood, 93–4, 96–9
businesswomen. see traders, women
Bywimble, Alice, 27

Caesarean sections, 17–19
Calais, 143, 146, 168

Cambridge University, 70, 71–2
Camden, William, 287
Campeggio, Cardinal, 163–4
Canterbury, 150–1, 168, 210–13
Carey, Robert, 324–5, 326, 328
Carre, Anne, 92–3
Catherine of Aragon, 23, 29, 57, 160, 176
and Henry, 147–8, 151–2, 164, 165
household of, 143–5
pregnancies and infant deaths, 148
reformist ideas, 226, 228–9
Catholicism, Catholics
recusancy, 262–7
restoration, 253–60
see also Barton, Elizabeth; monasteries, monks; nunneries, nuns; priests
Caxton, William, 70
Cecil, Robert, 275, 309, 310, 324
Cecil, William, 280–1
censorship, 171, 183
Chancery courts, 98, 109–10, 127
Chapuys, Eustace, 178, 179
charity, and old age, 293, 306, 313–22
Charles V, Holy Roman Emperor, 151, 234–5
and Mary I, 238, 239, 240, 244, 245–6
Cheese, Mary, 2, 15
Chelmsford, brothel-keepers in, 121–2
Chester, Church court, 87, 93, 213–14, 215–16
Cheyne, Margaret. see Bulmer, Margaret
child labour, 59, 68, 110–11
childbirth
Caesarean sections, 17–19

dangers of, 12, 15, 16, 280–1, 287
recovery from, 25–6
children
death of, 39–49, 77, 153, 298, 299
see also orphans
christening. see baptism
Church
on baptism of newborns, 16–17
position on sex/birth control, 89, 273
reform/reformists, 207–13
women's unofficial roles in, 191
on women/wives, 131, 132
see also churches; monasteries, monks; nunneries, nuns; Reformation
Church courts
on domestic violence, 132–3
on Henry VIII's first marriage, 170
on heresy, 211–13
on marriage and morality, 76–7, 87–8, 93, 213–16
on slander, 180–1
churches
attendance at, 214, 261–4
disputes over pews, 192–4
profits from, 253
churching, 24, 26
Clement VII, Pope, 151, 165
clergy, 42, 195–6, 202, 204–5, 214, 254
see also monasteries, monks
Clifford, Anne, 59, 275, 328–9
Clifford, Henry, 306–9
Clifford, Margaret, Countess of Derby, 283, 297
Clinton, Elizabeth, 31–2
Clitherow, Margaret, 264–7
cloth industry, 103, 107, 120
see also spinning wool

clothing
for childbirth, 9, 15–16
children's, 23–4, 34
purchasing of, 30, 37
fashion dolls, 36
royal, 276–7, 311
royal servants, 144, 145, 175
stitching and repairs of, 57–8, 293
theft of, 10, 128–9
Cobb, Thomas, 133, 135, 136
Barton's employer, 73, 74, 77, 78–9, 82
Colchester, Church court, 214
contraception, 89–92
cooking, cooks, 99–101, 187
Cooper, Elizabeth, 74, 257–8
cosmetics, 278–9
cradle, rockers of the, 11, 22, 28
Cranmer, Thomas
and Barton, 172–3, 176
break with Rome, 170
imprisoned, 255
on prophetesses, 160, 161
and reformists/radicals, 209, 213, 233, 239, 240, 241
Craythorn, William, 38, 94, 96–7
Cremor, Thomas, 123, 124–6
crime, female, 128–9
see also infanticide
Cromwell, Thomas
and Barton, 172–3, 176, 177–9
church reform, 195
Croydon Assizes, 128–9, 262, 298, 299
cucking stools, 139–41

Danse Macabre, 43–4
Davy, Alice, 28, 29
Delft, Francis Van der, 234, 235–9, 240, 244–6
Derby, Margaret Clifford, Countess of, 283, 297

diarists, 274–6, 322
diseases, 40, 44, 278, 279, 322
    venereal, 91, 153
divorce, 3, 159, 163–4, 219,
    224–5
dolls, 35–6
domestic violence, 132–3
Dormer, Jane, 58–9, 305–9
dowries, 95, 96
drapers, 103, 105, 106
    Drapers' Company, 115–16,
        124–6, 127, 130
    see also Fenkyll, Katherine
dressmakers, 104–5
Dryver, Agnes, 122–3
Dubois, Jehan, 244, 245, 246–9
ducking stools, 139–41
Dudley Castle, contraceptives at,
    90

East Anglia, cloth industry, 103
    see also Norwich
Edmund, Prince, 23, 39
education, 207–8, 268, 322
    at home or 'placing out', 54,
        55–6, 57, 58–63, 64–7, 197
    royal, 64–6, 174–5
    in school, 54–5, 67–70, 314
    see also universities
Edward IV, 9, 26
Edward VI, King, 57, 58, 66,
    131, 232, 239
    and Mary I, 235, 237, 249, 250
Elizabeth, Princess, 20–49, 62
Elizabeth I, Queen
    accession and Protestant
        settlement, 261–4, 298, 306
    Alençon and other suitors, 276,
        277–88, 301–2, 309
    appearance and aging, 271,
        276–7, 278–9, 311
    attends Catholic services, 260
    birth of, 173–4, 184

death and funeral, 275, 327–9
    and Edward VI, 57–8
    household, 59, 65, 66, 174–5
    old age, 291–2, 300–3, 305,
        309–12
    and the succession, 324–6
Elizabeth of York, 20–2, 29
    and childbirth/children, 12,
        15–17, 20, 40
    death, 143
    as a mother, 30, 32
    postnatal recovery, 25–6
    pregnancy and fertility, 7, 9,
        13–14, 45, 89
Eltham Palace, 26–7, 33–4, 35, 37
Elton, Alice, 262–4
embroidery, 56–8, 66–7
English Bible (1539), 207–8, 217,
    219, 234
entrepreneurs. see traders,
    women
Erasmus, Desiderius, 30, 31, 35,
    54, 77, 220
Essex, Robert Devereux, Earl of,
    301–2, 309
execution, forms of, 186–8,
    205–6, 210
    see also hanging
Exeter, Marchioness of, 166, 179

feasts, 115–16, 130, 144, 210
femme sole, 3, 109–10, 221
Fenkyll, John, 81, 106–7
Fenkyll, Katherine
    in business, 97–8, 116–17, 120,
        123–8, 130
    as a trader's wife, 81, 102, 103,
        106–7, 111
Fish, Simon, 167
Fisher, John, Bishop of
    Rochester, 70, 162, 181–2,
    222
Fisher, Rose, 320

fishing industry, 111
Fitzroy, Henry, 64, 145, 148
food/diet, 34–5, 91, 99–101
    see also feasts
Foxe, John, 56, 239–40
France, 37, 120, 276, 281
    see also Alençon, Duke of;
    Calais
fraudsters, 126–8
funerals, 45–7, 244, 275, 329
furnishings, royal, 11, 12–13,
    24–5, 34

gardens, 33–4, 124
Gardiner, Stephen, Bishop of
    Winchester, 225
gentry. see nobility and gentry
Germany, toys and games, 35, 36
Godalming, witches in, 298, 299
Godeson, Elizabeth, 128–9
godparents, 24, 25
Gold, Henry, 176, 177, 178
Gooderidge, Alice, 294–5
Greene, Robert, 20–1
Greenwich Palace, 26, 282–3
Grey, Henry, 250, 251
Grey, Jane, 250–2
Guillimeau, Dr, 8, 18

Hadley, William, 134, 178
Hall, Edward, 182–3
Hampton Court Palace, 39, 159
hanging, 11, 42, 43, 128, 129,
    183
Hatfield House, Hertfordshire,
    175
Hattersley, Jane, 42–3
heiresses, 86–7
Henry VII, King, 7, 26, 71, 221
    at Bosworth, 60
    fatherhood, 37, 44
    temperament, 27, 45, 60, 97
    and wetnurses, 29

Henry VIII, King, 125, 138,
    172, 298
    birth and childhood, 9, 24, 27,
    28, 29, 34, 35, 62
    births of children, 64, 66,
    173–4, 184
    character and appearance, 147
    coronation, 29, 142
    head of English Church, 167,
    184, 195, 207. see also
    monasteries, monks
    made Duke of York, 37–8
    and servants, 144, 145, 167
    and the succession, 250
    wives and mistresses, 87, 143,
    147–51, 154, 162–4, 168–9,
    220
heresy, 137, 232, 241
Hickman, Rose
    flees England, 254–6, 260–1
    Protestant education, 56,
    218–19
    widowhood and remarriage,
    273–4, 296
Hoby, Margaret, 274–5, 322
Hoghton, Katherine, 215–16
Horne, Joanna, 109–10
hospitals, 72, 103, 229, 274, 303,
    315–23
housewifery, 55, 99–101, 105,
    108
Howard, Catherine, 89, 92, 220
Howard, Elizabeth. see Boleyn,
    Elizabeth
Howard, Muriel, 61–2
Huguenots, 277
Hunsdon, 66
Hyrde, Richard, 54

illegitimacy
    and infanticide, 40–3
    of royals, 64, 65, 66, 145, 148
infancy, 33–4

infant mortality, 39–49
infanticide, 40–3, 77, 153
innkeepers, 110, 214
Ipswich, age and poverty in, 3,
    292–3, 303, 315–17

James I, King (James VI of
    Scotland), 300, 326, 328,
    329
Jane, Queen, 250–2
John XXI, Pope, 89–90
Johnson, Joanne, 97–8
jousting, 14, 15, 38, 142

Kitchin, John, 140

ladies-in-waiting, 58, 143–5,
    174–5
lady mistresses, 64–6, 174–5
land confiscation, 263
Latimer, Hugh, Bishop, 86, 131,
    233, 255
Latimer, Lady. see Parr,
    Catherine
Latin, 67, 68, 208
law, legal system, 122, 140, 242
    assizes, 10, 42, 80, 128–9, 262,
    298–9
    on sexual and domestic
    violence, 79–81, 132–3
    women/wives' status in, 94,
    97–8, 109–10, 126–8
    see also Church courts;
    Parliament; sheriffs
Leicester, Robert Dudley, Earl of,
    277, 280, 282, 283, 285
Lincoln, 197, 217–18
Lincoln, Elizabeth Clinton,
    Countess of, 31–2
livery companies, 104, 115–16,
    117, 130, 315
London
    City, 102, 103, 106–7, 108–10

hospitals and almshouses, 103,
    229, 274, 314–15, 318–23
    as international, 119–20
    law and Church courts, 117,
    122, 214
    libraries, 17, 250
    museums, 23, 57, 99
    Newgate prison, 225, 226
    population and structure of,
    117–20
    poverty and suicide in, 242–3
    religious reform in, 218–19,
    254
    schools, 68
    sex trade, 122–3
    Smithfield, executions at,
    187–8, 205–6, 225, 240–1,
    256
    trade and life in, 115–28, 130
    see also Tower of London
Louis XII, King of France, 87
Ludlow, 65, 193
Luther, Martin, 68, 198

Maldon, 246–7, 249
manuals
    on ailments, 40
    on breastfeeding, 30–1
    on childbirth, 16, 17
    on conduct, 67, 94
    on sexual abstinence, 89–90
    on weaning, 34–5
Margaret, Princess, 24, 28, 38,
    62
Markham, Gervase, 100–1, 108
marriage
    abandonment, 88, 110, 274
    annulment, 87–8, 93, 151, 170
    breakdowns and adultery,
    215–16
    of clergy, 254
    divorce, 3, 159, 163–4, 219,
    224–5

forced, 86, 87, 217
in old age, 273–4
and property, 92–3, 94–9
women's status in, 92–3, 131–3
martyrologists, 239–40, 268
Mary, Princess, 34, 48, 87, 250
Mary, Queen of Scots, 300
Mary I, Queen, 58, 64–6, 174, 176
Catholicism and, 234–9, 253–4, 256
death, 261
escape attempt, 244–9
and Jane Grey, 250, 251
succession of, 253
masques, court, 44, 144, 291
Massey, Alice, 16, 17
Masters, Richard, 77–8, 133–5, 137, 150, 181, 182
Medici, Catherine de', 277, 288
medicine
birth control remedies, 89–90, 91–2
treatment, funding, 317
women practise, 108, 322–3
see also diseases; physicians; surgeons
memorials, 47, 48–9, 71
menopause, 272–3, 293
merchants, 208–9, 218
midwives, 16–17, 22
Mildmay, Grace, 56, 91–2
mobs/riots, 151–3
monasteries, monks, 39, 179
and prophetesses, 161, 165, 166
reformist, 167, 210
suppression of, 150, 195–6, 318
see also Bocking, Edward
More, Thomas, 30, 31
and Barton, 138–9, 156, 165–6, 183–4

daughters' education, 54
motherhood, mothers
daughters' education, 55–6, 145
and infanticide, 40–1, 42–3
Mulcaster, Richard, 55
murder, 40–3, 77, 153, 187–8
museums, 23, 36, 57, 99

nappies (breech-cloths), 22, 23
needlework, 56–8, 66–7
Netherlands, 120, 277, 287
Nevinson, Christopher, 211–13
nobility and gentry
girls' education, 54, 55–6, 58–63, 66–7, 69–70, 197
in queen's household, 143–5
women and political influence, 133
Norfolk, Thomas Howard, Duke of, 199, 201, 204, 205
Northampton, William Parr, Marquess of, 226, 236–7
Northumberland, John Dudley, Duke of, 235, 250, 251
Norwich
female traders in, 110–11
poverty and old age in, 110–11, 292, 303, 313, 317
Protestants burned at, 258–60
schools, 68
servants, 74
surgeons, 323
widows, 274, 292
nunneries, nuns, 69–70, 150–1
nurseries, royal, 26–30, 37, 44
nursing care, 320–1

old age, 272–4, 278, 291–8, 303–4, 305–9
and charity, 293, 306, 313–22
see also Elizabeth I, Queen
Ormes, Cicely, 258–60

orphans, 57, 69, 316, 317, 318,
   323
Oxenbridge, Anne, 28, 29
Oxford University, 70, 71

Paget, William, 236
pamphlets, 42, 134, 178, 241
parenting, standards of, 59
Parliament
   on Barton and associates, 181–2
   on crime and punishment, 187,
      298
   and Elizabeth I, 276, 310
   on heiresses, 87
   law limits women's access to
      Bible, 207, 217
   and the monasteries, 195
   opening of, 45
   women's influence on, 133
Parr, Catherine, 198, 219–20,
   230–1
Parr, William, 226, 236–7
Parry, Blanche, 58, 174–5
patronage, patrons, 70–2, 146
   see also apprentices
penance, public, 216
pensions, 29, 37, 66, 150, 314,
   316–17
Percy, Henry, 146–7, 159
Percyvale, Thomasine, 106
pews, 192–4
Philip II, King of Spain, 256,
   261, 282, 283, 300
Philpott, John, 241
physicians, 31, 308
pickpockets, 128
Pilgrimage of Grace, 195–206
pilgrimages, pilgrims, 158, 161,
   308
pillories (punishment), 122–3
pinmakers, 105
plague, bubonic, 40, 322
play, playmates, 33–4, 35–7, 58

poetry, poets, 43–4, 53, 288,
   300
   see also Skelton, John
poisoners, punishment of, 187–8
Pole, Margaret, Countess of
   Salisbury, 64, 143–4
poor relief, 41, 293
poorhouses. see hospitals
pottage, 99–100
prayer books, 220, 230–1, 250
pregnancy, 7–15
   confinement, 12–15
   diagnosis and gender, 7–9
   illicit, 76–7, 320
   'pleading the belly', 10–11, 41,
      129
   see also infanticide
priests, 68, 77–8, 153, 264–5,
   267
printers, 70, 171, 226
prophetesses, 158, 160–2
prostitution, 121–3
Protestantism, Protestants, 56,
   192
   burning of, 256
   England and, 232, 233
   exiled, 120, 254–5, 260
   in London, 120, 254
Purgatory, 313

rape, 79–81
recipe books, 100–1
recusancy. see Catholicism
Reformation, English, 161,
   191–2, 232, 235, 261–4
   and Church revenue, 193
   impact on charity, 313, 318
   and women's education, 268
relics, for childbirth, 12, 13
religious houses. see monasteries,
   monks; nunneries, nuns
remedies. see medicine
reputations, women's, 81, 85–6

Rich, Richard, 227, 240
Richmond Palace, 305, 310–11, 328
Ridley, Bishop, 240, 255
riots. see mobs

sacraments, 211, 223, 225, 226, 256
Salisbury, Margaret Pole, Countess of, 64, 143–4
Samuel, Alice, 11, 296–7
Sandwich Board of Orphans, 57, 69
Saxonia, Hercules, 91
Scaramelli, Giovanni Carlo, 311–12, 327
schools, 67–70, 314
scolding, 139–41
seamstresses, 104–5
servants, 106, 306–9
  and crime, 41, 187–8
  French (royal), 277–8, 281–2
  household/agricultural, 73–82
  illicit relationships/pregnancies, 75–7
  rape of, 80–1
  royal, 26–30, 34, 44, 64–6. see also ladies-in-waiting
  status in relation to family, 61
  wages, 28, 37, 44, 75
  see also wetnurses
sex trade, 121–3
sexual intercourse
  and birth control/abstinence, 89–92
  and disease, 91, 153
  and marriage consummation, 93
  pre-marital, 89
sexual violence, 79–81
Seymour, Jane, 18, 145, 184–5, 198–9
Shakespeare, William, 2, 33, 53, 85, 115, 241–2, 272, 291

Sheen Palace, 11, 25, 26, 310
Sheriff Hutton Castle, 53, 60–3, 66–7
sheriffs, 74, 97, 216, 239, 257
Simier, Jean de, 277–8, 281–2
Six Articles, Act of the (1539), 223
Skelton, John, 53, 62, 63, 66–7, 159
slander, crime of, 180–1
Somerset, Edward Seymour, Duke of (Lord Protector), 232, 235, 236
Spain, 285, 306
  see also Philip II, King of Spain
spinning wool, 68, 110–11, 292–3
St Bartholomew's Hospital, 319–21, 323
St Thomas's Hospital, 318–19, 322, 323
Stainhus, William, 200, 202–3, 204–5
Stuart, Arbella, 36, 329
Suffolk, Catherine Willoughby, Duchess of, 219, 227
Suffolk, Elizabeth, Duchess of, 46–7
Suffolk, Frances Brandon, Duchess of, 250
Suffolk, Henry Grey, Duke of, 250, 251
sugar, 100, 101, 301
suicides, 241–4
Supremacy, Act of (1559), 261
surgeons, 17–19, 322–3
Surrey, Elizabeth Tylney, Countess of, 53, 60–4, 66–7, 144–5
Surrey, Thomas Howard, Earl of, 60, 63, 94, 96
Surrey, witchcraft trials in, 298–9

Sutton, Thomas, 74, 257
swaddling, 22–3, 33, 49

Taylor, Alice, 3, 303, 316–17
theft, petty, 128–9
Thwaites, Edward, 133–4, 136,
    137, 138, 178, 182
Toftes, John, 210, 212
toilet, flushing, 27
Tooley Foundation, Ipswich,
    293, 315–17
torture, 227–8, 266–7
tournaments, 14, 15, 26, 38, 291
Tower of London, 60, 176–7,
    185, 227–8, 250, 251–2
toys and games, 35–7
traders, women
    in London, 102–4, 106–10,
    111, 115–28, 130
    see also specific trades
treason, crime of, 182
tutors, royal, 62, 175
Tylney, Anne, 63
Tyndale, William, 167, 207, 209

Uniformity, Act of (1559), 261
universities, 67, 70–2

Vives, Juan Luis, 29–30, 36–7,
    85

Warham, William, Archbishop of
    Canterbury, 134–5, 138, 150,
    154–5
    on Barton, 157, 160

death, 167
Waters, Agnes, 298–9
weaning, 34–5
Wentworth, Margery, 63, 185
Westminster, 38, 44, 45
Westminster Abbey, 46, 47
wetnurses, 20–2, 28–32, 33,
    34–5, 44, 48
    see also Burbage, Cecily
Whitehall Palace, 168, 275
Whitgift, John, 326–7
widows, 92–4
    and charity, 306, 315
    chaste, 220–2, 306
    employed in hospitals, 320–1
    in poverty, 110, 292–3
    remarriage, 273
    social/political powers of, 133
    as sponsors/entrepreneurs, 102,
    104, 116–17
    and witchcraft, 298
    see also Fenkyll, Katherine
Windsor Castle, 197, 291
witches, witchcraft, 11, 283,
    293–9
Wolsey, Cardinal, 125
    Anne and Henry's divorce, 147,
    154, 159–60
    arrest and death, 164–5
    and Barton, 154, 158, 160
Wolters, Thomasine, 57, 69
Women's Secrets, 293
Woodville, Elizabeth, 14
Wright, Elizabeth, 294–5
writers. see authors; diarists